CHRISTOPHER PENCZAK

The Goddess of the Cauldron

MAGICK, MUSIC, AND WITCHCRAFT
FROM TALIESIN AND CERRIDWEN

**COPPER
CAULDRON**
PUBLISHING

Credits

Writing: Christopher Penczak
Editing: Tina Whittle
Copy Editing: Kathy Pezok, Leeon Pezok
Layout & Design: Steve Kenson
Cover Art: Sellena Dear
Interior Art: Sellena Dear and Christopher Penczak

The Goddess of the Cauldron: Magick, Music, and Witchcraft from Taliesin and Cerridwen is copyright © 2025 by Christopher Penczak. All Rights Reserved. No part of this work may be reproduced, stored in a retrieval system, or transmitted in any form or by any means, without the express prior permission in writing of the Copyright Owner, nor be otherwise circulated in any form other than that in which it is published.

For more information, visit:
christopherpenczak.com
coppercauldronpublishing.com

ISBN 978-1-940755-16-8
First Edition

Disclaimer

Please note that the information in this book is not meant to diagnose, treat, prescribe, or substitute consultation with a licensed healthcare professional. Both the author and the publisher recommend that you consult a medical practitioner before attempting the techniques outlined in this book and assume no liability for any injuries caused to the reader that may result from the reader's use of the content contained herein. All readers should use common sense when contemplating the practices described in the work.

Keep pure your highest ideals.
Strive ever towards it.
Let naught stop you or turn you aside.
For mine is the secret which opens upon the door of youth;
and mine is the cup of the Wine of Life:
and the Cauldron of Cerridwen,
which is the Holy Grail of Immortality.
I am the Gracious Goddess who gives the gift of Joy unto the heart of Man.
Upon Earth I give the knowledge of the Spirit Eternal,
and beyond death I give peace and freedom,
and reunion with those who have gone before.
Nor do I demand aught in sacrifice, for behold,
I am the Mother of all things,
and my love is poured out upon earth.

— from *"The Charge of the Goddess"*

Other Works by Christopher Penczak

The Temple of Witchcraft Series

The Inner Temple of Witchcraft: Magick, Meditation, and Psychic Development (Updated 20th Anniversary Edition, Llewellyn, 2021; 1st Printing, Llewellyn, 2002)

The Outer Temple of Witchcraft: Circles, Spells, and Rituals (Updated 20th Anniversary Edition, Llewellyn, 2022; 1st Printing, Llewellyn, 2004)

The Temple of Shamanic Witchcraft: Shadows, Spirits, and the Healing Journey (Updated 20th Anniversary Edition, Llewellyn, 2023; 1st Printing, Llewellyn, 2005)

The Temple of High Witchcraft: Ceremonies, Spheres, and the Witches' Qabalah (Llewellyn, 2007)

The Living Temple of Witchcraft, Volume One: The Descent of the Goddess (Llewellyn, 2008)

The Living Temple of Witchcraft, Volume Two: The Journey of the God (Llewellyn, 2009)

Temple Series Audio Recordings

The Inner Temple of Witchcraft CD Companion (Llewellyn, 2002)

The Outer Temple of Witchcraft CD Companion (Llewellyn, 2004)

The Temple of Shamanic Witchcraft CD Companion (Llewellyn, 2005)

The Temple of High Witchcraft CD Companion (Llewellyn, 2007)

The Living Temple of Witchcraft, Volume One, CD Companion (Llewellyn, 2008)

The Living Temple of Witchcraft, Volume Two, CD Companion (Llewellyn, 2009)

Other Books by Christopher Penczak

City Magick (Samuel Weiser, 2001, 2012)

Spirit Allies (Samuel Weiser, 2002)

Gay Witchcraft (Samuel Weiser, 2003)

The Witch's Shield (book with CD, Llewellyn, 2004)

Magick of Reiki (Llewellyn, 2004)

Sons of the Goddess (Llewellyn, 2005)

The Gates of Witchcraft (Copper Cauldron, 2012)

Buddha, Christ, and Merlin (Copper Cauldron, 2012)

The Feast of the Morrighan (Copper Cauldron, 2012)

The Mighty Dead (Copper Cauldron, 2013)

City Witchcraft (Copper Cauldron, 2013)

The Phosphorous Grove (Copper Cauldron, 2013, 2017)

Foundations of the Temple (Copper Cauldron, 2014)

The Casting of Spells (Copper Cauldron, 2016)

The Witch's Hut (Copper Cauldron, 2021)

The Lighting of Candles (Copper Cauldron, 2021)

The Magickal Botanical Oracle with Maxine Miller (Lo Scarabeo, 2022)

The Mystic Foundation (Copper Cauldron, 2024)

Books with Christopher Penczak

Laurie Cabot's Book of Spells and Enchantments (by Laurie Cabot, with Penny Cabot and Christopher Penczak; Copper Cauldron, 2014)

Laurie Cabot's Book of Shadows (by Laurie Cabot, with Penny Cabot and Christopher Penczak; Copper Cauldron, 2015)

Laurie Cabot's Book of Visions (by Laurie Cabot, with Penny Cabot and Christopher Penczak; Copper Cauldron, 2019)

Anthologies Edited by Christopher Penczak

The Green Lovers (Copper Cauldron, 2012)

Ancestors of the Craft (Copper Cauldron, 2012)

The Waters and Fires of Avalon (Copper Cauldron, 2013)

Acknowledgements

Thank you to the amazing individuals and communities who worked with me through this material, including the Temple of Witchcraft, the Cabot-Kent Hermetic Temple, The Robin's Nest Community, and the Heart of the Morrighan Interfaith Community, to name just a few.

Thank you to my partners, Adam and Steve, my father Ron, my friends, family, and students. Thank you to my teachers and mentors over the years, including Laurie Cabot, Raven Grimassi, and Stephanie Taylor.

And special thanks to those who have taught me the ways of Cerridwen on a deeper level, in particular Bonnie Kraft, Glen Velez, Andrew Plummer, Jhenah Telyndru, Kristoffer Hughes, and Jocelyn Van Bokkelen.

Contents

Introduction 11
Part One: The Wisdom of the Cauldron 17
Chapter One: The Witch's Cauldron 19
    The Five Elements 20
        Cauldron Ointment *27*
    The Deities of the Witch 28
Chapter Two: The Cauldrons of Myth and Legend 35
    Cauldrons in Mythology 39
    The Cauldron of the Dagda 39
    The Cauldron of Bran 40
    Cauldron of Diwrnach 42
    Cauldron of the Head of Annwn 42
    The Cauldron of Cerridwen 43
    Cauldron of Ceres 44
    Cauldron of Medea 45
    Cauldrons in History 46
    Gundestrup Cauldron 46
    The Cauldron Treasures of Britain 47
    The Holy Grail 48
    Alchemical Crucible 49
    The Cauldron of Hecate 52
    Flying Cauldrons 52
    Inner Cauldrons 52
    Fivefold Nature of the Vessel 57
    Abundance - Earth 58
    Rebirth – Water 59
    Inspiration – Fire 60
    Healing – Air 60
    Transformation – Spirit 61
Chapter Three: Cerridwen and the Cauldron of Awen 67
        The Cauldron of Ceridwen *71*
    The Tale of Taliesin 73
    The Meaning of the Tale of Taliesin 76
    Mother of Darkness and Child of Light 77
Part Two: Initiation from the Cauldron 81
Chapter Four: The First Darkness of the Hut 83

The Recipe of Inspiration **87**
    The Chair of Taliesin *94*
    Poem of Nine Woods *96*
    Sweet Cauldron of the Five Trees *97*
Escape from the Hut **101**
The Nine Maidens of the Cauldron **102**
The Cracked Cauldron of Consequence **109**
The Stirring Rod **114**
The Creation of the Brew **115**
    Brew of Awen Formula *115*
    Notes *128*

Chapter Five: The Second Darkness of the Womb **129**
    The Alchemy of Initiation **130**
    The Animal Allies and the Elements **141**
        Hare *149*
        Salmon *149*
        Wren *150*
        Grain of Wheat *151*
        Greyhound *152*
        Otter *152*
        Hawk *152*
        Black Hen *153*
    Advanced Shapeshifting **166**
    Nine Months in the Womb **168**
    Reborn as the Child of Light **179**

Chapter Six: The Third Darkness of the Sea **181**
    Surrender to the Journey **182**
    Initiatory Names **185**
    Living Awen **187**
        The Song of Wandering Aengus *188*
    The Magicians of Poetry and Song **201**
        The Song of Amergin *209*
    The Great Song **209**
    Musical Correspondences **213**
    Sacred Vowels 214
    Scales 217
    Magick of Meters 222
    Instruments 223

Part Three: Mysteries of the Cauldron **227**

Chapter Seven: The Adventures of the Child of Light **229**
    Elphin ap Gwyddno Garanhir **230**
        The Excellence of the Bards *238*
        The Reproof of the Bards *240*

	The Spite of the Bards	*241*
	One of the Four Pillars of Song	*244*
The Company of Bran		**248**
King Arthur		**258**
	Caer Sidi	*260*
	Caer Pedryfan and Caer Fredwyd	*262*
	Caer Rigor	*263*
	Caer Goludd	*264*
	Caer Fandy-Manddwy	*265*
	Caer Ochren	*266*
The Prison of Arianrhod		**274**
Chapter Eight: The Hallow of the West		**281**
The Three Dolorous Blows		**284**
Restoration of Heaven		**289**
Five Miraculous Changes		290
	Chalice	*292*
	Spear	*292*
	Plate	*292*
	Cauldron	*293*
	Stone	*293*
The Elements and the Miraculous Changes		294
The Three Sacred Drinks		298
The Quest of the Grail		**300**
	The Wilderness of the Wasteland	*302*
	Taming the Questing Beast	*303*
	Crossing the Sword Bridge of the Abyss	*303*
	Guardians of the Gate	*305*
	The Grail Procession within the Chapel of the Castle	*305*
	Ritual Items:	*307*
	Grail Quest Incense	*307*
	Part One: Facing the Wild	*309*
	Part Two: Passing the Tests	*310*
	Part Three: Encountering the Grail	*313*
Becoming the Grail		**316**
Chapter Nine: The Cauldron of Resurrection		**325**
The Structure of the Cauldron		**328**
Bull at the Base Plate		332
Horned Animal Master (Plate A)		336
Goddess of the Chariot (Plate B)		338
The God of the Broken Wheel (Plate C)		343
The Sacrifice of the Bulls (Plate D)		345
Cauldron of Rebirth (Plate E)		347
The Judge of Heroes (Plate a)		351

    The Sea God (Plate b) 353
    The God of Three Figures (Plate c) 355
    The Stag Hunter God (Plate d) 356
    Divine Trinity (Plate e) 358
    Triple Goddess (Plate f) 360
    Goddess of Rebirth (Plate g) 361
Appendix: Invocatory Poetry 363
Bibliography 367
    Online Resources 371
About the Author 374

Introduction

Sometimes I feel like Cerridwen is following me. Or perhaps I'm preceding her in certain situations, like a booking agent making arrangements and checking things out for the true rock star's visit. Or the warm-up act to get everyone ready for her. Early on in my training, I learned a form of the magick circle ritual that involved calling upon "Celtic totems" in each of the four directions for the elements, followed by four Celtic deities. It was a modern ritual, mixing the various Celtic pantheons – the Gaulish horned god Cernunnos, the Irish Lugh, the Irish Macha, and the Welsh Cerridwen.

I credit this ritual for connecting me to my matron, Macha, and through her, the forces of the Morrighan. We did exercises to commune with the four directions and while my water experiences – starting with salmon as my totemic figure and later transforming into snake – were visceral, my experiences with Cerridwen were mostly subtle. For a year, I studied the *Mabinogi* with a scholarly Celtic Reconstructionist teacher and spent a year on the Welsh *Mabinogi*. Included in this training was the tale of Cerridwen and Taliesin, as many versions of *The Mabinogi* – more often called by the Latinized name *The Mabinogion* – included extra tales beyond the four traditional Branches. Yet her presence still was not profound, and my attention switched to the Irish and Celtic-Romano periods for further study, magickal work, and, eventually, into the realms of occult healing and alchemy.

Other deities took the forefront in my practice, even when I eventually began teaching the Craft to others. But I did notice that many people I worked with in class and in ritual would have very profound Cerridwen experiences, often with no prior experience or exposure to her. Sometimes they would get her complete name in the vision without having really known it before, and other times they would not get her name specifically, but had a profoundly striking image of a Witch Goddess in a hut, with a cauldron, and a fierce yet ultimately affectionate personality, like a stern mother or grandmother. She hit them over the head with her wooden spoon unexpectedly, complaining she didn't have anyone to help her stir anymore, then handed them the spoon, offering them a chance to stir and listen and learn. Sometimes she would feed them. More rarely, she would cook and eat them in their visionary journey, but in each case, some major transformation or healing would occur, even if it came with a bit of fright along with the magick. She certainly wasn't for the faint of heart or easily offended.

This continued for many years, until my experiences with my matron would morph and change. I got deeply involved in the quest to experience the Arthurian mysteries and suddenly my matron goddess, the Morrighan, had shades of Morgan or Morgana Le Fey from Arthurian myth. Arguably Morgan is the earliest recorded name and image of the Lady of the Lake, as evidenced in Geoffrey of Monmouth's *History of the Kings of Britain* and related prophetic Merlin material *The Prophecies of Merlin* and *The Life of Merlin*. With more and more frequency, I would commune with the Lady of Avalon, the Lady of the Lake. Most Irish Reconstructionist Neopagans would say that Morrighan and Morgana Le Fey have little in common, but she was there in my experience.

Soon after this, I was visited by Cerridwen who reminded me that, in many ways, she was the original "lady of the lake," living in her magick hut, stirring her cauldron, on an island in a lake. She was at the root of those mysteries. If I wanted the mysteries of the lake and the cauldron, I needed to see her. I needed to learn her ways. And so I did. Eventually I even made it to her island-less lake in Wales, getting to touch the waters that she touches, from her island withdrawn in the otherworld as there is no actual physical island on the lake.

I soon developed an intense relationship with a goddess figure who morphed from crow-cloaked war goddess, to island priestess, and finally, to the crone-mother in the hut. Each had a distinct personality, but they manifested in vision seamlessly, threading from one to the other in a shapeshifting flow. Rather than ponder the arguments of soft polytheism vs. hard polytheism and the merits of personal gnosis vs. traditionally established lore, I decided to go with it and see what the magick would reveal. There are those who believe in the fluidity of divinities, and while they are as distinct as people, people are not always as distinct and separate from nature, from life, and from each other as we'd like to think. Others would deny this experience simply because it is not their own or because of how they perceive the lore of the ancestors. I didn't care. I just wanted to learn and was willing to go through the door that was opened to me, be it the mists of Avalon or the curtain door of a crude hut.

From that point on, Cerridwen had a more pronounced experience in my visions and magick. Still doing a variation of the basic magick circle ritual, the western quarter became a stronger focus and my potion making and brewing deepened with my knowledge of the plants. While potion magick was an early and profound experience for me, my later medicinal knowledge circled back to my magickal potions. Under her guidance, the two sets of lore became one, deepening my own experience and impacting how I would administer potions, oils, and essences to others as a professional Witch.

Not long after that, I was asked to teach a workshop fundraiser for the charity Project Witches Protection, an equal rights and education group, for what would later become the Cabot-Kent Hermetic Temple. Being specifically Celtic focused and falling before the Mabon celebration that I would have a hand in leading, the event had me wondering what theme I should use for the workshop, as I wanted to craft something special for the occasion.

In meditation, Cerridwen came to me not so subtly – with a wooden spoon in hand – to suggest the mysteries of the cauldron and her teachings. From the flow of subsequent visions and books she led me to, as well as the direct psychic 'downloads' of insight, I crafted the first version of this day-long workshop that eventually expanded into a two-day event for future venues.

After the fundraiser, I traveled around teaching it at various shops and centers before putting it away. One day, after completing a book on the Morrighan, I was pondering my next project, clearly having other ideas in mind, when she came to me and told me that my next project was to write her book based upon the workshop because the mysteries of the cauldron needed to be shared. I think she would have been happy for me to drop everything to focus on this book then and there, nonstop, but I did manage to make it through the next project and was amazed at how guided and easy the process was, at least initially. There are times when the deities want something shared, and I feel this was one of those times.

But, like getting locked in the hut, the work ground to a stop as my life became busier and busier. The previously easy flow of inspiration dried up. I find it ironic that the book that is so much about inspiration is the book I struggled with the most in my entire career of, thus far, thirty books. But even this was a trial – for inspiration can come at a price – and my price was to enter once more the darkness of the hut to learn my craft, the darkness of the womb to dream, and the darkness of the waters to float me wherever they may lead. Only then could I share what I needed to share. After a lot of long breaks, false starts, profound doubts and fears, and even the shedding of many tears, I was able to complete this book.

While there will be lore, myth, and history in this book, this is not a book specifically and only on the lore, myth, and history of the Welsh goddess Cerridwen and her son Taliesin. There are many fine books that do this already far better than I can, not being a native Welsh speaker myself, nor an academic with expertise in Celtic lore, history, and language. We'll explore her story in great detail, but this is a shared journey, of the things I've learned from both the study of this goddess and through her directly. It incorporates other people's experiences with her. Since she is the goddess of inspiration, contained within will be classic poetry and prose, and newly created works. This is a book about the cauldron, the great powers the cauldron evokes in our life, and the Goddesses – Cerridwen and beyond – who are the keepers of the cauldron. It is a manual on how to approach and interact with these powers in both a personal and sacred manner, for the two are really one within the heart of the Witch.

Though I might reference the teachings of those I've studied with in a more Celtic Reconstructionist background, I am a Witch, teaching from the place of a Witch. While perhaps not technically Witchcraft, the lore, practices, and rituals will be in the ethos and style of the modern Witch through the lens of the Western occult traditions. Here you'll see the crossing of Welsh folklore and preserved poems with the four elements of popular magickal theory. You'll find cross-cultural comparisons of Cerridwen and Taliesin with other figures in myth and history. Those looking for carefully recreated ancient rituals have probably picked up the wrong book, but those looking for how the ancient can inspire them today through working with the spirits of nature and beyond – manifesting nature into what we might think of as super-nature – will find a helpful path before them.

I am borrowing from the romantic occultists of the past and adding my own brand of magick and mystery to the ever-changing brew. While some might claim it is not "traditional," we often have to invent and reinvent today what will become the traditions of tomorrow, as they all have to begin somewhere. In the very traditional poetry attributed to Taliesin, global and cross-cultural references are made beyond traditional Celtic lore, including references to both the Old and New Testaments, the fall of Lucifer, and to foreign lands beyond the British Isles. In poetry is the very spirit of occultism, seeking the consciousness that is not bound by a single culture or tradition, but universal. Occultists look to the mysteries that can incorporate all. While my own focus here has been on the Western Mysteries, and the migration of classical mythology across Europe, it is quite hard not to delve into Eastern comparisons when looking at medicine, alchemy, and even music.

We will be doing ritual, reciting poetry, and doing inner vision work to connect to a realm beyond our five physical senses. We will see the cauldron as the crucible, as the alchemist's athanor, to incite change and transformation on a deeper level within us. We look to it not only as a tool, but as an embodiment of the powers of the Goddess herself – life, sustenance, poison, initiation, death, and rebirth! Through this vessel we better understand the Goddess as the matrix of creation, the ground of being from which all things are born and return to upon completion.

Everything here has been explored first by me, then by a smaller group of experienced practitioners, and finally with the public, from across the United States, in the United Kingdom, and in Australia. Visiting Cerridwen's native land in Wales – and even visiting the lake where she dwelled, Lake Bala, also known by her husband's name, Lake Tegid – brought the teachings to a deeper level for many of us. While you do not need to be in any specific place to connect with this goddess, the spirit of place can certainly facilitate and deepen the connection, and help people like myself share it with a wider audience. Through this research we have worked with lore and technique to help many people make an inner contact with the primal power of the cauldron and its goddess, in whatever guise she might take.

I owe a great debt to many of the bardic traditions and authors who have done so much amazing work already around the Taliesin story as an initiatory model. In particular I thank John Matthews for his books *The Celtic Shaman, Taliesin: The Last Celtic Shaman* and *The Song of Taliesin*; R.J. Stewart for his books on Merlin; Alexei Kondratiev with *The Apple Branch*; Kevan Manwaring with *The Bardic Handbook: The Complete Manual for the Twenty-First Century Bard* and the more recent *The Way of Awen*; and Tom Cowan with his classic book *Fire in the Head*. Jhenah Telyndru's *Avalon Within: A Sacred Journey of Myth, Mystery, and Inner Wisdom* and Kristoffer Hughes's *From the Cauldron Born* are also powerful sources of inspiration and understanding.

It is my wish to continue in that vein, adding to our understanding of these mysteries, and I hope you enjoy working with the material of *The Goddess of the Cauldron*, this Pagan inner visionary alchemy, as much as I do sharing it with you.

Part One: The Wisdom of the Cauldron

Chapter One: The Witch's Cauldron

By fire, water, earth, and air
Seeking the depths of the mysteries
Going where few would dare
Lord of Darkness and Lord of Light
Ladies of Fate who shape cosmic night
Source of creation as the divine womb
and the destination of destruction as the divine tomb
Cauldron of Mystery, open the gate
So I may pass through you freely
And become a stirrer of fate.

For many of us on the path of the Witch, there is nothing more magical than the thought of Witches gathered around the cauldron, making their magick over the warming fire. Few of us get to truly act out the images of the chained cauldron hanging from a tripod over the fire, brewing up some magnificent potion. These days, the most common cauldrons are reduced to smaller incense burners, though there is still a romance to watching wisps of smoke rise out of the dark iron bowl standing upon three legs.

Despite its reduction in size, the cauldron does play an important series of roles in contemporary Witchcraft and magickal practices. For many of us, it has an all-purpose role when considered in relationship to the four elements, making it the ideal tool for the fifth element that combines the four, as well as deeper philosophical and theological symbolism regarding the nature of the gods and creation in Witchcraft – again linking it to the power of spirit, the fifth element, the source of creation.

The Five Elements

In terms of its more practical function, I place the mid-sized cauldron in the center of my altar, between the ritual objects for the four elements. Classically, the blade is the tool embodying elemental air. The wand embodies elemental fire. The stone embodies elemental earth, though the ritual dish, or peyton/paten is also a symbol of earth. In the suits of the tarot, the earth element is represented by coins, or simply by pentacles, five-pointed stars in a circle, looking like the coin or the peyton dish. With the five points, it too, like the cauldron, can embody the fifth element. Lastly, water is made manifest through the ritual cup or chalice, the representative of the Holy Grail. Out of all the four "hallows" or elemental weapons of the magician and Witch, the cup is most strongly linked with the cauldron. Both are rounded vessels for containing liquid and both have strong feminine associations – connecting them with the Goddess. At one time in the older myths, the cauldron and cup were one tool, but as traditions developed, they divided into two distinct paths of magick and mystery teaching.

Today my cauldron is found between my four other tools upon my own altar, as the natural link between them as well as my center piece. I usually have a white or red seven-day jar candle placed within, to represent the light and power of spirit. The cauldron adds a measure of safety for if the glass should crack, the wax, glass, and any flame is caught in its cast iron bowl.

The cauldron can contain water, so naturally it is a vessel of elemental water. We brew potions in it, warm mulled wines, and steam water for our magick. I have already mentioned the use of cauldrons in smaller forms to hold burning incense. Small blocks of charcoal sold in occult supply shops are lit and placed in a flameproof container, usually with sand or salt at the bottom, to disperse the heat. The days of brass thuribles and braziers for incense burners have passed for most occultists, who now favor the small cauldron. The incense cauldron holds heat quite well, and the lid lets you extinguish the charcoal and incense when the smoke gets to be too much. With the sand, soil, or salt in it, the cauldron makes an excellent symbol of the element of earth. Some Witches keep their crystals in the cauldron until they are used for healing or magick. In fact, while most occultists will associate the iron composing the cauldron with the element of fire and the iron-rich red planet Mars, iron is also considered to be the lifeblood of the planet Earth itself, and a substitute for blood by modern practitioners looking at rituals that would require such things. So we can see iron as an earth element association through the planetary being, Mother Earth, or as a component in blood, a water correspondence.

Lastly, the main function I learned to use the cauldron for from my own Witchcraft teachers was as a receptacle for burning paper spells safely. We would write petitions, read them aloud, burn them over the cauldron, dropping them in when we could hold the burning paper no longer. The cooled ashes would later be gathered and put into an ash pot, a vessel for these spent petitions and the ashes of incense and matches, to be scattered annually on the wind, in the sea, or buried in the ground.

With the associations of water, air, earth, and fire, we are reminded of the element of spirit. Spirit is the combination of all the elements, so this tool, as a combination of elements, can be used for the element of spirit. Spirit, the fifth element, is known by many names, particularly akasha, ether, or quintessence. I particularly like quintessence, the essence of five, for magickal theory says that the fifth element has two natures, usually termed active and passive. From active spirit, the four elements are generated and bring pattern, cycle, and form to the universe. The four elements interact with each other through the modifications of the qualities of temperature and moisture, according to the philosophers of ancient Greece, including Empedocles, who saw these elements as the "roots" of all things. Various gods and spirits were identified with them. Elements are classified as either warm or cold, and either wet or dry. Changing the scale of any one of these elements transforms the elemental energy.

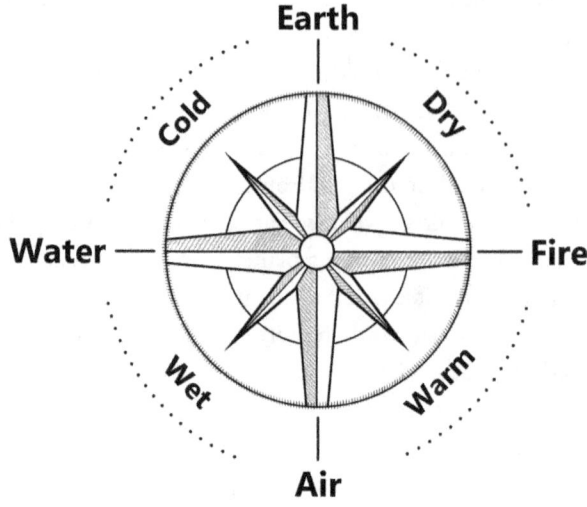

Figure 1: Alchemical Wheel

Earth	Dry	Cold
Fire	Dry	Warm
Air	Wet	Warm
Water	Wet	Cold

Chart 1: Elemental Qualities

The example most given is if you cool a flame (fire), you get ash (earth). If you add moisture to the ash, you get a solution (water) as the salts dissolve out. If you add heat to your solution, you get a water vapor (air), and when you add warmth to the air, usually to feed a flame, you sustain fire. This is considered the natural direction in the transmutation of the elements. In the opposite direction, if you add heat to a solid material (earth), the combustible components are set alight (fire). Before they are ignited, they are cooked, and in either case, when done long enough, reduced to their essential elements. If you add moisture to flame, you get smoldering smoke as the fire is extinguished and particles fill the air (air). Make the moist air cool, and the water precipitates out as rain (water), and draw out the moisture from water and the salts (earth) remain. This is sometimes considered the deathly rotation of the elements, or the path of initiation amongst the elements. It is considered a harder course of movement.

It is important to know that these physical symbols of the elements are not truly the power of the elements. The terrestrial symbols of the elements – stones, H_2O, atmospheric gases, and combustion – are simply the best tangible manifestations of the energetic principles of these forces of creation. Other systems align them with other divisions, including body/emotion/mind/soul, form/flow/pattern/idea, law/love/life/light or even gravity/strong atomic force/weak atomic force/electromagnetism.

These are the fundamental forces of creation, no matter how you look at them – spiritually, magickally, or scientifically – if you remember they are not literal, but symbols for higher patterns of energy. That was the mistake in the transition between alchemy to chemistry. The new chemists believed the elements were literal, so with the discovery of the atomic chemical elements such as hydrogen and helium, the alchemists' views seemed untrue. The discovery of the chemical elements does not invalidate the alchemical elements any more than the discovery of sub-atomic particles invalidates the chemical elements. They are all different things, different perspectives, within one greater system. But with the advancements of quantum physics and more esoteric sciences, the magickal worldview – particularly that of the alchemist, the observer who affects the outcome of the experiment – is firmly in play again. And when one thinks about the cauldron, a precursor to the more advanced laboratory equipment of the crucible, retort, and alembic, we again find a vessel to heat, distill, refine, and ultimately create something new.

As spirit, "active" quintessence is the force that generates. "Passive" or "receptive" spirit is the force that returns them to their original, undifferentiated state at the end of the cycle of creation. Alchemists taught about a "first matter" or first thing, found everywhere, but unseen to all. From this first matter, all things, including the fabled Philosopher's Stone of the alchemist, would be made. The stone would confer wealth by transforming lead into gold, bring healing, grant immortality, and even reveal the secrets of the universe. The Holy Grail, a later form of the Goddess' cauldron, was often a symbol or euphemism for the alchemist's Philosopher's Stone. This hints at some of the mysteries of the Pagan cauldron traditions mixed with the high esoteric arts of alchemy, as well as the Christian mysticism of the later grail romances involving King Arthur's court.

Exercise 1:
Consecration of the Cauldron

What kind of cauldron will you use for the workings of this book? I suggest a medium-sized cauldron, larger than the small incense burners. Pick something large enough to place a seven-day glass candle holder in, with some room to spare. Don't choose something so large you cannot easily transport or hold it. Ideally make sure the cauldron has three legs and a handle, and that you can carry it by the handle in one hand. Most commercially available cauldrons today, new and used, are iron, though with a little perseverance, you can find a cauldron in copper or brass. If at all possible, get a cauldron with a lid. Some fire pots are very cauldron-like and would work well.

Once you have chosen your cauldron, start by cleansing it of unwanted energies, particularly if you have chosen a used or antique cauldron. Bathe the cauldron in water. If you can, submerge it in water. You can place some flowers or essential oils into the water, just a drop or two. Scents such as lavender, lemon, pine, or sage work well to clear energies. If you cannot submerge it, wet a cloth with water and oils and thoroughly wipe it. In either case, make sure you dry it thoroughly with a cloth to prevent rust. When working with the water, call upon the spirit of water to aid you in the work of this cauldron. Think of your blood and the blood of your ancestors. Think of the blood of Mother Earth, of rivers and oceans, of streams and of lakes. Think of the water of the ladies of the lake – the faery women of myth and legend. Say this or something similar:

I call upon the spirits and powers of water, cool and wet,
to bless this vessel.
I call upon the spirits and powers of rivers and streams, of lakes and oceans,
to bless this vessel.
I call upon the blood within me, flowing from my ancestors,
to bless this vessel.
Blessed be.

Next, pass the cauldron through the smoke of a cleansing incense. Incense is a symbol of air, and can bring clarity of mind and perception. Many incense blends are said to be of a "high vibration," burning away unwanted vibrations that no longer serve a higher and deeper good. Blends such as frankincense and myrrh, or sage and cedar, work well, though if we want to be a little bit more primal and rooted in the northwestern European traditions, we might use a pine pitch or even dry pine needles as our clearing incense. While I prefer grain incense on charcoal, possibly in a smaller cauldron with some sand, as described before, you can also use stick incense, or the popular sage 'bundles' of herbs. Today there is concern about the use of sage and its endangerment, and the endangerment preventing indigenous people from having access to their traditional herb, so ask your local retailer about their source of sage and their ethical sustainability. Because of this, you'll find new herb bundles of lavender, mugwort, yarrow, and a variety of other cleansing and protecting herbs. Think of the breezes and the winds. Think of the clouds and the weather patterns within the Sky Father. Think of your breath and the life carried upon the breath. Say this or something similar:

I call upon the spirits and powers of air, warm and wet,
to bless this vessel
I call upon the spirits and powers of breezes and winds, of currents and storms,
to bless this vessel.
I call upon the breath within me, bringing the blessings of life,
to bless this vessel.
Blessed be.

Light a candle in honor of the spirits of fire. Traditionally a red taper would work, but any color you feel drawn to use will suffice. Bless the candle in the name of the spirits of fire and light it. Hold the empty cleansed vessel just above it. Think of the fire in the candle, in the blaze of a forest fire. Think of the fire deep within the Earth and in the heart of the Sun and stars. Feel the fire of your own metabolism burning within you, as if you were a star upon the Earth. Say this or something similar:

I call upon the spirits and powers of fire, warm and dry,
to bless this vessel.
I call upon the spirits and powers of hearth fires and lightning flashes, the deep earth fire and the stellar light
to bless this vessel
I call upon the fire within me, burning within me like a star upon the Earth,
to bless this vessel.
Blessed be.

You can now extinguish the candle and move to the earth's blessing. If you are outdoors, simply place the cauldron upon the land. If indoors, you might fill the cauldron with soil from your native land – the land where you live – or soil from another special place to you. Think of the element of earth in terms of the land, where all things grow. Think of the element of earth as an extension of the planetary being, Mother Earth. Think of all matter, anywhere and everywhere in the cosmos, as earth, bound by the physical laws of nature, and think of the earth of your body, crystalized as your bones. Recite this or something similar:

I call upon the spirits and powers of earth, cool and dry,
to bless this vessel.
I call upon the spirits and powers of land and soil, of fields and forests
to bless this vessel.
I call upon the earth within me, the earth within my bones
to bless this vessel.
Blessed be.

Finally, call upon the element of spirit to bless the cauldron. Feel the energies of water, air, fire, and earth coming together within you, and within the cauldron. Imagine the cauldron filling with light – an iridescent fire made from many colors, though often the dominant color is a prismatic violet or blue. Say this or something similar:

I call upon the blessings and powers of spirit, of akasha, ether, and quintessence
to consecrate this vessel.
In the name of the Many and of the One, the All and the Nothing,
I consecrate this vessel
By the powers and blessings of spirits within, by my ancestors, allies, and gods,
I consecrate this vessel to aid me in the work of illumination, transformation, and inspiration.
So mote it be!

Now your cauldron is ready for use in this work. You can repeat the cleansing and blessing whenever you like. If you plan on deeply exploring the mysteries of the Goddess of the Cauldron, make this cauldron a centerpiece in your own altar, or if you don't have an altar, start by arranging a special place for magickal tools, making the cauldron a primary part of it.

You can use the cauldron for any of the functions described in this chapter, from potions and incense, to placing a glass candle jar within for the light of spirit and inspiration. I have one magician friend, a crafter of magickal tools, who puts items into his cauldron to bless, charge, and empower them. New stones, vials of oil, jewelry – they all go into the cauldron for a time, and he pulls them out when it's time to work with them, or use the cauldron for another function. It becomes a functional "womb" for his future magickal and creative work.

To care for your cauldron, specifically your iron cauldron, you can "season" it as you would an old-fashioned iron skillet or frying pan. Gently heat the cauldron, which can be hard to do evenly, and spread it with either vegetable oil or lard. The oil creates a water resistant seal to prevent rust. Many believe you should season the cauldron after every use that involves water.

Other friends, owners of an online apothecary called Otherworld Apothecary, introduced me to the concept of "cauldron grease" – an unguent mixing oil and beeswax, with magickal herbs – to season a magickal cauldron. You can purchase cauldron grease or make a similar ointment.

Cauldron Ointment

3 Ounces of Olive Oil (regular or infused)Magickal Herbs. For Infused Oil – add a small amount of Mugwort, Nettles, Fennel, Vervain, and Rose Petals)
1 Ounce of Beeswax (by weight)
A Few Drops of Essential Oil (your choice)
3 Drops of Vitamin E Oil

As ointments are a mix of wax and oil, you might want to go slightly heavier on the oil to get a more grease-like consistency. You can use regular oil, or an herbally infused oil.

An infused oil carries the medicine, if not a strong perfume scent, of various magickal herbs. You can make a magickal infused oil by taking a canning jar and placing fresh herbs such as mugwort, nettles, fennel, vervain, and rose petals until the jar is full, or use dry herbs filling it 1/3 full. Then fill the canning jar with olive oil and let it steep out in the warm summer sunlight for a Moon cycle, roughly a month. If you are in a rush, you can gently heat the oil in a double boiler with the herbs on a low heat for thirty minutes. Let it cool, and strain the herbs out of the oil. Then store it in a clean glass bottle until you are ready to make the cauldron grease. For a balanced magick, I chose mugwort for water and the Moon, nettles for fire, fennel seed for air, and vervain for earth, though vervain has many versatile properties and correspondences. Rose is the plant of spirit in the Western Mystery traditions. You can choose different herbs, but if you plan on drinking anything from this cauldron, don't use anything toxic. Parsley can be an excellent herb due to its association with the gods of the underworld and cunning knowledge while still being edible.

Heat the oil in a double boiler on low, and slowly add the beeswax to it. When the wax is melted, stir well and pour into a small ointment jar. You can add essential oils to it then if you desire. Choose magickal oils that mean something to you and, again, if you plan to consume anything out of this cauldron, use non-toxic plants. It's traditional to use herbs like the deadly aconite in consecrating tools, but in this case, it would be ill advised due to the danger. You might add a drop or two of myrrh, frankincense, rosemary, patchouli, or lavender to the ointment. Put the lid over the jar, but do not screw it down until it cools fully. This loose covering will keep the oils in the mixture as the ointment cools, rather than partially evaporating away. Once cooled, you can use the greasy ointment to magickally "season" your cauldron.

If your cauldron should rust, you can rescue it by rubbing off the rust before you re-season it. If it's only a little rust, use a bit of sandpaper to remove it. For bigger problems, particularly on bigger cauldrons, you can use a steel wool brush, but I am generally hesitant to use hefty steel wool on my cauldrons. Make sure you never use soap and water to clean it, or put it into a dishwasher. When you do use water to clean, make sure you dry it right away to prevent rust from forming.

Some practitioners use an iron cauldron for many forms of magick, but use a copper or brass cauldron for brewing edible potions, teas, and anything resembling food. The seasoning grease works best for iron cauldrons, while copper and brass can be cleaned more normally with appropriate metal cleaners.

The Deities of the Witch

Like the properties of active and passive spirit, the cauldron itself is seen as the power of the Great Goddess in Witchcraft. It is representative of the womb of the Goddess and the tomb of the Goddess, as the universe, the Earth, gives us life, but our bodies are returned to the land, and upon the end of this world, what was once our atoms will be returned to the star stuff of the cosmic mother's universal body. Through her cauldron, we arrive and enter the world as consciousness, and our soul departs again for the next world through its darkness.

The entirety of deity in a Witchcraft context is explored in the cauldron. While the Goddess is considered central to Witchcraft and Wicca – as the ultimate creator and source, coming before all other deities – the role of the male divinity is equally important in balanced magickal traditions. In classic Wicca, the divinity is dual, with both Goddess and God, as the Goddess gives birth to her son and lover. Yet each side of the divine, male and female, has their own aspects and divisions.

Many traditions look at divinity as fivefold. The Goddess is triple in form. She is maiden, mother and crone, or goddess of the heavens, Earth, and underworld, or perhaps sky, land, and sea. Her triple nature is described in many ways, even as the Fates of past, present, and future. The three legs of most freestanding cauldrons represent her triple aspect. She gives support to creation, as creation is represented by the bowl of the cauldron. Without her, there is no universe.

Figure 2: Cauldron of Divinity

The handle of the cauldron connects in two points and forms an overarching bridge by which to grasp and carry the cauldron. The God is seen as dual, or double. He is two-faced like the Roman god Janus, and perhaps our Janus and Weaver deity imagery owes quite a bit to *The Prophecies of Merlin* text where such imagery is found. In Europe a number of "Celtic" head carvings survive, including the famous "Janus Stone" on Boa Island in Ireland. The God is both light and dark. He is the god of the Sun and the sky and the green plants, bringing life. He is the god of the hunter, and hunted. He is the god of the underworld, bringing death. Yet he is one, just as the handle is one. The god has two aspects, and the handle has two ends connecting it to creation, the cauldron. Together, the two gods are the Child of Light, Child of Hope, or Child of Promise, who is eternal and beyond space and time. And the Goddess and God are ultimately one, as these individual parts are still part of the greater whole of the cauldron.

The cauldron gives us a powerful model holding the paradox of the parts and the whole of divinity. Each is obviously separate, and can be pointed to as unique and individual. Yet they work together to support the entire container, and in fact, are part of the container, not separate. The model of the cauldron helps me delve into the mystery of the deities on a deeper level.

To attune with this triple goddess and dual god of the cauldron of creation, we can experience them through the use of magickal vision. Magickal vision is a time-honored tradition in both Western and Eastern Mysteries, involving visualization skills, but going beyond what many would think of as simple visualization or imagination. We use skills such as imagination and creativity to form a bridge through a deepening of consciousness. Through repetitive action and imagery, we trigger a trance state, allowing us to deepen our consciousness, and use imagery to connect beyond ourselves and relate to primal powers of the universe, including spirit allies, totemic animals, and the gods and goddesses themselves.

While we use words like visualization, vision, and seeing – all of which relate to our sense of sight – magickal journeys actually use a multitude of inner senses that parallel all our outer senses. We can magickally see, but also magickally hear, feel, smell, and taste. Many people don't "see" at all in their inner vision, but sense and feel "as if" they are experiencing something in the flesh. The more they go through the experience as if it were real, the more attuned their inner senses become to this new reality, and the deeper the experience goes. Truly we are perceiving no matter what the sensory experience and interpretation of information.

This form of magickal attunement and journey and simple accompanying rituals are the primary methods we will be using to attune to the cauldron powers in this book.

Exercise 2:
Vision of the Fivefold Divinity

Have your cauldron before you and place a candle in a container that will prevent the spilling of wax in your cauldron. Light your cauldron and any appropriate incense to help you relax and enter a trance state. Herbs such as sandalwood, frankincense, and myrrh are all helpful scents. I also favor mugwort burned upon charcoal to facilitate psychic and magickal abilities, but the scent is not as pleasing as the resins and woods. You can also play any appropriate mood music for relaxation and meditation. As we progress in this book and explore the mysteries of Cerridwen, what is popularly classified as "Celtic" music might set an appropriate tone. I also find some subtle harp music appropriate.

Start by getting into a comfortable physical position. I suggest you sit up in a relaxed state. Many who lie down fall asleep. Close your eyes and breathe deeply. As you breathe, give yourself permission to relax, starting at the top of your head and moving down your body. Relax all your muscle groups. Bring your awareness to the top of your head and give your head and neck permission to relax. Give your shoulders and arms permission to relax. Relax your chest and back. Relax your abdomen. Relax your hips. Relax your legs, all the way down to your feet. Feel waves of relaxation move through your body.

Relax your mind. Allow all thoughts to become like clouds upon the blue sky of your mind. Allow the clouds to gently blow away, leaving your mind like a clear, peaceful blue sky.

Open your heart. Feel the beating of your heart. With each beat, we feel the ideal of perfect love and perfect trust – the Witch's unconditional love beating through us.

Within your heart shines a flame of light – the light of your souls. This candle flame grows with your practice, and becomes like a torch, a beacon in the night to guide and protect you.

To deepen your trance state, count backwards from twelve to one. You can envision the numbers on the screen of your mind, imagining your screen like a set of curtains you can not only project images upon, but open and close like a gateway. When done, open the gateway into the blackness of space, and simply count with no visualization, down from thirteen to one, going into a deep level of trance.

State your intention, out loud or silently, with these or similar words:

I seek to attune to the Mysteries of the Cauldron.
I seek the Triple Goddess and Dual God who dwell within.

In the gateway screen of your mind, envision the cauldron you have put before you, with a single candle within it. Even though your eyes are closed, feel the presence of your consecrated cauldron, not just before you in the room, but before you in the cosmos. Be aware of the cauldron growing bigger before you. The light in the center grows brighter. The darkness grows darker. Soon you feel yourself becoming one with the light in the center of the cauldron. The center of the cauldron is the eye of the swirling of storms, the center of the rotating galaxies. Within it you find stillness and silence.

You are looking both at the rim of the cauldron far in the distance, all around you, and the rim of the universe, the edge of all that is known. To the furthest left and to the furthest right, you see two figures looming on the horizon edge of the cauldron. You feel their presence coming towards you as you seemingly float in the darkness of space like a lone star. You know that these figures are the two faces of the God. To your right dwells the Lord of Light and Life. To the left dwells the Lord of Death and Darkness. Let them approach you. Have no fear. They hold the key and the lock to the gates of mystery.

Commune with the God, each side in turn. Start with the Lord of Light. He might commune with you in words, thoughts, pictures, feeling, or a silent and still knowing. He might show you the mysteries of the Sun and his face as the Green Man growing upon the Earth. Ask any questions you have of him.

Then commune with the Lord of Darkness. Again, his method of communication might not be typical or linear, and often is different from the Lord of Light. He could show you the mysteries of the underworld, and his face as the Horned God, both hunter and hunted. He frequently manifests in primal emotions, not words. Ask any questions you have of him.

The two gods become one, a double-faced Janus-like god, with the light and younger face forward and the dark horned face looking backward. The God Who is Two opens the black space beneath your feet and reveals a world just beneath the world you know. There, waiting for you, are the Three Ladies.

They greet you as a Triform Goddess. They might be clad all in black, or in the colors white, red, and black. They are many things. You might sense them as the Maiden, Mother, and Crone. They also can manifest as the Goddess of the Heavens, the Goddess of the Earth, and the Goddess of the Underworld. One of their deepest faces is the Goddess of Fate, she who spins the thread of fate, she who measures out the line of life, she who cuts it when its time is over. She is Past, Present, and Future.

You are drawn down into the world beneath this cauldron, where the Three Who are One hold up the cosmos of what was, what is, and what will be. Commune with the Ladies. They will have questions for you, but will also give you a chance to ask your own. Usually you only get three questions, so make sure you ask clearly and truly to get the answers you need to understand your path into the cauldron mystery.

When your time with them is done, the Three Ladies will return you to the center of the cauldron, the center of your own life and world, yet you cannot operate in the world without understanding their presence and support beneath the cauldron of the cosmos. As they face from your direct awareness and you float in the darkness, take a moment to contemplate the void of space, the center of the cauldron, and your own place in the world and cosmos. Feel the profound peace that is found in the heart of the darkness of the cauldron, where all is potential, where all is possible.

Bring your awareness back to your flesh and blood, breath and bone. Feel your fingers and toes, ankles and wrists. Count up from one to thirteen slowly, and then close the veil of your awareness. Then count up from twelve to one. When ready, open your eyes and return your awareness to the world. Ground yourself as needed. You can imagine your feet growing like deep roots anchoring you to the Earth, or the base of your spine metaphorically and energetically "dropping anchor" to ground you to this spot. If you are truly light-headed, getting something to eat and drink can help bring your awareness back. Extinguish your candle and incense. Turn off your music. Record your experience in your magickal journal.

Chapter Two: The Cauldrons of Myth and Legend

By head, heart, and belly wise
Flowing with life, joy, and sorrow
To catch the emerald prize
Cauldron of Abundance and Cauldron of Rebirth
Prize of all prizes, both beyond all worth
Cauldron of Inspiration and Cauldron of the Grail
Bringer of awen and piercer of the veil
Cauldron of Transformation, the alchemist's holy stone
The secret of the royal road
that leads to our true home.

When one looks at the use of cauldrons in stories and legends, a few specific themes tend to arise. While at first they appear to be unrelated, when we look at all cauldron stories as stemming from the principles outlined in Chapter One – the elements and divinity, the sources of creation and destruction – we begin to see the divine links between all cauldron stories and grow closer to the heart of the cauldron mysteries.

In these stories, three obvious "substances" are made or contained within the cauldron. They are usually food, a potion, or a poison. These three substances detail three different ways to approach our understanding of the cauldron as a source of magick.

Food is the power of health and sustainment. It is the cornucopia found in other traditions, the never-empty horn of plenty. The Greek goddess Demeter, goddess of the grains and harvest, carries this horn of plenty, showing the abundance and blessings of the Earth. The cauldron of sustainment's magick is of prosperity, and the relationship of the people with the Goddess of Land to support their material needs, as represented by a feast of food.

Today, in the world of our twenty-four-hour supermarkets and pre-packaged treats, we forget the difficulty and scarcity of food. Though we still live in an agrarian society, it is an agrarian industrial complex where few have little direct experience with the difficulty and work required to grow and raise our own food. Food – harvesting it, raising it, hunting it, and gathering it – plays a huge role in the ancient myths and our relationships with the gods. And it is a mystery we forget as modern twenty-first-century people, but a mystery we should do better to understand and appreciate as our models of sustainment must change to more conscious and holistic patterns in the coming age. The gods are found in the very food we eat. They are embodied in the sacred grains, fruits, vegetables, and animals we consume. Through our relationship with food, we find the sacred.

The use of potions is for transformation. Many of our stories of potions deal with the use of a sacred liquid to cause change. One falls in love with another after drinking a love potion, putting into effect a series of changes for the story to unfold. Another potion might give the ability to shapeshift, transforming the recipient into an animal or unearthly creature. Sometimes the potion gives the knowledge of how to do such magick. Other times it's involuntary and spontaneous, revealing deep and hidden things about the imbiber of the brew. Potions can cause sleep, act as a magical "truth serum," make one invisible, or grant strength. All of these great abilities that people do not normally have – and often want – are within the purview of the Witch, Magician, and Sorcerer,

The most important of these, and the one most grounded in the reality of the Witch's potion, is the elixir that can cure illness. Most potions' origins start as traditional herbal medicines, transformed through alchemy to the Elixir of Immortality, the fabled medicine of all medicines, healing all illness, perfecting the body, and granting everlasting life. Magick is transformation, for magick is the power of change. The definitions of modern magick almost always involve Aleister Crowley's famous line: "Magick is the Science and Art of causing Change to occur in conformity with Will." Magick is change, and change is magickal. The magickal religions honor, observe, and participate in the changes of the seasons, the passages of the Moon, Sun, and Stars, and mark the changes in humanity through the three phases of female change also embodied by the Goddess – maiden, mother, and crone. It is important to realize while they are tied to biology, like the elements, they are embodiments of greater cosmic powers. The three embody the past, present, and future, or in a cosmic sense, initiation, sustainment, and ending. It doesn't mean you have to be a woman to do magick, or as a woman, you have to go through all three aspects of life. Nor do we necessarily have to replace them with other symbols to fit us personally, for they are a part of the cycles in the process of life, and embody the cosmic principles quite clearly.

The last item within our cauldron is described as a poison or toxin. That was the great fear people had concerning Witches, that they would hurt, curse, or kill you with their "black" magick. Most of that reputation stems from the ability of the herbal witch to poison. While I'm sure many historically plied their trade selling poisons, the understanding and use of poisons does not automatically make one malefic. One of the titles for a Witch in Roman times is Venefica, which many associate solely with "venom" though it is quite possibly related to Venus. Along with being the goddess of love, she is also the goddess of cultivated gardens and herbs. When her Greek counterpart, Aphrodite, rose from the ocean and stepped upon land, flowers bloomed in her wake. But the Venefica are associated with the poisoners because of this bias in fearing those who have the knowledge to kill.

To use herbs, you must be intimately aware of what will kill you as much as what will heal you, and what not to mix together. When harvesting wild carrot, it is easy for the novice to mistake it for deadly hemlock or water hemlock. Many things classified as dangerous poisons today were used in the past as sedatives for the ill, or anesthesia for earlier forms of surgery.

The deadliest of the Witch's herbs go into the flying ointment, the Unguent of the Sabbat, a mix of deadly and protective herbs to be rubbed upon the skin at sensitive areas, where the poisons would be absorbed slowly, ideally not enough to kill, but enough to induce an entheogenic trance with overtones of Eros and Thanatos, sex and death, the primary forces in the Witch's worldview. The sabbat mystery is another view of the womb and tomb, and all that is related to both. Life force comes in through sex and goes out upon death. They form the gates of incarnation and excarnation. The ointment simulates that force of sex and more specifically death, putting the Witch at the threshold point between the realms of flesh and spirit, where they can commune with the dead, the spirits of nature, and the gods. It is often used at threshold times, the sabbat days themselves, as they are between points on the calendar of seasons and astrological alignments.

Figure 3: Witch's Sabbat Woodcut

The ultimate goal of these religious poisoners is to use these poisons upon themselves in a form of spiritual death and rebirth, which is the mark of initiation traditions all across the world. Initiation rituals simulate death, as the experience is meant to change the initiate, giving perspective and communion with transpersonal forces and a new lease on life. This is the rebirth of the Goddess. This is the secret of the Holy Grail of Immortality. This is what ultimately "opens upon the doors of youth" being reborn and the "knowledge of the Spirit Eternal." The poisoned cup also contains the "Wine of Life" as we seek to truly understand the mysteries of "The Charge of the Goddess."

The tales of the poisonous cauldrons or potentially deadly sleeping potions inducing a magickal coma are about death and rebirth, surviving in some garbled and scarier form in fairy tales. The point is not to kill, but to test, and to show the secrets of rebirth and renewed life. Coma is also a time for spirit journey, or out-of-body travel. For those in a nature-based religion, the Earth, Moon, and Sun "die" frequently, only to be reborn. In the winter the Earth goes to sleep, with everything "dying" until spring. The Moon goes dark once a month, only to be reborn as a silver crescent. The Sun "dies" daily in the western horizon, and yearly through the shift of the solstices and equinoxes. Many of the Witch's deities are based upon the forces of the Earth, Moon, and Sun, for they are teachers of these mysteries. Magick is not just change, but the deepest forms of initiatory magick are the changes of death and rebirth.

Poisons – and tales of the poison cauldrons of death – are sometimes tales of initiation and rebirth, not murder. Those without the eyes to see what is really going on beneath the surface easily misunderstand the symbolic meaning.

Cauldrons in Mythology

Many of the more famous cauldrons of myth have a connection to modern Witchcraft traditions. Many Craft traditions look directly to Celtic lore as their inspiration or mythic source of origin. Celtic lore has several references to cauldrons- and one could argue, the Holy Grail tradition- while on the surface seeming entirely Christian, they are really rooted in the Celtic Pagan traditions of the cauldron and the other magickal 'hallows'. There are also other tales that evoke the cauldron's magick.

The Cauldron of the Dagda

One of the stories to relate the four tools traditionally found in ceremonial magick (blade, wand, cup and pentacle) to the worldview of the more nature-based Witch comes from Ireland. It is the tale of the fabled four cities. In the account of The Second Battle of Mag Tuired, the children of the goddess Dana, the Tuatha de Danann, were said to come from four cities in the north of the world, versed in all manner of sorcery. When they arrived in Ireland, they came with four treasures – a stone, spear, sword, and cauldron. Many believe this to be a potential mythic source for the four elemental tools used in Witchcraft and magick, though variations of them can be found in many places across the world, including the Mithraic traditions. The Dagda's cauldron – called the Undry, or un-dry, the coire ansic, as many magickal objects in ancient myths had their own name, personality, and spirit to them – was a cauldron of plenty, like the cornucopia, or horn of plenty, in Greek mythology, and left no one unsatisfied. The Dagda's cauldron ensured that none of the Tuatha de Danann went hungry when battling their enemies for control of Ireland. Modern occultists classify tools and traditions in terms of the four elements, but it's important to note that the ancient Celts didn't quite use our fourfold elemental system, despite the four tools and the four divisions of Ireland. While most occultists wanting to make elemental associations would make this cauldron of the four tools a vessel of water, in many ways it is also about earth and the body, for it sustains. But on the deepest level, the element of water is about containing – the concept of the vessel and the outpouring flow – so both water and earth can be appropriate associations for the Undry.

The Cauldron of Bran

In the tales of *The Mabinogi* is the Second Branch, Branwen, Daughter of Llyr. The tale features King Bran and his sister, Branwen. Most Pagan practitioners assume these two are gods, for Bran is described with a titanic stature, usually a sly indication of godhood when myths are recorded and re-recorded in the Christian era. Elder gods were often giants. Likewise, the Dagda is described as a giant, leading many to think that perhaps Bran is the Welsh equivalent of the Irish Dagda, both being giants with magick cauldrons. While they have different stories – and different associations – there are points in the story of Bran that subtly connect the mysteries of Ireland and Wales together through the tradition of the cauldron.

Bran marries his beloved sister Branwen off to King Matholwch of Ireland, to make an alliance between Wales and Ireland. Playing a key role in the wedding is Bran's Cauldron of Rebirth or Regeneration, also known as the Pair Dadeni. In a conversation with Matholwch, he tells the tale of receiving a cauldron from a strange couple, two giants named Llassar Llaesgyvnewid and Kymideu Kymeinvoll, originally hailing from Ireland. They escaped from an iron house that they were trapped in by the inhabitants of Ireland, who then heated it to torture them. They made their way to Wales with the cauldron and gave it to Bran. He would only give it to someone of responsibility from Ireland, and used the wedding as a means to return the cauldron to Ireland, as part of

Branwen's eventual dowry to the King. Based upon the name of Kymideu, some speculate that the couple was a form of Cerridwen and her giant husband Tegid Voel. We will learn more about Cerridwen later, as the primary story of the cauldron mysteries.

In truth, Bran gave the cauldron to Matholwch to settle an insult. Bran and Branwen's cousin, Efnysien, often considered the Welsh god of disruption or of social ills by modern interpreters, is angered for not being consulted over the marriage as a respected member of the family should have been. In his anger, he slaughters some of Matholwch's prized horses. Matholwch is of course upset by this, and is ready to call the wedding off. For the marriage to continue, Bran must offer Matholwch compensation. This comes in the form of the Cauldron of Rebirth that Bran owned. Matholwch, of course, accepted such an amazing gift, but it appears that he and his people did not quite forgive the insult given by Efnysien.

This cauldron has the ability to resurrect the dead. It is the cauldron of regeneration. Place a dead body within the cauldron, and it will emerge alive, yet silent. Esotericists say this is a remnant from the concepts of initiation. One who experiences the underworld, the deep initiation of death and rebirth, is silent, for no amount of talking about it will adequately explain it, but two who undergo it never need to talk about it for them to recognize a silent understanding between them. Perhaps, like other mystery traditions, there are vows of silence extracted as well, as in today's British Traditional Wicca and various lodges of ceremonial magick.

Others read this tale and envision a necromantic zombie ritual of the cauldron, regenerating mindless corpses for battle, but not true resurrection with the retention of individual memories and mind. The magick is only of bodily reanimation. This is magick gone awry, taken out of the God's hands, akin to Prometheus stealing fire from the gods, but without the same liberating effects. People look at Arthur's quest for the cauldron in the same light. That's why they are silent. Those who emerge from the cauldron seem like silent shells of their former selves. Strangely, the resurrected never play a major role in the story, so we never get any information from their perspective. We have to remember that these tales were written in a Christian era, and any overt Pagan magick and mystery would be obscured.

Sadly, Branwen is mistreated by the king of Ireland and his people. The reason cited is the ire the people and king still have over Efnysien's disrespect. After continual abuse and beatings, Branwen learns to tame the birds, considered otherworldly beings and messengers. She sends a starling bird messenger to her brother, beginning a war between the two lands that ends in disaster, the destruction of the cauldron, and the death of Bran. Efnysien's own actions destroy the cauldron. His work results in the death of many Irish, and when he realizes Matholwch is using the cauldron to resurrect them, Efnysien hides among the Irish dead and is placed in the cauldron himself, destroying it from within as he is a living creature, not dead. The living cannot be put into the cauldron of the dead. On one hand, you can interpret it as a redeeming act for his cousins. On the other, the destruction leads to further imbalance between the realms of magick and mortals, leading to the death of Bran and most of his army.

Cauldron of Diwrnach

In the story of Culhwch and Olwen, there is the cauldron of the Irishman Diwrnach. The story is collected in versions of *The Mabinogion*, though not one of the four traditional branches of the work. Some would consider this one of the earliest recordings of a grail-esque myth, for it involved the illustrious King Arthur, cousin to Culhwch. Culhwch's mother dies in childbirth, and his new stepmother tries to marry him to her own daughter – whom he rejects. In retaliation, the stepmother curses him, so the only one he can marry is Olwen, the daughter of a fierce giant. Despite never seeing her, Culhwch becomes obsessed and seeks Arthur's aid. King Arthur lends him six knights, and they go forward in a search of Olwen. They do eventually find her, and she is receptive to the courtship, but cannot marry without her father's approval. Her giant father, Ysbaddaden Bencawr, the chief of the Welsh giants, is fated to die after his daughter is married, so he assigns forty impossible tasks to Culhwch. One of these tasks is to obtain the cauldron of the Irishman Diwrnach. Diwrnach is the steward to Odgar, the son of Aedd, the King of Ireland in this tale. Arthur goes to request it and is refused. His warriors battle the Irish and manage to steal the cauldron and leave Ireland with it. The cauldron is compared to a cauldron of plenty, but in the tale, its power, if any, is unclear. It bears in name a striking similarity to one of the Thirteen Treasures of Britain – the Cauldron of Dyrnwch the Giant.

Cauldron of the Head of Annwn

The Head of Annwn is the Chief of the Otherworld, considered by many to be the underworld. It is depicted most clearly in the First Branch of *The Mabinogion*: "Pwyll, Prince of Dyfed." In this tale, the seemingly more human figure of Pwyll ends up in Annwn while chasing game during a hunt. He encounters Arawn, possibly the god of the dead, or at least a king of the otherworld, and through the tale, ends up changing places with him, becoming the ruler of Annwn for the course of the year and defeating Arawn's enemy, Hafgan, in combat. Arawn/Pwyll and Hafgan are reminiscent of the battles of the Oak and Holly Kings. Later, Pwyll marries the goddess Rhiannon, and their son, Pryderi, is stolen and lost. An alliance is formed between the lands of Annwn and Dyfed.

In other tales, the god Gwyn Ap Nudd – a name meaning "Light, Son of Darkness" – is considered the head of Annwn. Gwyn is seen as the Faery King, God of Light, Horned God, and King of the Underworld, depending on his depiction.

In the tale of Preiddeu Annwfn or "The Spoils of Annwn," we find the Cauldron of the Head/Chief of Annwn. This cauldron is compared to many of the Welsh and Irish cauldrons of myth, but beyond this cryptic early Arthurian poem, we don't know more about it:

Am I not a candidate for fame, if a song is heard?
In Caer Pedryvan, four its revolutions;
In the first word from the cauldron when spoken,
From the breath of nine maidens it was gently warmed.
Is it not the cauldron of the chief of Annwvn? What is its intention?
A ridge about its edge and pearls.
It will not boil the food of a coward, that has not been sworn,
A sword bright gleaming to him was raised,
And in the hand of Lleminawg it was left
And before the door of the gate of Uffern, the lamp was burning
And when we went with Arthur, a splendid labour,
Except seven, none returned from Caer Vedwyd.
— from Book XXX, *The Book of Taliesin*

The distinguishing characteristic is the association with nine maidens, sometimes seen in Neopagan circles as nine Witches, akin to the nine sisters in the earliest tales of Avalon and the nine Maidens of the Wells whose rape creates the Wasteland of later Arthurian lore. This cauldron seems to have something to do with words and speech, akin to inspiration, as well as cooking food for heroes, not cowards.

The Cauldron of Cerridwen

Cerridwen's Cauldron of Awen, of Inspiration, is possibly the most famous of the cauldrons, and forms the foundation myth for most of this book and for most cauldron mysteries of modern Witchcraft. Essentially, we have a Witch with a cauldron, living upon an island with her husband, a giant named Tegid Voel and her son and daughter. She also obtains servants, or slaves, one a young boy and another an old man. The stature of her family, other than her husband, is never really described, so we are not sure if they are all giants or not. The hut and cauldron are not described in gigantic proportions, so perhaps Cerridwen can alter her size at will.

Cerridwen is making a magickal potion of knowledge and wisdom for her ugly son, whom she fears no one will love due to his unsightly appearance. Her magick for some reason cannot transform him physically, but she believes that if he is eloquent and knowledgeable, if he knows story, song, and most importantly magick, he will be accepted and loved despite his appearance. Through the aid of her servants, she concocts a potion known as *greal*, designed to give him this knowledge, yet her plans go awry when her servant boy, Gwion Bach, "accidentally" receives the blessings of the potion, not her son. He escapes his mistress through a series of animal shapeshifting experiences and is pursued until caught and later reborn as the bard Taliesin.

In many ways, Cerridwen's cauldron fulfills all three functions of mythic cauldrons. Her cauldron's power, or at least her potion, is one of magick and transformation, but it is also poison, for the remainder of the brew does turn toxic and ends up poisoning water and animals. Though not an obvious source of food, the cauldron gives spiritual sustainment, as it's meant to help an ugly boy survive in a tough world – providing him the means to relate to others, to socially and emotionally sustain him in community, if not a means of nutritional sustainment. In Pagan sacramental ceremonies inspired by The Church of All World's use of Robert Heinlein's book *Stranger in a Strange Land*, when we say "may you never hunger" and "may you never thirst," we mean it both in the physical sense of starvation and dehydration as well as in the spiritual sense of never being empty of a higher form of energetic and inspirational nutrition.

Cauldron of Ceres

The cornucopia, or horn of plenty, has become associated as a symbol and tool of many of the Earth and grain goddesses of the Mediterranean, including Gaea and Demeter/Ceres, even though classical myth associates it more properly with Zeus' nursemaid Amalthea and the Roman goddess Abundantia, the goddess of abundance. But it is the inner mystery traditions of Demeter and Ceres, those of Eleusinian and related sects, that interest us here. In the inner mystery traditions associated with Ceres, the Roman name of Demeter, sea water was mixed with barley, flowers, and other ingredients in a cauldron to form the sacrament of the mystery traditions – insight and knowledge of life after death. We know in the story of Demeter and Persephone that Demeter, in mourning for the loss of her daughter to the underworld, would eat or drink nothing except kykeon, considered a peasant's drink of barley, water, and herbs, in this case, pennyroyal, controversially considered a somewhat dangerous herb for those pregnant, but with digestion-aiding properties, also now associated with mystery initiations. Kykeon became known as the initiatory drink of Eleusinian rites, breaking their fast, and many believe that they used a particularly powerful psychoactive version of it. The most popular contemporary theory is that the barley was infected with ergot, a psychoactive fungus with LSD-like properties. Others believe it was a form of entheogenic mushroom or involved opium poppies.

As in the story of Cerridwen, where the brew of greal is made from sea foam and the remains of it considered poison, only initiates are said to drink this brew of Ceres. Some say the nine muses must blow upon the fires of the cauldron of Ceres, akin to stories of the nine maidens or nine witches who must blow upon the pearl-rimmed cauldron found in "The Spoils of Annwn." Due to these similarities, many eighteenth-century folklorists like to make a clear connection between the mysteries of Ceres and the mysteries of Cerridwen. While we tend to say in modern English a soft C in Ceres, as in "cereal," there is evidence of ancient pronunciation with the hard K sound, just as we say in the names Cerridwen and Celt. Because of this similar sound and story, parallels are drawn between two different mystery traditions. Perhaps they are in harmony in spirit and in myth, but we have no direct worldly evidence linking the bards and Druids of Wales to the mystery schools of Greece and Rome. Yet to the occultist's eye, everything is connected on some level.

Cauldron of Medea

Medea is a figure in the Greek story of Jason and the Argonauts, usually depicted as a Witch, priestess of Hecate, and villain, but who also appears in some tales to be a descendent of the gods, a niece of Circe, and the granddaughter of the Sun Titan, Helios. She is a controversial figure, as she is clearly depicted as a murderer in most stories, though modern Neopagans and feminists want to understand the layers of her story, and wonder if there are older, richer, and more positive tales beneath the ones written by Greek men. Like other dark goddess figures, her story is a difficult one for modern Witches to reconcile.

Medea had a cauldron, which, like Bran's cauldron, renews life and restores vigor. She would mix a wide variety of herbs, seeds, stones, sand, frost, and animal parts, and stir it with an olive branch. When the olive branch sprouted leaves and fruit, she knew the brew was ready. She would either dismember an animal and place it into the cauldron to revive it, younger than before, or slit the throat of a human, usually a man, place his blood in the cauldron and then feed him the brew, resurrecting him and transforming him into a younger version of himself. Of course, she shows this trick to the daughters of Pelias, who are unsuccessful at reviving their father, helping further Medea and Jason's plans with his death. Medea is, however, successful with Jason's father, Aeson, restoring him to youth, so he could participate in the celebrations of the Golden Fleece. In many ways, Hera orchestrated the death of Pelias, making Jason fall in love with Medea in hopes that Medea would kill him. Like most Greek tales, the motivations and actions of gods and humans are tangled and difficult to clearly apply in modern spiritual context.

Cauldrons in History

Just as we can find cauldrons of myth, we can look to their physical correspondents in history – and in some cases pseudo-history or mythic history – and find similar themes to the myths we have learned. These items, while usually physically unverifiable, are considered by some to have a stronger root in physical reality than some of the cauldrons of the previous myths, even if no one has been able to produce all of them. They present tantalizing threads of our mythic history, and many could relate to actual objects.

Gundestrup Cauldron

Most famous of the historic cauldrons is a Celtic artifact known as the Gundestrup cauldron, as it was found in 1891 in peat moss near the hamlet of Gundestrup, Denmark. Scholars are conflicted over the origin of the cauldron. By craftsmanship, it looks to be Thracian, though the art appears Celtic, suggesting perhaps a Gaulish origin. The cauldron is formed in several pieces, and was found disassembled in the peat moss bog in a way that suggests the peat grew up around it after it was deposited. Most likely it was offered in a bog, and the peat grew around it over time. The various plates depict intricate scenes of what scholars believe are both human and divine figures. They appear to demonstrate acts of sacrifice, rebirth or initiation, blessings, and the mastery of nature.

*Figure 4: **Gundestrup Horned God***

One of the most famous depictions, believed to be a horned god figure such as Cernunnos, is beloved by modern Pagans, though alternative theories say it is simply a ritualist in a horned costume. In any case, the images and mystery continue to inspire the magick of modern Pagans. The Gundestrup cauldron and its art will be focused upon in Chapter Nine.

The Cauldron Treasures of Britain

In Arthurian mythology, there is a list of thirteen treasures of Britain hidden from the world by Merlin, until the world is again ready for them. Each tantalizingly suggests forgotten tales in their name, relating them to mythic characters and stories lost, and four of the thirteen treasures have interesting associations akin to the mythic cauldron mysteries, even if they are not specifically cauldrons or cups. While these are listed in the mythic histories of Britain as actual objects, no artifacts related to them have ever been found and verified, so they are mythic history at best. The four treasures relating to cauldrons, plus the familiar fifth Cauldron of Annwn, are:

The Hamper of Gwyddno Long-Shank – This hamper, or basket-like container, could turn one meal placed into it into a hundred meals, multiplying the food. It is akin to the horn of plenty, though it has the interesting twist of needing an amount first, a seed or blueprint, before replicating the food. Such magick is reminiscent of the Christian miracle of the multiplying loaves and fishes by Christ. They were not conjured out of thin air, but replicated from a base amount. This follows the principles of alchemy. Unlike other forms of mythic magick, something cannot be made from nothing, but multitudes can be produced from a "seed" material. This demonstrates an alchemical principle known as multiplication.

The Cauldron of Dyrnwch the Giant – This cauldron presents a test or challenge to the user. It will heat and boil the food of a hero who places his food into the cauldron without any outside work. No lighting of any fire. But if a coward places food into the cauldron, nothing happens. The food remains cold and uncooked.

The Horn of Bran from the North – This simple drinking horn of plenty provides any type of drink the user desires. No requirements are asked of it. The desired drink magickally appears in the cup.

The Crock of Rhygenydd the Cleric – Like the Horn of Bran from the North, this crock requires nothing from the user and will simply manifest the favorite food of the person using it. It grants the food wishes of anyone who holds it.

Cauldron of Annwn – Preserved in *The Book of Taliesin*, in the text of *Preiddeu Annwn* or "The Spoils of Annwn" is an account of King Arthur's descent into the otherworld, Annwn, to seek a magickal cauldron, from the Chief, or Head, of Annwn. It is rimmed with pearls and will not boil the food of a coward. Though considered "historic" as we look at King Arthur as a semi-historical figure of Britain, this is one of the most magickal and mythic of the thirteen treasures.

The Holy Grail

The Holy Grail is considered historic in the sense that many believe it is a possible – and not only a possibility, but an eventuality -- to find a physical relic that is the Holy Grail. Those who look to Biblical history as an undeniable fact believe that the cup of the Last Supper existed, and due to its holy nature, most likely still survives. Interestingly enough, a lot of the magician's "hallows' have made their way into Christian occult mythos, such as the Spear of Destiny, and find a home in the Christian-Pagan mix of Arthurian lore.

While the Holy Grail's Christian origin is either a cup that caught the blood of Christ upon the cross, or the cup Jesus used in the Last Supper, its place in Arthurian lore has always been a little strange. In some tales, the same cup was used for both functions. Myth tells us that Joseph of Arimathea came to Glastonbury, England, and established the first British Christian church. He either buried the Holy Grail within Chalice Hill, magickally giving rise to the red iron spring associated with the blood of Christ by Christians, or he buried two cruets, one filled with Christ's blood to create the red spring, and one filled with tears, to create the calcium-rich white spring.

In the more esoteric sagas of the Grail Quest, the Holy Grail itself can take many forms, not always in the shape of a vessel. It's described at various times as a cup, cauldron, plate, cube, stone, lance, rose, or even a severed head. A popular theory among occultists and modern Pagans is the name of the potion in Cerridwen's cauldron, greal, gives us the name of the grail. Her Cauldron of Inspiration was the original template for the Celtic grail myths. An enticing theory for many of us, but not necessarily historically accurate, or at least not provable.

Many believe the quest for the Holy Grail is the spiritual quest for redemption, and the grail is not a physical historic relic, but an inner experience that cannot be put into true words, so a symbol must be used. In the Christian context, it is the Holy Spirit, restoring virtue and healing the land. In a Pagan context, it is the love of the Goddess, restoring balance, granting inspiration, and healing the land. The association with the

Goddess' cauldron points to a potential Pagan origin.

Others look to the word play in French between san greal – holy cup – and sang real – royal blood – and have the theory that the Grail is not an object, but a person, or a blood line, directly connected to Jesus Christ. Perhaps the blood is not of Christ, but simply refers to the royal bloodlines of sacred kingship. Turn-of-the-century occultists concerned about the teaching of Atlantis claimed the lore of Arthurian romances had links to the dragon king mysteries of Atlantis, and the figures of Merlin, Morgan, and Arthur all played archetypal ritual roles in the sacred balance of power. They were manipulating the bloodlines of the descendants of the Atlantean kings who migrated to this new world.

The otherworldly origin of these experiences or objects is attributed to the realm of Avalon. Avalon is described as an isle in a lake, surrounded by mist and mystery. The sword Excalibur explicitly comes from the realm of Avalon. The grail's origin is not so explicit, but it stands to reason if one magickal "hallow" tool, the sword, comes from Avalon, perhaps the others do as well. The original inhabitants of Avalon were nine sisters, led by Morgan, a sorceress and healer. In a later version of the Arthurian mysteries, nine maidens, keepers of sacred wells, were raped, and that transgression against the divine feminine created the Wasteland. Perhaps the nine maidens relate to the nine sisters, and the wells are a form of grail. Both are considered to be otherworldly faery women, not mortal women at all, in the esoteric interpretations of the tales. The lake itself, now believed by many to be the lands around Glastonbury, absent their water, is like a caldera, a cauldron, where the magick is made. The well in Glastonbury from the red spring is also considered to be the scrying pool and cauldron of the chief sister, Morgen. The whole isle, now the town of Glastonbury, is a literal nexus, a metaphorical cauldron of magick and spiritual traditions. It is a cauldron of healing, for the waters, red and white, are said to miraculously heal and rejuvenate. Traditions from across the world – from mainstream and esoteric Christian to various Pagan, Wiccan, Goddess and Witchcraft, with Buddhist, Hindu, Qabalist, Voodou, and New Age – all mingle in this cauldron of a little town.

Alchemical Crucible

The crucible is historically documented in the work of the European alchemists. This vessel, among a few others, was used in the process to prepare the Philosopher's Stone, equated with the Elixir of Life. When depicted as a physical substance, the Philosopher's Stone was described as a green stone, a liquid, a white powder, or a red powder, descriptions also associated with the grail. It had the power to transmute metals, notably lead into gold, and to confer healing and immortality depending upon the dose and use. Many believe that as in the stories of the grail and cauldron, this all spiritual allegory. The green stone, the heavenly emerald, is one of the forms of the grail, said to be the emerald from the crown of Lucifer. Transmuting lead into gold was what we might call the transformation of sin, or karma, into enlightenment. In the era of Jungian psychology, it is easy to see this as entirely metaphorical, but if that's the case, the ancient alchemists and philosophers still spent a lot of time in their laboratory, praying and working with real chemicals, flasks, athanors, retorts, and crucibles, in service of a metaphor. They worked with natural items too—herbs, animal remains, chemicals, and metals—seeking to unlock the wisdom of nature. Modern alchemists think many processes were occurring at once, within and without, and seek to emulate the alchemists of old. Processing the laboratory reflects internal processes, but both are connected – and both are necessary. Successful laboratory operations indicate the sufficient changes within. It really speaks back to our modern quantum understanding of the observer effect on that which is observed. There, the observer is really a participant, and that which is being observed, the chemical reaction, is also causing change within the alchemist.

Figure 5: Alchemist Laboratory

The prime directive of the alchemist is to "dissolve and coagulate," meaning to break apart, purify, and reunite. It is written in the arms of the occult image of Baphomet from Eliphas Levi. Another way this directive is written is through the code of VITRIOL, standing for Visita Interiora Terrae Rectificando Invenies Occultum Lapidem. This translates as "Visit the interior of the Earth to find and rectify the hidden stone." While alchemists did use vitriol chemically, they were also seeking to break down spiritually and visit the "interior of the Earth," the underworld, where things are formed, and to experience the Philosopher's Stone through perfecting the self. When one looks at the variety of cauldron myths, with journeys to the inner otherworld, western land, island, or underworld, it is easy to see a continuation of the theme in alchemy. Many see the imagery of the Temperance card in the major arcana of the tarot is a pictorial description of some of the mysteries of alchemy and the cup-cauldron.

Figure 6: Art-Temperance-Alchemy Tarot Card

The Cauldron of Hecate

Another not-so-historic image is three Witches gathered around the cauldron, famously documented in William Shakespeare's *Macbeth*. The image of three Witches around the cauldron was not unfamiliar to the audience of Shakespeare, and while definitely works of fiction, plays such as Shakespeare's documented ideas and practices of their time and pointed to some truths. Witches from which he drew inspiration – or Witches who later drew inspiration from him – use the cauldron as a means to call to Hecate, the Goddess of Witches. Before the Weird Sisters give their prophecy to Macbeth, they summon Hecate by delivering the famous lines "Double, double toil and trouble; Fire burn, and cauldron bubble." Though Hecate with a cauldron is a popular folkloric image, the ancient primary sources do not typically show her with a cauldron. Her symbols are torches, knives, swords, keys, gates, dogs, and crossroads – to name a few. But there is something about the Witch prophesying over the cauldron steam that rings true to us today – that must have rung true then as well – to become such a familiar cliché that it ended up in *Macbeth*.

Flying Cauldrons

Despite the popular notion of Witches flying on brooms, there is a wide variety of devices they flew upon, from steeds such as goats and rams to pitchforks, stangs, and – often forgotten – cauldrons. The most famous folklore akin to the flying cauldrons comes from the myth of Baba Yaga, where the Witch flies the night sky in a mortar, steering with a pestle. Modern Witches look at this as a potential symbol for consciousness, as the cauldron becomes the vessel or chariot for consciousness, not unlike the chariot of Jewish Kabalistic mysticism, the Merkavah, or its modern association with the New Age Merkaba. Through it, one can ascend or descend through the levels of reality, just as many see the Witch's flight as a symbol for astral travel.

Here is another historic example of a tale involving the flying cauldron with someone dressed all in white, this one from the Synodic Archives of Kazan University in Russia: " ... met a stranger dressed in white who took him to a flying cauldron. He ... visited another world, and then returned to Earth."

Inner Cauldrons

In some traditions, the energy centers of the body are described as cauldrons or vessels, which contain and transform energy. They are akin to, but often described differently than, chakra points. Eastern traditions, particularly the Chinese Taoists and Tibetan Tantriks, describe inner energy experiences as a form of biological alchemy. With their cauldrons and warmers, they use terminology that sounds like devices in a laboratory to describe aspects of the inner etheric anatomy.

They bear a striking possible parallel in the Celtic Irish tradition, in a little known poem known today as "The Cauldron of Posey," describing three possible energy centers paralleling the Taoist triple cauldrons of their Dan Tian, or dantian. Dan Tian means "red field" and refers to cinnabar, a red mineral of sulfur and mercury, two key alchemical ingredients. Modern alchemists influenced by Daoism can refer to the three centers as the Fields of Cinnabar. The similarity between the Celtic system (assuming it is an esoteric system originally) and the Chinese system is striking.

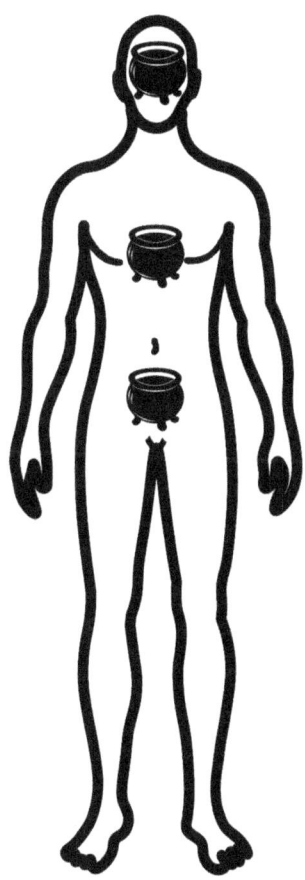

Figure 7: Three Cauldrons in the Body

The Celtic cauldrons are described as the mechanism by which a poet or bard gains their skill. The lower cauldron, Coire Goiriath, is the Cauldron of Warming, considered a cauldron of life, found in the lower abdomen or belly. It is what sustains life. In Taoism, the Lower Dantien is called Xia Dantien, meaning the Golden Stove, and is sometimes called the Sea of Chi. Brewed within this cauldron is an elixir of vitality, created when Jing, or Essence, is purified into Chi, or life force.

The second cauldron, presumed in the heart, Coire Ernmae, is the Cauldron of Vocation or perhaps Motion. While Coire Goiriath is always upright in the living, most people have Coire Ernmae on its side, or even upside down, and it must be turned by joy or sorrow, strong emotion, to be upright and functioning. The Middle Dantien of the Taoist is Zhong Dantien. It transforms Chi into Shen, or Spirit, and stores Shen, keeping the internal organs healthy.

The last cauldron – believed to be the skull, Coire Sois – is the Cauldron of Wisdom, Knowledge, and Inspiration. It is upside down, and is only activated once the middle cauldron is active. While a different strain of Celtic wisdom than the Cerridwen myth, it finds nice parallels with our studies of her myth here. The Upper Dantien, or Shang Dantien, transmutes Shen into Wu Wei, or the emptiness of enlightenment, what Western magicians might refer to as the void. Wu Wei embodies the great mystery.

In Raven Grimassi's book *The Cauldron of Memory*, the three cauldrons from lower to higher are called the Cauldron of Regeneration, Cauldron of Abundance, and Cauldron of Enlightenment. In my own work in the Temple of Witchcraft community (TOW), we simply refer to them as the Cauldron of Life, the Cauldron of the Heart, and the Cauldron of Inspiration.

Location	Traditional Name	Daoism	Grimassi	TOW
Belly	Coire Goiriath – Warming	Xia	Regeneration	Life
Heart	Coire Ernmae – Motion	Zhong	Abundance	Heart
Head	Coire Sois – Widom	Shang	Enlightenment	Inspiration

Chart 2: The Three Cauldrons

Exercise 3:
Three Cauldron Activation

While you can ritualistically have a cauldron – or even three cauldrons – before you, this working can be done with nothing at all before you, for it truly works with the inner energies in your own body. If you choose to work with tools, incense, and music to set the atmosphere of the exercise, I suggest aligning three cauldrons prior to the ritual, with the largest in front of you, the middle-sized one behind it, and the smallest behind that, furthest from you. In the large cauldron, place water. In the second cauldron, put a charcoal and burn powdered incense resin, such as frankincense, allowing the smoke to trail upward. In the smallest cauldron, put a small white taper, votive, or tealight candle.

Bring yourself to a comfortable sitting position, with your spine upright. With your eyes closed, breathe deeply, allowing your body to get into its own rhythm as you relax your muscles, from your head down to your feet. Feel the waves of relaxation move through you as you give your entire body permission to relax.

Clear your mind, allowing all thoughts to become like clouds floating away from the blue sky of your mind. Open your heart and feel the beating of your heart filled with perfect love and perfect trust. Within your heart is the secret fire of your souls, illuminating your entire body, guiding and protecting you.

Deepen your trance by counting backwards from twelve to one, envisioning the numbers on the screen of your mind. Then count from thirteen to one, with no visualization, to get to your deepest level and set your intention:

I seek to activate and align my Three Inner Cauldrons.

Breathe deeply, activating all three parts of your lungs. As you breathe, you should feel the bottom of your lungs fill first, near the abdomen, followed by the middle part of the lung, the thoracic, finally getting to the upper part of the lung closest to the shoulders, known as the clavicular lung. The deeper you breathe, the more you feel your abdominal area, the belly. Each breath is stoking the fire of the belly, as if adding fuel and air to the fire beneath the Coire Goiriath, the Cauldron of Warming. This is the Cauldron of Life, our seat of power and life force. Feel as if there is a cauldron, a swirling energy center in the belly. With each breath, you are filling up the belly, as it brews the elixir of life force. It fills you with a warmth that spreads to all points within your body, revitalizing you. Breathe deeply and allow this energy to build.

Once the lower cauldron feels as "full" as you can make it, take a deep breath, and as you inhale, raise the power up to the middle Cauldron of the Heart, Coire Ernmae, the Cauldron of Motion. It is said that this cauldron is tipped on its side. Joy or sorrow can turn it over, and once you begin filling it, it brews an elixir of well-being, radiating out well-being for not only you, but with love and concern for others. Take a moment as you breathe to allow a memory of something with great emotion, great joy or great sorrow, to be conjured in your heart. Let the memory rise like an ocean wave, peaking, cresting, and coming down, filling you. Feel the cauldron turn and feel with this emotional energy. Allow it to pass, and use the power to energize the Cauldron of the Heart. This is the energy of motion, the motion of the heart and the wheels of life. This is what powers our day-to-day life, beyond the animal existence. With each breath, you balance and brew a new vital elixir within you. Rest within the Cauldron of the Heart for a time.

Then with your next deep breath, inhale and rise up to Coire Sois, the Cauldron of Wisdom, Enlightenment, and Inspiration. This is usually turned down in most people. The open heart will lead to great sources of inspiration, turning it to be open to a flow from above. Only then, once it's turned by initial inspiration, can it catch the drops of the elixir from above, the potent drops of heavenly ambrosia, and mix them with the elixir from the heart. As you breathe, be inspired. Think of the moments where you have truly felt heaven touched, ideas and inspiration coming out of nowhere. Be open to them again. Turn the cauldron. You might even imagine three rays of light, the traditional image of the Druidic awen coming into your skull. Allow the light to descend and fertilize the elixir in your head cauldron, like wine or mead touched by yeast to ferment. Only with this addition will you truly rise and age like a fine wine. Feel the light, warmth, and inspiration fill your head.

Figure 8: Traditional Awen Symbols of the Three Rays

You might even feel the Cauldron of the Head overflow, and its energy seep down, filling the heart cauldron, which in turn overflows and fills the lower belly cauldron. Allow this reciprocal flow of steaming vapors to flow upward with the excess flowing downward, circulating the light and energy within you like an alchemical laboratory.

When you feel the experience is complete, bring your awareness back to the belly cauldron, gathering and storing any excess energy for your highest good and healing.

Then bring your awareness back to your flesh and blood, breath and bone. Feel your fingers and toes, ankles and wrists. Count up from one to thirteen slowly, and then close the veil of your awareness. Then count up from twelve to one. When ready, open your eyes and return your awareness to the world. Ground yourself as needed. Extinguish your candle and incense. Turn off your music. Record your experience in your magickal journal. Practice this exercise to induce both health and preparation for deeper experiences of inspiration.

One can't help but also notice parallels between the cauldron motif and the concept of the three primary "souls" or soul parts popularized in modern Hawaiian Huna and found in Witchcraft traditions, Voodou, Esoteric Christianity, alchemy, early Jewish mysticism, and ancient Greek and Roman thought, as well as modern psychology. Essentially, it states our consciousness operates in three levels, called the higher soul or higher self, the middle soul, and the lower soul. The lower soul is more animalistic and primal, sometimes referred to as the Fetch. The middle soul can sometimes be described as the most human of the souls, the personality. The higher soul is the part that is most divine, what many think of as the true soul, existing above and beyond space and time, fully aware, but not always able to communicate clearly with the other two parts. It is the source of higher guidance and inspiration. Like the lower cauldron, the lower soul provides the raw energy and connecting link between the three parts.

Fivefold Nature of the Vessel

While there are three primary kinds of substances in the cauldron – sustenance, potion, or poison – not unlike the alchemists' teachings of the three primary states of matter – salt, sulfur and mercury – the nature of the cauldron, when looking at the myths and legends, can really correspond to the fivefold division of the elements. The three potions are worked in the five elements just as the three primary matters of the alchemist must manifest through the five elements. The fivefold nature is of abundance, rebirth, inspiration, healing, and transformation.

Nature	Element	Cauldron from Myth
Abundance	Earth	The Cauldron of Dagda – Undry
Rebirth	Water	The Cauldron of Bran – Pair Dadeni
Inspiration	Fire	The Cauldron of Cerridwen – Cauldron of Awen
Healing	Air	The Holy Grail – San Greal
Transformation	Spirit	The Alchemical Crucible

Chart 3: Fivefold Cauldron Powers

Abundance - Earth

The cauldron is a vessel of abundance, and therefore the element of earth. The Dagda's Undry, as a horn of plenty, along with five of the Thirteen Treasures of Britain, clearly illustrate the generative, physical power of food and drink. Likewise, there is a sexual nature to it. The religions of Wicca are based upon the principles of divine and physical fertility. Abundance is a sign of the fertile Earth. The God's union with the Goddess is the key to that fertility and abundance, and is re-enacted in ritual through the token use of the blade/wand with the cup/cauldron or in fact through ritual sexual sacrament in the Great Rite. In a version of the Summer Solstice ritual from The Gardnerian Book of Shadows:

Magus comes forward sunwise and takes wand with kiss, plunges wand into Cauldron and holds it upright, saying, "The spear to the Cauldron, the lance to the Grail, spirit to flesh, man to woman, sun to earth."

He salutes High Priestess over Cauldron, then rejoins people, still bearing wand. High Priestess takes aspergillum, stands by Cauldron, says, "Dance ye about the Cauldron of Cerridwen the Goddess, and be ye blessed with the touch of this consecrated water, even as the sun, the lord of light, arriveth in his strength in the sign of the waters of life."

The legends of the Dagda mating with the Morrighan, a goddess of war and death, but also of the land, speaks of this. As in the stories of Arthur, we are taught the king and the land are one, as the queen is the representative of the Earth Goddess. When things are right between the people and the land, with the king as their sacred representative to the Goddess, abundance will reign. When it is not, the "grail" is lost and the Wasteland is formed all around us. While the historic validity of the ancient kingship teachings is under debate by scholars (at least in terms of the ancient British people where these myths take place), we see evidence of sacred kingship in many other Pagan cultures. The mythic truth of this rings strongly with us today.

Rebirth – Water

With the Cauldron of Bran, the Pair Dadeni, we see the most clearly mythic demonstration of rebirth in the lore. Literally the bodies are placed in the cauldron dead and come out alive, emphasizing not just the womb-tomb formula for the cauldron goddess, but the tomb-womb mechanic of rebirth. Every death in the physical world is a birth in the spirit world. Every birth in the physical world is like a death in the spirit world. We sacrifice all knowledge and memory to enter the flesh, and if this cauldron's teaching is code for initiation, then we are able to get the wisdom of death and rebirth without losing the line of memory and sense of past self as we forge a new post-initiation identity. The Gunderstrup cauldron's image of dipping the line of soldiers into the cauldron and returning them out again is so reminiscent of this motif, even if the original artist's intention was not as such, that it takes on this meaning in our Neopagan world.

Though in some traditions the element of Earth and the direction of north are the realms of the dead – connected to the North Star road of the ancestors and ancient psychopomps associated with the pole stars – in many other traditions, the west – the land of the setting Sun and the western seas – is the realm of the spirits and the dead. Ancestor altars and shrines often face west, and the reflective element of water is associated with the underworld. In the threefold division of the universe – the shamanic Upper World, Middle World, and Lower World – the realms were embodied by the sky, land, and sea, and in most of the Indo-European traditions, the great sea was envisioned to the west. The Theosophical and occultist motherland, Atlantis, was the western isle of the Atlantic Sea. Even for those of us on the east coast of the Americas, if you go far enough west to the unknown, you hit the foreign sea, making the realm of the setting Sun still have ancestral significance for us. The motherland prior to Atlantis, according to Theosophists and New Agers, was in the Pacific, where Hawaii is today, as the land of Lemuria or Mu. Like Atlantis, it may or may not be a literal truth as there is little evidence to support it, but its mythic quality lends psychic weight to those of us working with the mysterious islands to the West. To the Western occultist, the tales of Atlantis and Lemuria are akin to Shambhala and Shangri-La of the East, ideas whose stories teach us.

Inspiration – Fire

Inspiration is the quality best demonstrated by the Cauldron of Awen, brewing the greal of Cerridwen. Inspiration means quite literally to be "in spirit" and Cerridwen later became known as the mother and matron to the bards, for their ability to speak with the spirit tongue, to truly prophesize. One can wonder how much was prophecy and how much was spellcraft put into motion by their prophecy, but the bards were described in various Celtic traditions as having "fire in the head." They would flow with a magickal fire, an inspired knowledge that illuminated them. While air is associated with words and poetry, with communication, this fire is the pure fire of creativity, the fire of spirit, the fire of soul, that flows directly with little to no conscious thought. In the magick and miracles of Gwion Bach/Taliesin, his transformations were not learned skills, but things that intuitively came to him in need, for he possessed the flow of knowledge from all things. Cerridwen's terrestrial cauldron was not the source of his rebirth, but her own living cauldron womb was. Her cauldron gave rise only to his inspiration. His name describes his shining, or fiery, brow. We can also wonder about other traditions with spirit tongue, from the Pythias, the prophetic priestess of the Temple of Delphi, to the evangelical Christians speaking in tongues, and wonder if the same fire in the head phenomenon is working. It is from this direct line of intuitive inspiration that the bardic magick flows.

Healing – Air

Though healing can be associated with water – for the healing powers of love and the heart – or with earth – for remedying the illness of the body – air is an appropriate elemental choice for healing, for true healing comes when the original and perfect pattern is restored. Then healing can flow from the highest levels of fiery spirit to the realm of the heart and body. But when the pattern is damaged, any energy put into healing will be equally warped. In angelic magick, the elemental archangel of air, Raphael, is known as the divine physician. While technically a god of communication and messengers, Hermes-Mercury has associations with medicine through a misunderstanding between the Caduceus (communication symbol of two serpents) and the Rod of Asclepius (healing symbol of one serpent). But is not the basis of healing the appropriate communication between all our parts on a cellular level? It is this aspect that makes Hermes-Mercury an excellent patron for holistic health.

In the lore of the cauldrons, it is the Arthurian forms that hold the greatest promise of healing. It is the mysteries of the elder races of Avalon, withdrawn and more perfected than the common counterparts in the world of form, that hold the key. Morgan is a great healer due to her knowledge of herbs, magick, and anatomy. It is not necessarily compassion that is her mechanism of healing. It is esoteric lore and understanding. It is the promise of the Holy Grail, the healer of the Wasteland. While obviously a water image, what does the grail do? It restores the right relationship between the people and the land. What is this relationship based upon? An appropriate and respectful form of communication, ritualized through folk tradition. Communication is air. What must the grail knight do to retrieve the grail once found? Ask a question. "For whom does the grail serve?" is the appropriate grail knight question, yet few communicate it. The speech of the grail heals. The grail itself is described by modern seekers as a blueprint or matrix for life, time, and creation, akin to what many occultists would consider the mental plane or what cutting edge biologists would call morphogenic fields of consciousness, or biological information fields to help creatures sustain and evolve. Anything based on information and communicating is rooted in the element of air and can therefore restore health and balance.

Transformation – Spirit

Just as the fifth element is the source and end of the four, the last function of the cauldrons embodies all of the cauldrons. Each has the power of transformation. Abundance transforms the state of need to a state of fulfillment, restoring connection and faith in the material world. Rebirth transforms the state of the dead into the living, and in the case of initiation, the state of the spiritually sleeping, the living dead, to the truly awakened and alive. Inspiration transforms a lack of connection to one of flow and magick, evidenced by the many shapeshifting transformations that Gwion Bach experiences once imbibing the Greal of Inspiration. Healing transforms the living status of an individual, community, or land from losing life force and the resulting disconnection to gaining life force and the resulting flow. All the cauldrons transform in some way, for transformation is at the heart of magick.

One of the best symbols for this transformation is the alchemist's vessel, often a crucible. It is a vessel that can withstand heat, allowing the substances placed inside to undergo the transformation by heat. The athanor is the alchemical furnace that provides the constant and even heat of the alchemical processing, allowing substances to digest and transform within it. The alembic and retort are used to distill and refine chemical substances, catching the vapors and condensing them into a new vessel.

Along with the laboratory experiments, alchemists would meditate on these tools and their associated symbols, elements, and animals, and envision themselves being subjected to the chemical forces, likewise transforming their consciousness as well as their material substances in the laboratory. The laboratory is a vessel in itself as well, a container for the transformations of all these "cauldrons."

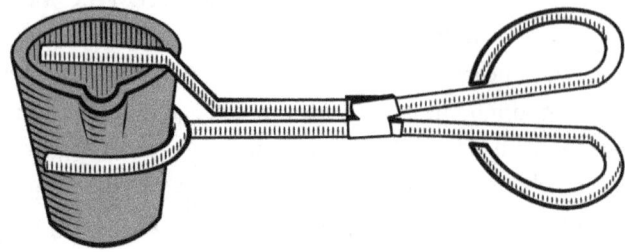

Figure 9: Crucible

Figure 10: Athanor

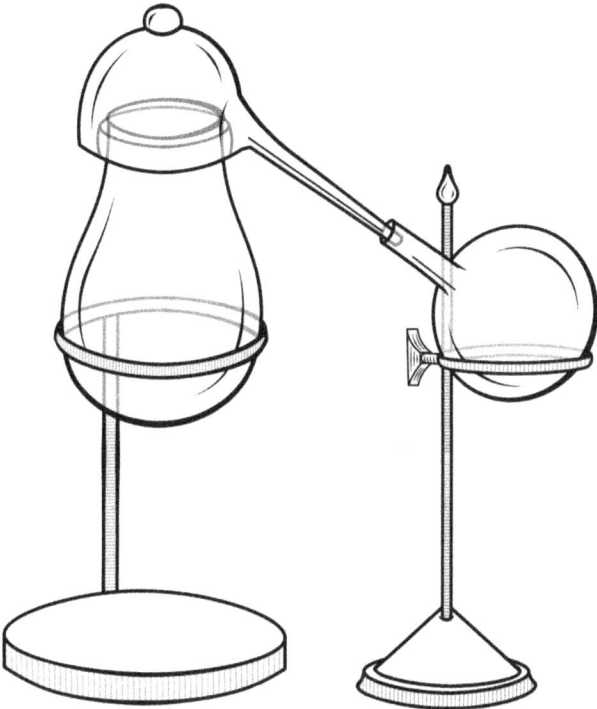

Figure 11: Alembic

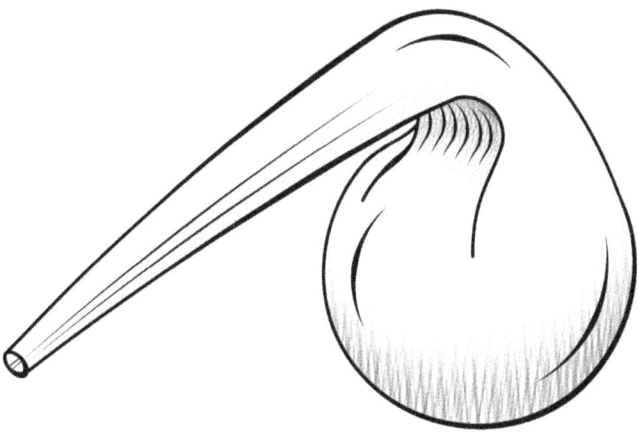

Figure 12: Retort

Exercise 4:
Fivefold Cauldron Blessing

Set your altar before you, with the cauldron in the center. Have five items for the five elements. For this exercise, I suggest the following elemental tokens, all to be cleansed prior to their use by either sprinkling pure water upon them or passing them through the smoke of a purifying incense.

Earth	Coins – Foreign coins, as opposed to native coins, are ideal for magick
Water	Water – Pure water either from a sacred site in nature or from your home area.
Fire	Candle – A simple white votive in a glass holder will do.
Air	Incense – Either stick incense or loose incense on charcoal in a heatproof vessel.
Spirit	Flower – A single cut flower, such as a rose.

Chart 4: Elemental Tokens

Start by quickly going through the steps of **Exercise 3: Three Cauldron Activation**, as a primary method of achieving a balanced sense of trance prior to the exercise. State your intention, out loud or silently, with these or similar words:

I attune myself to the fivefold blessing of the Cauldron.

Hold out the coins above the cauldron. Feel your energy mix and mingle with the coins, and charge them with your intention of prosperity:

In the name of the Undry, the Cauldron of the Dagda,
May the Cauldron grant me the blessings of abundance and prosperity.
May I and my family have all the resources needed for health and happiness.
So mote it be!

Drop the coins into the cauldron, and listen to them clack upon the metal.

Hold out the bowl or bottle of water above the cauldron. Feel your energy mix and mingle with the water, imprinting your intention over the water's own patterns:

In the name of the Pair Dadeni, the Cauldron of Bran the Blessed
May the Cauldron grant me the blessings of rebirth and renewal
May I be able to resurrect myself after all difficulties, reborn wiser.

So mote it be.

Pour the water into the cauldron, enough to cover the coins, but do not fill the cauldron completely.

Hold the candle above the cauldron space, unlit, but with matches or lighter handy. Infuse your intention into the wax of the candle:

In the name of the Awen, brewed in the Cauldron of Cerridwen
May the Cauldron grant me the blessings of divine inspiration and illumination
May I be ever flowing with divine light and magick
So mote it be!

Place the candle into its holder if not already there, and then light the candle. Place it in the cauldron, balanced upon the coins and within the water, so the flame is above the water, reflecting off its surface. You have now created the water that burns and the fire that flows, one of the sacred mysteries.

Take the incense and hold it over the cauldron, letting the incense be illuminated from the light below. Charge the incense with your intention:

In the name of the San Greal, the Holy Grail of the Mysteries
May the Cauldron grant me divine healing and restoration
May I be renewed in my connection to all that is holy
So mote it be!

Sprinkle the incense upon the charcoal, or light the incense stick, and then let the smoke waft. With your breath, blow the incense smoke into the cauldron, upon the waters and fire, careful not to blow out the candle flame.

Hold the flower over the cauldron, taking a moment to smell its scent and charge it with your intention:

In the name of the Crucible, the Alchemical Vessel of Transformation
May the Cauldron grant me transformation and purification
May I be initiated into the mysteries of the Elixir of Life
So mote it be!

Either place the flower stem into the water and prop the flower on the lip of the cauldron, or gently tear off the petals and float them upon the water of the cauldron.

Take a few moments to reflect on the fivefold blessing. Welcome the blessings and changes of the cauldron in all its forms, and allow yourself to start on a journey within this sacred container that will bring abundance, renewal, inspiration, healing, and ultimately initiation into the mysteries.

Extinguish the candle. You can keep it for other workings in this book. And you can repeat this whole exercise and reconsecrate a new candle when that one burns down. Continue to use the incense in future rituals and meditations. Keep the coins someplace safe, as a talisman for prosperity, or bury the coins near your front steps. Pour the water out around your home, along with the flower petals.

Chapter Three: Cerridwen and the Cauldron of Awen

By the daughter of blessings
By the son of disgust
By the mother of wisdom whom none could trust
Father of Giants unseen and unheard
Blind man of the hut barely speaking a word
Boy thrown into darkness stirring without end
Divine nectar to mix and nectar to blend
Releasing three holy drops, enchanted and charmed
The secret brew of the lady
Used to heal and to harm

Cerridwen is a mysterious figure in the lore of the Witch Goddess. While today we do consider her a goddess, her nature and role, like many of the Celtic deities, is unclear. In her stories she could simply be a sorceress or Witch, not necessarily a divine figure. Though she is married to a giant and has at least two children, presumably by him, suggesting a giant or size-changing ability befitting an elder divine power, it is not explicitly stated. Giants in these myths are considered to be a hint of elder godhood, the gods before the more "mainstream" or human-like gods, akin to the Titans of Greek myth who preceded the Olympians. Unfortunately for modern Pagans studying the Celtic traditions, the race of each being is not as clearly identified as it is in the Greek and Roman records, as those were written in a more explicitly Pagan time in a more linear culture.

As her myth grew, the idea of her being a goddess of magick and inspiration grew. In *The Triumph of the Moon*, author Ronald Hutton theorizes that her original, more Pagan image, was transformed by the poet Gogynfeirdd in the twelfth century, though she does appear with her cauldron of inspiration in other texts. Her interpretation as goddess was popularized by Robert Graves, who influenced much of the modern Wiccan and Neo-pagan revival, as she makes it into Doreen Valiente's reworked "The Charge of the Goddess" for the Gardnerian Book of Shadows, later distributed in various forms to many Wiccan and Pagan traditions. For modern Witches, it's hard not to think of her as a powerful, complex, and multifaceted goddess.

Some traditions with a passion for alliteration look to Cerridwen and Cernunnos as the primary images of the Goddess and God, though Cerridwen is from Welsh myth and folklore and the horned god Cernunnos, another mysterious historic figure, is Gaulish in origin. There is no particular folkloric tradition linking the worship or stories of the two. Yet I know I've been to rituals when both have been called on as the primary names of the cosmic creatrix and her consort, to great effect for all involved.

Cerridwen appears in a variety of Welsh tales, including "The Tale of Taliesin," which contains the most complete aspects of her myth and is often included in versions of *The Mabinogion*. She is also referenced in the poetry of *The Book of Taliesin* attributed to Taliesin himself, *Cynddelw Brydydd Mawr* by Gogynfeirdd, and *The Black Book of Carmarthen* under the name of Cyrridven, not specifically Cerridwen:

I will address my Lord,
To consider the Awen.
What brought necessity
Before the time of Cerridwen.
  — from "Juvenile Ornaments of Taliesin" from Book IX, *The Book of Taliesin*

I will adore the love-diffusing Lord of every kindred
The sovereign of hosts manifestly round the universe.
A battle at the feast over joyless beverage,
A battle against the sons of Llyr in Ebyr Henfelyn.
I saw the oppression of the tumult, and wrath and tribulation
The blades gleamed on the glittering helmets,
Against Brochwel of Powys, that loved my Awen.
A battle in the pleasant course early against Urien,
There falls about our feet blood on destruction.
Shall not my chair be defended from the cauldron of Cerridwen?
   — from "Song Before the Sons of Llyr" from Book XIV, *The Book of Taliesin*

Sovereign of the power of the air, thou also
The satisfaction of my transgressions
At midnight and at matins
There shone my lights.
Courteous the life of Minawg ap Lleu,
Whom I saw here a short while ago.
The end, in the slope of Lleu.
Ardent was his push in combats;
Avagddu my son also.
Happy the Lord made him,
In the competition of songs,
His wisdom was better than mine,
The most skillful man ever heard of.
Gwydion the son of Don, of toil severe,
Formed a woman out of flowers,
And brought the pigs from the South,
Though he had no pig-styes for them;
The bold traveller out of plated twigs
Formed a cavalcade,
From the springing
Plants, and illustrious saddles.
When are judged the chairs,
Excelling them (will be) mine
My chair, my cauldron and my laws,
And my parading eloquence, meet for the chair.
I am called skilful in the court of Don.
I and Euronwy, and Euron.
I saw a fierce conflict in Nant Frangeon

On a Sunday, at the time of dawn,
Between the bird of wrath and Gwydion
Thursday, certainly they went to Mona
To obtain whirlings and sorcerers.
Arianrod, of laudable aspect, dawn of serenity
The greatest disgrace evidently on the side of the Brython,
Hastily sends about his court the stream of a rainbow,
A stream that scares away violence from the earth.
The poison of its former state, about the world, it will leave.
They speak not falsely, the books of Bede.
The chair of the Preserver is here.
And till doom, shall continue in Europa
May the Trinity grant us
Mercy in the day of judgment.
A fair alms from good men.
– "The Chair of Cerridwen" from Book XVI, *The Book of Taliesin*

In the earliest version, the meaning of Cyrridven's name is associated with the word for "bent" or "crooked," so she is sometimes known as the crooked woman. That epithet is a poetic vindication to those of us who call the path of the Witch the Crooked Path. Her later spelling relates to gwen, the word for "white" and "blessed," shortened simply to "wen" in her case, making her the bright, white, and blessed woman. Because of the association of gwen with the faery realm, it is possible that Cerridwen was a faery woman, an otherworldly being. Depending on the myth and time period, the gods are often synonymous with the faery races and not the diminutive, winged creatures so many today exclusively equate with the faery races. Many correspond the faery races of Ireland with the deities known as the Tuatha de Danann, so it's possible that similar myths and beliefs exist in Wales.

Some in modern Wicca try to associate her with the Moon specifically, but other than sometimes being described in terms of a crone or hag, as well as an enchantress – one of her totemic forms being described as a "corpse eating" white sow – there are no specific lunar associations in her myth, though one could see the white of the pig as the white of the Moon, and the death eating a reference to the waning darkness of the Moon. In the tale of Lleu Llaw Gyffes in the Fourth Branch of *The Mabinogion*, "Math the Son of Mathonwy," it is a flesh-eating sow that leads the magician Gwydion to his nephew Lleu, who is injured and stuck in the form of an eagle. The pig is in the roots of the tree devouring the falling flesh from the injured eagle, and many see this totemic connection as a nod to the goddess Cerridwen, aiding the magician Gwydion and taking a role in an initiatory tale for Lleu. Cerridwen is often treated as a cognate to other dark crones and magickal goddesses, such as Hecate and the Morrighan. As the sow, she is at the roots, or underworld, of the tree.

In the Victorian era, poet and author Thomas Love Peacock, contemporary and friend of famous author Percy Bysshe Shelley, wrote a poem of Cerridwen entitled "The Cauldron of Ceridwen" in 1829. Retelling the tale of Taliesin, he clearly separates the characters of Morvran and Avagddu, often seen as one character in the more modern retellings of the tale, and relates Ceridwen as a "sage" or wise one. Peacock's poetry captures many of the images and themes that inspire modern Pagans today.

The Cauldron of Ceridwen

By Thomas Love Peacock

"The Cauldron of Ceridwen
The sage Ceridwen was the wife
Of Tegid Voîl, of Pemble Mere:
Two children blest their wedded life,
Morvran and Creirwy, fair and dear:
Morvran, a son of peerless worth,
And Creirwy, loveliest nymph of earth:
But one more son Ceridwen bare,
As foul as they before were fair.

She strove to make Avagddu wise;
She knew he never could be fair:
And, studying magic mysteries,
She gathered plants of virtue rare:
She placed the gifted plants to steep
Within the magic cauldron deep,
Where they a year and day must boil,
Till three drops crown the matron's toil.

Nine damsels raised the mystic flame;
Gwion the Little near it stood:
The while for simples roved the dame
Through tangled dell and pathless wood.
And, when the year and day had past,
The dame within the cauldron cast

The consummating chaplet wild,
While Gwion held the hideous child.

But from the cauldron rose a smoke
That filled with darkness all the air:
When through its folds, the torchlight broke,
Nor Gwion, nor the boy, was there.
The fire was dead, the cauldron cold,
And in it lay, in sleep uprolled,
Fair as the morning-star, a child,
That woke, and stretched its arms, and smiled.

What chanced her labours to destroy,
She never knew; and sought in vain
If 'twere her own mis-shapen boy,
Or little Gwion, born again:
And, vext with doubt, the babe she rolled
In cloth of purple and of gold,
And in a coracle consigned
Its fortunes to the sea and wind.

The summer night was still and bright,
The summer moon was large and clear,
The frail bark, on the spring-tide's height,
Was floated into Elphin's weir.
The baby in his arms he raised:
His lovely spouse stood by, and gazed,
And, blessing it with gentle vow,
Cried TALIESIN!'
Radiant brow!'

And I am he: and well I know
Ceridwen's power protects me still;
And hence o'er hill and vale I go,
And sing, unharmed, whate'er I will.
She has for me Time's veil withdrawn:
The images of things long gone,
The shadows of the coming days,
Are present to my visioned gaze.

And I have heard the words of power,
By Ceirion's solitary lake,
That bid, at midnight's thrilling hour,
Eryri's hundred echoes wake.
I to Diganwy's towers have sped,
And now Caer Lleon's halls I tread,
Demanding justice, now, as then,
From Maelgon, most unjust of men."

The Tale of Taliesin

In some versions of *The Mabinogion*, an extra branch of the book is created, beyond the traditional and clearly marked four sections, by including "The Tale of Taliesin" as a fifth section to this book of Welsh mythology. While the tale is the most complete account of a figure that shows up in many Welsh tales, it has subsequently been told and retold so many times, particularly in the context of Neopagan teachings and ritual, that it has taken on a life of its own and has, in some ways, mutated. The number of Cerridwen's original children is particularly unclear. In the *Hanes Taliesin*, it clearly appears to be three in the English translation, not including Taliesin, but Afagddu is later explained as a nickname of Morfran, rather than two distinct figures.

The following is a simple account, told much the way I first heard it. Though it is consistent with the basic elements of the tale, a person looking for a truly orthodox version should read a direct translation, available in many versions of *The Mabinogion* in print as well as online. We often fall in love with our first serious study of the work. Most of us in the occult world learned primarily from the translation by Lady Charlotte Guest published in 1877, really preserving and popularizing the tales. For that, Guest should be honored, and her translation is freely available and beyond copyright concerns, making it the most often quoted version (and the one I will be using when quoting *The Mabinogion*, unless otherwise noted). Though from a linguistic perspective, many would point out a lot of errors in details as our understanding of Celtic language and culture has grown. My more serious Celtic mentor used *The Mabinogi and Other Medieval Welsh Tales* as translated and edited by Patrick K. Ford, which I highly recommend as it has a great translation of both the four main branches and the other tales often included, particularly Taliesin.

There was a Witch who lived on an island in the middle of the lake of Bala, with her husband, the giant known as Tegid Voel. So famous was this Witch woman and giant husband that some knew the waters as Lake Tegid. The couple had two children.

The first was a girl named Creirwy. She was the loveliest girl any had seen. All those who saw her, who talked with her, loved her. She radiated light and blessings to all. One could not help but love her. Their son, named Morfran, was a strange and ugly child. Covered in dark fur or black feathers, his appearance was frightening. All who saw him were repulsed and turned away. He was renamed Afagddu, or Utter Darkness, due to his blighted appearance.

Cerridwen was a great Witch, and she used all her magick to transform her son from an ugly child to match the beauty of Creirwy. She failed. No matter what she did, not only could she not make him beautiful, she could not even make him ordinary in his looks. Her magick had no effect on his appearance at all. But she was the keeper of the Cauldron of Inspiration, of awen. And she was determined to brew a potion in it that would give her son the blessing of eloquence, storytelling, memory, song and magick. With all these talents, all would love him despite his appearance, and his life would be good. She found her lore in the *Book of Fferyllt*, but the potion's formula was complex. It needed continual stirring and constant supervision of its heat, not getting too hot and not getting too cold. So she obtained two servants, some say unwilling slaves.

The first servant was a blind old man named Morda. He had a sensitivity to the heat due to his blindness, and was able to tend the fire very effectively. The second servant was a boy named Gwion Bach. He knew nothing, so she had him stir the cauldron continuously. Both worked in her dark hut upon the island of Lake Bala.

Cerridwen traveled by her magick, flying to the corners of the globe, adding herbs and ingredients to her potion at the appropriate season and astrological time, including sea foam. It took a year and a day to brew this potion with constant heat and stirring. She would travel back to the hut, add her new ingredients, speak her charms over the brew, and leave again on her quest. All proceeded according to her plan.

One day, almost at the end of the yearly cycle as the potion neared completion, Morda got careless with the fire. He stacked too much wood, and the fire grew too hot. Young Gwion also got careless and tired. As the potion boiled, he did not notice. It bubbled and frothed until three enchanted drops flew out of the cauldron upon his thumb. Instinctively he stuck his burning thumb into his mouth to cool and soothe it and suddenly all the power of the potion was contained in those three drops and went into him. He received all the power meant for Afagddu. He immediately knew he would be in trouble with Cerridwen, as with her preternatural powers, she would know what happened and return to kill him for wasting all this time and effort. The potion remaining in the cauldron turned to poison and split the cauldron in two. Its contents ran out of the hut, into the lake, down the river, and into a weir, where the horses of

Gwyddno were drinking. Poisoned, the poor creatures immediately died from the effects of the potion.

With his new knowledge and magickal power came the knowledge and ability to shift his shape. Gwion became a hare, and escaped Cerridwen's land, moving so swiftly upon the ground that he felt she would never catch him.

Cerridwen investigated the hut where only Morda remained. In her fierce anger for the loss of this year and the loss of a precious gift for her son, she struck Morda so hard with a piece of wood that his eye fell out upon his cheek. Morda admonished her, for he had done nothing, and she agreed, realizing the fault lay with Gwion Bach. She began her hunt.

Being a master of magick, Cerridwen left the island and turned herself into the even faster greyhound to apprehend Gwion as the hare. Just as the greyhound's jaws would snap around the hare, the two approached a stream, and Gwion jumped up to become a salmon, diving back down into the water. She followed him into the water, becoming an otter herself. As she again was about to catch him, Gwion's salmon jumped into the air to transform into a tiny wren and fly away. The otter shape-shifted into a hawk, and she again pursued her prey. The wren led the hawk onto the threshing floor of a granary, and in an act of cleverness, Gwion transformed himself into a grain of wheat, a seed, hiding amongst thousands of other seeds. Cerridwen then became a black hen and ate all the seeds.

As soon as she did, she realized her mistake. Rather than digesting the seed, she had become pregnant with Gwion Bach. Nine months later, she gave birth to this new child. Seeing Gwion's soul through its eyes, she refused to name it anything for its new incarnation. Though she wanted to kill the child, she could not. But in fairness to her sad son Morfran, and her own nature, she could not keep him in her family. Cerridwen wrapped the child in a leather satchel, placed him in a coracle, a small rounded boat, and floated him upon the water. She left his fate to the mercy of the sea. He followed the stream as the poison did, and ended up in the same weir of Gwyddno.

He was fished out by Elphin, son of Gwyddno, who was urged by his father to visit the weir on this special day. Elphin's luck had always been poor, being born under an ill-fated star, and the weir upon May Eve could grant luck, bringing something new to start one's life with the yield of good fish. But Elphin found no fish. He, and others, feared his ill luck had destroyed the virtues of the weir. Yet he did find a strange leather satchel. As Elphin opened the bag, the light struck the child's brow and was reflected brightly. He exclaimed "radiant brow" which in Welsh is Taliesin, and Taliesin became the child's name. Taliesin immediately began speaking to Elphin as if an adult. He grew rapidly and eloquently to be the bard in the household of Gwyddno, Elphin's father, bringing them many blessings and rectifying his debt from the horses until his own fate and adventures took him further afield, serving with King Arthur. He became Britain's chief bard and Cerridwen from then on became known as mother of the bards.

The Meaning of the Tale of Taliesin

The tale of Taliesin can be read in many ways, but to me, the most important view is to look at the tale as one of initiation. It's the origin story of the 'first' bard, but really a cognate for the magician, the Druid, the sorcerer, or Witch through the Goddess as the mother of bardic sorcerers. Each of the characters in the tale is an aspect of the initiate divided, what we might psychologically view as sub-personalities or impulses given form. But each is not just an inner experience, but a power of the deep mysteries of the land, and the consciousness that resides within and beyond the land itself. Each are contact points for otherworldly forces as embodied by the island.

In the tale, Cerridwen takes the form of the initiator, above all the other characters in power and importance. Someone acting as such an initiator can also be a terrestrial teacher to the living initiate seeking the mysteries, but terrestrial teachers are always mediating a higher magickal force. In this tale, Cerridwen is really the mediator of awen, of divine inspiration, the true initiator bringing the inspiration, the fire in the head which initiates and changes Gwion Bach into Taliesin. Like any good initiation tale, there is hard work, lessons from nature in the form of animal shapeshifting, and literal rebirth, before being sent out into the world to fulfill his mission as first and chief bard of Britain. From that moment forward, all bards become an aspect of Taliesin, and Cerridwen becomes the mother to them all.

The tale of Taliesin is the tale of life, of our journey that can lead us to an unexpected place. Would one guess that poor Gwion Bach, by these circumstances, become a great bard? Probably not. We, too, do not always know where the magician's Will is leading us, but when we listen, we come to the right place at the right time. I know I believed my Will was taking me into music, not writing and certainly not teaching Witchcraft, but here I am.

Regeneration is a theme. How many lives does Taliesin go through? He experiences Gwion Bach, a hare, a fish, a bird, and a seed. He is reborn as Taliesin, new and fresh, through several trials and the womb of the Goddess. The poetry of The Book of Taliesin relates him to be an almost universal figure, reborn again and again, witnessing history. He has always been here, and he will always be here, though his home is the "region of the summer stars." Each new life regenerates himself with new lessons.

It is a tale of wisdom, of waiting and learning, and accepting the unexpected blessings life has to offer, even if they come with dangers and difficulties. Our measure is found in how well we handle them.

And lastly, it is, quite literally, a tale of inspiration. We are meant to be inspired, to seek our own cauldron, our own Cerridwen, and find our own purpose and muse, even in unlikely places. We are inspired to learn for a year and a day and let that journey take us into unexpected avenues, listening to the voice of inspiration and using what wisdom we find within ourselves after we've taken our three drops.

Mother of Darkness and Child of Light

The initiatory tale is one of the most compelling and complex of the themed myths of what I call the Mother of Darkness and the Child of Light. Many similar tales and fragments of tales exist, but you do not quite see the same clear initiatory formula as the three specific periods of darkness found in the Taliesin story. The story of Finn MacCool is quite similar, with a salmon eating the hazelnuts of knowledge replacing the cauldron, but that initiation yields more of a warrior-adventurer-hero than a master magician. But by looking at other initiatory tales between mother and son or simply Goddess and God, we gain a great appreciation for the inner alchemy that is occurring.

From a warrior's perspective, you have the initiatory tale of Arianrhod and Lleu. In character, I don't think Arianrhod is any less harsh than Cerridwen. Perhaps she is not as murderous, but in the tale she is vengeful. In modern times Arianrhod is often joined not only with Cerridwen, but also with Blodeuwedd as a triple goddess of Wales – Blodeuwedd as flower maiden and wife, Arianrhod as Mother and Moon Goddess, and Cerridwen as dark crone of the cauldron.

Our knowledge of this link comes from the story of Lleu and Arianrhod, with the Cerridwen reference from the corpse-eating sow that devours the flesh of a transformed eagle of Lleu. While I love the poetic interpretation, there is no historical, folkloric, or religious documentation of the three being linked as a triple goddess. Many of our modern ideas of the triple goddess are traced to the author of *The White Goddess,* Robert Graves, yet they still make a poetic sense to us, cutting across time and culture as we craft our current traditions.

In a rite of kingship to become the foot-holding maiden of King Math, Arianrhod jumps over Math's rod and gives birth to two beings. The first is clearly the sea god Dylan. The second is described as a formless mass, which is quickly scooped up by her brother, the magician Gwydion, and taken to a chest where it incubates. Through his care comes his nephew, Lleu. Already humiliated by her very public birthing in the court of King Math, when Gwydion presents her new, fully-formed son to her, she is furious.

Many esotericists suspect that some fertility rite is going on there, with possible incestuous themes regarding Math and/or Gwydion, and this is partly what compounds her anger. The test of jumping the rod is a test of virginity, though the "rod" itself might be a sexual reference. The subsequent immediate birth of two beings shows Arianrhod is not the virgin she claims to be and is therefore unqualified to hold the feet of King Math in peacetime.

Just as Taliesin experiences three darknesses, Lleu experiences three curses, each in turn. Arianrhod curses him to not have a name unless she names him, and then refuses to do so. Gwydion tricks her through his illusions into naming Lleu based upon his "skillful shot" that she observes with a bird. Literally his name Lleu Llaw Gyffes means "the fair-haired one with the skillful hand."

Arianrhod then curses Lleu to not bear arms unless she arms him. Again Gwydion disguises them with illusions and then makes the pretense that her castle is being attacked, so she arms all able-bodied men, and unknowingly, arms her son. Here is what we today call the shadow self in modern popular psychology, but the concept is known in occult circles, from a form of the Dweller on the Threshold to the Egyptian concept of the shew or swt.

Arianrhod curses Lleu a third and final time to not have a wife from any of the races upon the Earth. To get around this particular curse, Gwydion and Math build him a bride made from flowers, creating the woman Blodeuwedd. Blodeuwedd however, did not want to be married to Lleu (a question no one asked her) so she finds a lover in Pebr, and they conspire against Lleu. Blodeuwedd convinces Lleu to tell her what his magickal weakness is, how he could be killed, and he reveals the strange liminal circumstances around his potential death by a magick spear. She and Pebr conspire to create those circumstances so they can be together. Pebr mortally wounds Lleu with the magickally forged spear, as Blodeuwedd betrays Lleu's trust as his wife with this secret knowledge.

Lleu escapes through a transformation into his totemic form, an eagle, and the rotting flesh that falls from his wounded body is eaten by the white sow. Gwydion heals Lleu and curses Blodeuwedd by turning her into an owl, a bird shunned by all other birds, but known for its flower-like face feathers.

Other pairs of deities with an initiatory structure also exist, but none so complex or complete as these Welsh tales. We can look to the tale of Mabon and Modron, though the original is only fragmentary in nature. In the surviving versions, it is King Arthur who rescues Mabon from the otherworld. And to do so, he has to encounter five animals, the five oldest living creatures: the blackbird, the stag, the owl, the eagle, and the salmon. The salmon links this teaching to that of Finn MacCool and the salmon of wisdom.

Arthur himself has an initiatory relationship with the Lady of the Lake, originally Morgan, echoing Cerridwen as a lady of the lake. In other Welsh tales, the story of Rhiannon and her lost son, Pryderi, echoes the loss of Mabon from Modron, but the tale "Pwyll, Prince of Dyfed" – found in the First Branch of *The Mabinogion* – is really more of the trials and initiations of the mother rather than the son, whom she would name "trouble," which is the translation of Pryderi. You can also look to the tales of Branwen and Bran as initiatory for both siblings, though again, not a tale of mother and son but of brother and sister. We'll be exploring Bran and his cauldron further.

Looking beyond the Celtic countries, we can find other mother-son myths as models for initiation. I look to the tales of Dionysus. While our modern era emphasizes his mortal mother Semele, other tales see a more divine mother in the form of Demeter/Ceres or her daughter Persephone/Proserpina. We see a myth of protection, light, death, and descent in the Norse tale of Frigga and Balder. Frigga makes all things in the nine worlds promise to never harm her son, the beautiful, light-filled Balder, yet she forgot the mistletoe, and a dart of mistletoe leads to his death and descent into the underworld. We also have the myth of Horus and Isis. Her son is the child savior and solar figure after the death of his father Osiris, destined to triumph over his uncle Set. We even see these themes time and again in Christianity with Mother Mary and the reborn Jesus Christ.

Any of these tales could be a wonderful exploration of the Mother and Child mythos, though for our work here, we shall focus on the mysteries of the cauldron and the matrix of the Cerridwen and Taliesin story.

Part Two of *The Goddess of the Cauldron* is devoted to the three periods of darkness, the three degrees of initiation in this powerful tale, and the lessons that each contains. Many systems of magick, ceremony, and Witchcraft divide themselves into three primary degrees, and the story of Cerridwen gives us a similar pattern with different teachings. It can be an effective addition or substitution to other types of training in the magickal communities.

The first darkness embodies the plant wisdom of the teachings, and how the plants can be great catalysts and initiators, being an intermediary between the realm of animals and humans and the mineral consciousness of the deep Earth. The plant wisdom, through the potion, initiates the process of change. The second darkness comes from a place of red tooth and claw, the animal wisdom of the Witch where one must eat and be eaten. This is embodied by the chase and the shifting of shapes leading to rebirth in a new womb. The third darkness leads to the transpersonal vision among the tides and stars, to then return from this dream and use it to guide one's life work as the bard, magician, or sorcerer.

We shall look at them through the lens of myth and poetry, alchemy and occult theory, and then experience them in ritual and pathworking, integrating their life, regenerations, wisdom, and inspiration in our own lives.

Exercise 5:
Calling to Cerridwen

Since Cerridwen is the preeminent teaching spirit around the mysteries of the cauldron in the context of modern magick and Witchcraft, if you plan on working with her, it is best to petition her. By politely establishing a request to enter into a relationship with her to explore these mysteries, she is more likely to take an active interest in your development, and be more fully present as you work with her, following the path of Taliesin.

Place your cauldron before you and put a single votive candle in the center, ideally in a glass holder so the wax does not spill into your cauldron. Light it. Perform Exercise 3 to attune to the cauldron powers within you. And then simply recite this, or something similar from your own inspiration, to call to the goddess Cerridwen:

I call to Cerridwen
Lady of the Cauldron
I call to Cerridwen
The Mother of Bards
I call to Cerridwen
The Crooked Lady
I seek the Mysteries of the Holy Earth
I seek the Mysteries of the Heavenly Stars
Lead me into the Hut of Darkness
Follow me through the fourfold chase
Lead me into your Womb of Rebirth
And out to the Seas to Find my own place
Blessed be!

When done, take a few moments to reflect. See if you sense her presence connecting to you. It can take time for some, while others feel a connection almost instantly. Extinguish your candle and pay attention to your dreams and ideas in the coming days and weeks. Look for ways that Cerridwen might be reaching out to you, to accept your invitation.

Part Two: Initiation from the Cauldron

Chapter Four: The First Darkness of the Hut

By the darkness of the hut
In the school of the cave
Where the cauldron boils hot by the work of the slave
Balms of the field, banes of the hedge
Diving deep these waters we dredge
Day after day and week after week
Searching for that which none may speak
Cracking the cauldron and poisoning the plot
Seeking the light of freedom beyond
By remembering all we've forgot.

As the initiate, we begin our tale as Gwion Bach, Cerridwen's slave or servant boy. He is brought to the hut sheltering her cauldron upon the island in the lake. Though we enter the story by Gwion's path, in reality, we are like all of the characters in the story. Each aspects a different part of our self, of our souls. Each is like a soul part, a distinct essence fulfilling a particular function in our initiation into magick and life. While some of these entities can be considered vast transpersonal powers – titans both within the landscape of the planet and beyond the realms of time and space, affecting us, but not truly of us – the "three" children of Cerridwen are most certainly all connected, and in her children, I include her slave "child" Gwion Bach.

The children of Cerridwen relate in many ways to the three selves found in us all. Creirwy is the light side of the self, when looking at things in polarity. She is brightness, light, and all that people are attracted to and long to be. She is the anima, the idealized opposite of the very mortal Gwion Bach. In a more vertical view of reality, she is the higher self, the perfected self. She is the gold of the alchemist. Strangely she has very little to do in the story. Other than being announced as beloved, her part in the tale is done, or at the very least unseen. I always wondered if she had a story that continued onward in some other tale, where she was the hero, but if so, that tale has not readily survived.

Morfran, also known as Afagddu, is her opposite. He is the shadow to her light. He is the darkness and lead of the alchemist seeking to be transformed. He is like a lower self, but the self that contains all that is unloved and repressed. He is what we today call the shadow self in modern popular psychology. In some ways he can be considered the lower self in a three-soul model of the self, though he's really the shadow of the lower self, not just that which is child-like and innocent, but that which has been rejected. He is described as dark, as his name Afagddu means "utter darkness," though some interpret Afagddu as still another sibling, distinct from Morfan. Morfan is described with either dark fur or dark feathers or with hair like a stag's upon his face. Both are magickal creatures with deep lore, but speak to the lower, animal nature. Many make associations with him as a crow boy or crow baby. Crows have a deep connection with mystery, magick, and the otherworld. Stag and deer are creatures of the forest. Many conceive the Pagan horned god as a stag god, such as our interpretation of the Gaulish Cernunnos. Unlike his sister, Morfan/Afagddu seems to survive the tale, and go on to other stories. He is one of the three survivors of the battle of Carlann and one of the "three irresistible knights" along with Sanddeff, who is described like Morfan's sister, Creirwy, as beautiful as Morfan is ugly.

Gwion Bach, the young slave boy, is essentially the personal human self. He is the one stuck in the toil of everyday life, stirring the cauldron. He is the one not embodying an extreme or free to go about his own business. He is bound by either slavery, employment, or some other obligation to Cerridwen, much like many of us who feel bound, even enslaved, by the life we have unconsciously agreed to in our society. It's not unlike the jobs of toil we have all gone through on the path of life, perhaps not seeing the blessings and lessons in the day-to-day work and what it has to teach us if we had but the eyes to see and the ears to learn. Gwion has great potential, which he does fulfill, but the potential is not obvious upon first glance. Others are inclined to see the treatment of Gwion as akin to physical or emotional child abuse, but it's good to keep in mind the stories are of mythic proportions, not advice for everyday human behaviors.

Morda, the blind man keeping the fires, is an interesting character. Although Morfan is considered by some a "lower self" due to his darkness, if we look at him more like the shadow, then Morda takes the classic role of the lower self in three-soul cosmology, with a higher all-knowing self, a middle human self, and a lower instinctive or animalistic self. While Morda is no animal, he's a man, he plays this role well. He is described as either blind, or eventually with just one eye, reminiscent of the Norse god Odin, who sacrifices an eye in this world for the wisdom of the other world. Odin is a trickster magician god who deepens his power through this sacrifice. Morda has to let instinct guide him. He can't see, so he relies on his other senses, such as the feeling of the heat. His actions are repetitive, fulfilling a pattern as he keeps watch over the fire. Morda is also a village name near the border of England and Wales, and a river name, suggesting an association with a genus loci, or a spirit of the land. One might see him taking the role of elder wise man to Gwion Bach, not passing on the high intellectual knowledge of the priest or Druid, but the day-to-day instinctive wisdom of the man living on and with the land itself. He is not that different from Gwion, another slave, but has lived a life longer than Gwion doing things – and before blindness, perhaps seeing things – that give him greater understanding and insight. Like the lower self, he guides Gwion into the mysteries. How does he do that? It is his error in stoking the fire that lets the brew get too hot in the first place.

This first movement, the first darkness of the tale, leaves us only with the mysterious Tegid Voel – mostly un-described, who, like Creirwy, plays little to no part in the actual tale – and Cerridwen herself. Tegid Voel is usually depicted as a giant, and giant status is "code" for a divinity, possibly an elder god, a chthonic force of the land before this cycle of life. The Greeks knew such forces as Titans. He is associated with the island in the lake, Lake Bala or sometimes called Lake Tegid. His power comes from the land before the land we know now, the deepness of the elder Earth. Locally there is the tale of the townsfolk turning against the harsh and cruel rule of Tegid.

Cerridwen is not specifically described as a giant, but if her husband has that titanic status, then she must be beyond our ordinary ken. Scholars will rightly insist that, like other Celtic divinities, nowhere is she described as a goddess, simply a Witch or sorceress, but Witches and Wiccans today will insist that she is a goddess, or at the very least, an elder power. To Gwion Bach, she is master or mistress, pseudo-teacher, enemy, mother, and ultimately, the higher power acting as initiator.

Through this cast of characters, we have expressed aspects of male and female; beautiful and ugly; light and dark; young and old; foolish and wise; careful and careless; human and god; and giant and child. We have a trinity of higher self, lower self, and middle self, with shadow and the transpersonal forces to bring them into alignment. Cerridwen and Tegid can be seen as the higher, wiser, or deeper selves to our more accessible higher selves.

Figure	Role	Purpose
Gwion Bach Middle Self Pre-Initiate	Human Identity Learning Discipline Learning by Listening and Watching	Breaking Imposed Limitations (Servitude)
Creirwy Higher Self	Anima or Gold of the Alchemist	Model of Divine Beauty and Goodness
Morfran/Afagddu Shadow	Lower Self or Lead of the Alchemist What is rejected and feared	Model of Divine Darkness
Morda Instinct Lower Self Connection to Land	Elder Wisdom Trusting senses other than sight Intuition and Inner Guidance	Guide with Wisdom from experience
Tegid Voel Lower Transpersonal Land Titan	Primordial Self Embodiment of the Lake/Island from an earlier age.	Pre-Human Consciousness of Land/Creation
Cerridwen Tutelary Spirit Initiator Higher Transpersonal	Matron Goddess Taskmaster and Teacher Gateway to Rebirth and the Mysteries	Divine Goddess to Creation/Destruction

Chart 5: Tale of Taliesin as Soul Complex

The Recipe of Inspiration

As traditional initiatory training in many forms of Witchcraft and magick is based upon three degrees, the first is usually considered the education of the neophyte, the new student. The first year is filled with learning foundational skills and the basics of rituals, history, and correspondences. In the tale of Cerridwen, this level of training is depicted by the year and a day in the dark hut. While at first this scene appears to depict slavery and punishment, it's been interpreted as a time of training. The initiate, as Gwion Bach, is sequestered away from the world. One might think of it as a type of cloister, focused upon meditative work. In both Celtic traditions, with the hero's quest being a year and a day and the traditional minimum Wiccan period of a degree training being a year and a day, Gwion learns daily discipline with the stirring of the cauldron. It's a slow, rhythmic, meditative practice that will teach patience and perseverance. It will teach the basic methods of trance and vision, by turning inward through the repetition. It is also the teaching of alchemy. Stir and be stirred. Boil and be boiled. As without, so within. The alchemical processes work on many levels at the same time.

Gwion is cloistered away with an elder, finding a wise guide in Morda, or is Morda simply the elder, wiser part of himself guiding the process? It's open for interpretation when understanding magickal realities, but his own companion is an elder man with a similar intuitive chore. But the chore of fire stoking takes more awareness, patience, and timing. Morda's chore is a bit more dangerous for both himself and Gwion. Fire, as a magickal force, can easily get out of control and cause great damage. The stirring is more rote, more automatic. Yet the frustration is much like those earlier lessons in meditation, mindfulness, and simply sitting before the altar with basic repetitive practices. Morda's role is more subtle and requires greater skill.

The outside education occurs through the return of Cerridwen, adding new material that was properly picked according to the astrological times and cycles. The knowledge was said to be held in the mythic *Book of Fferyllt,* for the Cauldron of Inspiration and Science.

Sadly, there is no real manuscript of the *Book of Fferyllt,* though that has not stopped some authors from citing it as a historic Welsh manuscript, such as Douglas Monroe in his immensely popular yet critically panned *21 Lessons of Merlyn*. "Fferyllt" is most likely a Welsh spelling of Virgil, which would make it the "Book of Virgil." This famed poet was considered a powerful magician in both the Christian and Pagan communities, and his work would be used as a form of bibliomancy, or divination with a book. Referencing the *Book of Fferyllt* would be like referencing a book of sorcery and divination for Cerridwen to find the answer to her problem. Some consider the mythic *Book of Fferyllt* to be akin to the Akashic Records, the Formulary of the Heart of the

World, the astral repository of all knowledge and arcane wisdom.

"So she resolved, according to the arts of the books of the Fferyllt, to boil a cauldron of Inspiration and Science for her son, that his reception might be honourable because of his knowledge of the mysteries of the future state of the world.

"Then she began to boil the cauldron, which from the beginning of its boiling might not cease to boil for a year and a day, until three blessed drops were obtained of the grace of Inspiration.

"And she put Gwion Bach the son of Gwreang of Llanfair in Caereinion, in Powys, to stir the cauldron, and a blind man named Morda to kindle the fire beneath it, and she charged them that they should not suffer it to cease boiling for the space of a year and a day. And she herself, according to the books of the astronomers, and in planetary hours, gathered every day of all charm-bearing herbs. And one day, towards the end of the year, as Caridwen was culling plants and making incantations, it chanced that three drops of the charmed liquor flew out of the cauldron and fell upon the finger of Gwion Bach. And by reason of their great heat he put his finger to his mouth, and the instant he put those marvel-working drops into his mouth, he foresaw everything that was to come, and perceived that his chief care must be to guard against the wiles of Caridwen, for vast was her skill…"

— from "Taliesin" in *The Mabinogion*

Though the text makes no mention of it specifically, we have to wonder if she told Morda and Gwion what she was putting in – and why – as they tended the cauldron. If so, it would be considered a period of intellectual education along with the practice of discipline and quiet. Sometimes a teacher won't specifically start a "lesson," but if you are wise, you learn by listening and watching. The best lessons can happen not in the covenstead or temple, or in a workshop or class, but in the kitchen and garden, or over tea. It takes someone who is mindful to realize a lesson is being presented. Here in the hut, Gwion and Morda learned the mechanics of the Craft, of how to brew the potion of awen. Sad for us, the origin tale has no explicit list of herbs or instructions for brewing, though some other texts give us hints.

Other texts suggest the ingredients in the brew of awen, and those who believe this tale codes a bardic teaching think the brew was entheogenic nature, akin to the kykeon of the Eleusinian Mysteries, perhaps of a psychoactive mushroom, or ergot fungus. Since the story claims she "gathered every day of all charm-bearing herbs," the likely ingredients are three hundred and sixty-five in number, one for every day of the year. This is symbolic of how the brew could have all the wisdom of the world within it. Yet the brew reached a boil just before it was completed, so perhaps Gwion Bach didn't get "all" the knowledge possible, causing him to strive just a bit more.

This is similar to an idea found more overtly in the tale of the Irish Celtic goddess Airmid. Patroness of herbal healing, she buried her brother, and rising from his grave were three hundred and sixty-five herbs for every ailment of the body, a bounty she gathered in her cloak. Like the specific brew of the cauldron, her knowledge was lost as her jealous physician father scattered the herbs, so now one must evoke the spirit of Airmid to intuitively regain that specific knowledge of plant-based healing. If there was a formal system taught, the myth now tells us that it is lost to us, though I know quite a few people on the hunt to perhaps reconstitute it.

Modern spellcasters inspired by the lore use a more simplified version of twelve ingredients for the zodiac, or thirteen for the thirteen moons of the lunar year, or perhaps twenty-six ingredients for the thirteen full Moons and thirteen dark Moons. There is no "right" formula as we know, for no specific formula is recorded, but various traditions – particularly those citing the poem "The Chair of Taliesin" from *The Book of Taliesin* and the suppositions of occult academics, mostly from an earlier era – hold that some of the ingredients included the following:

Vervain (Taliesin's Cresses) – Vervain is the enchanter's herb, versatile in use, with powers including protection, love, money, sleep, purification, and health. Though ruled by Venus, the planet of love, it is also used to break harmful enchantments. Supposedly the vervain of Cerridwen's cauldron had to be "borne aloft and kept apart from the influences of the Moon."[1] This refers to a supposed Druidic tradition of vervain harvesting, particularly under the influence of the dog star, Sirius, where libations of honey had been poured forth as an offering to the spirit of the plant. In the tales of Cerridwen, the folk name "Taliesin's cresses" is said to be synonymous with vervain. For an obvious chronology of the story, the plant could not have been called by this name prior to the birth of Taliesin, so perhaps there is a lost story or bit of lore clearly linking the bard to the magick of vervain.

Cowslip (Pipes of Lleu) – Cowslip is an early blooming plant that is magickally known for its ability to help one absorb all the effects of the other herbs mixed with it in a potion, making it a catalyst of sorts. Associated with Beltane, it is used to protect cows from faeries and malevolent Witches, allowing them to produce healthy milk blessed by the magick of the flower. It is another herb of Venus, used for its soothing qualities. Medicinally it has a history as a sedative. The flowers are reminiscent of keys, and the magick involving cowslip can include the process of unlocking something to reveal a hidden treasure. In the Cerridwen lore, the apparent folk name of this plant is the pipes of Lleu, named after the son of the goddess Arianrhod, foster son of the magician Druid god Gwydion. Many see Lleu as a sacrificial figure who (almost) dies and rises again in his tale with the flower maiden Blodeuwedd.

Fluxwort (Gwion's Silver) – One of the problems with folkloric formulas written prior to or disregarding Latin botanical names is that when we research them today, we sometimes don't know what they meant. Even during modern times, in relatively close regions in the United States, the same folk name can mean different species in different regions. And that brings us to the mysterious fluxwort, also known in the literature of Cerridwen as Gwion's silver, indicating that it is most likely a silvery white plant or flower. *The Alphabet of Medical Botany for the Use of Beginners* by James Rennie only has one reference to it, listing its Latin botanical name as *Nerium antidysentericum*. This plant's modern Latin reclassification is said to be *Wrightia antidysenterica*. Strangely, Wrightia is a white five-petalled flower, native to Sri Lanka and found in India, the Philippines, and other areas of Southeast Asia where it is used in the medicines of Ayurvedic tradition. Its Sanskrit name is Kutaja. Kutaja is in the same family as the dangerous oleander, and is most often used as a dermal or oral antimicrobial. It should not be used internally as its effects can be toxic, like all in the Apocynaceae family. As the Nerium oleander is related to the star jasmine, both being in the Apocynaceae family of plants, I wonder if the original Gwion's silver was something akin to a jasmine-like flower. Perhaps Cerridwen's hunt for magickal plants was truly worldwide, bringing this Welsh goddess to Sri Lanka and beyond.

Hedgeberry (Borues of Gwion) – Like fluxwort, hedgeberry is another mysterious plant referred to as the borues of Gwion. References to it might be the "ruddy" or red gem, indicating a red berry. Prunus padus – another red-berried plant commonly known as hagberry or bird cherry – could be it, but cherry trees do not make the best hedges, though they can be maintained in a bush-like form. In Scotland, it was known as a Witch's tree, with the berries being very astringent. The bark is used as a charm to ward off illness when put over the door. If not bird cherry, then hedgeberry might be the more common, but very magickal, raspberry or blackberry hedge. Both are associated medicinally with women's reproductive health and esoterically with the Mother Goddess. Blackberry as a flower essence can be used to face darkness and confront your personal fears. Whether it is the Witch's cherry tree or the berry bush, it is interesting that it is associated with Gwion, the earlier, immature form of Taliesin. The themes of darkness, protection, and confrontation would certainly fit his story.

Mistletoe – The preeminent herb of the Druids, mistletoe harvests were described in detail in the Roman records of Pliny the Elder. Today we consider mistletoe a parasite, but its presence on a tree was considered holy, with no combination more holy than oak and mistletoe. Since it did not grow from the Earth, but hung from the tree as if appearing magickally from the heavens, it was considered to be the fruit of lightning. Pliny said they would harvest it on the sixth day of the Moon cycle, after sacrificing two white bulls. The mistletoe would be cut with a golden (most likely brass or bronze) sickle and caught with a white cloth to keep it from touching the ground. This empowered mistletoe was used to heal illness and cure infertility, and later was considered a powerful protective charm. Today, though considered toxic, Mistletoe is used homeopathically as an anti-cancer agent, fighting off parasitic diseases. Magickally we say it is ruled by the Sun and Jupiter, though we could also see a Moon influence due to the harvesting rituals and white berries.

Frankincense – Not native to the British Isle, frankincense was considered a sacred resin in the temple traditions of the Middle East particularly. A yellow, sticky substance dried into "tears" that harden, this plant is ruled magickally by both the Sun and Jupiter. Burning it and inhaling the scent or smelling the essential oil lifts the spirits, as the magick of frankincense lifts away unwanted spirits and vibrations. It is not usually recommended for consumption in tea, tincture, or oil, despite the call for it in the potion. Instead it is used in incense, oils, and balms. Perhaps the cauldron brew was purified in the smoke of such offerings of frankincense, myrrh, and aloe, rather than ingested.

Myrrh – Another resin not indigenous to the British Isle, myrrh is the dark counterpart to the brighter energies of frankincense. Ruled by the Moon and Saturn, the burning of myrrh incense is slightly reminiscent of burning rubber when alone, but is quite pleasing when used in combination with frankincense and other resins and woods. Its nature is preserving, protecting, and trance-inducing, forming an energetic barrier. Unlike frankincense, myrrh can be taken internally, best via a high-proof alcohol tincture, for its antimicrobial properties that fight infections.

Aloe – In this reference, along with frankincense and myrrh, aloe most likely refers to wood aloe, or lignum aloes, rather than the succulent African plant we are familiar with in the form of aloe vera. When particular species of Asian evergreens are infected, it produces a resinous heartwood to protect the rest of the tree from the infection, creating the aloeswood, which is subsequently used in perfume and incense. It's become a staple in many traditional incense and oil formulas, confusing many modern occult students unfamiliar with the term. Like frankincense and myrrh, it is referenced in the Bible as an aphrodisiac. Magickally it is ruled by Jupiter, used in good fortune magick, as well as for love and protection.

Hedgeweed – According to the English herbalist Nicholas Culpepper, hedgeweed most likely refers to the species *Erysimum officinale*, also known as hedge mustard in our current era, though Culpepper saw the two as separate plants. It is not a plant commonly used in modern Witchcraft today, and in any case, is distinct from the traditional mustard plant. Medicinally it is used as a cure for food poisoning and perhaps other forms of poisoning. It can soothe the stomach and the throat. Culpepper labels the hedgeweed as an herb of Mars, and describes its action as astringent and hot. The seeds are the best part to use medicinally, but the juice or a decoction of the root can be used as well.

Primrose – Primrose, *Primula vulgaris,* is a Eurasian primrose species known as common primrose or often English primrose, and is most likely the plant referred to in this story and is closely related to cowslip. In my own formulation, I must admit I used evening primrose, *Oenothera biennis*, before realizing it was unrelated to common primrose, being native to North America but established across the world. This yellow flower blooms at night with a lovely scent, and is associated magickally with the night, the Moon, and faeries. Due to its association with Diana, it is used in hunting magick, both literal and metaphoric. With the chase of Cerridwen and Gwion, this makes a certain amount of sense to have such an herb in the brew of awen. Primrose is also an herb of shapeshifting, so it is doubly appropriate. Medicinally, evening primrose oil is often cited, somewhat controversially, as an aid to women's health, particularly alleviating the symptoms of premenstrual syndrome, and many women who use it swear by its effectiveness.

Cress – Cress can refer to a small, spicy-leafed plant used in garden salads, or it can refer to the watercress, or *Nasturtium officinale*. Both are related to mustard and radish. Watercress is also related to the Moon due to the watery influence, and associated with a clear mind, psychic and physical protection, and the fertility we associate with the cycles of the Moon. Medicinally it is said to be a great tonic and heals the liver.

Selago – Selago actually refers to a genus of plants, not a single one, with many native to Africa. It is described in the esoteric lore of Taliesin: "The selago, a kind of hedge hyssop, was a charm as well as a medicine. He who gathered it was to be clothed in white – to bathe his feet in running water – to offer a sacrifice of bread and wine – and then with his right hand covered by the skirt of his robe, and with a brazen hook to dig it up by the roots and wrap it in a white cloth."[2] Hyssop is a purifying herb, used to clear and cleanse, and in particular used to clear away guilt or "sin" in folk magick and is even is mentioned in the Bible. So perhaps this "selago" has a similar quality to it magickally.

Segyrffyg (Trefoil) – Possibly referring to a species of trefoil that magickally protects the owner or wearer from illusion,[3] "trefoil" simply means a three-leaved plant, like a clover. It can have magickal associations with any trinity, though in the Christian era in the British Isles, it has most commonly been associated with the Christian trinity of the Father, Son, and Holy Spirit. Modern Pagans today see it as maiden, mother, and crone, and some of a less religious persuasion see the symbolism of mind, body, and spirit. A surviving bit of lore describes a specific charm to use it for protection from "Witches" as defined as malevolent practitioners:

"Trefoil, Vervain, St. John's Wort, Dill,
Rob Witches of their Will."

Wort – Wort, from the Old English "wyrt," is another name for a plant, though many plants have retained the term "wort" in their proper name, such as mugwort, lungwort – and probably most famously in this age – St. John's wort. Mugwort is a lunar herb used to both clear unwanted spirits and to open one's psychic abilities. Lungwort is primarily used as a respiratory herb in herbal medicine. St. John's wort is a powerful magickal plant filled with sunlight. Medically, it alleviates trauma and depression, and magickally it is a protective herb, dispelling nightmares and unwanted forces. It brings in heavenly light to guide you when times are dark.

Silver – Assuming this reference is to the metal silver, or argentum – and not a silvery plant such as silverwort, mugwort, Gwion's silver (fluxwort), or lunaria (also known as honesty and money plant) – silver is related to the Moon, psychic abilities, intuition and healing. Colloidal silver is used as an antimicrobial, though silver jewelry is used to stimulate magickal powers.

Sea Foam – Sea foam is the consistent ingredient in all versions, paralleling the cauldron of Ceres. The ocean is the source of life as we evolve out of the ocean. In myth, we see it as a realm of power and spirit. In Celtic myth, the spirit world is depicted as a realm, an island, to the western shore. Modern Witches use a base of water and sea salt to make and preserve many magickal potions. For this potion, sea foam becomes the matrix of magick for the potion.

Magic Mushroom (Psilocybe mushroom or Amanita muscaria) – Though never stated outright in the literature of Taliesin, many researchers feel there must be an active entheogenic component in the brew of Cerridwen, and the story indicates a cultus devoted to initiatory practices using the entheogen in a ritualized context. As a practitioner, I highly favor this interpretation, but there is no hard evidence for such a thing by academic standards. The mythos can nonetheless inspire us to create such a thing today. The speculated available entheogen, making a link to the Hindu Soma, is usually considered to be a species of Psilocybe mushroom, or the famous recapped *Amanita muscaria*, commonly known as the fly agaric. Both are associated with faeries, elves, and the otherworld and divine inspiration. *Ploughing the Clouds: The Search for Irish Soma* by Peter Lamborn Wilson makes an argument for the historic use in a Celtic context.

The Chair of Taliesin

I am the agitator
Of the praise of God the Ruler.
With respect to the concerns of song,
The requisites of a profound speaker,
A bard, with the breast of an astrologer.
When he recites
The Awen at the setting in of the evening.
On the fine night of a fine day.
Bards loquacious the light will separate.
Their praise will not bring me to associate,
In the strath, on the course
With aspect of great cunning.
I am not a mute artist,
Conspicuous among the bards of the people.
I animate the bold,
I influence the heedless

I wake up the looker on,
The enlightener of bold kings.
I am not a shallow artist,
Conspicuous among kindred bards,
The likeness of a subtle portion,
The deep ocean (is) suitable.
Who has filled me with hatred?
A prize in every unveiling,
When the dew is undisturbed,
And the wheat is reaped,
And the bees are gentle,
And myrrh and frankincense,
And transmarine aloes.
And the golden pipes of Lleu,
And a curtain of excellent silver,
And a ruddy gem, and berries.
And the foam of the sea.
Why will the fountain hasten
Water-cresses of purifying juicy quality?
What will join together the common people?
Wort, the nobility of liquor.
And a load that the moon separates
The placid gentleness of Merlyn.
And philosophers of intelligence
Will study about the moon.
And the influence of an order of men,
Exposed to the breeze of the sky.
And a soddening and effusion,
And a portion after effusion,
And the coracle of glass
In the hand of the pilgrim,
And the valiant one and pitch,
And the honoured Segyrffyg,
And medical plants.
A place of complete benefit,
And bards and blossoms.
And gloomy bushes,
And primroses and small herbs,
And the points of the tree-shrubs.
And deficiency and possession,

*And frequent pledging.
And wine overflowing the brim,
From Rome to Rossed.
And deep still water,
Its stream the gift of God.
Or if it will be wood the purifier,
Fruitful its increase.
Let the brewer give a heat,
Over a cauldron of five trees,
And the river of Gwiawn,
And the influence of fine weather,
And honey and trefoil,
And mead-horns intoxicating
Pleasing to a sovereign,
The gift of the Druids.*
– from Book XIII, *The Book of Taliesin*

Along with the named ingredients included in the list above, the poem also cites anonymous berries, blossoms, bushes, herbs, and tree-shrubs that may or may not be a part of the brew. With such a lack of information, it's impossible to know what these were exactly, if they were anything, and if they were a part of some recipe for the brew of awen.

"Let the brewer give a heat/ over a cauldron of five trees," is believed to signal that the fire is created from wood of five sacred trees, most likely found in the Celtic Ogham system with tree associations with lined symbols. It's not unlike the surviving Wiccan prose, "The Poem of Nine Woods," where nine different kinds of woods are burned in, not under, the cauldron, for magickal effect.

Poem of Nine Woods

(Traditional)

*"Nine woods in the Cauldron go,
Burn them fast and burn them slow;
Birch in the fire goes,
To represent what the Lady knows;
Oak gives the forest towers might,
In the fire brings the God's insight;
Rowan is the tree of power,
Causing life and magick to flower;*

Willows at the waterside stand,
To aid the journey to the Summerland;
Hawthorn is burned to purify,
And draw faerie to your eye;
Hazel, the tree of wisdom and learning,
Adds its strength to the bright fire burning;
White are the flowers of Apple tree,
That brings us fruits of fertility;
Grapes that grow upon the vine,
Giving us both joy and wine;
Fir does mark the evergreen,
To represent immortality seen;
Elder is the Lady's tree,
Burn it not or cursed you'll be!"

Poet and writer Robert Graves, author of *The White Goddess*, considered the five trees to be birch, rowan, ash, alder and willow. They are associated with the five vowel sounds, and one with each finger of the hand. They are the primary magickal pillars, and each is associated with a host of magickal expressions. The magickal fire beneath the cauldron might not be a fire at all, but a reference to the magick of the hands. While the historic truth of this is unlikely, as Robert Graves' work is an amazingly inspired poetic work, not an academic historic work of Celtic reconstructionism, we can use such poetic possibilities to expand our own magick and craft.

Sweet Cauldron of the Five Trees

by Robert Graves

"Tree powers, finger tips,
First pentad of the four,
Discover all your poet asks
Drumming on his brow.

Birch peg, throbbing thumb,
By power of divination,
Birch, bring him news of love;
Loud the heart knocks.

Rowan rod, forefinger,
By power of divination

Unriddle him a riddle;
The key's cast away.

Ash, middle finger,
By power of divination
Weatherwise, fool otherwise,
Mete him out the winds.

Alder, psychic finger,
By power of divination
Diagnose all maladies
Of a doubtful mind.

Willow wand, ear finger,
By power of divination
Force confessions from the mouth
Of a mouldering corpse.

Finger-ends, five twigs,
Trees, true-divining trees,
Discover all your poet asks
Drumming on his brow."

— from *The White Goddess*

Notice that the system given on **Chart 6** uses associations that were not traditional in Irish Celtic society, such as the elemental scheme of Earth, Air, Fire, Water, and Spirit, as well as the outer planets of Uranus and Neptune, which have become associated with the Ogham through the use of it as a modern occult calendar system and astrological method. Though certainly not the intention of the inventors of the Ogham as far as we know, there is merit to the systems, as many, myself included, find illumination from it. But it does differ greatly from other esoteric systems involving the hands. More traditional would be the associations given on **Chart 7**.

Tree	Ogham	Finger	Letter	Color	Element	Planet	Meaning
Birth	Beithe	Thumb	B	White	Spirit	Sun, Venus	Energy, Vitality, The Power of Growth, New Beginnings, Birth, Purity
Rowan	Luis	Forefinger	L	Gray	Fire	Uranus, Sun	Foresight, Healing, Inner Vitality, Inspiration, Spiritual Strength
Alder	Faern	Middle Finger	N	Crimson	Earth	Mars, Saturn	Foundation, Strength, Shield, Inner Confidence, Inner Guidance
Willow	Saille	Ring Finger	S	"Fine-colored"	Water	Moon	Intuition, Psychic Powers, Prophecy, Enchantment, Healing, Emotion, Cunning
Ash	Nuin	Little Finger	F	Clear	Air	Neptune	Rebirth, Transformation, Happiness, Seeing the Big Picture, Universal Order, Balance

Chart 6: Tree Finger Ogham

Finger	Element	Planet	Meaning
Thumb	Spirit	Venus	Spirituality
Forefinger	Water	Jupiter	Wisdom
Middle Finger	Earth	Saturn	Patience
Ring Finger	Fire	Sun	Energy
Little Finger	Air	Mercury	Communication

Chart 7: Traditional Finger Mudras

Elements previously are based upon the distribution of elemental energy according to traditional palmistry finger correspondences. Other systems will vary, with the elemental associations of thumb/spirit, index/fire, middle/air, ring/water and little/earth being popular. Thumb/spirit, index/air, middle/earth, ring/water, and little/fire is another system popular amongst ceremonial magicians. Some systems use the middle finger for spirit, rather than the thumb. For our purposes here, the point is that the five points of the finger correspond with five fundamental powers, even if people disagree on which fingers correspond to what powers.

Occult author Lewis Spence looks at "The Chair of Taliesin" as a code to the initiatory rites of a Cerridwen cult, comparing it to the rites of Ceres in his book *The Mysteries of Celtic Britain*. Added to the potion, according to Spence, was a sacramental drink used by the Druids that contained a mix of wine, honey, water, and malt, which he compared to devotees of Ceres using a blend of wine, barley, water, and meal. We can see some of these ingredients referenced in the poem. But while it's an important text in a collection of amazing Taliesin poetry, it's important to remember that we don't really know who wrote it or their level of magical and initiatory knowledge, and that Spence and Graves, despite good intentions, are today considered out-of-date with their interpretations of Celtic culture and religion, like many occultists and romantic poets of this time. Their work, however, has influenced the way many modern occultists, Witches, Wiccans, and magicians view these mysteries, and new rites have been created around the poetic interpretations of the British occult revival.

Wine – Made from the fermentation of grapes – or the vine, as "vine" is considered a "tree" in the Irish Ogham system – red wine is associated with blood and regeneration. Depending on the dose, it brings joy, melancholy, or madness, all states associated with the poets and mystics of all traditions.

Honey – Made by bees from flowering plants, honey is considered to be a solar power. Sacred for its healing and magickal virtues, it brings eloquence and sweetness to our words, making us "honey tongued." Mead is honey wine or fermented honey water, and is associated with divine inspiration and madness, particularly in the Norse tradition.

Malt – Malt is germinated cereal grains, with the corn or wheat being a part of the Taliesin tale as Gwion's last shapeshift turns him into a kernel which is then eaten by Cerridwen. His seed later "sprouts" in her womb, and she becomes pregnant. Malted grains are used in the making of various alcohols, baked goods, and candies. The grain springing forth with life is a potent symbol in many mystery traditions, for the grain usually sprouts in darkness first, and must reach forward to the light.

An occultist could almost make a comparison between these three sacred substances and the primal ingredients of the alchemists – Mercury, Sulfur, and Salt. Wine has the dissolving, flowing, liquid associations of Mercury, the symbol of the connective force. Although not volatile like Sulfur, honey has both its golden and solar associations. While not crystalline like Salt, malt is the most terrestrial and seemingly fixed, yet alive, of the three ingredients.

Escape from the Hut

The Cauldron of Inspiration overheats as it brews, thought to be either error or a divine and purposeful "mistake" on Morda's part, setting into motion the fate of Gwion Bach, just as our own inner wisdom sometimes arranges challenges and "mistakes" that forever alter the course of our lives, like the "three drops of the charmed liquor" that land on Gwion's thumb and then past his lips as he sucks his thumb to relieve the pain of the hot liquid. He immediately foresees Cerridwen's anger in a flash of magickal vision, and flees the hut.

We can see this sequence through an initiatory perspective. After a period of successful training, an elder priest administers the sacramental drink given in the darkness of the hut-cave-temple. The initiate has now undergone the first trial, displaying the successful discipline and fortitude to make it through the training of the hut. Many would-be Witches never make it through their year and a day. In traditional coven training, the drudge work wears them down. It's a deterrent to remove those unsuitable for initiation. The idea of being required to learn to meditate, to read lore, to aid in ritual before actually doing spells and magick makes the process lose its luster, and those without the proper dedication quit. This is exactly why difficult teachers do it. If you don't want to learn the mysteries of magick, if you are easily deterred, your magick will go awry anyway, so best not to learn it. Safer for yourself, and safer for those around you, to quit. Eastern teachers do the same thing, turning away seekers until they ask three or more times, and when they are finally accepted, they end up like indentured servants for a long while, with little teachings being slipped into everyday tasks, to see if they notice the teaching. The process of "asking three times" was even adopted into the lodges of ceremonial magicians.

With the drinking of the brew, Gwion completes that phase of training. Now he prepares to enter the second gate of mystery. The sacrament of the cauldron also grants a certain freedom, a perception that is invisible to the uninitiated. Gwion Bach can leave! He has the freedom of choice to go or stay, but seemingly doesn't realize it until imbibing the three drops. We too have the freedom to go or stay in any area of our life.

Any seemingly forced servitude or responsibility must be accepted. Sometimes there is greater good in taking on such responsibility, but you must acknowledge your willingness to do it.

The escape from the hut can also be analogous to the escape from Plato's Cave. In this allegory, the cave is a metaphor, a teaching about the Theory of Forms, a realm of purer and more ideal reality. He likened humanity to prisoners chained in a cave, without the ability to move our heads. There is a fire behind us all, and the fire casts shadows upon the wall from puppets held by puppeteers behind the "prisoners" of humanity. The puppets are "real" and the shadows and echoes are unreal, but we believe the unreal shadows to be true reality. We have no concept of what is making the shadows. The concept of what we actually can name and understand, the shadow, is not the same as the reality of Forms. And beyond the puppeteers and the fire casting shadow is a whole world beyond the cave.

Our work as initiates is to free ourselves from the chains, to be able to turn our heads and perceive "real" objects, the fire and eventually the world beyond the cave. Many then seek to return to the cave to free their fellows, only to be misunderstood, rejected, feared, and ridiculed, for the ideas of life beyond the cave sound preposterous to those who have no concept of such things. Some do this with philosophy, while others might find ritual magick the tool for finding a world beyond the cave. On some level, this is what happens to Gwion Bach, leaving the hut and being opened to a whole new world, seeing it in a whole new way, and having an understanding of shape, form, and idea that he'd never had before the drops of the cauldron touched his tongue.

When Cerridwen returns, she punishes Morda, who remains on the scene. She strikes him with a piece of wood, and one of his blind eyes falls out of its socket, hanging upon his face. This gruesome image is reminiscent of other gods such as Odin or Wotan, who sacrifices his eye at the Well of Mimir to gain wisdom and knowledge, wells and cauldrons having a mythic resonance to each other, being not dissimilar. Odin's myth is filled with sacrificial imagery, including hanging himself from the World Tree for nine day and nine nights to learn the secrets and magick of the runes. Wells and cauldrons have a mythic resonance to each other, being not dissimilar. With Morda, the force of sacrifice is not a well of wisdom, but a goddess of the cauldron.

The Nine Maidens of the Cauldron

In "The Spoils of Annwn," the Cauldron of Annwn, rather than being stoked by an old man, is said to be warmed by the breath of nine maidens. Comparisons with other sets of nine, particularly in the grail mythos, abound: the Nine Witches of Gloucester who appear in the Welsh tale of Peredur, the Nine Maidens of the Wells in the French poem known as "The Elucidation," and the Nine Sisters of Avalon mentioned in Geoffrey of Monmouth's work *The Life of Merlin*, listed as Morgen, Moronoe, Mazoe, Gliten, Glitonea, Gliton, Tyronoe, Thiten and Thiten cithara notissima (or Thetis). To comparative mythologists, these nine figures could all relate to the same principles, and to the occultist, the same spiritual entities.

Outside of the scope of Celtic and grail lore, the nine are compared to the Nine Muses of Greek mythology, influencing the course of Western civilization. While the nine are not given detailed depiction in the Celtic tales, the Greek muses have fairly clear descriptions:

Calliope – Muse of epic poetry and eloquence, and the superior muse. Her symbol is the writing tablet. She, like all the muses, is the daughter of the Olympian god Zeus and the titan Mnemosyne, indicating their nature being between the primal and the civilized. Reportedly she was Homer's muse when he wrote *The Iliad* and *The Odyssey*. Calliope gave birth to and mothered Orpheus, who was fathered by the god Apollo. She taught her son to sing, and he later inspired the Orphic Mysteries.

Clio – Muse of history. Her symbol is the scroll. She is the proclaimer, making heroes and historic figures famous. Her son is Hyacinth, the lover of Apollo. She is also associated with the musical instrument the lyre.

Erato – Muse of the cithara (a lyre-like instrument) and lyric poetry, particularly love poetry. A wreath of myrtle and rose is one of her symbols, along with doves and golden arrows. She is also associated with, and sometimes depicted, accompanying the god Eros, as their names share a common root.

Euterpe – Muse of the flute and musical instruments. The aulos, an instrument like a double flute, is her symbol.

Melpomene – Muse of tragedy. Melpomene started as a muse of singing, but became synonymous with tragedy. She holds the tragedy mask of the actor and is depicted carrying a club in the other hand.

Polyhymnia – Muse of sacred songs, hymns, and the art of mimicry. She is also associated with geometry and meditation, and seen as the most serious of the nine muses. Her symbol is the veil or the cloak.

Terpsichore – Muse of dance and poetry. She holds the lyre and plays for the dancers who accompany her.

Thalia – Muse of comedy and science. She carries a comic mask and wears a crown of ivy.

Urania – Muse of astronomy and the heavens. She is considered the eldest of the muses and the most regal, with beauty, grace, power, and love. She is associated with universal notions of love and spirit. Her symbol is a heavenly globe she points to, and she uses astronomy/astrology to predict the future. She raises people up to the heavens, later associating her somewhat strangely as the muse of Christian writers and philosophers. Her symbol is a cloak embroidered with star patterns.

There is an occult tradition of correspondences relating with the muses and their place in the greater classical cosmology. Starting with their descriptions in Hesiod's *Theogony*, much later occultists and philosophers continued their descriptions. Martianus Capella, one of the first innovators of the seven liberal arts in Late Antiquity, assigned them to the classical planets and fixed stars in his work *The Marriage of Philology and Mercury*. In 1482, Ramis de Pareja assigned notes to the muses in his *Musica practica*, which was later repeated by Franchinus Gaffurius in 1518, in his *De Harmonia Musicorum Instrumentorum Opus* and later in the work of famed occultist Cornelius Agrippa in *Book II* of his *Occulta Philosophia* published in 1533. To our modern magickal mind, some of these associations can seem confusing, but it can be good to honor the past and discover why those who came before us made these patterns.

Later occultists have related the muses to the Qabalistic Tree of Life and concepts found in comparative mythology. One can even relate the Nine Sisters of Avalon, today associated with points on the Neopagan Wheel of the Year, to the muses. Though the mythic correspondences are not quite a match, meditating upon their potential links can be quite an illuminating process on the nature of the nine guardians, and gives us a more British link to the classical tradition in the context of the cauldron.

This unusual division of the year gives us a system of dividing the year under the rulership of a single muse for approximately 40 days, with some minor adjustment (40 x 9=360) to account for the last five days of our Gregorian calendar. By Sun sign degree or birthdate, you can find out which of the nine muses "rules" your birthday and influences your life.

Muse	Avalon	Astrology	Sephira	Note	Zodiac Degree	Date
Thalia	Gliton	Earth	Malkuth	Silent	1 Aries	March 21
Clio	Thetis	Moon	Yesod	A	11 Taurus	May 1
Calliope	Gliten	Mercury	Hod	B	21 Gemini	June 10
Terpsichore	Gitonea	Venus	Netzach	C	1 Leo	July 23
Melpomene	Monroe	Sun	Tiphereth	D	11 Virgo	September 2
Erato	Mazoe	Mars	Geburah	E	21 Libra	October 13
Euterpe	Tyronoe	Jupiter	Chesed	F	1 Sagittarius	November 22
Polyhymnia	Thiten	Saturn	Binah	G	11 Capricorn	January 1
Urania	Morgen	Fixed Stars	Chokmah	–	21 Aquarius	February 9

Chart 8: The Nine Muses

In the Avalonian scheme, the nine sisters are divided among the eight Pagan sabbats with one in the center of the mystery. Many of the new correspondences with the Avalonian sisters are found in the Glastonbury Goddess tradition depicted in the work of Kathy Jones, particularly in her book *Priestess of Avalon Priestess of the Goddess: A Renewed Spiritual Path for the 21st Century*. Notice how the many of the traditional correspondence schemes with elements, directions, tools, and totems is quite different in this tradition, shying away from the more familiar earth/north, east/air, south/fire, and west/water or even the less popular alchemical orientation of earth/north, east/fire, south/air and west/water.

Are these nine figures who tend the fire of the underworld cauldron implied in some way in the Taliesin tale as embodied in Morda, tending to the cauldron fire? Internally, Morda or the Nine Maidens, would work with the lowest cauldron of life, a place within our etheric anatomy where life force is raised to induce health, inspiration, creativity, and psychic phenomenon. I often wonder if there was another depiction of the cauldron warmer, or if the nine Avalonian ladies of the lake had anything to do with the story of this island goddess of the cauldron. They are healers. The muses do induce creativity. The psychic resonances abound. One can meditate on the nine qualities of these spirits to go deeper before entering into the first initiatory working of this book at the end of this chapter.

Sister	Sabbat	Direction	Element	Tool	Animal Spirit
Tyrone	Winter Solstice	North	Air	Sword	Wren, Eagle
Thiten	Imbolc	Northeast	–	Spindle	Swan, Snake, Cow, Wolf
Gliton/Cliton	Spring Equinox	East	Fire	Wand	Bear, Hare, Hen, Cat
Thetis	Beltane	Southeast	–	Comb, Mirror	Mare, Horse, Dove, Swan
Gliten	Summer Solstice	South	Water	Chalice	Dolphin, Whale, Salmon
Gitonea	Lammas	Southeast	–	Loom	Dear, Stag
Monroe	Autumn Equinox	West	Earth	Stone, Orb, Crystal	Boar, Badger, Fox
Mazoe	Samhain	Northwest	–	Cauldron, Sickle, Scissors	Crow, Sow, Toad
Morgen	–	Center	–	–	–

Chart 9: Nine Sisters of Avalon

EXERCISE 6:
The Nine Maidens of Inspiration

Before you begin, gather nine small pebbles that will fit into your cauldron. Set up your ritual space with your cauldron before you, filled at least halfway with pure water. Place the stones before the cauldron in a pleasing arrangement. Place a candle behind the cauldron for illumination, and burn any incense you find appropriate. Lunar or faery incenses, such as jasmine, mugwort, myrrh, camphor, rose, or sandalwood are ideal, and play any soft, still trance-inducing music.

Sit before this altar, and start by quickly moving through **Exercise 3: Three Cauldron Activation** to align, balance, and achieve a trance state. State your intention with these or similar words:

I seek to call on the Nine Maidens of Inspiration
I seek to contact the Nine Ladies of the Mystery
I seek to commune with the Nine Sisters of the Cauldron

Whose breath warms the pearl-rimmed cauldron of the Underworld.
May there be peace and blessings between us.
Blessed be.

One by one, call the nine ladies. With each, gently drop a pebble into the cauldron until all nine are called.

I call upon the Sister of the Earth, of the Equinox, of comedy and of science.
Hear my call.

I call upon the Sister of the Moon, of May Day, of history and of proclamations.
Hear my call.

I call upon the Sister of Mercury, of the Summer, of poetry and of eloquence.
Hear my call.

I call upon the Sister of Venus, of the harvest, of dance and of poetry.
Hear my call.

I call upon the Sister of the Sun, of the balance, of song and of tragedy.
Hear my call.

I call upon the Sister of Mars, of the hallows, of lyrics and of loves.
Hear my call.

I call upon the Sister of Jupiter, of the rebirth, of music and rejoicing.
Hear my call.

I call upon the Sister of Saturn, of the awakening, of silence and of the hymns.
Hear my call.

I call upon the Sister of the Stars, of the heavens, of astronomy and the universe.
Hear my call.

Gaze into the light reflecting off the water and the stones from the cauldron. Gaze deeply, letting your thoughts diffuse as you focus on the cauldron. Then close your eyes. Even with your eyes closed, feel the presence of the cauldron, the light, and the nine stones. Envision the cauldron growing larger in the room, as it expands outward. The dark waters reflecting light are an energy that gently envelops you, and you feel yourself becoming one with the darkness of the cauldron.

In the depths, you see nine faint lights, and you find yourself moving towards them. You could feel as if you were swimming towards them in the watery darkness, or the landscape may have become a cavern or tunnel in which you climb down. However your will directs you, move towards the nine lights.

As the lights grow brighter, you realize it is the nine flame tips of one fire, beneath a pearl-rimmed cauldron hanging from a tripod in the dark. As your eyes adjust to the increasing light, you realize that in the darkness around the cauldron are nine Witches, nine priestesses, or nine faery women. It is hard to understand who they are, as their shapes seem to flicker like flames. They are fluid in form, morphing from one thing to the next. They are the sisters of Avalon. But they are also the muses of old. They are the nine Witches of Annwn. But they are also the nine Maidens of the Wells. No matter who they are to you, they tend the cauldron.

The chief of the sisters takes the lead. How does she treat you?

What does she communicate to you?

The chief of the sisters leads the other eight to interact with you. What does this council of cauldron guardians say or do? They might require you to solve a riddle, or present a challenge for you, as only the most worthy may drink from the cauldron.

Experience the nine in their role as guardians of the cauldron, and if you pass their tests, they shall grant you a blessing from the underworld. You could experience a new creative impulse, healing, or an influx of magickal power.

When your time is done, they will release you from their secret chamber of Annwn. They will urge you to go back the way you came, from the darkness, into the light again, climbing out of the cauldron, which will soon regain its normal proportions. Close the portal of the cauldron, as if you were spiritually putting a lid on it.

Bring your awareness back to flesh and blood, breath and bone. Count back upwards slowly, one to thirteen, then one to twelve. Open your eyes and return your awareness to the world. Ground yourself. Extinguish your candle and incense. Turn off your music. Record your experience in your magickal journal.

When fully back, pour the water out somewhere in nature as a blessing to the Earth, and either retain the stones for future working with the nine, or return the pebbles to nature as well. Reflect on which sister was most prominent in your vision. Does she correspond to the muse of your birthday, or the muse currently ruling this time of year?

The Cracked Cauldron of Consequence

And lastly, while looking at the aftermath of the first third of the myth, we must ask, "Why does the cauldron crack?" and "Why are the remains poisonous?" The cauldron itself cracks and the poisonous dregs that remain after the three magical drops are removed from the brew flow outward, down the river and into a weir, poisoning the horses of Gwyddno Garanhir.

The cracking is reminiscent of votive offerings – sacrificial items left in the ground, fissures, graves, lakes, and bogs – like the Gundestrup cauldron, returned to the Earth as an offering, later found dismantled in the land which later became a bog. Weapons and other offerings are usually broken when offered, so no human can retrieve them and use them at a later date. Their use is strictly for the gods and spirits now. Breaking them, thus "killing" them, sends the object to the spirit world, where they are whole. Does the cracking send the cauldron to our world, or return it to the spirit world, like a votive offering?

In the Eleusinian Mysteries, the remains of Demeter/Ceres' cauldron were also said to be poisonous, and also said to have a base of sea water. It shows that these mysteries are those of life and death, and that one skirts the edge of death when entering the mysteries. Seas are the source of life, but also potential death. One must be careful. There is an inherent danger to the seeker. Anyone who tells you differently is lying. We speculate on the literal dangers of the more ancient mystery schools of Egypt and Greece. If you were unworthy, you would not survive. Like those who use the Witch's flying ointment, a poisonous balm used to seek the mystery of the otherworlds, we must be careful. A misstep can be fatal.

Lastly, this cracking and subsequent poisoning can be interpreted in a sacrificial lens beyond the votive offerings of sacrifice. The cauldron is filled with all possibility, all potential, and the highest and best is refined into three drops of magickal elixir. All the rest of the brew contains the sins, the pain, the illness – what one might call the karma – of the world. The weight of this force is too much, forcing the cauldron to crack. The potential to brew the mix again is lost, in the hopes that the one who imbibes the brew will be able to redeem, inspire, and enlighten all.

As Gwyddno's horses are killed, he, his son, and the weir shall play an important role in Taliesin's future. This episode teaches the lessons of balance, reciprocity, and redemption. Before Taliesin can go out into the world, he must first redress this debt he owes to Gwyddno. Sometimes our actions have unintended consequences. We'd like to think we are not responsible because we meant no malice, but ultimately, we are responsible. If we don't take responsibility for our own actions, intended or otherwise, who will? We must take responsibility for even our unknown and unintended actions if we are to be truly free to fulfill our mission. It's part of the training of the bardic magician as a full initiate. Only when we reach a state of balance, working out these obligations, can we reach a higher attainment. It's Taliesin's first step in redeeming the results of that cracked cauldron of karma flowing out in the world, using his personal responsibility to transform the world on a more transpersonal level.

Exercise 7:
Lower Cauldron of Life and the Five Woods

Start as you would start **Exercise 3: Three Cauldron Activation**. You don't need any tools other than your own body, but if you desire, you can set an altar with cauldrons, candles, incense, and music, but the primary purpose of this rite is to move the energy within your body. The intention of this rite is to focus on the lower cauldron of the body.

In my own experiences of the three cauldrons, the lower cauldron relates to what ceremonial magicians refer to as the microcosm, the terrestrial world, the realms of the elements. The middle cauldron relates to the powers of the heavens, the macrocosm, and what we call the planets, or wandering stars. The upper cauldron works primarily with seemingly abstract powers, the primal powers of the three rays, also known as the powers of love, will, and wisdom. But before one can reach for these higher powers, the lower foundation must be secured. Like Gwion and Morda in the hut, one must stoke the fire beneath the cauldron and stir the pot, warming the cauldron by raising the vital energy of life, before further initiation can occur.

To conjure the elements, we'll be using a combination of seed sounds with the hand positions known in the east as mudras. We will be combining the Ogham consonant sounds with the occultist's correspondence of the vowels with the elements, using U for spirit, I for fire, A for earth, O for water, and E for air.

Prepare your body and posture, then put your fingertips together. Place the tips of your index fingers together. Place your middle fingertips together. Then your ring fingers together, little fingers together, and thumbs together. Place a slight pressure, but nothing taxing or uncomfortable. The position is much like a prayer position, but with fingers outstretched. Only your fingertips are touching, not the palms of your hands. Your fingers can point upward or outward before you, whichever is most comfortable for you. This contact and pressure will activate the five elements within you and kindle the power of the first five tree powers from the Ogham. Make sure your arms are comfortably supported, depending on your seated position. If you're in an armed chair, your forearms can be supported on the chair arms, or if sitting without such support, forearms can rest on your thighs.

Close your eyes. Begin to breathe deeply. Relax yourself as you prepare for the trance of energy work. Clear your mind. Open your heart and seek the secret fire that illuminates your souls, guiding and protecting you. Count backwards twelve to one, envisioning the numbers drawn on the screen of your mind. Then release that image to the void, and without visualization, count downward from thirteen to one to get to a deeper level. Set your intention:

I seek to activate and align the five elements with my Lower Cauldron.

As you breathe, focus upon Coire Goiriath, the lower Cauldron of Warming. Focus upon this Cauldron of Life that warms and sustains the entire body, providing the foundation for your being in this lifetime. Draw deep breaths into the belly. Feel them in the lower cauldron.

With each breath, you are filling the cauldron with vital life force. You are enhancing your strength and health. With the sensation upon your fingertips, we invoke the five powers to fill and stoke the cauldron center with power. It is as if the power of the woods themselves are burning beneath the cauldron, kindling the blessing of the tree and its element into your belly. You are kindling the cauldron of five trees within you in preparation for the brew of awen.

    Bring your awareness and slightly more pressure to your thumbs.
    Focus upon the thumbs' sensation, and activate the power of birch.
    Birch, known as Beithe, bringer of new growth and new beginnings.
    As you breathe out, think or speak out loud the "B" sound of "Bu." Then repeatedly chant "Bu."
    Invoke the power of spirit as you breathe.
    Spirit is the element of creation, destruction, and liberty.
    Feel the power of spirit, and of the birch, enter your cauldron, giving you new life, new beginnings, new potential.
    Relax your thumbs but keep them touching.
    Stop the vibration of your sound.

    Bring your awareness and slightly more pressure to your forefingers.
    Focus upon the forefingers' sensation, and activate the power of rowan.
    Rowan, known as Luis, granter of protection from unwanted forces and the gift of foresight.

As you breathe out, think or speak out loud the "L" sound of "Lie." Then repeatedly chant "Lie."

Invoke the power of fire as you breathe.

Fire is the element of identity, passion, life force, and light.

Feel the power of fire, and of the rowan, enter your cauldron, giving you the blessing of protection from ill forces.

Relax your forefingers but keep them touching.

Stop the vibration of your sound.

Bring your awareness and slightly more pressure to your middle fingers.

Focus upon the middle fingers' sensation, and activate the power of alder.

Alder, known as Fearn, granter of inner strength and guidance.

As you breathe out, think or speak out loud the "F" sound of "Fay." Then repeatedly chant "Fay."

Invoke the power of earth as you breathe.

Earth is the element of security, sovereignty, prosperity, and law.

Feel the power of earth, and of the alder, enter your cauldron, giving you the blessing of confidence and foundation.

Relax your middle fingers but keep them touching.

Stop the vibration of your sound.

Bring your awareness and slightly more pressure to your ring fingers.

Focus upon the ring fingers' sensation, and activate the power of willow.

Willow, known as Saille, granter of prophecy and enchantment.

As you breathe out, think or speak out loud the "S" sound of "Soh." Then repeatedly chant "Soh."

Invoke the power of water as you breathe.

Water is the element of emotion, intuition, relationship, and love.

Feel the power of water, and of the willow, enter your cauldron, giving you the blessing of intuition and emotion.

Relax your ring fingers but keep them touching.

Stop the vibration of your sound.

Bring your awareness and slightly more pressure to your little fingers.

Focus upon the little fingers' sensation, and activate the power of Ash.

Ash, known as Nuin, granter of rebirth and balance.

As you breathe out, think or speak out loud the "N" sound of "Nee." Then repeatedly chant "Nee."

Invoke the power of air as you breathe.

Air is the element of communication, truth, thought, and life.

Feel the power of air, and of the ash, enter your cauldron, giving you the blessing of transformation and universal order.

Relax your little fingers but keep them touching.

Stop the vibration of your sound.

Feel your lower cauldron become so full as to be overflowing with the blessings of the elements and the tree spirits. Rather than crack and burst, as many mythic cauldrons do, we must transform the brew of your life.

Swirling in the cauldron, reflect on your life. Reflect on all the good and the bad. Reflect on your choices and relationships. Look at the things that give you strength and warmth, and those that sap your vitality and passion. Explore all the consequences of your actions over the course of your lifetime.

Feel them swirl around in the cauldron. We must refine and transform them, so these experiences can teach us and serve a greater good by raising our energy up to the next level, to the next cauldron. One might say we are looking at the pool of our past actions, or karma, and transmuting that lead, if not to gold, at least to a lighter metal such as tin, iron, or copper.

Begin a more rapid breath supported from the diaphragm. This breath can come out your nose or out your mouth, depending on what is more comfortable to you. You should feel a bit of a pumping sensation in the lower body, performing a "breath of fire" or "bellows breath" as if the rapid breath is stoking the heat of the fire, to distill and refine the life force now with the cauldron.

Start a rapid breath, equal on the exhale and inhale. It is powered by the belly/solar plexus point, but is not a pumping of the belly. It's relatively shallow compared to our deep, full yogic breaths, and can almost feel like hyperventilating. If you begin to feel that way, slow down the breath and work your way up to the faster speeds. The chest is lifted and stays still. The spine should not flex.

When you feel you have the hang of it, you can add a two-syllable mantra to the breath, the first on the inhale and the second on the exhale. I prefer the mantra of "Ah-Za" for the alpha and omega, the beginning and the end of our modern alphabet, A and Z. It can give your mind a clear focus while breathing.

Only do this for a few minutes to start, to purify your cauldron. In the kundalini yogic tradition, the Breath of Fire is ended with a position known as the mulbandh, or root lock, which is helpful here. The posture locks the energy in the body for a moment, causing it to circulate, purify, and revitalize the self. To perform the root lock, inhale fully and contract the rectum, sex organs, squeezing the naval back to the spine. Hold for three to five seconds. Exhale fully. Once you have the hang of it with practice, repeat the root lock three times, and on the third exhale, hold the root lock again after the exhale out, and then relax. This is a powerful stimulation of the lower cauldron, what some see as the lower three chakras of the more traditional Vedic and modern metaphysical teaching.

Relax your hands. Just place them, without the fingertips touching, upon the belly. Rest. Allow yourself to relax afterwards, and then, when ready, reflect again on the past in your cauldron. Does it feel any different? Is the response in your body any different? Over time, as you repeat this exercise, you will notice a transformation. It can take many times to really transmute the karma of our actions. And when you practice **Exercise 3** alone again, you should notice some subtle differences as we refine the lower cauldron.

When you are ready, complete your experience by bringing your awareness back to the world around you, beyond the circulation and refinement of your inner energy. Feel yourself return to flesh and blood, breath and bone. Count up from thirteen to one, then twelve to one. Feel your fingers and toes. Open your eyes and ground yourself as needed. Record your experience in your journal. Practice this exercise regularly until you feel a shift and believe you are ready for the last initiatory experience of this chapter.

The Stirring Rod

In this work, it can be helpful to have a wooden "wand" or rod specifically used for stirring the brew of awen and other magickal mixtures. Originally I started with a glass stirring rod, not seeking to contaminate any mixture, but over time, I saw the value of adding a connection to the wood spirits. Perhaps you will find a stirring rod from one of the five sacred woods listed here, or from another set of correspondences.

If possible, take it from a living tree, with permission from the tree spirit. Make an offering of beer, wine, milk, cream, or something else the tree spirit requests. When you cut the branch, leave a little natural oil on the wound of the tree to help heal it. If you find a fallen branch, ask the tree spirit from where it fell to bless and empower it. Peel the branch and dry the bark. You can use it later as a base for an empowering incense. Sand the branch. Oil it with a natural oil. Then rub it with beeswax or a beeswax and oil ointment mix to seal it. Empower it in a simple ritual in sacred space in whatever way you see fit. Then use it for your cauldron work, both as a stirring rod and possibly as a form of magick wand.

The Creation of the Brew

Now that we are educated in the linear teachings of the hut, the only task left to us is the creation of the brew. While one could take a year and a day to deeply study the herbs as spirit allies and practice the discipline of the visionary techniques, the yearlong training for those following the text can be more metaphorical, as many of us will come to our Craft with previous experiences and training.

The creation of the brew, of greal, is both inner and outer. Yes, we shall create a sacramental drink in our work. But like the Chinese Taoist alchemists believed, some brews must be distilled internally. With the application of the previous rites, one will start to change both the energy, and thereby the physical indications of the energy center, or chakras, within the body. These markers are the hormones of our endocrine system. As each chakra is tied to a prominent gland, that gland's secretions are a physical anchor for that chakra's power in our body. So in truth, we are like a little laboratory, secreting new chemicals as we change our hormonal balance. Meditation alters our hormone balance and our nervous system response in their most simple forms. Focused energy workings like those found in the three cauldrons–which link the traditional lower three chakras with the Cauldron of the Belly, the heart chakra with the Cauldron of the Heart and the upper three chakras to the Cauldron of the Head– most certainly alter our biochemistry, at least according to esoteric tradition. So we are brewing within the "hut" of our body and consciousness, as well as the "hut" of our workspace. Thus when we consume the sacrament, we are activating powers already generated within us, waiting to be signaled through our ritual.

While the classic ingredients are fascinating, they are not altogether practical for our work, though we do try to include as many as we possibly can use. My own vision working with Cerridwen has yielded a formula that serves us here, though it might lack either the physical shapeshifting powers of the myth or the speculated psychedelic influence of a soma-like brew. Yet when made with clear intention and in alignment with the plant spirits, it can grant potent experiences.

Brew of Awen Formula

1 Pinch of Ginger Root (Aries)
1 Pinch of Nettle Leaf (Aries)
1 Pinch of Rose Hips (Taurus)
1 Pinch of Cowslip or Lady's Mantle (Taurus)
1 Pinch of Fennel Seeds (Gemini)
1 Pinch of Skullcap (Gemini)
1 Pinch of Primrose (Cancer)

1 Pinch of Mugwort (Cancer)
1 Pinch of Bay Leaf (Leo)
1 Pinch of Rosemary (Leo)
1 Pinch of Vervain (Virgo)
1 Pinch of Rowan Berry (Virgo)
1 Pinch of Yarrow (Libra)
1 Pinch of Raspberry Leaf (Libra)
1 Pinch of Wormwood (Scorpio)
1 Pinch of Basil (Scorpio)
1 Pinch of Lemon Balm (Sagittarius)
1 Pinch of Garden Sage Leaf (Sagittarius)
1 Pinch of Solomon's Seal (Capricorn)
1 Pinch of Mullein Leaf (Capricorn)
1 Pinch of Mistletoe (Aquarius)
1 Pinch of Elderberry (Aquarius)
1 Pinch of Hyssop (Pisces)
1 Pinch of Jasmine (Pisces)

1 Cup of Spring Water
1 Cup of Salt Water (8 Ounces of Water with 4 Tablespoons of Sea Salt)
1 Pinch of Malt
3 Tablespoons of Honey
3 Tablespoons of Brandy

Incense of Frankincense, Myrrh and Copal (Equal Parts)

    While trying to remain true to our knowledge of the brew–and create something workable in the modern world that is associated with the yearlong cycle–I've used two herbs for each zodiac sign, signifying one for the time when the Sun is in that sign, and the other for when the full Moon is in that sign, though obviously many plants will not be in growth or bloom at those specific times, particularly depending on your region. The first twenty-four ingredients are truly a nod to the "year and a day" cycle.

    I know some Witches who suggest a formula of 365 ingredients, one for each day of the year, akin to the Irish myths of Airmid, a goddess of herbal healing. The herbs grew on the grave of her brother, Miach, one year after his death. She watered the grave with her tears of grief, and perhaps, imparted a bit of her own magick to the site. She gathered in her cloak the three hundred and sixty-five herbs, one each for the joints, sinews, and organs of her brother. Perhaps each herb grew "near" or "on" the corresponding body part it healed. She created a pattern in her cloak to learn the blessings of the herbs, but her father – the physician Dian Cecht, who, jealous of his children's healing magick had slain her brother – scattered the herbs so the true and complete secrets of the herbs would be lost. This attitude reminds me somewhat of the antagonism between modern medicine and herbal wisdom.

Other Witches, astrologically minded, suggest a formula of three hundred and sixty herbs, one for each degree of the zodiac, thirty for each of the twelve signs, though of course we know that none of the ancient Celtic traditions followed the same zodiac system we use today. Others will divide each of the twelve zodiac signs into the traditional three decans of the zodiac, and thus choose thirty-six herbs.

In order to balance effectiveness with practicality, I suggest the formula above. Here is some additional magickal information on each of the herbs:

Ginger Root (Aries) – Ginger is a fiery root herb also associated with the Sun, and known for its medicinal properties to boost the metabolism, digestion, and immune system. It helps generate the inner fire, particularly in the lower cauldron, that can then be coaxed into the upper cauldron to produce greater awareness and inspiration.

Nettle Leaf (Aries) – Nettle leaf is known for its tiny stingers, making its common name stinging nettle very appropriate. While the painful stings can be used to alleviate aches and pains, nettle's magick helps us learn to let go of pain, and it is also an herb associated with faeries and protecting the bounds of faery lands.

Rose Hips (Taurus) – Roses are the primary herb in the Western Mystery traditions, based upon a petal pattern of five, like the pentagram, and also showing up in the Tudor rose symbol, Witch's pentacle design, and the ceremonial rose cross. It is an herb of both personal and cosmic love. Rose hips contain a high amount of vitamin C, stimulating the immune system, which is ruled by the thymus gland, the gland of the heart chakra/cauldron.

Cowslip (Taurus) – Our traditional "pipes of Lleu" is chiefly known as an herb that can help harmonize and catalyze the divergent properties of other herbs that it is mixed with, making it perfect for a complex brew like this. Our past entry on the pipes shows it is associated with Taurus through its holiday Beltane, which occurs when the Sun occupies the sign Taurus, and it is an herb of Venus. It's not a common herb used in modern American herbalism, so find a substitute if you must – lady's mantle would work since primrose, a relative of cowslip, already appears in this formula.

Fennel Seeds (Gemini) – Fennel seeds, like many plants that produce large numbers of seeds, is associated with Mercury and therefore Gemini or Virgo. Herbally, fennel quells a nervous stomach. Magickally it can create wealth, for it produces so many seeds. And spiritually, fennel is about the quickness of the mind and the multiplicity of our thoughts.

Skullcap (Gemini) – Skullcap is known as a tonic herb for the nervous system and is generally said to be good for the skull, or brain. While the herb relaxes us from stress, magickally it helps improve memory, a necessary skill for future bardic seers who must memorize great poems and sagas.

Primrose (Cancer) – In our previous section on the traditional lore, we learned of the faery and lunar associations with evening primrose. It is also protective from all the mysterious creatures of the night that might do harm. Baths made from evening primrose are said to reveal your inner beauty, linking it to some of the previous teaching on shapeshifting. Evening primrose is the version most likely found for sale in the United States, as it grows profusely in the wild, though the traditional primrose, related to cowslip, is also often available.

Mugwort (Cancer) – Mugwort is a green plant with green nondescript flowers, often overlooked as a noxious weed and not a deeply magickal plant, but when it gets close to maturing in its power, the leaves take on a silvery hue, and it stands out upon the light of the full Moon. Used in tea, oil, or incense form, mugwort helps develop the powers of a seer or psychic, and some consider its effects to be reminiscent of a mild psychoactive substance. Mugwort is also considered by some to be spiritual/psychically protective and a defense against poisons.

Bay Leaf (Leo) – Bay leaves are of the Sun and were used in the ancient solar temples of prophecy. The leaves would be burned and the fumes inhaled to help give greater sight and inspiration. Bay leaf potions can also help stimulate the inner psychic light of the third eye and crown, so we can see things more clearly and make our prophecies.

Rosemary (Leo) – Rosemary is well known for its powers of memory, both in magick and medicine. Sniffing rosemary or rosemary oil is said to increase our natural ability to remember things. It's used in handfastings, or Pagan weddings, to help the couple remember their commitment and love on that day. It's used in potions to stimulate the memory center, as well as being a favored culinary flavor.

Vervain (Virgo) – Vervain is our "Taliesin's cresses" or enchanter's all-purpose herb. Today, we usually find American blue vervain, which is a substitute for the classic European white vervain referred to in more traditional texts and Pagan tales. They share similar properties and can be used somewhat interchangeably, though blue vervain has a stronger air element to it, and thereby Mercury associations, while white vervain is stronger with spirit and Venus.

Rowan Berry (Virgo) – Rather than hedgeberry for our "ruddy" or red gem berry, we are using rowan as one of our red berries, along with raspberry, though with rowan, the actually berries rather than the leaves are used medicinally and magickally. Rowan is also high in Vitamin C, like rose hips, but the berries form a natural five-pointed star, as the flowers are five-petalled. The red-orange berries were used as a charm against ill magick, and people today still hang them with red thread to avert harm and protect a home. Though said to be protective against Witchcraft, many Witches use them as a simple but powerful protective charm, for protection on a physical and spiritual level.

Yarrow (Libra) – Yarrow is an herb of boundaries, associated with both Venus and Mars. Medicinally it rules the flow of blood, staunching blood when cut and regulating the flow of blood in the circulatory system. Magickally it can attract or repel things and people. Spiritually it controls the flow of energy in and around us, strengthening our energy field, our aura, when it's too weak or damaged and relaxing it when we are too tense and contracted. It helps us measure the appropriate personal space. It also helps us "craft" the vessel of our energetic boundary, to contain the new energies of initiation and to successfully perform spirit journeys.

Raspberry Leaf (Libra) – Raspberry is another "ruddy" gem of a berry, and besides being quite a treat, it is medicinally associated with feminine mysteries and the Goddess. Ruled by Venus, it is used in fertility and fidelity magick, helping a woman get pregnant as well as keeping a man from wandering. The prickly barbs and red berries also associate it with blood, both the blood of feminine cycles and the blood of the ancestors, of the past, within us all.

Wormwood (Scorpio) – Wormwood is considered to be the fiery "brother" to the more watery mugwort, though they are both artemisias, so they have sacred qualities associated with Artemis, the Moon goddess. Wormwood medicinally kills off parasites, things attached to us, and magickally that power can be extrapolated to also include unwanted people and entities in our life. It is also known for calling the spirits and helping facilitate communication with otherworldly entities. It is one of the chief ingredients in the popular alcoholic spirit absinthe and is the reason for the unusual stories involving its use and the perception of "green faeries."

Basil (Scorpio) – Basil is a fiery herb associated magickally with both passion and money. The passion comes from its use as a spice in culinary magick, while the money is due to its associations with literal bills of green money when it is freshly chopped and used in oils and floor washes. Spiritually, basil involves sexuality and healing wounds around sexuality and shame, working in a similar way to jasmine by raising up the energy of the root, or lower cauldron.

Lemon Balm (Sagittarius) – Lemon balm's Latin name is *Melissa*, giving association with both honeybees and the temple priestesses aiding the Pythia, or the oracular prophetess in Delphi in ancient Greece. Medicinally it helps restore and relax without sedating. Magickally it is said to be an herb filled with life force, but working gently to restore us. Like cowslip, it also enhances any other herb it is mixed with, making it essential in larger combinations.

Sage Leaf (Sagittarius) – Sage leaf here refers to garden sage, not the various Native American burned sage bundles of brush sage or white sage. Garden sage has similar cleansing properties, but is more suited for ingestion as it is also a culinary herb. It helps restore the respiratory system by clearing the lungs, and magickally it removes all psychic debris, allowing our energy to flow smoothly.

Solomon's Seal Root (Capricorn) – A powerful root herb that resembles a spine or the joints of the knuckle, depending on how it grows, Solomon's Seal is used medicinally for issues of the spine and connective tissues, helping tone and strengthen them. Magickally it is very protective, being an herb ruled by Saturn, providing psychic structure and support. Its flowers are six-petalled bell flowers, associating it with the hexagram or Star of David. It is found in ceremonial magick and tied to King Solomon in traditional myth.

Mullein Leaf (Capricorn) – Mullein is a biennial herb that takes two years to flower on long tall stalks. The stalks were dipped in paraffin in the fall and used as makeshift

Halloween candles known as hag's tapers. They are said to illuminate not only in this world, but in the otherworld as well, as a guide for spirits traversing to and fro. Mullein flower in oil helps ear infections, and spiritually, mullein helps us hear on all levels; its leaf in incense can be used to commune with the dead. It has a "old wise man" energy to it, guiding, but not forcing. Medicinally it is most popular as a respiratory herb, but it can also be used to promote muscle/skeleton alignment, relieve pain from injuries, and support lymphatic movement.

Mistletoe (Aquarius) – Many people, knowing mistletoe is considered toxic, would shudder to think of a pinch of mistletoe going into this potion, but if one is otherwise healthy, with no particular herbal allergies, the recommended amount in a two-cup base, with the dosage of the potion being three drops, makes this potion perfectly safe for our uses. Mistletoe is considered to be the herb of heaven, descended down by lightning as a gift from the gods. The powers of inspiration are described much the same way.

Elderberry (Aquarius) – Elder is the Lady's Tree, associated with the white goddess, the dark goddess, and the faery queen, depending on the tradition. While Wiccans are prohibited from burning the wood – and honestly, it's a prohibition also from harvesting without proper intent, offerings, and blessings – the flowers and berries are used medicinally, particularly for flu infections and respiratory illness. Magickally elder is a plant of protection and blessings, as well as curses. If honored, an elder tree was said to care for the people, protect them, and bless them with gifts. If dishonored, it would bring harm to the people. Spiritually, elder is said to help rejuvenate us, or bring "immortality" by revivifying the body, particularly our appearance. Witches are said to look young again through the use of elderflower water.

Hyssop (Pisces) – As our replacement for the "selago" ingredient, we use hyssop primarily as an herb to cleanse and clear. As a plant spirit, it is said to clear away issues of guilt and repression, and the oil and herb is used in baths when we are feeling like we cannot forgive ourselves for a mistake. A wash of it can also purify our homes or workplaces, but internally, it helps purify the inner temple of our spirit.

Jasmine (Pisces) – For our fluxwort substitute, we'll be using simple jasmine flowers, like the kind you'd find in jasmine tea. Jasmine is a plant of the Moon, hence a substitution for "Gwion's silver" even though the flowers are usually white, giving an association with the Moon. Jasmines of all kinds are said to raise the frequency of anything, raising our lower energies to higher ones, particularly in sexual, or tantric, rituals. Here, we are using it to raise the energies of the lower cauldron to create a shift and change as they rise up to the higher cauldrons. Jasmine also helps improve psychic ability and empathy.

Incense of Frankincense, Myrrh, and Copal – This incense blend evokes the previously mentioned powers of frankincense and myrrh, but instead of wood aloe, which has become a little less in favor in modern magick, we are using another powerful resin that is more easily found by today's magician, copal. Copal simply means "incense" and refers to a number of Central and South American resin trees, all with powerful clearing and healing properties, making them complimentary with frankincense and myrrh. I suggest either black copal, gold copal, or white copal. Grind to a powder and mix equal parts together to burn upon charcoal.

Read **Exercise 8** thoroughly before attempting it, to make sure you have all the things you need and understand all the parts to it. I suggest practicing the swaying and chanting techniques several times before using it alone in this ritual working.

Exercise 8:
First Initiatory Working – The Creation of the Brew

The final exercise of this chapter – and the first of our initiatory workings in the tale of Cerridwen and Taliesin – involves three basic factors. The first is the actual making of the brew itself, the concocting of the potion upon the physical plane. The second is the visionary work induced by the trance. The third is the communion with the plant spirits, the green allies, initiators, and teachers within the brew, as facilitated by the visionary trance. It is not an introductory practice, and I suggest those partaking it should be fully familiar with basic ritual, trance work, and the process of crafting herbal potion. All the written calls and poetry here are suggestions to attune to the forces. As inspiration is the guide, if you are inspired to say something else, do so, but remember part of the first dark mystery is training – following what was – before allowing inspiration to lead you into new and uncharted waters.

Along with the herbs and other ingredients from the formula above, you will need:

Heatproof Brewing Vessel/Cauldron
Support for Cauldron (potpourri stand, fondue dish, hanging rack)

Heat Source (tea-light candle, alcohol lamp, or Sterno)
Stirring Rod (glass or wood)
Incense Burner/Thurible/Small Cauldron
Charcoal for Incense
Lighter/Matches
Sealable Bottle or Jar
Funnel
Filter (unbleached coffee filter or cheesecloth)

I prefer this brew be made in ritual, in formal sacred space, rather than over a kitchen stove. To do this, you can use a variety of flameproof vessels. A larger potpourri simmering dish heated by a tea-light candle can easily and safely be used and will warm the water sufficiently. Warming dishes or fondue dishes also work well. I like to use an antique copper cauldron that sits nicely upon a warming dish stand. In any case, your vessel should be able to hold about two cups (sixteen ounces) of liquid. If your primary magickal cauldron from **Exercise 1** would work, then use it. If not, keep it out as a focal point in the ritual, but use another, more practical, vessel for brewing the potion. Some prefer a traditional iron cauldron to brew, while others prefer vessels of copper or brass, feeling iron is best for protective and cursing magick. Ceramic and Pyrex work well too. It's up to you to follow your own intuition about the vessel.

Have out all the tools and ingredients you will need, from the practical – like candles for illuminations and matches/lighter to light them – to any of your previous tools, music, and incense to attune you to the intention of your working. You can have your ingredients for the brew in little jars, small cups, or bowls. I have a large number of small wooden condiment bowls, made to be used at picnics and parties, that I use for my potion ingredients. I arrange them in a line from left to right in the order in which the formula calls for the ingredients. Since you will only be using a pinch of each, use whatever is practical for you.

Once your altar is set, create a sacred space through ritual. If you come from a tradition that has its own methods for creating sacred space, and those methods would be appropriate for this cauldron working, then use them. If not, a very simple method of creating a magick circle – one in tune with the five elements and gods of the craft of the Witch, along with the powers of the cauldron – is below.

Hold your consecrated cauldron form **Exercise 1**. Face a direction of power for you. Usually it is north or east, but for cauldron workings, west would also be appropriate. Facing your direction, move clockwise three times as you hold your cauldron aloft. Feel as if the cauldron is "spinning out," as if the "lip" of the cauldron surrounds you like a circle so that you and your ritual space are dwelling within the cauldron. If the cauldron is too awkward or unorthodox to cast the circle, use your stirring wand, making sure you have previously cleansed and consecrated it for this purpose.

Say:
By the Sacred Cauldron that dwells within the heart of Annwn, I cast this cauldron circle.
I call upon the Waves of Creation to flow from within me, about me, and all around me.
I call upon the powers of the cauldron to guard me from all harm. So mote it be.

Holding the cauldron aloft in the center, evoke the powers of the two and the three:

By the vaulted arch of the cosmos,
I call upon the Lord of Death and Darkness to my left
And the Lord of Light and Life to my right.
May you ever hold the cauldron's brew.
Hail and welcome.

By the fires warming the cauldron below,
I call upon the Three Ladies, the Three Who Are Nine Who Are Three Again.
Maiden, Mother, Crone
Stars, Earth, Underworld
Future, Present, Past
May you ever initiate change.
Hail and welcome.

In this sacred space, you are prepared to brew your potion. Light the candle or other fire source beneath the cauldron. Add the pure spring water and say:

I call upon the fresh pure waters of life, sustaining, rising from the Earth.

Add the salt water and say:

I call upon the ancient salt waters of life, creating, flowing from the Sea.

Allow the waters to warm and heat while you go deeper into trance and commune with the plant spirits in the darkness of the hut. Light your incense charcoal and put a little bit of your frankincense, myrrh, and copal mix upon it. Smell the rich, resinous scent. Allow it to take you deeper. Quickly move through **Exercise 7: Lower Cauldron of Life and the Five Woods**, which includes **Exercise 3: Three Cauldron Activation**, to begin.

With your five fingers still together from **Exercise 7**, begin to sway using a powerful yet simple movement trance technique. Move your torso in a rotating motion, as if your spine were like a stirring rod in the cauldron of your body. Most will move clockwise, what is known as deosil or sunwise in the Northern Hemisphere, though if you are called to move counterclockwise or widdershins, meaning against the Sun, then do so. Widdershins is also known as tuathal, or star-wise, and can be appropriate for the wisdom of Taliesin (note: the traditional directions are reversed in the Southern Hemisphere with deosil being counterclockwise and widdershins being clockwise.) Essentially you are "stirring" yourself, the repetitive movement inducing a deeper trance without losing touch with the body.

Once you feel like you have entered into a natural rhythm and sway, add to it the mantra of inspiration. Written as "awen" but chanted as "ah-ou-en," "Ah" rhymes with "la" in the musical scale, "ou" rhymes with "boo," and "en" sounds like the letter N in English. Time the chant with your swaying motion, perhaps doing one full awen for each rotation around. Then, with eyes closed, enter the vision working.

• • •

You are in the darkness of the cosmic cauldron. Feel that darkness surround you. As you stir your own cauldrons within your body, you are stirring the cauldron of the cosmos. Gaze into the darkness, and let it gaze back into you.

There, in the darkness, you see a dim light flickering. You move towards that light. In that light, you see the shadowy outline of a hut, and you realize, floating in this sea or lake of darkness, is the Isle of Inspiration, the Isle of the giants Cerridwen and Tegid, and their children, the daughter of beauty and the son of utter darkness. If you choose to enter the hut, then you are choosing a time of service, to be a servant to the light of the divine brew and the Mother of Darkness. Will you accept this service and enter the hut?

In the hut, the light is a bit brighter, with fiery embers beneath the cauldron. There is the old blind man Morda tending the fire, and the stirring rod is sitting in the brew. You start to stir the cauldron in time with your own body's movements. The old man says nothing. You say nothing. You just gaze into the waters of the cauldron.

The dark lady returns, and she too is silent. She carries in her apron many herbs, and she places them into the waters with love and blessings. Perhaps she announces the name and purpose with an incantation. Perhaps she doesn't. They all go into the cauldron. They all get stirred by you. And she leaves again.

As you stir, you call upon the plant allies. You call upon the plant spirits who act as healers, initiators, and teachers. By the seeds and roots, by the stems and leaves, by the buds, blossoms, and fruits, you call upon the plant spirits.

As you do, the spirits of the plants rise from the brew. The spirits of the plants begin to commune with you, in their sacred green tongue that is not a tongue, with words that are not words. They teach you about their mysteries, beyond those which you can learn in books or from teachers. They teach you directly in the mysteries of their own work, individually, and how they are working together in the formula of awen. You continue to stir your body, and stir your brew, until the plants are done communing with you.

• • •

While maintaining your sense of self in the hut, in the darkness, gently open your eyes. Place the physical ingredients of the brew, one by one, into the cauldron. You can name them or remain silent. Stir each one into the now warm waters. Continue to stir them until they are well mixed, and when you are ready, close your eyes again. Use the stirring motion to continue the trance. You can return to the rotating body motion and chanting of awen, or simply sit in a deeper silence, whichever you prefer at this point. Enter again into vision.

• • •

As you continue to stir, you gaze into the fire below the cauldron. The embers have grown to a flame as Morda stacks the woods, the five woods of your five fingers. Into the fire goes birch, rowan, alder, willow, and ash, releasing the blessings of spirit, fire, earth, water, and air.

Within the light of the fire, you see the light of the eyes of the child, the Child of Light within the hut of darkness. Gaze deeply into the eyes of light and darkness and these eyes will gaze into you, and awaken something long slumbering.

Stir, and you are stirred!

Boil, and you are boiled.

Feel the blessings of awen. Take these blessings of awen, and know that you release what doesn't serve you into the cauldron, to be returned to the Earth when the vessel cracks. That which is needed will rise to the top, distilled in a few drops. That which is unnecessary will fall below, dead and poisonous.

• • •

When you feel this exchange is done, again gently open your eyes and come to stillness. Burn more of the frankincense, myrrh, and copal mix on the charcoal, and blow the smoke with your breath towards the brewing cauldron, as a blessing and offering to the new brew of magick. You can snuff the fire and let the brew cool, either while remaining in a circle or after releasing your sacred space. To release the sacred space, follow the instructions below, or release in the manner that is appropriate for your tradition and the method by which you created it.

If your consecrated cauldron from **Exercise 1** is also your brewing cauldron, you can simply hold out your hands or use your stirring wand, as the brew will still be uncomfortably hot to hold. If this is not the case, then hold your cauldron and say:

By the cosmic fires of the deep below,
I thank the Three Ladies, the Three Who Are Nine Who Are Three Again
Crone, Mother, Maiden
Underworld, Earth, Stars
Past, Present, Future
I thank you.
Stay if you will, go if you must.
Hail and farewell.

By the Vaulted Arch of the Cosmos
I thank the Lord of Light to my right hand
and I thank the Lord of Darkness to my left hand.
Lords of Life and Death
I thank you.
Stay if you will, go if you must.
Hail and farewell.

Facing your starting direction, and moving in the opposite rotation of how you created your sacred space, hold out your hands or hold your cauldron aloft and say:

By the Sacred Cauldron that dwells within the Heart of Annwn, I release this circle.
May all things return to their place and time,
Yet may the changes in this cauldron reverberate throughout the cosmos.
So mote be it.

When the vessel is cool enough to touch and use, put your funnel in your bottle or jar and line it with your filter. I prefer unbleached coffee filters. Pour the liquid through the filter into the jar. The filter will catch the herbal material. Do not pour the entire volume of liquid into the bottle. Leave at least one fourth of it by volume, along with the herbal matter. This is now the "poison" of the cracked cauldron. With your will, heart and mind, send forth into the dregs all that doesn't serve you, all that you seek to transform or transmute upon your breath. Then go out into nature and release this material, asking Mother Earth, the land spirits, and the Soul of the World to help you transform all that does not serve as you take responsibility for your actions in this life and all others.

Keep the bottled potion for the next chapter, or if you are prepared and have read ahead, you can go directly into the second initiatory working of the next chapter. The potion can be used as a sacramental drink, taking three drops upon the thumb. It can also be used to anoint candles and ritual objects, usually with anywhere between three to nine drops, for magickal inspiration and purpose.

If you wanted to deepen the process through the course of a year and a day, you could repeat this ritual twenty-four times, twice a month on the full and dark Moons, adding each herb individually to a measure of 80-proof or less alcohol in a jar, creating a tincture. Reseal the jar after every use and keep it in a dark place. This experience will give you a chance to work with the plant spirit of each ingredient in a deeper way. On the twenty-fifth time, on the final day of your year and a day, you would add the tinctured liquid to the two cups of pure and salt waters, mixing honey and malt into the brewing vessel. Heat gently, making sure not to ignite the alcohol.

Notes

1. Spence, Lewis. *Mysteries of Celtic Britain*. p. 82.
2. Reade, W. Winwood. *The Veil of Isis; or, Mysteries of the Druids.* Chapter X: Priestess. 1861.
3. *The Land Book of the Vale*, published by T. Thomas James Street, 1852. p. 70.

Chapter Five: The Second Darkness of the Womb

By hare and salmon, bird and seed
By dog and otter, hawk and hen
To the threshing room floor and the bitter end
Chased on the Earth and chased in the deep
Running to avoid the eternal sleep
Chased in the air and chased on the floor
Womb, tomb, gate, door
Red mad mother seeking my guts
Tricking and turning and twisting
All to escape that dark hut.

Once poor Gwion Bach has burned his finger and imbibed the blessing of the great brew, the most famous portion of the story occurs – the chase! A common motif among magicians in fairy tales, myths, movies, television, and comics is the shapeshifting duel, and while not so much a duel, as Cerridwen is clearly the more powerful of the two, the chase is a battle of wits between Gwion and Cerridwen, between student and teacher, initiate and initiator. Such battles are confrontations, as well as tests to clearly demonstrate the student's level of practical progress and deeper insight.

In the psychic formula for initiation found in most magickal traditions, a necessary step is the separation. One must separate the identity from that of the home, family, or community, everything considered the old life, and enter the new magickal life of the initiate. We can say that Gwion does this when he is taken as a servant, or neophyte, by Cerridwen. But it must happen again, as the student identifies with the new role, new community, new family, and often with the teacher. Any serious student on the path – and any teacher worth their salt – knows this all too well. When the process is well-supported and contained by rituals, ceremony, proper boundaries, and clear intention, the process can be quite amazing. When those boundaries break down – whether on the side of the student or teacher or sometimes both – the process becomes very messy. Unhealthy family dynamics are replicated, and the thread of initiation can become obscured. Many well-meaning teachers don't understand the process themselves, and repeat the same mistakes over and over again, not comprehending that separation and loss is a necessary step for all involved.

The Alchemy of Initiation

There are many systems and formulas for spiritual initiation, though the basic premise here is found most eloquently in the alchemists' teaching: solve et coagula. This means dissolve and coagulate, and can be found written on the arms of the image of Eliphas Levi known as Baphomet as mentioned in the alchemical crucible of Chapter Two and in our first exploration of the elements. While many first see the Devil figure of Christianity in this image, an occultist and initiate will see many interesting things pointing to deeper teachings on the nature of life and spirit. In particular, the blend of masculine and feminine qualities within what might be expected in a usually "male" Devil figure gives the first hints at something deeper.

Figure 13: Baphomet

Many state this saying is short for *solvite corpora et coagulate spiritus,* which means "dissolve the body (matter) and coagulate the spirit (energy)." This sums up a series of seven to twelve alchemical operations found both in the laboratory and in the consciousness and life of the alchemist, but in many ways, they can be summed up as various processes of separation, purification, and return.

Is this not the world of the cauldron? Separate things are brought together, the ingredients of the brew. They are joined together, dissolved in the waters of the cauldron and in the psychic sea of the initiate's consciousness or the collective consciousness of the tradition. Then the best part is drawn off and purified, as the dregs like poison fall to the bottom of the cauldron. We see this with the distilled essence of awen in the three drops and the cracked cauldron.

The inner cauldrons of our bodies reflect an inner alchemy within our psychic centers. The outer cauldrons reflect a process in nature that we mirror as we progress along our spiritual path of transformation. Is this not what happens to our poor Gwion Bach? By looking at the process of the cauldron through the lens of alchemy, through the art and science of initiatory matter, we can deepen our own understanding of the cauldron mysteries. Cerridwen is an alchemist with her potions and herbs, her fire and water. The stages of alchemy are not just for alchemists, but reflect a universal process all initiates must go through in some form in the search for deeper wisdom.

Chakra	Planet	Element Essential	Operation	Definition	Metal
Lower Cauldron of the Belly					
Root	Saturn	Fire	Calcination	Burning to ash	Lead
Belly	Jupiter	Water	Dissolution	Dissolving in water	Tin
Solar Plexus	Mars	Air	Separation	Dividing one from another	Iron
Middle Cauldron of the Heart					
Heart	Venus	Earth	Conjunction	Uniting parts	Copper
Upper Cauldron of the Head					
Throat	Mercury	Sulfur	Fermentation	Decay and new rising	Quicksilver
Brow	Moon	Mercury	Distillation	Refinement of essence	Silver
Crown	Sun	Salt	Coagulation	Perfect unification	Gold

Figure 14: Alchemical Process of the Planets, Chakras, and Three Cauldrons

The seven-process alchemical work repeats the process of separation and unification in several different arenas, using different chemical processes and their psycho-spiritual metaphors. Let's look at the stages more closely.

Calcination – Calcination is the process of using the element of fire to reduce something to its fundamental structure, with everything else taken out. To calcine is to reduce to "bone" or "bone ash," referring both literally to bones in animals and the structures within any substance. In plant alchemy, calcination reduces the plant to its basic salts, devoid of water, oils, and other chemicals. In life, it is the destructive process of heat that reduces us to our essentials, often through traumatic experiences. This process of purification is the result of something we have done previously, and must now accept the consequences of our actions – indicating the influence of Saturn, as the planet of karma and the hard teacher – in our lives. Sometimes we seek to escape the consequences of our actions, but that never works out in the long run. The process teaches us patience. In a laboratory, it can take a while for black ash to be heated enough that it turns gray and finally white, requiring patience in our lives. The root is the chakra, for in the Eastern traditions, we say that the root is the source of kundalini, or the fire serpent of awareness coiled within our base. Its awakening is initially a fiery calcination experience leading to the potential of greater consciousness. We can see many of the themes of the hut of Cerridwen in this operation.

Dissolution – Dissolution is the process of dissolving something in the element of water, or emotion, to allow all that can be dissolved by this simple "acid" to be dissolved. Like sugar or salt in water, it seems to disappear, but one taste will indicate its invisible presence universally through the liquid. Dissolution is a stage of unification, bringing things together, after the period of calcination, as the salts are then dissolved in a liquid as the second stage of a laboratory operation. Jupiter is the planet associated with this operation, for its great gravity welcomes everything it can into its collective gaseous planetary mass. It is a planet of benevolence, forgiveness, good fortune, and a sense of coming home, a return to what is safe, a catharsis that can occur after the initial emotional overwhelm. The belly, the digestive system, is what dissolves our food into a digestive acid soup, letting it all become one before nourishing us. The process of dissolution is the epitome of the stirred cauldron.

Separation – Separation is the process of dividing one thing from another, usually one part being more purified than the other. Depending on the laboratory form it takes, it can also be considered a form of filtering, as the purified substance will pass through the filter, while the material that is not pure will be blocked. In alchemy, this process is associated with Mars, a planet astrologically associated with fire and water signs (Aries and Scorpio), yet the operation is considered the function of air, for air – like the sword in the tarot – is the tool of discernment and dividing. The digestive system helps us discern and separate out nutrition from waste; therefore the stomach, adrenal glands, gallbladder, and liver, the largest filter within the body, are all associated with the solar plexus, the traditional chakra of this third operation. Separating the charmed drops from the poisonous dregs of the cauldron is one example of separation in the Tale of Taliesin.

Conjunction – Conjunction is the process of uniting separate parts, usually after their purification process. Sometimes it is described as thickening, allowing the substance to cool, bringing all the parts together. It is associated with the heart chakra, being the great uniter between the upper and lower cauldrons. The heart chakra's planet is Venus, the planet of love, but also of magnetic attraction, uniting things with magnetic pull. The element is earth, bringing the first four operations to a semi-conclusion in the solidness of the earth. The first four operations together are said to craft the Lesser Stone, and the Lesser and Greater Stones are considered grail symbols. The Lesser Stone also deals with work in the vegetable kingdom of alchemy. Venus is the goddess of nature in all her forms, born of blood and violence, rising from the ocean and making the world bloom. So while we tend to associate her with plant life, she is also associated with the oceans from which all life, including animal life, rises. Uniting the wisdom of the animal totems could fall under the operations of conjunction within the Cerridwen cycle of initiation.

Fermentation – This fifth operation is the first associated with the upper cauldron and the traditional throat chakra. Fermentation is the process of allowing decay, technically the sub-operation of putrefaction, and through that putrefaction new life rises from the fermentation. In the chemical process, an invisible – and seemingly secret – substance is added: a yeast. In the spiritual process, this is the invisible touch, the additional blessing or grace bestowed by contact with a higher reality. This triggers the new process. This can be the blessing of a teacher, a ritual of initiation, or the influence of a deity. Despite the traditional planet associated with this fifth operation being the planet Mercury, it is said the necessary power of the three alchemical forms is the power of sulfur. Its nature is volatile and individual, illuminating. Much of the fermentation mystery imagery is about rising to life after death. Alcohol is known as a rising spirit because it is aged in caskets, mixing the life, death, and resurrection imagery in simple wine- and beer-making. The seed returns to the womb, the womb of the Goddess, to be nourished by the new life of her own body. This connection triggers a new form, a resurrection from the old, when the seed falls away to reveal a new child. In the tale of Cerridwen, this is the gestation of the seed of Gwion Bach.

Distillation – Distillation is the refinement of a liquid through the process of rising and falling. In laboratory operations, a fermented liquid, such as wine, is distilled through heating and cooling, and that refinement would yield brandy. The brandy is a stronger, sharper, more "wise" form of the wine because it has gone through so many deaths and rebirths. We go through a similar process of rising to the heavens and returning to the Earth. The Moon is the "planet" of astrology associated with this operation, as it clearly rises and falls most nights, though the alchemical principle necessary for this stage is alchemical mercury, or quicksilver, as its nature is mercurial, easily adapting, rising and falling as circumstances dictate. Along with the Moon, which rules psychic abilities, the brow chakra, or third eye, is the point within the body resonating with the sixth operation. In our tale of Taliesin, it is the return to the seas, rising and falling with the flow of the tides and the rush of the waters. The reborn child is not quite "done" and needs to grow wise in darkness, concentrating power, one last time.

Coagulation – The seventh and final stage in the alchemical operations is coagulation. It is associated with the pinnacle of the chakra ladder, the crown at the top of the head, corresponding with enlightenment, the Sun, and perfection. In coagulation, the various parts are united in perfection, with the best qualities of all substances and none of the flaws. In metallic alchemy, gold – being solid yet shapeable, conductive and non-corrosive – is the true symbol, while lead is at the lowest rung with the root, Saturn and calcination. The last of the alchemical triad, salt, the principle of purity and fixedness, is necessary for the unification of coagulation, as the final product of the seven operations is described as a stone or crystal. The bright and shining brow of the reborn Taliesin is revealed to the world. It resonates with the magick "stone" or "bone" placed by the spirits in the body of a newly initiated shaman.

While it might seem overly complex, one can use this basic formula for understanding the process found in many initiatory tales – even fairy tales – containing deeper esoteric truths.

Aries	Calcination	Burning to mineral ash
Taurus	Congelation/Conjunction	Thickening by cooling
Gemini	Fixation	Trapping volatile as liquid or solid
Cancer	Dissolution	Dissolving of solids in liquid
Leo	Digestion	Extended continuous warming
Virgo	Distillation	Rise and fall of a liquid
Libra	Sublimation	Rise and fall of a solid
Scorpio	Separation	Isolation of solid from liquid
Sagittarius	Ceration	Softening hard substance
Capricorn	Fermentation	Biological animation
Aquarius	Multiplication	Increasing potency
Pisces	Projection/Coagulation	The mysterious power of the stone

Figure 15: Alchemical Processes of the Zodiac

Along with the seven-rung "Ladder of the Heavens" found in most forms of initiatory alchemy, the operations can be expanded to correspond with the twelve zodiac signs. The twelve operations of the zodiac, repeating the seven processes outlined above, will be covered in more depth in the rebirth section of the chapter. They clearly show similar operations, yet reveal a different pattern and process that is equally important.

Preparing for this level of initiation is like adolescence. A teenager is not quite ready for the magickal world all on their own, but more ready than when they began. Boundaries begin to be tested. When a student once readily agreed with a teacher, issues of dissent, whether magickal or personal, begin to grow between them. Warnings are ignored, and like the cracked cauldron, mistakes are made, but those mistakes ultimately serve the greater good of the initiate, for each mistake provides a true opportunity for learning. One might say they are divine mistakes, propelling us along at a deeper and faster rate than if we simply played it safe.

At some point in the process, there is this seeming battle of wits, where the student believes they can outsmart the teacher and do better, just as Gwion, who has absorbed all the knowledge of the world, knows that Cerridwen will be murderously angry at him for drinking the three drops even though it was not his intention or even his fault. He must know that he cannot outrun her, yet tries to both outrun and outsmart her. While it's not his "fault," he knows he will nonetheless be held responsible for the actions that occurred on his watch, yet in his adolescent stage, he seeks to escape that responsibility. His fate, however, is pre-ordained in the formula of initiation. All that has been separated will be coagulated again.

In their day-to-day relationship, the teacher must often push the student to begin mentoring and teaching, to experience things a bit from the side of the instructor. The student might be asked to carry more responsibilities, to see how those responsibilities are handled. That added pressure functions like the pressure created in an alchemical vessel, helping cook and refine the consciousness of the student. Sometimes the release means a student leaves responsibilities for a time, to find their own way and seek their own path. But, as with Gwion, in true initiation, there is return. Sometimes the return is not to a specific teacher or tradition, but to the greater initiator of life, the Tradition with a capital "T" that oversees all our spiritual traditions from the inner planes. But the process of separation, ruled by Mars and its image of the discerning blade or sword, can be traumatic.

Part of our work in the lower cauldron was stoking the fire of life force found in the belly. We used the five woods – found in the fingers – for the five elements, and ignited our fire. Now, as we approach a new level of maturity, we must go beyond and integrate the powers associated with the seven planets, showing we have a clear flow, if not yet mastery, over the seven centers in our body, the interior stars associated with the planets. The cauldron of the heart, being the bridge between the inner and outer, can actually help us do that. One of the symbols in both the West and East for the heart center is the hexagram, the six-pointed star. The six points plus the center stand for the seven planets in the Hermetic ceremonial traditions, as well as a union of the macrocosm and the microcosm. The middle cauldron unites the upper and lower cauldrons. Once we have this greater flow between all parts, we are prepared to face the elements again, this time refined in the form of totemic guardians.

Exercise 9:
The Alchemy of the Middle Cauldron of the Heart

If you wish to focus primarily on just the heart cauldron, start as you would start with **Exercise 3: Three Cauldron Activation**, or if you want to build upon your cauldrons, perform **Exercise 7: Lower Cauldron of Life and the Five Woods** and then move into **Exercise 9**. Like these previous exercises, no tools other than your own body are required, but you can set the space with an altar and whatever tools you desire.

This working of union with the seven planets prepares us to fully follow the threads of initiation in our life to greater completion. The heart links the lower world of the elements, embodied by the lower cauldron, to the upper world of the abstract powers. It helps us understand and accept the responsibilities of the path with an open heart, and balance our worldview between student and teacher, realizing the paradox that we are both, at once, but allowing us to assume the role that is most appropriate in any given situation.

Place your hands in the "five wood" position of each of the corresponding fingertips touching (**Chart 6: Tree Finger Ogham**), but with no pressure on any particular finger. Close your eyes. Breathe deeply. Feel this connection and the connection of the elements to the lower Cauldron of the Belly. Prepare yourself for the trance state of energy work. Clear your mind. Open your heart and seek the secret fire that illuminates your souls, guiding and protecting you. Count backwards twelve to one, envisioning the numbers drawn on the screen of your mind. Then release that image to the void, and without visualization, count downward from thirteen to one to get to a deeper level. Set your intention:

I seek to activate and align the seven planets with my middle cauldron.

As you breathe, focus upon Coire Ernmae, the Cauldron of Motion, of Abundance. Focus on the Cauldron of Heart that links all parts of yourself. Breathe deep and focus on the beating of your heart and the flow of blood through your veins.

The teaching of the Cauldron of Heart is one of joys and sorrows. Joys and sorrows, deep and genuine emotion, opens the heart of the potential bard and rocks the tilted cauldron from its side to a fully upright position. Only through an honest experience and understanding of the depth of human emotion can the bard relate the legends, myths, and sagas in a way that will move the listener's heart. Only through this understanding of the human realm can the magician then tackle the mysteries of the deep Earth and holy heavens. We cannot leave either our joys or sorrows unacknowledged, but must embrace them.

I evoke the teachings of Saturn, planet of karma and consequence.
Show me your joys and your sorrows.
Grant me understanding and empathy.

Perceive your heart filling with a dark black "light" or color, as this is the color of Saturn. Feel the heaviness of lead within your heart and recall times in the past when you were faced with the consequences of your mistakes. Recall the times when you tried to escape the consequences of your actions and how that turned out for you. Focus upon times when you have taken on responsibility, and there were difficulties and pressure. Recall times of deep grief and sadness. Recall depression. Focus upon how all of this felt for you as your consciousness dwells within the black light of the heart.

Feel the black light of the heart become like a black flame, a flame of calcination that burns through the heaviness, to reveal the clear white light of the truth of the experience, without anything that is unnecessary.

I evoke the teachings of Jupiter, planet of mercy and blessing.
Show me your joys and your sorrows.
Grant me understanding and empathy.

Perceive your heart filling with a royal blue "light" or color, as this is the color of Jupiter. Feel the brittleness of tin within your heart and recall times in the past when you were faced with acceptance and forgiveness, or asked by someone for acceptance and forgiveness. Recall all the times of benevolence and mercy, both received and given. Think of a time when you failed to give forgiveness or acceptance to another, and think of a time when you too were failed by another. Remember all your homecomings, all the times when you were loved and accepted unconditionally. Recall your sense of family and home, good or ill. Focus upon how all of this felt for you as your consciousness dwells in the blue light of the heart.

Feel the blue light become like water, a water that washes over your heart and purifies and heals your heart on all levels, washing away all that doesn't serve your highest and deepest heart.

I evoke the teachings of Mars, planet of action and protection.
Show me your joys and your sorrows.
Grant me understanding and empathy.

Perceive your heart filling with a red "light" or color, as this is the color of Mars. Feel the strength of iron within your heart and recall times in the past when you were faced with using your power to take action. Recall the times when you have actively sought out your desires, what you wanted, and how that turned out for you. Focus on times that you have had to draw a strong boundary, end something, or destroy something because it was necessary, or because you lost control and misused your power. Recall times of strength or lack thereof. Focus upon the consequences of your actions and how all of this felt for you.

Feel the red light of the heart become like a strong wind, a wind drawing a boundary around you, allowing some things to pass and some things to be blocked, protecting your heart from all that doesn't serve.

I evoke the teachings of Venus, planet of love and relationship.
Show me your joys and your sorrows.
Grant me understanding and empathy.

Perceive your heart filling with a deep green "light" or color, as this is the color of Venus. Feel the shininess of copper within your heart and recall times in the past when you were in love, in a relationship. Relationships can be romantic or sexual, friendships or simply social connections. Think about the blessings of those relationships and all the joys and euphoria. Think about the difficulties of relationship, and the vulnerability, pain, and sorrow that accompany them. Focus upon how all of this felt for you as your consciousness dwells within the green light of the heart.

Feel the green light of the heart become like an emerald, shining bright, strong and solid. The emerald light reveals the true heart that beats in time with the heart of the Earth Mother, matching your love with her love.

I evoke the teachings of Mercury, planet of thought and speech.
Show me your joys and your sorrows.
Grant me understanding and empathy.

Perceive your heart filling with an orange "light" or color, as this is the color of Mercury. Feel the fluidness of quicksilver within your heart and recall times in the past when you were challenged to speak your truth and how that felt for you. Recall times when you failed to speak truly. Recall times that you were forced to listen to challenging truths from others. Reflect on education, formal and informal, when your mind has been filled and patterned. Recall times of inspiration and creativity, as well as times of anxiety and stress. Focus upon how all of this felt for you as your consciousness dwells within the orange light of the heart.

Feel the orange light of the heart become like a spark of light, a seed, entering your heart and catalyzing something new, something clear, that will grow over time and in the fullness of your own bardic voice.

I evoke the teachings of the Moon, planet of emotion and family.
Show me your joys and your sorrows.
Grant me understanding and empathy.

Perceive your heart filling with a violet purple "light" or color, as this is the color of the Moon. Feel the reflectiveness of silver within your heart and recall times in the past when you were faced with strong emotions, strong feelings, about yourself, family, friends, and particularly your mother. Recall times of reactiveness, where you felt you were unconsciously responding to people. Focus upon times when your intuition was strong and clear, when you could trust your feelings, and how that was different from when you were unconsciously reacting to difficult things. Focus upon how all of this felt for you as your consciousness dwells within the violet light of the heart.

Feel the violet purple light of the heart become like an ocean wave, a tide coming in and out of your heart in a rhythm, with a soothing, rocking motion. This aligns the beating of your heart to the tides of the stars.

I evoke the teachings of the Sun, planet of health and perfection.
Show me your joys and your sorrows.
Grant me understanding and empathy.

Perceive your heart filling with a golden yellow "light" or color, as this is the color of the Sun. Feel the lightness of gold within your heart, and recall times in the past when you were faced with issues of health for yourself and for others. Recall issues of fearing death, fearing loss, and fearing failure. Focus on times of happiness, of success and recognition. Reflect on the process of seeking perfection, doing what you are here to do in the world. Focus upon how all of this felt for you as your consciousness dwells within the golden light of the heart. Feel the yellow light of the heart become like a clear crystal, reflecting the light of the Sun. Your heart becomes like quartz, like a diamond, like the clearest, most beautifully cut stone, dazzling in all the reflected facets, reflecting all things in all directions.

Feel your Cauldron of the Heart open and ready to receive the blessings of the heavens and the Earth. The above and below are joined within your heart, and you are prepared to fill your heart until it becomes the inexhaustible well, as your cup shall runneth over.

When you have reflected and energized all seven wandering stars within your heart, relax your hands. Rest. Reflect. As a whole, how do you feel? You can repeat this exercise, like the lower cauldron work, to bring greater awareness and stability to these changes. At different times, one of the seven planets may have a deeper experience for you than the others.

When ready, bring your awareness back to the world around you, to your flesh and blood, breath and bone. Count up from thirteen to one, then twelve to one. Feel your fingers and toes. Open your eyes and ground yourself as needed. Record your experience in your journal. Practice this exercise regularly until you feel a shift and believe you are ready for the last initiatory experience of this chapter.

The Animal Allies and the Elements

For many people, the core of the Taliesin tale is the shapeshifting chase. Even with little to no esoteric knowledge, it is easy to intuit that something important, something incredibly deep and profound is happening, even beyond the fantastic magick of shapeshifting that is presented in the tale.

"And she went forth after him, running. And he saw her, and changed himself into a hare and fled. But she changed herself into a greyhound and turned him. And he ran towards a river, and became a fish. And she in the form of an otter-bitch chased him under the water, until he was fain to turn himself into a bird of the air. She, as a hawk, followed him and gave him no rest in the sky. And just as she was about to stoop upon him, and he was in fear of death, he espied a heap of winnowed wheat on the floor of a barn, and he dropped among the wheat, and turned himself into one of the grains. Then she transformed herself into a high-crested black hen, and went to the wheat and scratched it with her feet, and found him out and swallowed him. "

— from "Taliesin" in *The Mabinogion*

Though differing from our Celtic reconstructionist counterparts who would not look to find the four Greek roots, or elements, of the philosopher Empedocles in a native Welsh tale, occultists and Witches easily see the fourfold pattern of the chase as indicative of the four elements and their powers, though we might not always agree on our interpretations of the symbols. While our Western understanding of the elements is from Greek philosophy, parallels of these terms are found all over the world, particularly in Hindu Ayurveda, and the concepts have become a staple of the Western Mystery traditions. Adepts of these Western Mysteries were the first to popularize and bring the classic Celtic tales into the spiritual light of the modern esoteric traditions. While they might not have been working with the deepening linguistic and historic knowledge base we have today on the Celtic cultures, they did understand the patterns of truth and spirit, and applied them in their understanding.

We prepare the Cauldron of the Heart in this chapter for it represents a culmination of the four elements, as the fourth step of alchemical initiation in conjunction, or bringing things together. The chase also serves to bring the four elements together through trials and transformations that require a certain level of mastery over fire, water, air, and earth.

Usually the first transformation, hare and greyhound, is associated with fire for the swift and powerful movements initiating the chase. The second with water, as both creatures – salmon and otter – swim. The third is obviously air, for both animals – wren and hawk – fly. The last is most often associated with earth, with the grain being from the Earth itself, and the hen being a source of food, both eggs and meat, and the process of eating resonating with the lessons of earth.

Some switch the first and last, believing the land-running animals represent earth, and the strange consumption of the seed is more indicative of the transforming fire. Personally I disagree, favoring the first interpretation of fire, water, air, and earth. It fits the already established alchemical patterns quite well with the associated element of calcination, dissolution, separation, and conjunction.

Yet on an alchemical level, both patterns are very initiatory. Today the pattern is harder to see, as modern magickal traditions favor the Golden Dawn orientation of the elements and directions, with earth in the north, air in the east, fire in the south, and water in the west. This works best with the corresponding four archangel associations, and those of the seasons in modern-day ceremonial magick.

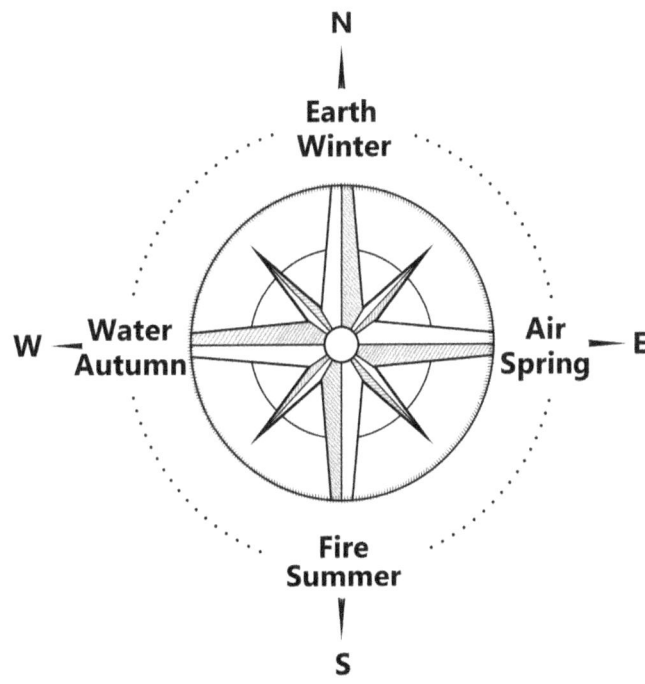

Figure 16: Modern Elemental Alignment with the Directions and Seasons

The older Greek traditions used a different mandala, with fire and water – as the primal pair – opposing, and earth and air – as the more complex pair – opposing. Each pair represents a male/female dynamic, with the male elements represented by an upward triangle in Hermetic alchemy, while the female elements are symbolized by a downward triangle. Complex elements have a horizontal line, while primal elements lack this line.

This also aligns the two qualities of the elements. Each element is said to be either warm or cold, and each element is said to be either wet or dry. When placing them upon a circle in the four directions, the primal elements must oppose, and the complex elements must oppose.

These qualities lead to the cycle of creation and destruction rotating around the wheel. Much like practitioners of Traditional Chinese Medicine, or TCM, use a five-pointed pentacle mandala to show how each interpretation of the elements can encourage elemental growth or diminish an elemental power, and then use this imagery in their diagnosis and treatment, ancient Greek medical practitioners, as well as occult initiates, would use it as well.

In its most simple, almost literal, demonstration, one can start with fire, warm and dry. Diminish the warmth as the fire burns out, and you are left with ash, now cool and dry. Ash is ruled by the earth element for those qualities. Adding to the wetness of the ash adds moisture, and if you add enough moisture, you will have a solution of ash and liquid, with the dissolvable plant salts becoming part of the water, and the insoluble dropping out of the solution. You have thereby created a cold and wet substance, ruled by water. Add heat to the cool and wet water, and the water will evaporate, leaving the salts behind, but then entering into the atmosphere, being technically warm and wet, and ruled by the element of air. Lastly the air goes to feed the spark igniting the fire, and becomes dry as it's consumed, leading back to fire. Through manipulation of the two axes of qualities, you transmute the elements – both in life, and in ourselves – using their energetic equivalents.

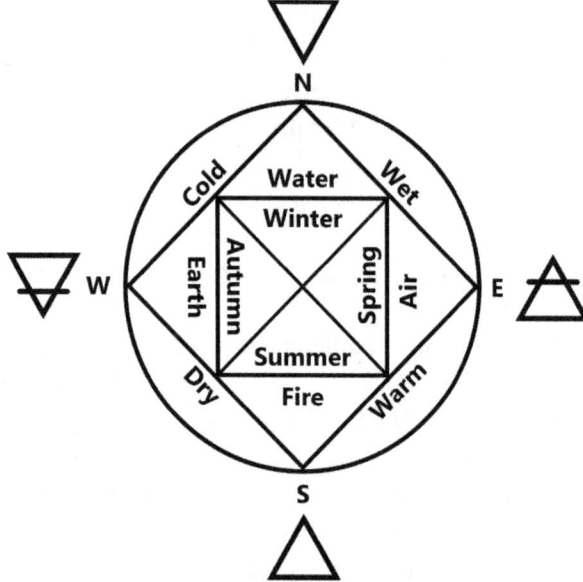

Figure 17: Greek Mandala of the Elements with the Qualities and Hermetic Triangle Glyphs

Some modern magickal traditions, like the Cabot Tradition of Witchcraft and the Temple of Witchcraft, seek to reconcile these two ideas by keeping the northern alignment of Earth (popular in many magickal traditions oriented to the Earth and stars), but then changing the alignment to suit the alchemical qualities, putting fire in the east and air in the south, altering two of the four traditional points found in modern Wicca and most styles of ceremonial magick. While the ancient Greeks might have placed them differently around the circle (if they used such circles), this is a pattern I learned from my own Witchcraft teachers and pass on to my students today. There is some evidence outlined in *Practical Elemental Magick* by David Rankine & Sorita d'Este that this might have actually been an older formula of the Medieval grimoire traditions such as *The Greater Key of Solomon*, all the way back to the writings of Zosimos of Panopolis, and it was Éliphas Lévi who popularized the switch between the directions of air and fire.

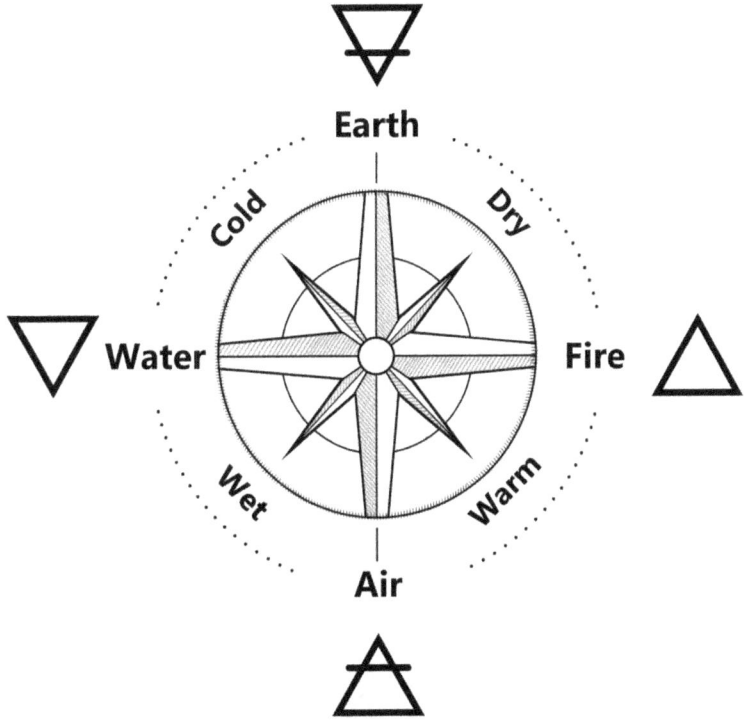

Figure 18: Modern Elemental Mandala with the Qualities and Hermetic Triangle Glyphs

With these associations and modern models in mind, we see both interpretations of the elements and the shapeshifting chase give us some deep imagery and energies to contemplate and experiment with.

If using the patterns I favor – of fire, water, air, and earth – you are working with the primary pairs, creating a cross of sorts across the mandala. In Qabalistic lore, the elements in their order of creation are fire (the spark), water (the form), air (the breath of life), and earth (the manifestation). One is in a position of confrontation with the opposite, which is essentially what Cerridwen is seeking to do, to confront poor Gwion. Many good initiators, literally or ritually, must be confrontational, and the student, seeking to avoid confrontation, soon finds out they have nowhere to go. A guardian of the gate, the dweller on the threshold, prevents one from passing further until the demands are met. In British Traditional Wicca of the Gardnerian and Alexandrian variety, one is held blindfolded and bound, challenged by the cold steel of a sword point to give the password for entering the circle of initiation.

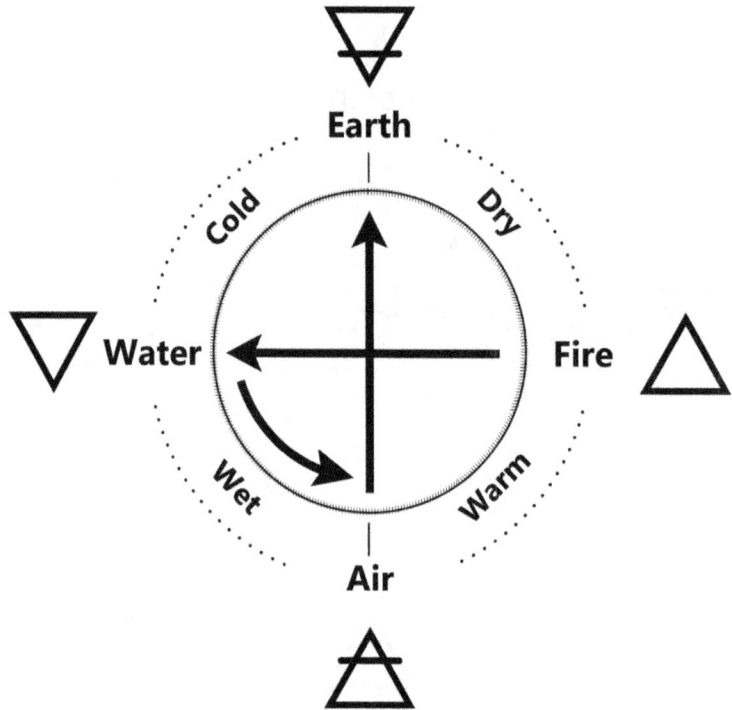

Figure 19: Mandala of Initiation through Confrontation

For those who favor starting with earth – the common point in the world where we all begin – and moving to water, air, and fire, the practitioner is elevated through levels of density. Earth is considered to be the densest element, with fire as the most ephemeral, for its symbol, combustion, is literally not matter in any form, but the process of changing matter to energy. Water and air, though somewhat ephemeral, are nonetheless physical states of being, liquid and gas. In this sequence, one goes around the modern mandala counterclockwise, unwinding the self and returning to the center. Witchcraft can be described as a path of unmaking, as we ultimately unmake ourselves, peeling away all that is false to identify with a true, essential core. In some ways, that could be said about most introspective, mystical spiritual paths. And certainly it could be said about the path of Cerridwen, for those who wish to be reborn as bards. Then one must reforge and walk a path of re-making, which is really the mystical heart of the "craft" in our Witchcraft, the crafting of the true self at work in the world. What becomes our vehicle we forge to experience the world? That is another stage of initiation in the rebirth of the self to the new. Here are the various integration phases of the alchemical journey, the conjunctions and coagulations.

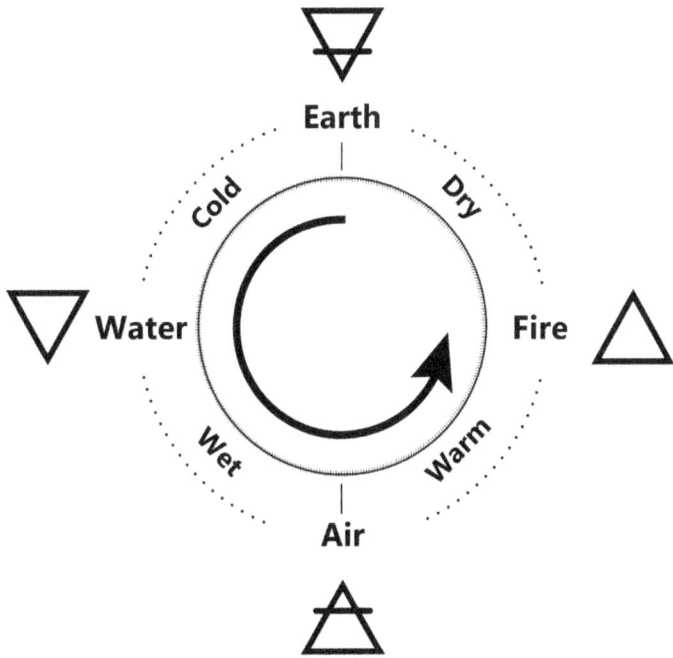

Figure 20: Mandala of Initiation for Unwinding

The process of confrontation or unwinding, however you see to choose it, is guided by the spirits of the animals in this sequence. Each pair provides a pattern to the process. Each pair holds the gates to a mystery necessary in the training. All adepts go through elemental training, whether they call it such or not. The initiation of the Goddess and the cauldron is no different.

Element	Magickal Training
Fire	Establishing Will, Directing Desire, Harnessing Energy, Maintaining and Increasing Vitality, Finding and Acting upon Passions, Using Creativity
Water	Generating Compassion, Getting in Touch with Emotions, Balancing Relationships, Healing Family Wounds, Accessing the Unconscious
Air	Seeking Truth, Learning of Lore and Patterns, Improving Memory, Greater Understanding, Listening and Speaking, Quieting the Mind, Storytelling
Earth	Seeking Sovereignty, Conditioning the Body, Discipline, Security and Independence, Stability, Grounding, Practicality, Health, Diet

Chart 10: Elemental Training

In modern metaphysics (which seems to borrow from the Indigenous tribes of the Americas, but is really working with some universal themes), each animal is said to have a "medicine," meaning a teaching or energy that helps restore balance in an individual missing that teaching. Animal medicines are considered in light of both the animal's literal behavior and habitat, as well as the mythology and folklore surrounding that animal. Primal traditions from across the world see animals – and animal spirits – as teachers, guardians, and primal ancestors, helping humanity on its course and attributing our present difficulties, at least partly, to our inability to listen and work with the spirits of nature and align with our own deeper animal wisdom. As illness is something that brings disharmony and takes us out of balance, medicine is something that returns the balance within us. Sometimes our spiritual journeys with animals in shamanic vision help restore physical healing, but more often than not, they bring healing, wisdom and balance to the souls.

Here is the medicine of each of Gwion's transformations:

Hare

The spirit of the hare is all about survival, be it survival of self or survival of species. No wonder it was the first creature chosen by Gwion. The two key themes that come up time and again for the hare (or rabbits in general) are fertility, for these animals multiply rapidly, and fear, for they are quick to flee a confrontation since they have little fight capabilities against bigger predators. They can dart rapidly in a crooked line to evade predators and rarely counterattack. Likewise, people who have strong hare energy in their makeup do the unexpected, taking unusual twists and turns to get to safety. Some hares and rabbits generate such a strong fear response that their systems induce a heart attack when they are captured by a predator rather than be eaten alive. Hares are known to survive by finding the best hiding space, digging small burrows to live and hide from their dangerous enemies.

Hares are associated with the powers of the Moon, and in particular, white hares are creatures of the Moon. The gestation period of the pregnant hare is the short twenty-eight day Moon cycle, unlike our own human nine-month cycle. Hares quickly mature and can soon be on their own, much quicker than rabbits, and unlike rabbits, are often loners apt to be less social.

Mythically, hares embody the spirit of the trickster who wanders alone, a rebel by nature. Tricksters also like to shake it up and do the unexpected, often going where they are not always wanted. With both the Moon associations and their crooked-path chase response, hares have become creatures associated with Witchcraft, with medieval Witches said to go to the Sabbat in the form of a hare. They can walk between worlds like a shamanic practitioner, and travel along the astral. Like many tricksters, hares have been associated with a variety of creation myths.

Salmon

In Celtic myth, the salmon is known for its wisdom, creating some interesting cognitive dissonance with other Western Mystery traditions. We tend to associate all water totems with emotions, healing, psychic ability, and family, not wisdom or intelligence, and the salmon, being a fish and obviously associated with water, seems to fit this pattern. Technically, however, while Gwion's transformation was simply into a fish, most poetic renderings have turned this fish into the bardic salmon. The salmon is said to feed upon the nuts from the Hazel of Wisdom, and grow wise. The Salmon of Knowledge lived within a sacred well that overflowed into a river. The salmon plays this role of wisdom keeper in the Irish tale of Finn MacCool. In the Welsh tale of Mabon, the son of Modron, the salmon is the oldest and wisest of creatures, surviving from the first age.

The wisdom of this creature is said to come from its life cycle. In studying the salmon's patterns, it returns to where it was spawned, typically swimming upstream to get there. We observe it from the outside as it swims against the current, and we think that is foolishness, particularly those of us looking to the root of the word Wicca as a wisdom to follow, to "bend or shape" and go with the flow with the energies that are already present rather than against them. Yet the salmon uses the undercurrent beneath the surface to move upstream, showing a depth and level of wisdom that is not apparent to the surface observer. One must get into the situation, the river, to find that deeper current.

Salmon are determined to get there, taking little food or rest on the journey. They avoid predators, and can even jump quite high over obstacles, into higher water sources from the down-flowing river. They seek to return to their source, a metaphor for us on the spiritual journey, and will not stop or get distracted. Once they get there, the salmon spawn and then die, returning to the cycle of life through this death. Perhaps on some level Gwion was preparing to die and reenter the cycle of life even as he consciously used the salmon's tenacity to avoid Cerridwen's otter.

Wren

Again the description of Gwion's transformation was simply into a "bird of the air," yet is poetically described today as the tiny wren, a bird with rich magickal lore. This tiny brown bird is a powerful creature, its nature and its myths both demonstrating resourcefulness, boldness, and confidence, yet it rarely shows itself out in the open air and will build its nests upon the ground or close to the ground, along with decoy nests to lure predators away. Their nests often fit into places unsuitable for other birds. The wren will sing from dawn until night, with a voice much louder than expected for a bird of this size. With this confidence, a wren will attack a much larger threatening bird or other creatures, human included, seemingly not realizing its own size in the match. Their medicine teaching really involves how size does not matter in the issue, but resourcefulness and boldness can win the day.

A myth illustrating this, depending on the version, involves the King of the Birds. One day, the birds gathered together and called for a king. While trying to determine the best way to choose a king, the birds consulted the owl, the wisest of birds. Yet the wren thought he was wiser still, and loudly suggested that the bird that flies the highest should win the title of king. Each of the birds flew up and returned down to their nests, until the eagle flew the highest of all before him. But before he could claim kingship, the wren, tucked under the feathers of the eagle, popped out and flew just higher, above the eagle, and as they flew down, the wren claimed kingship. Some end the tale there, with the lesson being those who dare, win. Other versions of the tale say that the collective of birds, undecided, went back to the owl, who determined that the wren did not, in fact, fly on his own, and named the eagle as king, with the wren learning humility and the value of staying close to the Earth.

Grain of Wheat

The seed is technically a "grain of wheat" or corn, for in this context, corn is not American maize, but any of the cereal grains familiar in the British Isles and Europe. Wheat is a sacred substance, symbolizing life, sustenance, death, and rebirth. The sacrificial gods were associated with the life cycle of grain. The green gods of vegetation become golden ripe and then are cut down to feed their people. This is the mythos of John Barleycorn. Some feel this association makes Taliesin, whose initiatory name refers to his golden brow, a sacrificial vegetation god. As he can be all things, perhaps he is, but he is not only a sacrificial figure, nor is that his traditional role.

In the Eleusinian Mysteries sacred to the Goddess Demeter (and her Roman form, Ceres) and which have occult associations with Cerridwen, the grain is a symbol of rebirth, for she is the grain mother. Images of triune wheat are a symbol of the Eleusinian Mysteries, and one theory holds that the special ingredient to their sacrament was the psychedelic fungus ergot, which grows upon grain. Its poison is similar to LSD in composition and effect. So the grain has associations with otherworldliness.

Yet beyond the more esoteric associations, the seed is a source of food, a point of potential growth, and a symbol of abundance. This transformation takes Gwion from the realm of the servant to the rebirth that fulfills his divine potential.

In this cycle of transformations, Gwion moves from the survival mechanism of the hare to run rapidly away to the determination of the salmon to return. Determination turns to confidence in the boldness of the wren, as if he could possibly get away, and the cleverness of the wren leads to his plan of hiding as the seed.

Each of these spirit medicines builds upon the other, from pure survival to the potential of the seed. The elemental associations that I tend to favor follow the sequence of the alchemical operations, with calcination/fire/hare, dissolution/water/salmon, separation/air/wren, and conjunction/earth/seed.

And here are the spirit medicine meanings for all of Cerridwen's transformations:

Greyhound

Not simply shifting into any dog, Cerridwen takes the shape of the greyhound, a dog known today for its racing speed, though these hounds have a rich history in hunting and sport. Greyhounds originated in ancient Egypt, where they were highly prized and honored. From Egypt, they were then honored in ancient Greece, figuring into the iconography and myths of Hecate and in the tales of Artemis. In the tale of Actaeon the hunter, he, with his forty-eight greyhounds, came upon Artemis bathing and stared at her naked body rather than avert his eyes. For this insult, she transformed him into a stag, and his own hounds ripped him apart.

Celtic hounds were known as guardians of the roads and crossroads and guides to lost souls after death. They appear in some form in Celtic knot work and artistic designs. Likewise they have become associated through this myth with Cerridwen, and embody not only speed and the hunt, but nobility and companionship.

Otter

Traditionally otter wisdom is not so concerned with the hunt, as the otter of Cerridwen is, but with playfulness and joy. Yet otters, both sea and river otters, primarily eat fish and spend much of their time hunting for food. While fish is their primary diet, they aren't picky, and will eat just about anything appropriate for them including crabs, crayfish, frogs, small birds, and even lizards when upon land. They use all their senses in hunting and are in particular sensitive to vibration in the water through their face whiskers, while their claws are deadly to their prey. People watching otters hunt describe it as "fun" as they float and dive. This is one of the reasons otter medicine is said to be of playfulness, joy, and going with the flow, wherever the waters of life take you. Otter is also associated with the divine feminine energy, and with the Goddess. Otters hunt so much because food is associated with the Great Mother, but also nursing otters caring for their young need a lot of food to produce enough milk, as they frequently nurse for eight hours a day. When exploring otter magick, it is a message to reconnect with the divine mother, but also to have fun while taking responsibility for your work at the same time. Chores can be playful. Be sensitive to vibrations and flow with what's around you.

Hawk

Hawks are predatory birds, with a keen ability to see the ground below from far above. They can see the details and remain detached, soaring through the heavens, and then strike when the time is right. Unlike falcons, hawks kill their prey with their talons, rather than their beak. Fledgling hawks learn to hunt at a very early age, having strong instincts. Hawk magick indicates an ability to lead, to take decisive and effective action quickly. Hawk medicine is one of focus. With the ability to perceive both the big picture and the small details, hawk is also a teacher of the greater vision, which includes the larger spiritual insights and psychic vision.

Spiritually, hawks, like many larger predatory birds, are considered to be divine messengers. Flying so high, they touch the realm of the heavenly spirits, and can indicate a message returning from the heavens or take our prayers and messages to the sky realm.

Black Hen

Generally the magick of the hen is one of the divine feminine, of fertility and sexuality. Hens embody both the mother archetype and abundance, as they are both grain devourers and a source of food to humans and animals. Hens are about the enjoyment of the "house" or domestic life. There is a distinct "pecking order" to the world of chickens, and the medicine lesson is understanding your place in the scheme of things around you. Yet on the darker side, hens are neurotic and poorly tempered. They can lash out, be greedy or lazy, and warn us about similar traits.

The "high crested black hen" that Cerridwen transforms into has a long association with magick and mystery. According to Witch hunters, the Devil could never resist a black hen. The Witch's Ladder or Witch's Garland used black hen feathers in the knots of the cords to make magick. Traditionally it was for baneful cursing magick, though some practitioners use it simply to gather power. Today black hen feathers and eggs are used both to cleanse and heal, and to curse. All our associations with the dark goddesses can apply to the magick and mystery of the black hen.

In many ways, Cerridwen's transformations were more specific than the generalized ones of Gwion. They show the savvy of the teacher prepared rather than the student jumping from one scene to the next in the escape attempt with only improvisations, not preparations. Each of the animals is in alignment with Cerridwen's essential nature. The speed of the greyhound is followed by the playfulness of the otter. She's not worried that she won't succeed and will take time to enjoy the hunt. With the third escape, she becomes a bit more serious, more powerful, with the hawk form. Then she trumps Gwion's seeming cleverness in hiding as a grain of wheat by becoming the devourer of wheat, the black bird that embodies the devouring goddess. Yet the trick is laid upon her, with her unexpected pregnancy. Teachers can be surprised.

Likewise I see the elemental sequence of calcination/fire/greyhound, dissolution/water/otter, separation/air/hawk, and conjunction/earth/hen. This process matches that of the student, paralleling his development and pushing him further on the path of initiation.

In the center of these two animal wheel mandalas is the mystery. For us as practitioners, it's finding our own central animal ally. In many metaphysical traditions, there is a belief that everyone has a primary animal ally, though the teachings around it differ, depending on the tradition and teacher. Some feel your primary animal ally is the one that embodies qualities you do not yet possess, that you are here to learn. Others feel, myself included, that this is the role of other allies as spirit teachers, and your primary ally embodies the traits you already possess and carry into the world. They are already a part of your nature.

Witchcraft traditions have a wide range of animal teachings. Some call your animal ally your familiar, or familiar spirit, after terms popularized in the Old Testament that were used by Witch hunters against those they sought to persecute during the Witch trials. A Witch was defined as one with a familiar spirit, which originally might have meant any kind of intermediary spirit acting as a go-between for the Witch and the spirit world. Later, because the traditions associated with Medieval Witchcraft were most likely remnants of a European shamanic tradition, the term got associated with mundane and otherworldly animals, as shamanic traditions have a core association with spirit animal allies. Today, many Witches refer to their beloved pets as familiars, but such familiars have to have a special magickal relationship with their Witch. Just any domesticated animal will not do.

A more primal teaching in the Craft involves the many parts of the soul. As the Taliesin myth can be viewed as a soul complex integrated with spirit allies, the simplest associations of the soul divide ourselves into a higher soul, lower soul, and middle soul, with various associations. The lower soul is considered to be the most primal, child-like, and animalistic. Drawing its traditions from the Norse soul part known as the fylgja, it comes into Traditional Witchcraft as the English word "fetch." Some see the lower soul as the fetch, and express it as a core animal that represents who you are on an animalistic level, rather than who you aspire to be. While it can be considered animalistic on its own, others see it linked to an animal spirit that is united with it, a fetch beast, that becomes an ally bonded to you through the lower soul.

Work with the lower cauldron and the initiatory cycle of the four animal allies brings you to a deeper understanding that could reveal your fetch beast. This is a major key to the mysteries of the Craft. One might say the white sow is the primary animal of Cerridwen, but this creature isn't even in the Taliesin story.

Prior to the next exercise, you can work with the individual animals, one by one in sequence, looking to communicate with them to learn their wisdom and teachings before you attempt shapeshifting. Start with the Gwion cycle, and then the Cerridwen cycle. Ideally take one Moon cycle for each animal, giving you four to eight months to do this animal work before going deeper.

You can also do meditative journey work to find your own personal and individual animal ally in each of the four directions/elements, a practice in many core shamanic traditions.

Once you feel you have a deeper understanding of animal spirit medicine and working with animal spirits and teachers and allies, attempt the shapeshifting journey below.

Exercise 10:
Second Initiatory Working – The Hunt

The second initiatory working of this book involves the formula that leads to the gestation of the second darkness, the chase of the animals. It starts with a ritual honoring the animals associated with each of the elements, using the elemental mandalas in conjunction with the four cardinal directions. Once the animal spirits have been evoked and been petitioned to bring their medicine teachings, we enter a visionary journey state. Unlike the guided journeys of Western occultism, with clearly suggested imagery in a sequence of events, the vehicle for journey will be the shamanic drumbeat.

Though the term "shamanism" is used widely and perhaps should only be applied to specific areas of Siberia and Asia, the core techniques are found across the world in what is now referred to as "core shamanism" detached from specific cultural expressions. I believe the same core techniques are found at the heart of Celtic and Witchcraft spiritualities, and the corrupted teachings of the Medieval Witch are the misunderstanding of an indigenous form of European shamanism. Central to these teachings is the use of a fast, rather than slow, repetitive beat, often through a drum or rattle, usually at 120-140 beats per minute. The effect of the fast repetition is atavistic; it awakens something primal in us, and despite seeming counterintuitive, the quickness actually lowers our brain waves, allowing us to enter a trance state and perceive non-ordinary reality. In this primal trance state, we seek to directly experience the magick of shapeshifting. We perceive our form becoming something else, ideally either one of the four animal spirits of Gwion Bach or four unique and individual animal spirits, each one a teacher and ally on our own path with something to share with us about the journey and possibly requiring something from us in their own journey, for the rule of the spirit world is reciprocity and exchange.

To facilitate the experience of shapeshifting, I'm going to suggest another piece of ritual technology that is not necessarily a part of established core shamanism, but perhaps will be at some point. This technique is known as ecstatic body posture.

Ecstatic body posture is a technique intuited by anthropologist Dr. Felicitas D. Goodman of the Cuyamungue Institute. Through study of and experimentation with postures depicted in ancient art, she believed the body postures of the art depicted keys for shamanic experiences encoded by these cultures. While holding the body posture and listening to the rapid shamanic beat, different and possibly deeper trance occurred, and each position held a similar type of journey.

While core shamanic journeyers would traditionally lie flat on their backs to listen to the beat, the posture builds up an internal psychic energy and directs it in a specific way. Many shamanic practitioners have difficulty experiencing shapeshifting in trance, but Goodman categorized one group as "metamorphosis" postures that essentially aid with shapeshifting in general, or with specific shapes and teachers of nature.

Two powerful ones for the work of the Goddess of the Cauldron and the hunt of Cerridwen are called the Corn Goddess position and the Gundestrup Cauldron position.

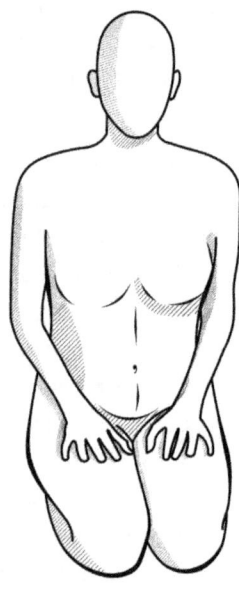

Figure 21: Corn Goddess Position

Figure 22: Horned Man of Gundestrup

The Corn Goddess posture is drawn from Aztec art. While it aids in animal shapeshifting, it can also bring one into contact with the shape of insects, plants, fungus, and other primal aspects of nature that are interconnected.

To perform, kneel with your buttocks resting upon your heels. Place your hands palm down upon your thighs, with the heels of your hands resting at the point where your thighs meet your torso and hips. Keep your fingers together and point the tips of your fingers down towards your knees, resting upon the thighs. Keep your arms close to your body, shoulders stiffened and slightly raised. Face ahead, closing your eyes.

The Gundestrup Cauldron figure is sometimes known as the Cernunnos position, or the Horned Man of Gundestrup in the Cuyamungue teachings, for it is the well-known horned "god" position found on the famous Gundestrup Celtic cauldron. This position is another shapeshifting one. Cernunnos is referred to as the Lord of Animals and upon the cauldron is surrounded by animals, but this is another position that might lend to shapeshifting not only in the animal realm, but beyond. It opens to the three worlds of the shaman and the patterns of life. The strange hand positions help one "steer" through these journeys.

To perform, sit on the ground with your spine and sit bones touching the floor. Do not cross your legs, but rather bring the heel of your right foot to the groin. The left leg is similarly bent but not touching the groin, a bit further out from the right leg. Arms are at the side of the body, held in a "V." In the art, the right hand is grasping a Celtic neck ring or torc, while the left hand holds a ram-headed serpent. You can use ritual props or simply pretend to hold these items. The head is slightly bent forward, gaze downward.

You may decide in advance if you wish to use either of these positions for your initiatory working in the hunt. In experimenting with them in the Cerridwen and Taliesin work, and in general with the techniques of shamanic Witchcraft, I've found them to be invaluable aids. If these postures are not right for your own body and health, you can do the journey in a simple comfortably seated position or lying down flat on your back.

Once the shape-shifting journey is complete, the animal allies will be honored, thanked, and released ritually from this sacred space and the second initiatory rite shall be ended.

For this ritual, you will need:

Shamanic Drum/Rattle Music (or an assistant to play the drum)
Offerings for the Spirits (wine, mead, other alcohol, grain, milk, butter, cheese, or sacred herbal smoke)
Offering Bowls (one for each direction if experiencing this ritual inside)
Brew of Awen (previously created)
Chalice
Blindfold/Eye Covering

Set up an altar before you to the work of the cauldrons. Have a chalice filled with your previously concocted Brew of Awen. Light your candles. Light your incense. You can prepare yourself by doing **Exercise 3: Three Cauldron Activation**.

If you come from a tradition that has its own method of creating sacred space, and it would be appropriate for this type of working, feel free to use or adapt as called. If not, a simple magick circle ritual from the modern Witchcraft traditions works very well.

Using a consecrated wand, your cauldron stirring stick, or simply the fingers of your outstretched hand, envisioned drawing a ring of light, starting in the north and moving clockwise. This is simply another way of "spinning out" the cauldron around you as done before in previous rituals.

Say:
By the Sacred Cauldron that dwells within the heart of Annwn, I cast this cauldron circle.
I call upon the Waves of Creation to flow from within me, about me, and all around me.
I call upon the powers of the cauldron to guard me from all harm. So mote it be.

Holding the cauldron aloft in the center and evoke the powers of the two and the three:

By the vaulted arch of the cosmos,
I call upon the Lord of Death and Darkness to my left
And the Lord of Light and Life to my right.
May you ever hold the cauldron's brew.
Hail and welcome.

By the fires warming the cauldron below,
I call upon the Three Ladies, the Three Who Are Nine Who Are Three Again
Maiden, Mother, Crone
Stars, Earth, Underworld
Future, Present, Past
May you ever initiate change.
Hail and welcome.

Now call upon the animal powers. We will circle again three times, first calling upon the animals of Gwion Bach. Then we shall call upon the animals of Cerridwen, and lastly we shall call upon our own unique animal alignments, even if they are unknown to us. You can use the calls written here or use your own poetic license to embellish and adapt as you see fit.

At each station, make an offering, a gift of some sort to the quarters. One simple and traditional gift is a bit of alcohol, including beer, wine, mead, or distilled alcohol. Foodstuff works as well. I use cornmeal or wheat flour. If you are indoors, you can have four small bowls for each of the directions to pour the offerings in and then leave them outdoors when finished with the entire ceremony. Sacred smoke from incense or loose herbs can also be an offering. The important part is honoring the animal teachers with blessings and gifts. The offering itself is a medium through which we transfer energy and strengthen our psychic connection to the tutor animals.

Start by facing east, and evoke the spirit of the east.

To the east, I call upon the spirit of the Hare, swift and cunning.
Please bring your magick to this circle, and teach me the ways of escape.
Hail and welcome.

Face south, and evoke the spirit of the south.

To the south, I call upon the spirit of the Wren, confident and bold.
Please bring your magick to this circle, and teach me the ways of bravery.
Hail and welcome.

Face west and evoke the spirit of the west.

To the west, I call upon the spirit of the Salmon, ancient and wise.
Please bring your magick to this circle, and teach me the ways of deep memory.
Hail and welcome.

Face north and evoke the spirit of the north.

To the north, I call upon the spirit of the Wheat, sustenance and rebirth.
Please bring your magick to this circle, and teach me the ways of return.
Hail and welcome.

Repeat the cycle again with the animals of Cerridwen.

Face east and evoke the spirit of the east.

To the east, I call upon the spirit of the Greyhound, swift and strong.
Please bring your magick to this circle, and teach me the ways of the hunt.
Hail and welcome.

Face south and evoke the spirit of the south.

To the south, I call upon the spirit of the Hawk, focused and sharp.
Please bring your magick to this circle, and teach me the ways of vision.
Hail and welcome.

Face west and evoke the spirit of the west.

To the west, I call upon the spirit of the Otter, playful and sensitive.
Please bring your magick to this circle, and teach me the ways of joy.
Hail and welcome.

Face north and evoke the spirit of the north.

To the north, I call upon the spirit of the Black Hen, dark and fertile.
Please bring your magick to this circle, and teach me the ways of the mystery.
Hail and welcome.

And repeat the cycle for a third and final time, for your own personal animals. If you know the animals, replace these open calls with more personal ones based upon your own animal relationships. If not, keep it open to see which animal, if any, shows up intuitively in the opening ritual and in the deeper vision.

Face east and evoke the spirit of the east.

To the east, I call upon the animal teacher that stands in the east for me.
Please bring your magick to this circle and to my life.
Hail and welcome.

Face south and evoke the spirit of the south.

To the south, I call upon the animal teacher that stands in the south for me.
Please bring your magick to this circle and to my life.
Hail and welcome.

Face west and evoke the spirit of the west.

To the west, I call upon the animal teacher that stands in the west for me.
Please bring your magick to this circle and to my life.
Hail and welcome.

Face north and evoke the spirit of the north.

To the north, I call upon the animal teacher that stands in the north for me.
Please bring your magick to this circle and to my life.
Hail and welcome.

• • •

Once your final evocations and offerings are made, you are almost ready to journey. You must first take the sacrament. Recall Gwion Bach in the hut with Morda. Recall your own work in creating the brew. Recall the herbs that went into it, and what they all mean, and the stirring of the cauldron. Then place your thumb into the chalice of the brew and say, "Uisce beatha." I was taught to pronounced it as "ISH kah BAH hah" meaning "the waters of life" (also found in everyday usage as either as a toast or a reference to whiskey). Bring it to your lips, taking a drop. Do this three times.

• • •

You can start your music or have your assistant start playing. Assume either one of the two positions suggested, or lie down flat on your back in the ritual space. Using a blindfold or other eye covering can aid the depth of the experience, blocking out extraneous and distracting light. Listen. Let the pulse race. Ride the waves of the beats like you are running, like you are being chased. Allow the vision to carry you through the teaching of the animal spirits, and allow yourself to shift your shape into different forms.

The important part is the ability to let go of the human form and the human identity as your sole identity. You are beyond any one form and must experience that directly to move onto the next lesson. You must embody the shape of four things, to bring the four elements together properly and prepare you for rebirth.

The music can play for ten, fifteen and even up to thirty minutes, until your experience is complete. When you feel it is finished, relax your posture. Turn off the music. Sit upright and reflect for a time before bringing the ritual to a close and releasing the space.

• • •

Thank and release the animal spirits that have guided you in this working. Start first with your own personal allies. Again, if the animals were not clear, keep your quarter releases open or adapt them as you see fit to align with the relationships you have to the spirits of each direction.

Face north and release the spirit of the north.

To the north, I thank and release the animal teacher that stands in the north for me.
Thank you for bringing your magick to this circle and to my life.
Hail and farewell.

Face west and release the spirit of the west.

To the west, I thank and release the animal teacher that stands in the west for me.
Thank you for bringing your magick to this circle and to my life.
Hail and farewell.

Face south and release the spirit of the south.

To the south, I thank and release the animal teacher that stands in the south for me.
Thank you for bringing your magick to this circle and to my life.
Hail and farewell.

Face east and release the spirit of the east.

To the east, I thank and release the animal teacher that stands in the east for me.
Thank you for bringing your magick to this circle and to my life.
Hail and farewell.

Then, thank and release the spirits of Cerridwen's totems.

Face north and release the spirit of the north.

To the north, I thank and release the spirit of the Black Hen, dark and fertile.
Thank you for bringing your magick to this circle, and for teaching me the ways of the mystery.
Hail and farewell.

Face west and release the spirit of the west.

To the west, I thank and release the spirit of the Otter, playful and sensitive.
Thank you for bringing your magick to this circle, and for teaching me the ways of joy.
Hail and farewell.

Face south and release the spirit of the south.

To the south, I thank and release the spirit of the Hawk, focused and sharp.
Thank you for bringing your magick to this circle, and for teaching me the ways of vision.
Hail and farewell.

Face east and release the spirit of the east.

To the east, I thank and release the spirit of the Greyhound, swift and strong.
Thank you for bringing your magick to this circle, and for teaching me the ways of the hunt.
Hail and farewell.

Lastly, thank and release the spirits of Gwion Bach's totems.

Face north and release the spirit of the north.

To the north, I thank and release the spirit of the Wheat, sustenance and rebirth.
Thank you for bringing your magick to this circle, and for teaching me the ways of return.
Hail and farewell.

Face west and release the spirit of the west.

To the west, I thank and release the spirit of the Salmon, ancient and wise.
Thank you for bringing your magick to this circle, and for teaching me the ways of deep memory.
Hail and farewell.

Face south and release the spirit of the south.

To the south, I thank and release the spirit of the Wren, confident and bold.
Thank you for bringing your magick to this circle, and for teaching me the ways of bravery.
Hail and farewell.

Face east and release the spirit of the east.

To the east, I thank and release the spirit of the Hare, swift and cunning.

Thank you for bringing your magick to this circle, and for teaching me the ways of escape. Hail and farewell.

Thank and release the divine powers of the cauldron.

*By the cosmic fires of the deep below,
I thank the Three Ladies, the Three Who Are Nine Who Are Three Again
Crone, Mother, Maiden
Underworld, Earth, Stars
Past, Present, Future
I thank you.
Stay if you will, go if you must.
Hail and farewell.*

*By the Vaulted Arch of the Cosmos
I thank the Lord of Light to my right hand
and I thank the Lord of Darkness to my left hand.
Lords of Life and Death
I thank you.
Stay if you will, go if you must.
Hail and farewell.*

Facing your starting direction, and moving in the opposite rotation of how you created your sacred space, hold out your wand, stirring rod, or your hand, and while expanding the circle infinitely, say:

*By the Sacred Cauldron that dwells within the Heart of Annwn, I release this circle.
May all things return to their place and time.
Yet may the changes in this cauldron reverberate throughout the cosmos.
So mote be it.*

Extinguish any candles and incense as needed. Ground and balance yourself as needed. Take this time to reflect, write in your journal, and rest. Give yourself a bit of time to process the experiences beyond your flesh and form before moving onto the rest of the chapter, but don't wait too long, as the work of the womb will help support the deep changes going on within you.

Advanced Shapeshifting

In the poetry of Taliesin, he takes far more shapes than the animals of Gwion Bach in the chase. When Taliesin was asked what he was by Elphin's father, Gwyddno Garanhir (or possibly Elphin himself due to a transcriber error in the manuscript), Taliesin answered:

First, I have been formed a comely person,
In the court of Caridwen I have done penance;
Though little I was seen, placidly received,
I was great on the floor of the place to where I was led;
I have been a prized defence, the sweet muse the cause,
And by law without speech I have been liberated
By a smiling black old hag, when irritated
Dreadful her claim when pursued:
I have fled with vigour, I have fled as a frog,
I have fled in the semblance of a crow, scarcely finding rest;
I have fled vehemently, I have fled as a chain of lightning,
I have fled as a roe into an entangled thicket;
I have fled as a wolf cub, I have fled as a wolf in a wilderness,
I have fled as a thrush of portending language;
I have fled as a fox, used to concurrent bounds of quirks;
I have fled as a martin, which did not avail;
I have fled as a squirrel, that vainly hides,
I have fled as a stag's antler, of ruddy course,
I have fled as iron in a glowing fire,
I have fled as a spear-head, of woe to such as has a wish for it;
I have fled as a fierce bull bitterly fighting,
I have fled as a bristly boar seen in a ravine,
I have fled as a white grain of pure wheat,
On the skirt of a hempen sheet entangled,
That seemed of the size of a mare's foal,
That is filling like a ship on the waters;
Into a dark leathern bag I was thrown,
And on a boundless sea I was sent adrift;
Which was to me an omen of being tenderly nursed,
And the Lord God then set me at liberty.
 — from "Taliesin" in *The Mabinogion*

He can shift his shape beyond those simple animal forms into the abstract. The poetry is not unlike the Irish shapeshifting poetry attributed to Amergin the bard, as in "The Song of Amergin." While the lower cauldrons unlock our animal, or primal, fetch nature, the mystery of the upper cauldrons unlocks the secrets of the universe and how we are all connected to them, and at one with them. Our consciousness can take any shape, any form, and thereby we know that aspect of the universe better. We are anything and everything. Shapeshifting helps break us out of the sense of separation and fear, showing us the unlimited potential of the consciousness that runs through us all. This is the true mystery we seek as aspiring "Taliesins" ourselves:

I have been in a multitude of shapes,
Before I assumed a consistent form.
I have been a sword, narrow, variegated,
I will believe when it is apparent.
I have been a tear in the air,
I have been the dullest of stars.
I have been a word among letters,
I have been a book in the origin.
I have been the light of lanterns,
A year and a half.
I have been a continuing bridge,
Over three score Abers.
I have been a course, I have been an eagle.
I have been a coracle in the seas:
I have been compliant in the banquet.
I have been a drop in a shower;
I have been a sword in the grasp of the hand
I have been a shield in battle.
I have been a string in a harp,
Disguised for nine years.
in water, in foam.
I have been sponge in the fire,
I have been wood in the covert.
I am not he who will not sing of
A combat though small,
The conflict in the battle of Godeu of sprigs.
   — from the "The Battle of the Trees," *The Book of Taliesin VII*, from *The Four Ancient Books of Wales*

As you continue on your magickal journeys, and particularly if you continue to experiment with the metamorphosic ecstatic body postures, you could find your shapeshifting going beyond the animal and into the vegetable and mineral kingdoms. All have been part and parcel of the alchemist's initiation – ingredients in medicine and in magick. But soon, your experience moves beyond the material and terrestrial, and the shapes you take become abstract forms. You enter Plato's realm of Ideas or Ideal Forms, and better know the deeper reality upon which our seeming consensual reality is based. And behind the world of forms that supports our own reality is a world of forces we cannot often give shape or name.

Nine Months in the Womb

After the grain is consumed by the black hen, the goddess realizes she has made a mistake. Or has she? Rather than destroying the seed, and thereby Gwion Bach, she has taken the seed with herself, and is pregnant with the essence of Gwion found in the seed, but the essence no longer has the form of Gwion. Growing within the rich fertile matrix of this dark mother goddess, a new form can take shape. She desired to be the tomb, the end of Gwion, but in truth she returned him to the womb. And in reality, even a tomb is a new womb, for a death in this life is a birth in the world of spirits. And a birth in this life is a death to the realm of spirits. Womb and tomb, like life and death, are two sides of the same coin.

Initiates are called "twice-borns" meaning they are born not once in this life, but twice, leaving behind an old life without necessarily losing their memory of that life. Sometimes "twice-born" refers to those with memories of past lives, but more often, it is a mark of the initiate. An old mystical teaching most popularly found in the work of the Sufi poet Rumi is to "Die before you die" or more broadly in Islamic teachings, "To truly live, you must die before you die." The teaching is not restricted to the mysticism of the Islamic Sufis, but is found in the mystery schools all across the world, including those that inspire the Wiccan and Neopagan revivals.

Sometimes this first death and rebirth is through the initiations of life, circumstances that can utterly change us, depending on how we handle them, and the shifts within that we embrace while experiencing them. For others, there is a formal death and rebirth ritual in the form of initiations in the mystery traditions. To go through a specific ritual makes you a brother or sister of all those who have gone through the same ritual before you, all being reborn by the same spiritual Mother, even if a specific goddess tradition is not involved. Some mystics, myself included, even look more broadly to all traditions stemming from a perennial wisdom, what we call the Tradition with a capital T, and this links all initiates as brothers and sisters regardless of the form the initiation took. For those with this universal perspective, mystics in one faith thereby have kinship with those of any other mystical tradition. While the expressions are different, the essential mysteries of death and rebirth are the same. We learn to recognize each other by the shape and feel of the consciousness, not necessarily the outer signs and pass codes.

The "twice-born" theology speaks of a second initiation or elevation, for the first step is induction into the order, as Gwion Bach was inducted into the mysteries of the hut. This multiple initiation is not unique to this Welsh mythos. It's found all over the world, but since many believe you can only be truly initiated once, subsequent rituals are known as elevations, attunements, or empowerments. This second stage or second birth is truly the initiation of rebirth regardless of initial induction into the mystery, with the death and rebirth bringing one outside of space and time. We find it in an old version of the tale of Dionysus.

Dionysus is known as "twice-born." He is the son of Zeus and Persephone in the older versions of the myth. Zeus' wife, Hera, jealous of any offspring from his dalliances, seeks to end little Dionysus and persuades the wild Titans to eat him. They lure him away with toys, and then cook him up in their cauldron. They tear apart his body limb-from-limb until all that is left is his heart. Zeus learns of what is happening and kills them all with his lightning. The heart is saved by a goddess – Rhea, Demeter, Persephone, or Athena in different versions – and Zeus puts the heart into his thigh to give the child a second birth. Zeus goes on to make humanity out of the remains of these elder gods. Each new human, therefore, has a bit of Dionysus and the more primordial Titans inside, showing the dual nature of humanity. Dionysus, reborn, leads the way for humans, who are a mix of the nature of the old and new gods, also to be reborn again through the mysteries of rebirth.

The key to this stage of rebirth and awakening is the incubation that happens within the womb. A major mistake that occurs in terrestrial initiations is the rushing forward from the rebirth into a new life, with no time to truly be "properly prepared" as initiates in the British Traditional Wicca sects would say. "Properly prepared" does not mean having all the right jewelry, clothes, or even lessons, but having time to grow and the inner and outer conditions to support that growth. The rank neophyte, a beginner on the path or tradition, literally means "newly planted," and anything newly planted needs time to grow its roots. It needs water and minerals. The seed of Gwion Bach needs time in the womb of the goddess to slumber and dream, to grow wiser, clearer, and more powerful before setting forth into the world. Even after birth, like any infant, he is still not ready. The time of the womb dissolves the old self, like salt, leaving the old body behind for some new form to manifest.

Gestation of a human child is traditionally seen as a nine-month cycle, or three sets of three Moon cycles. Threes are associated with triple forms of the Goddess, be it the current images of maiden, mother, and crone, or the triple fates, or even the goddess of the sky, land, and underworld. Our growth occurs on all these levels simultaneously.

In esoteric astrology, it can be helpful to look back upon the Sun sign of your conception, assuming you were carried to a full nine-month term, as it is to know your classical birth sign. Nine signs preceding your own birth sign indicates the sign that has the seed of your own life and energy within it. In esoteric medicine involving homeopathic use of cell salts, there is a belief in twelve universal "salts of salvation" necessary for our clear functioning. Each sign rules a particular cell salt, and the salts of the three signs ruling the months you were not in the womb might be deficient in your own makeup, and the theory states you might require supplementation.

The pattern of nine signs, beyond their esoteric healing correspondences, can be quite helpful to meditate upon. Doing dream work and meditations upon the signs, their alchemical associations, and the cell salts associated with them (including any other correspondences – herbs, flower essences, stones, colors, alchemical operations, or talismanic images) can help us be "properly prepared." Between the last meditation vision of the chase and the next of rebirth, you should take your time, incubate, and dream your new life of wisdom and blessings.

Sign	Alchemical Operation	Element	Quality	Cell Salt
Aries	Calcination	Fire	Cardinal	Potassium Phosphate
Taurus	Congelation/Conjunction	Earth	Fixed	Sodium Sulfate
Gemini	Fixation	Air	Mutable	Potassium Chloride
Cancer	Dissolution	Water	Cardinal	Calcium Fluoride
Leo	Digestion	Fire	Fixed	Magnesium
Virgo	Distillation	Earth	Mutable	Potassium Sulfate
Libra	Sublimation	Air	Cardinal	Sodium Phosphate
Scorpio	Separation	Water	Fixed	Calcium Sulfate
Capricorn	Fermentation	Earth	Cardinal	Calcium Phosphate
Aquarius	Multiplication	Air	Fixed	Sodium Chloride
Pisces	Projection/Coagulation	Water	Mutable	Iron Phosphate

Cell Salt	Physical Issues
Potassium Phosphate	Restlessness, insomnia, bad breath
Sodium Sulfate	Water retention in hands and feet, flatulence with foul smell
Potassium Chloride	Coughing, white mucus, high fever
Calcium Fluoride	Chapped skin, tooth enamel problems
Magnesium Phosphate	Muscle spasm, muscle cramps, hiccoughs
Potassium Sulfate	Yellow discharge, variable and changing symptoms
Sodium Phosphate	Oily skin and hair, brittle hair, acne, skin issues
Calcium Sulfate	Open infections and sores, boils, yellow discharge
Silica	Sensitive to cold and light, sweaty hands/feet
Calcium Phosphate	Nosebleeds, headaches, late teeth in children
Sodium Chloride	Sensitive to Sun, respiratory congestion, cold sores
Iron Phosphate	Low fever, sore throats, cold, flu, nosebleeds

Cell Salt	Mental-Emotional Issues
Potassium Phosphate	Nervousness, tension, moodiness, anger, self-pity
Sodium Sulfate	Inclination to head injuries, depression with wet weather
Potassium Chloride	Irritable, apathetic, longing for home, wistful, hypochondria
Calcium Fluoride	Poor self-image, indecisive
Magnesium Phosphate	Overly sensitive, rash
Potassium Sulfate	Nightmares, bothered by noise, anger, irritability
Sodium Phosphate	Depression, drowsiness, poor self-esteem
Calcium Sulfate	Fatigue, inertia, imaginary or self-created problems
Silica	Shyness, hypersensitivity to others/environment
Calcium Phosphate	Weak mind, lack of motivation
Sodium Chloride	Isolation and separation, control, grief
Iron Phosphate	Easily overheated/over stimulated, followed by exhaustion

Cell Salt	Common Foods
Potassium Phosphate	Beets, celery, lettuce, cauliflower, spinach, onion, mustard greens, watercress, radishes, carrots, cucumber, dates, apples, walnuts, lemons
Sodium Sulfate	Spinach, beets, Swiss chard, cucumbers, cauliflower, onions, cabbage, pumpkin, radishes
Potassium Chloride	Green beans, asparagus, beets, carrots, cauliflower, sweet corn, celery, apricots, peaches, plums, pineapple
Calcium Fluoride	Milk, cheese, yogurt, kale, watercress, savoy and red cabbage, pumpkin, onions, oranges, lemons, egg yolks, raisins, rye bread
Magnesium Phosphate	Almonds, rye, lettuce, apples, plums, figs, lemons, coconut, cucumbers, blueberries, walnuts, onions, red wine
Potassium Sulfate	Chicory, endive, whole wheat, oats, rye, cheese, almonds, lean beef
Sodium Phosphate	Carrots, asparagus, beets, yellow corn, brown rice, figs, apples, strawberries, peaches, blueberries, almonds, raisins
Calcium Sulfate	Onions, asparagus, kale, garlic, watercress, mustard greens, cauliflower, leeks, radishes, figs, black cherries, prunes, gooseberries, coconut
Silica	Figs, strawberries, prunes, Scotch oats, parsnips, brown rice, cherries, marjoram, mallows, agrimony, sage
Calcium Phosphate	Cabbage, asparagus, spinach, lentils, brown beans, celery, almonds, cucumbers, strawberries, figs, blueberries, plums, barley, egg yolk, lean meat, whole wheat
Sodium Chloride	Cabbage, spinach, asparagus, celery, radishes, carrots, corn, lentils, strawberries, apples, figs, seafood
Iron Phosphate	Lettuce, strawberries, radishes, cucumbers, almonds, walnuts, raisins, spinach, lima beans, beef liver, lean beef

Chart 11: Cell Salts and the Zodiac

As each of the zodiac signs are associated with a more detailed alchemical operation, the zodiac signs have their own elemental and quality correspondences along with one of the twelve cell salts. A focus upon the cell salts also helps us dive into the mineral consciousness necessary to go deeper into the wisdom of the Earth. We have explored the plants in the cauldron, and the animals of the chase. Now we look to the body and bones of the Earth for their wisdom.

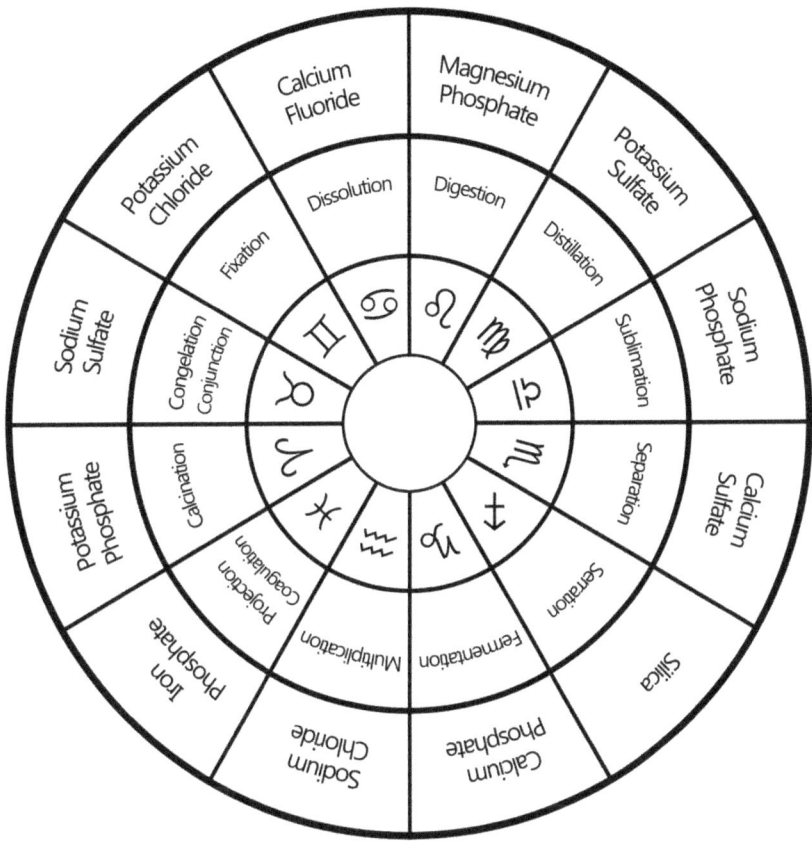

Figure 23: Mandala of Signs, Operations and Cell Salts

An expanded understanding of the twelvefold operations of alchemy can help us in understanding our ninefold birth cycle.

Calcination – Calcination is the first of the seven-step operations found in some alchemical traditions, and as previously discussed, is the process of burning and heating something down to white ash or "bone." Essentially, you are reducing it down to its barest minerals, devoid of other chemicals. Though the "first" operation in both sequences, it is often done after other chemicals, such as essential oils in plants, have been extracted from their base material in a laboratory working. Quick burning aligns the operation with Aries.

Congelation/Conjunction – While conjunction is the fourth of seven steps, here it is equated with congelation and is the second step, corresponding with Taurus. To congeal something chemically is to slow it down and allow it to thicken or gel. The essential trait is what makes the substance, or the alchemist, more viscous. Substances that are more viscous can flow, but are less at the whim of whatever forces are around them. They move slowly and deliberately. Think of the difference between water and honey. And many viscous fluids, like honey, are considered divine! Viscosity is a very Taurean trait.

Fixation – Fixation is the process of taking something volatile, or unstable, and shifting its form, usually making it a solid or liquid, but stabilizing it. Volatile substances tend to either easily vaporize and disappear, or explode. There is no lasting quality to them. Essential oils, in their pure state, are considered volatile, as the oil will easily evaporate and diffuse into an environment, but that quality makes them effective medicine in aromatherapy. Volatile people are often angry, erratic, or irrational. Today, due to modern psychology, many assume fixation means an unhealthy attachment and as such should be avoided, but this is a stabilization of something that was previously reactive to outside forces. Gemini is a sign of volatility, being mutable or changing air, but it uses these skills to ultimately find the more stable, fixed truth.

Dissolution – The second of the seven steps previously outlined, dissolution is the immersing of solids into a liquid solvent, often water, but sometimes acid. That which is soluble will dissolve and merge with the liquid, and that which is not will sink. This is seen in the turning of the sea, the first saltwater solution, and aligns with the sign of the sea mother Cancer.

Digestion – Digestion is the process that occurs in our stomach, one of the parts of the body associated with Leo via the solar plexus. Essentially it is the application of a low and continuous heat to break down a substance, usually one that is in a solution. We eat food, and it mixes with stomach acid and is subjected to a higher body heat. Between the blood rushing to our abdomen and the chemical reactions, food that appears insoluble breaks down. Continuous "heat" in our lives during this process helps unnecessary structures break down within us and be integrated.

Distillation – Distillation is the sixth step of the sevenfold alchemical system, and it refers to the purification of a liquid through its rise and its fall. Alcohols are distilled into refined spirits, with the most noted example of wine becoming brandy. The distillation process increases the potency and concentration. In the twelvefold system, it is associated with Virgo, as Virgo is a sign of regenerated purity, and distillation is a purification process. The volatile is separated from the rest of the liquid, much as the intestines, the anatomical correspondence of Virgo, separate nutrients from waste product.

Sublimation – Sublimation is the process of converting a solid substance into a gas and letting it return back as a liquid or solid. We most commonly see sublimation in nature when snow, due to pressure and temperature, converts directly to a foggy mist instead of melting into a liquid. Psychologically, sublimation is the conversion of one type of behavior, usually not acceptable to society, into another type of behavior, usually of greater benefit to society. Rather than being denied or extinguished, the energy of the impulse is converted into something else. Modern psychology focuses on sexual impulses, but all sorts of behaviors can be linked to sublimation. Libra, its corresponding Zodiac sign, is a sign of justice, balancing that which does not serve society with that which does. In the most metaphysical view, justice is really adjustment, a rebalancing of forces to their proper place.

Separation – Separation is the third of the sevenfold alchemical processes, a filtering of solid matter out of a liquid, thus separating the two. It is associated with Mars for action, but also the element of air for discernment, and the zodiac sign Scorpio. In traditional astrology, Mars also ruled Scorpio. Scorpio is the sign of transformation, leaving behind the old, that which has been separated, and the new rising up to another reality, symbolized by the scorpion and snake transforming into the eagle or phoenix. All of these diverse animals are totems for the sign of Scorpio.

Ceration – Technically, ceration is the process of adding liquid to a hard, dry substance while heating it, softening the material. It is sometimes mistaken for incineration, or what is alchemically referred to as calcination. It is sometimes also confused with serration, using the teeth of a saw to cut a substance into smaller pieces. Sagittarius is a mutable heat, flexible in its work, gentler than the fires of Aries or Leo, making it a perfect sign for this softening process.

Fermentation – Fermentation is the fifth of the seven traditional stages described previously. This process is often seen as "animation" by a biological agent, for the yeast of fermenting alcohol, or the microbes of other processes, seemingly brings the substance to life for a time, with biological consumptions, waste, and cell division occurring until a new substance is created. Cardinal Earth, Capricorn, is the sign of creating something new in the physical world, as in the rising of mountains from the depths, releasing new matter upon the Earth.

Multiplication – In mathematics, multiplication is an operation, but in alchemy, multiplication refers to increasing the power and potency of a substance. It is a mysterious process, usually described as exposing the final product, the Philosopher's Stone, to the repeated processes that originally created it, increasing its potency or even its volume and weight. Multiplication was strongly associated with the creation of gold and silver from baser metals, but the mystical lore hints that the true multiplication occurs internally in the alchemist's biological laboratory. This multitude, or potential of sharing for all, is aligned with the socially conscious Aquarius.

Projection/Coagulation – While coagulation is the seventh of the seven classical processes, it is also the twelfth step, associated with Pisces, and sometimes referred to as projection. Projection refers to the power of the Philosopher's Stone or Philosopher's Powder, used to project, or transmute, base metal into noble metals like silver and gold. A small portion of the Philosopher's Stone is put into molten metal, and the molten metal transmutes as it cools into the "higher" metals. Though if multiplication occurs internally, many speculate the true power of projection occurs internally as well, simultaneously filling our matter with a golden light.

Other minor processes not listed in the major twelve, yet necessary parts of the major processes, include putrefaction – or letting something rot – and circulation – putting a gently heated liquid through a distillation process, but rather than separating the distilled essence, allowing it to circulate from vapor to liquid and back to vapor repeatedly. The substance "dies and resurrects" many times and grows wise.

Exercise 11:
Growing Wise in the Womb

Take time out to properly prepare yourself, using the nine-month pattern of the tropical zodiac signs and the missing three signs of your own birth. An illuminated bard must be able to speak on every part of the cycle of mysteries, so this second rebirth is an opportunity to experience, supplement, and deepen the forces you may have missed in your "first" birth. In a ritual context, we will be preparing for rebirth over the course of nine days rather than nine months.

In the theory of cell salt healing, you use up the mineral corresponding to your Sun Sign the most, but also the two following signs. These three together represent the missing energies you need to align with in order to properly function. Look up the cell salts of your Sun sign and the following two signs.

Birth Sign	Traditional Conception Signs	"Missing" Signs
Aries	Cancer	Aries, Taurus, Gemini
Taurus	Leo	Taurus, Gemini, Cancer
Gemini	Virgo	Gemini, Cancer, Leo
Cancer	Libra	Cancer, Leo, Virgo
Leo	Scorpio	Leo, Virgo, Lbra
Virgo	Sagittarius	Virgo, Libra, Scorpio
Libra	Capricorn	Libra, Scorpio, Sagittarius
Scorpio	Aquarius	Scorpio, Sagittarius, Capricorn
Sagittarius	Pisces	Sagittarius, Capricorn, Aquarius
Capricorn	Aries	Capricorn, Aquarius, Pisces
Aquarius	Taurus	Aquarius, Pisces, Aries
Pisces	Gemini	Pisces, Aries, Taurus

Chart 12: Zodiac Conceptions

These three salts are your "cell salt bridge." The physical and emotional issues associated with the corresponding cell salts tend to manifest in your life. While we might want to count our "missing signs" starting with the one after our Sun sign, the established tradition of cell salts starts with the birth sign. For those born in the middle of a zodiac sign, some healing practitioners will "prescribe" a cell salt bridge of four salts, and for those of a premature birth, up to six for those nearing a two-month premature period. For those with a greater education in astrology, these signs are the ones the Sun in your "progressed chart" would most likely go through during a typical lifetime.

Your conception sign would start with the same quality (cardinal, fixed, mutable) as your birth sign, which is easily available through simple calendars, and if you were born on a day of transition, through researching online astrological data to determine your birth Sun sign. Most magickal practitioners are already aware of their Sun sign. While your conception sign shares the same quality, it will be different by element.

To better prepare yourself in this nine-day time period, start by working with the cell salts of the cell salt bridge. Many health food stores have homeopathic prepared cell salt kits. Avoid those that have all twelve in one dose, but look for the ones that separate out each individual mineral and only take the ones that correspond to your bridge. I suggest starting in the morning with the Sun sign salt. Then mid-day with the second, and in the evening the third. The homeopathic versions of the salts are not truly mineral supplements, but are therapeutic in the sense they are said to help us absorb the minerals more easily from our food and make use of them in our body. It can be helpful to supplement our diet at this time with the foods that contain our deficient cell salts.

Over the course of the nine days, contemplate the signs of conception through birth, one per day. Contemplate the associated alchemical operation and the physical and emotional qualities of the appropriate cell salt. For example, if your birth Sun sign is Taurus, you'd be taking the cell salts for Taurus, Gemini, and Cancer, which are Sodium Sulfate, Potassium Chloride, and Calcium Fluoride. Then, your daily ritualized contemplation would be as given on **Chart 13**.

Write out your own pattern of nine days and use it as a focus for reflection and contemplation while taking your cell salts. On the tenth day, perform **Exercise 12**.

Those who wish deeper knowledge beyond the basics of the cell salt bridge might also look to the individual horoscope. Look to the signs of the Moon, Saturn, and the South Node of the Moon. Their corresponding cell salts are quite helpful in the spiritual evolution of the initiate, as well as dealing with physical healing issues. They are particularly helpful when dealing with karmic challenges in this lifetime.

Day	Sign	Operation	Cell Salt
1	Leo	Digestion	Magnesium Phosphate
2	Virgo	Distillation	Potassium Sulfate
3	Libra	Sublimation	Sodium Phosphate
4	Scorpio	Separation	Calcium Sulfate
5	Sagittarius	Ceration	Silica
6	Capricorn	Fermentation	Calcium Phosphate
7	Aquarius	Multiplication	Sodium Chloride
8	Pisces	Projection	Iron Phosphate
9	Aries	Calcination	Potassium Phosphate

Chart 13: Example of Nine-Day Birth Pattern

Reborn as the Child of Light

From the second darkness of the womb, transformed, the child must enter back into the light of the world with his rebirth through the Goddess herself. The process of growing wise in the womb will hopefully heal and transfigure issues that were from the previous life, allowing you as an initiate to enter a new state of awareness through this rebirth.

Modern New Age traditions cite a technique of breathwork known as Rebirthing. It was invented by Leonard Orr who experienced a spontaneous "rebirth" while in a bath, and he felt it healed childhood trauma, particularly around the trauma of birth, healed repressed memories of abuse, relieved chronic pain, and healed disease. It's been panned as a medical or even psychological technique by scientists, psychologists, and anti-cult experts, though some still find value in the healing of the original "birth trauma." Rebirthing therapy evolved out of this work to include an almost ritualized form of restraint with psychological patients suffering from reactive detachment disorder, whereby the patient is wrapped in sheets and surrounded by pillows and forced to be reborn through the restraints. This method has been outlawed due to the death of a patient via asphyxiation.

These techniques are very different than the gentle and loving rituals of rebirthing ceremonies held by doulas who seek to help heal trauma between mother and child from medically difficult births, or the Goddess rebirthing ceremonies found in some predominantly feminist spiritualities that help heal the emotional difficulties between a child and its estranged or distant mother, looking to re-envision the Goddess as primary mother.

Initiatory rebirth in the context of the cauldron is different still, usually involving visionary work, though it does involve directed breath work and an evocation of the Goddess. It can be done alone, with no pressure placed upon the body directly, and is perfectly safe for anyone of reasonable, average health.

Exercise 12:
Rebirth Ritual

Perform this ritual upon the tenth day of your reflection on the cycle of the womb. For this rite, you will need:

Dark Cloth or Cloak (big enough to cover your face and body)
Cauldron Filled with Water

Essential Oils (such as rose, spruce, vanilla, vetiver, ylang-ylang)

Set your altar. Light your candles. No incense is needed. Any music you desire will work, though soft and meditative is best. Fill your cauldron with water and add a few drops of the oils to the surface of the water. Create a simple sacred space to hold yourself and your intention. Evoke Cerridwen or simply the Dark Goddess, to rebirth you into the world anew.

When ready, lie down flat on the floor and place the cloak over you. Reflect upon the potion from the hut. Reflect upon the hunt of the animal transformations. Reflect upon your nine days and the process of gestation. Breathe deeply and fully but relax. Your inhale is active, and your exhale is passive. Both are more or less equal. Allow the breath to deepen, and imagine it reaching into every area of your body, releasing all stress, tension, and all things held back within you.

If you are ready to go deeper, curl yourself into a fetal position, and then cover your face and body with the cloth. Feel yourself tight in the womb. How does it feel? Comforting? Difficult? Does it bring up issues of our own terrestrial mother? Does it bring up issues you have with the Goddess herself? What rises in this womb time for you? Stay in this space as long as it feels right.

When you are ready to be reborn, stretch out from the fetal position and uncover yourself, removing the cloth as if taking off the caul that so often wraps the face of the seer as a second veil. Take off your "caul" and know that you will be able to see in all worlds. Gaze at the candlelight. Rise up and place yourself over the cauldron. Stir it, and release the sweet aromas. Breathe them in deep like the first breath of a new life that shall inspire you.

When done, give thanks. Release your sacred space. Extinguish the candles. Pour the water and oils out into the land. Ground and reflect. With this rite, you will be ready to move onto the third darkness of the sea.

Chapter Six: The Third Darkness of the Sea

By the flowing of the river
In the darkness of the bag
Taken to the shores far from the hag.
Rescued by a fool right upon the weir
Light from darkness dispelling all my fear
Hold me up as the radiant brow
and I fulfill an unspoken vow
To him I shall be loyal and true
Till my time unfolds once again
And I'll know exactly what to do.

The journey of the sea is the third and final initiatory darkness to prepare the new child for his special role in the world. The third darkness can be analogous to the third elevation or initiation in many traditional systems. While the first inducts you into the order, and the second is the personal confrontation to re-order your psyche, the third is what moves your perspective from the more personal to the greater transpersonal vision of the world. It is in the third degree in Wicca where one is prepared to teach and lead a coven as a High Priestess or High Priest. This role is one of service to the spirits as a priest or priestess, and of service to the greater good of the community, including the commonwealth of the land, plants, animals, minerals, and the entire world, not just people. The travels upon the wave into the greater world place our child of light into the proper context to come out into the world.

When Cerridwen gave birth after nine months, she had a change of heart. Until this point, we assume her plan was to still take revenge on the new incarnation of Gwion Bach, whoever he might be. But like a new incarnation, when he is born, he has a new lease on life. The consequences of his actions are not wiped away, but do not have an immediate and lethal effect for him either. They unfold through the fields of time, just like the teaching of the East on karma would predict. And his last challenge, while not a true darkness, allows him to repay Gwyddno Garanhir and aid Elphin before going out into the world on his mission as the chief bard of Britain.

"And, as the story says, she bore him nine months, and when she was delivered of him, she could not find it in her heart to kill him, by reason of his beauty. So she wrapped him in a leathern bag, and cast him into the sea to the mercy of God, on the twenty-ninth day of April."

— "Taliesin" from *The Mabinogion*

In his rebirth, he gains a new gift: beauty. Gwion Bach was never described as a beauty. Perhaps this is the beauty we see in all newborn babes, but I think it must be something more, something magickal, to move Cerridwen so. I think of the Platonic idea of Beauty, along with the virtues of Truth and Goodness.

Surrender to the Journey

His beauty is not so great that she decides she must keep him, though. She compromises with herself and his fate. She decides to wrap him in a leather bag, not unlike a second, artificial womb. We assume the construction of this bag makes it waterproof and seaworthy, for he does not die in the tale. Rather than a bag, it can be described as a coracle, a small wicker basket-like boat found in Wales and Ireland. In this new vessel, this escape pod of sorts, she cast him into the sea. It's not clear if she casts him from her original isle, and he eventually follows the trail of the poison from the cracked cauldron, leading out to the weir where the horses drank. Technically, the horses drank from a stream, but we assume there is proximity to where the horses were to where Elphin later fishes the babe from the waters. Perhaps she came to the shores of the greater land, and not her island, and cast him out to the depths, to eventually be caught in the weir on May Eve, also known to us as the eve of Beltane.

Whenever I relate the story of Taliesin, someone in the group always thinks that this tale shows that the Christians stole Pagan ideas and put them into the Bible in the very similar tale of Moses. But I have to point out that the tale of Moses was originally Jewish, and our written accounts of it pre-date all our written accounts of Taliesin's own journey on the sea. But there is a deep mythic resonance of the child magician floating upon the waters:

"Now a man of the tribe of Levi married a Levite woman, and she became pregnant and gave birth to a son. When she saw that he was a fine child, she hid him for three months. But when she could hide him no longer, she got a papyrus basket for him and coated it with tar and pitch. Then she placed the child in it and put it among the reeds along the bank of the Nile. His sister stood at a distance to see what would happen to him.

Then Pharaoh's daughter went down to the Nile to bathe, and her attendants were walking along the riverbank. She saw the basket among the reeds and sent her female slave to get it. She opened it and saw the baby. He was crying, and she felt sorry for him. "This is one of the Hebrew babies," she said.

Then his sister asked Pharaoh's daughter, "Shall I go and get one of the Hebrew women to nurse the baby for you?"

"Yes, go," she answered. So the girl went and got the baby's mother. Pharaoh's daughter said to her, "Take this baby and nurse him for me, and I will pay you." So the woman took the baby and nursed him. When the child grew older, she took him to Pharaoh's daughter and he became her son. She named him Moses, saying, "I drew him out of the water."

— Exodus 2, Verses 1-8 (NIV)

While not necessarily born of a goddess, Moses is adopted by Egyptian royalty, a strange fate for a Hebrew child. Biblical tradition tells us that at this time, newborn Hebrew children were being killed to reduce the population of Hebrew slaves to prevent the possibility of rebellion against the Egyptians. Like Taliesin, he was under threat of potential death, and his watery journey was what really saved him.

Whatever his Hebrew birth name, he was renamed by his rescuer, the daughter of the Pharaoh, who "drew him out from the water" and named him after a variation of this phrase – Moses. It's not unlike the renaming of the babe Taliesin based upon what his founder first says about him as the light strikes his brow.

Before Moses fled for killing a slave master who was beating a Hebrew worker, esoteric tradition tells us that he was educated in the royal courts and learned the magick of the ancient Egyptian priests, possibly better than they did. It was this magickal education, even from his people's oppressors, that served him, as did his connection to the Hebrew god Yahweh, when he came back to free the Hebrew slaves and lead them to a new land. Perhaps it was his skill as a magician as much as his prophecy that created the conditions of the plagues of Egypt. Taliesin's own punishments on local authorities were not quite so deadly, but both served similar roles, using their magick against abusive authority figures. Moses is attributed as the author of the Torah, and is considered the lawgiver to the Hebrew people as one of the chief prophets in the religion, usually with esoteric skill. He communed with the burning bush and brought down the tablets of the law. Archetypally, we can align him with figures such as Thoth as the giver of letters, and with Orpheus, the teacher through song and myth. These are not so different attributes than the ones we give Taliesin if we look at the prophet's function more as a seer, poet, bard, and magician than absolute lawgiver. But it is important to note that in traditional Celtic cultures, the Druids and their various subdivisions such as the bard and ovates were the lawgivers and arbiters of legal disputes. So again it is a similar resonance if we think of Taliesin as having links to the Celtic Druidic past.

Both children end up in places, in situations, they might never have dreamed of, with resources and responsibilities far beyond the usual. Being an initiate in the mysteries requires a delicate play of taking action like a magician, developing the will, or choosing consciously to not take action, to surrender, let go, and see where the divine current is taking him. The true adept has to balance doing and not doing, speaking and listening, acting and observing. Sometimes the wisest action is no action at all, realizing that the time is not right for fighting against what is. But we can also be in danger of surrendering too much, of never taking action, of never speaking our truth, and ultimately, never getting out of the bag or basket to fulfill our destiny.

Seers, visionaries, magicians, shamans, and Witches all need time to rest and incubate. We need time to dream and see what visions visit us in the dream. But to do so, we need to take that time and space to simply be open without agenda or control. As we proceed into life, we have to surrender to the flow, bringing us not only to where we would decide to go consciously, but guiding us to where we need to be to fulfill our work in the world.

Initiatory Names

A tradition found in many magickal cultures is taking a new name. Going back to our most tribal rituals of coming of age, where a child name might be discarded in effort to take an adult name. The change in the name shows the change in relationship between the individual and the community. The community members' willingness to call the new adult by a new name demonstrates the community has accepted this person in a new role, with new blessings and responsibilities as childhood is left behind.

In magickal traditions, such names can serve a similar purpose, but one less frequently talked about purpose is secrecy. In times past when secrecy was more paramount (though in many traditions it still is), the use of magickal names meant you could never reveal someone publicly if you were caught practicing Witchcraft, because you didn't know the legal names of those you were practicing with. The name created an additional layer of safety. On an esoteric level, it also represented leaving the mundane life and persona behind, to assume the magickal persona in the group and ritual.

Today the names used reflect either inherent qualities the person was said to exhibit in the tradition or qualities the initiate aspired to embody. In more shamanic-oriented traditions, the first path is chosen, and "medicine" names are given, using animal, plant, and other nature-based terms that embody the wisdom and medicine the individual brings to the group.

In more occult and Pagan traditions, the name is one from mythology and folklore, and embodies the divine qualities the initiate seeks to embody. Sometimes the name has something to do with a deity that has a strong influence in the initiate's life and practice. That is why you might find new initiates taking names such as Apollo, Thor, or Cerridwen, though many Pagans and Witches will still take on animal, plant, and other nature-based names too. Some consider using deity names as magickal names offensive, while others find it quite honoring, so it all depends on the group and tradition. I prefer non-deity names myself, but I am not offended by what anyone chooses to call themselves. I simply think deity names can come both with a lot of expectation and a lot of baggage that you might never resolve, for it is part of the eternal story of that name.

In many ceremonial lodges, the magickal name is one of an abbreviated "motto" that sums up a magickal philosophy or perspective. They were also aspirational, and could be in Latin or another foreign language, or abbreviated in some way. Some of the more famous examples include Dion Fortune, an abbreviation of Deo, non fortuna meaning "God, not chance," and Aleister Crowley's Golden Dawn name Perdurabo, meaning "I will endure" or "I will endure to the end."

Egyptian magick, among others, teaches the power and importance of names. Many magickal traditions believe that to have the true name of something is to have power over it. With the name, you can forge a magickal link. That is why some, for protection, would use public and private Craft names, never revealing their private, true name, to the untrusted and uninitiated. The Egyptians believed so thoroughly in the power of names they taught that one aspect of the soul, the ren, was the true name, given at birth. A kind of immortality could be conferred as long as the name was still spoken. Occultists today think of the ren as not simply what is given at birth on a terrestrial level, but your "true name" or "soul name" which is the divine sound that embodies the essence of who and what you truly are. This is the secret name. In one tale, the goddess Isis tricks the creator god Ra out of his secret true name, and with it, she has access to the magick of creation.

In the Taliesin myth, the unnamed babe in the coracle gets renamed, much like Moses. He is discovered in the water by Elphin, and is named on the observation of his radiant brow. In this magick, it is the innocent fool who names him.

"And the next day when Elphin went to look, there was nothing in the weir. But as he turned back he perceived the leathern bag upon a pole of the weir. Then said one of the weir-ward unto Elphin, "Thou wast never unlucky until to-night, and now thou hast destroyed the virtues of the weir, which always yielded the value of an hundred pounds every May eve, and to-night there is nothing but this leathern skin within it." "How now," said Elphin, "there may be therein the value of an hundred pounds." Well, they took up the leathern bag, and he who opened it saw the forehead of the boy, and said to Elphin, "Behold a radiant brow!" "Taliesin be he called," said Elphin. And he lifted the boy in his arms, and lamenting his mischance, he placed him sorrowfully behind him. And he made his horse amble gently, that before had been trotting, and he carried him as softly as if he had been sitting in the easiest chair in the world."

— from "Taliesin" in *The Mabinogion*

One of the last parts of taking a magickal name is also not often discussed, but clearly demonstrated in the tale of both Taliesin and Moses, and that is the question of "who names you?" For most magicians today, we are self-named. The act of self-naming, of self-declaring, is one of empowerment. We are typically coming from a mainstream religion in an over-culture we do not resonate with. The quest to find our authentic self is one of self-determination. This is a very magickal idea, and a very modern one. Not all traditions and cultures subscribe to it.

Some believe that a teacher, mentor, or community can see you more clearly, or see what you are aspiring to, and give you the gift of a new name. Do you have such a relationship? Before going onto **Exercise 14: Third Initiatory Working – The Sea**, give some thought to your magickal name, if you currently have one. Does it still suit you? Are you seeking another? Are you fine using your birth name? And be open to the idea that the appropriate name, regardless of what you might consciously choose, could manifest in the vision of the third initiatory working.

Living Awen

The true purpose of the initiation of Cerridwen is to live in awen. What does this mean? Living in awen is to be in a perpetual state of gnosis, of inspiration. Awen is the mysterious flow of the three rays within from the heavens and all of creation. But to be inspired does not simply mean to be creative and produce art, music, writing, dance, or other mediums of self-expression, though those who are inspired do seem to have an inexhaustible flow of creativity. The problem, in fact, can be moderating that inspiration to other areas of life and service. To be inspired from the perspective of English is to be "in spirit." Inspiration is living in the constant flow of spiritual contact which supports and guides all that you do. Awen is an awareness that does not simply transcend the world, but helps create it, through your own art in the world.

Other traditions have similar ideas, with perhaps different connotations. It is not unlike the mystical experience of being touched by the Holy Spirit and the gifts of the Holy Spirit as described in many forms of Christianity. It can be the first stages of "Knowledge and Conversation with your Holy Guardian Angel" as practiced in the ceremonial traditions of magick. It is like the Lesser Stone of the alchemists, preceding the true enlightenment of the Philosopher's Stone.

To live with this connection radically reorients your worldview and ideas of life, work, and purpose. It is not unlike popular notions of The Force in the *Star Wars* series, as silly as it might sound. George Lucas studied with master mythologist Joseph Campbell, who saw the mono-myth behind all mythologies, particularly articulated as The Hero's Journey. The concept of The Force is not unlike the Chinese concept of the

Tao, guiding the flow and unfolding of all of creation. It is ever present, our trainings and initiations hopefully making us more aware of it and more willing to flow with its guidance.

The consciousness of inspiration, of awen, is described in elemental terms. Those versed in ceremonial magick will likely see that the elements are the same ones associated with the Hebrew Mother Letters – the elements of fire, water, and air – as they come to the material reality of the earth element with their subtle blessings.

We start with the description of Taliesin himself. He has a "radiant brow." Radiant suggests light, gold, and fire. Occultists see the radiant brow as a reference to the third eye or crown chakras, opening the higher energy centers of the upper cauldron, to receive the light of the higher realms, and like a crystal lens, focus it into vision. Many would believe that is the true function of the pineal gland, the inner eye. That new inner "vision" is the guiding force of inspiration, constantly fed by the light of the otherworld.

In Irish myth, awen was known as imbas, and a variety of gods and heroes were described as burning with fiery power or inspiration, such as Brid and Cúchulainn. In one version of "The Song of Amergin" from the Irish tradition, a line usually translated as "I can shift my shape like a god" is translated as "I am God who fashions Fire for a Head."

This image was cleverly depicted by the poet William Butler Yeats in his poem, *The Song of the Wandering Aengus,* and has gone on to inspire many a new Celtic shaman, bard, and Witch – myself included. The poem is filled with a summary of classic Celtic otherworldly inspiration. The fire in – or radiating from – the head has obvious parallels to the radiant brow of Taliesin, fulfilling a similar function. The light of the head acts as a guide, like a lantern in the darkness of normal human consciousness, revealing new shapes of thought, idea, and art. It is akin to the Christian and Buddhist icongraphy of glowing hallows or a nimbus of light:

The Song of Wandering Aengus

By William Butler Yeats

I went out to the hazel wood,
Because a fire was in my head,
And cut and peeled a hazel wand,
And hooked a berry to a thread;
And when white moths were on the wing,
And moth-like stars were flickering out,
I dropped the berry in a stream

And caught a little silver trout.

When I had laid it on the floor
I went to blow the fire a-flame,
But something rustled on the floor,
And someone called me by my name:
It had become a glimmering girl
With apple blossom in her hair
Who called me by my name and ran
And faded through the brightening air.

Though I am old with wandering
Through hollow lands and hilly lands,
I will find out where she has gone,
And kiss her lips and take her hands;
And walk among long dappled grass,
And pluck till time and times are done,
The silver apples of the moon,
The golden apples of the sun.

 Not as obvious in the myths but subtly present in our understanding of inspiration is the idea of flow, and with flow comes the concept of liquid and thereby water. The Christian concept of the Holy Spirit is described as both fire and water. As the fire or light descends, the water rises up. Rituals all across the world use fire and water. Deities of inspiration can have water and fire associations as well. Cerridwen herself is associated with the cauldron, and thereby liquid, but has a hot, volatile nature in much of her story. The Irish Bridget is a goddess of poetry and inspiration, of creativity and crafting, and has the symbols of the fiery forge and the healing well. The fish, the salmon, is a source of inspiration and knowledge, found in the waters. And at the most basic level, when we now speak of our own inspiration and creativity, we describe it as a flow, and when we are having difficulty, we think of our inspiration as "drying up" or being "blocked" like a poorly plumbed pipe. The flow of awen is the flow of the river that takes the coracle of Taliesin. It not only carries him from place to place, it also flows through him, descended like the three rays of the Druidic awen symbol into his skull and coming through his eyes, his tongue, his hands, and his feet. One can think of it as the flow of the cosmic river, of the Great Goddess, guiding us all in what we are doing and where we are going, as part of the greater whole. One who is living awen simply knows and responds to this more consciously, and doesn't necessarily fight to swim upstream to satisfy the ego.

While fire is the creative element and water the emotive, it is the air that allows us to express these things in terms of words, shapes, ideas, and forms. It is the intellect, filled with agreed-upon symbols, that allows us to bring the intangible out into a form that others can perceive and interact with. Awen itself comes from an Indo-European root word that means "to blow" and is linked to a Welsh word, awel, that refers to the "breeze," so the Welsh concept of awen has always had an air component, as do other cultures' words associated with life force. Terms such as prana, chi, ki, pneuma, and ruach are often translated as life force or vitality, but have connotations of breath and air along with spirit. The air of awen isn't limited to logical linear thought; it is also the divine madness, the power of the divine fool who does seemingly strange things for divine reasons, sometimes consciously and sometimes unconsciously. While the blade is classically the magician's tool for air, within our bodies, air and intellect are often expressed by the double-edged power of our tongue.

In our understanding of the Celtic bards and poets, it's said that those who attained the highest skill in the art, such as the Irish Fili, attained the "tongue that cannot lie." This is akin to our living awen consciousness, living with an insight or constant sense of inspired connection. Mythically, one whose tongue cannot lie utters prophecy constantly. The poetry is not just creative or beautiful, but truly inspiring in the sense that reality corresponds with the verse. Often delivered in lines or sung in lyrics, this poetic prophecy links awen to the song of creation. For Witches and magicians, this brings up interesting questions, much like riddle of the chicken and the egg, of which comes first. Is the poet with the tongue that cannot lie casting a spell with intention, therefore making things happen? Or is the poet so in tune with the nature of reality that everything is a correct prophecy? At that level of consciousness, is there a difference? The prophecy is often in verse, or sung, giving associations of awen to the song of creation.

One must prepare the vessel to receive this inspiration of fire, water, and air, but the source of awen, while flowing from a single presence, is also described as triune. While we can call upon its nature as described as fire, water, and air, the source of it is so much more. As three drops came out of the cauldron, and three rays of awen descend, the source is also a trinity, a three in one. Many of the texts, written in a post-Christian area, are decidedly filled with Christian imagery, but there are other ways to look at it. To Christians, this is Father/Son/Holy Sophia, but they drew their wisdom from the lands of Khem where it was Osiris/Isis/Horus. The triune source is Brahma/Vishnu/Shiva in India, or Maiden/Mother/Crone to the modern Witch. To the alchemists its sulfur/mercury/salt. To me, it's power/love/wisdom.

Exercise 13:
The Living Cauldron of Awen

If you wish to focus primarily just on the Cauldron of the Head, start as you would with **Exercise 3: Three Cauldron Activation**, or if you want to build upon your cauldron experience, perform **Exercise 7: Lower Cauldron of Life and the Five Woods** and then move into **Exercise 9: The Alchemy of the Middle Cauldron of the Heart**. Then you will be prepared for **Exercise 13**. Just as before, no other tools are required beyond your own body, but you can use an altar and any setting to create an appropriate atmosphere conducive to the work.

Make sure your hands are in the "five woods" position, with each of the corresponding fingertips touching (**Chart 6: Tree Finger Ogham**), but with no pressure on any particular finger. Close your eyes. Breathe deeply. Feel this connection and the connection of the elements to the lower cauldron of the belly. Feel the connection to the seven planets of the chest. Prepare yourself for the trance state of energy work. Clear your mind. Open your heart and seek the secret fire that illuminates your souls, guiding and protecting you. Count backwards twelve to one, envisioning the numbers drawn on the screen of your mind. Then release that image to the void, and without visualization, count downward from thirteen to one to get to a deeper level. Set your intention:

I seek to activate and align my Upper Cauldron with the Source of Awen.

Focus all your awareness beyond your reach, in a direction that you know, but cannot be pointed to. In this place beyond, in this infinite source of awen, a field of consciousness that supports and permeates all that we know, reach for its pure heart. This heart is triune, triple, and you reach for it, however you perceive the triple force.

As you breathe, draw down the first force. It is like fire and light. It is like power. It is like sulfur. Its source is the father. Draw down this power until it reaches your Coire Sois, your Cauldron of Wisdom in the head. The fiery power heats and illuminates the cauldron.

As you breathe, draw down the second force. It is like water and darkness. It is like quicksilver. It is like love. Its source is the mother. Draw down this power until it reaches your Coire Sois, our Cauldron of Wisdom in the head. The watery power fills the cauldron.

As you breathe, draw down the third force. It is like air and clarity. It is like rock crystal. It is like the song of wisdom. Its source is the child. The airy power fills the cauldron, feeding the fire, bubbling the liquid, as all three come together within your head as one. Feel the union in the cauldron of the head.

The three coagulate as one within your upper cauldron filling you with wisdom and inspiration. The cauldron's contents multiply. The liquid overflows and seems to self-generate a vast blessing. This flows down into your heart until the heart cauldron is filled and overflowing. All the planetary powers are activated within your heart. You feel the blessings touch the powers of Saturn, Jupiter, Mars, Sun, Venus, Mercury, and the Moon within you. From the heart, it overflows into the belly. You feel all the elemental powers activated and blessed within you. You embody the blessings of fire, air, water, and earth. It fills the belly and flows into the entire body, filling all your flesh. It fills the body and flows outward into your energy body, filling every fiber of your aura. Soon all of your being is at one with the awen of the head.

When ready, bring your awareness back to the physical world around you. Bring your awareness to your flesh and blood, breath and bone. Count up from thirteen to one, then twelve to one. Feel your fingers and toes. Open your eyes and ground yourself as needed. Record your experience in your journal. Practice this exercise regularly until you feel a shift and believe you are ready for the third and final initiatory experience of this work.

While it would be nice for a series of exercises in a text to promise the illumination of living awen for all time, unfortunately it doesn't work that way. Material from a book, tradition, or teacher can create a path, forge alignments within you, clear blockages, and give techniques, but no one event will bring permanent awen. It's a long process and a constant choice to live "in spirit" and allow the cosmic flow to guide and inspire you. Our third and last initiatory working hopes to forge those alignments. The intention is the third birth, the seeking of a vision of true purpose and inspiration. The vision might not make sense, but if the working is done properly, images and ideas formed might guide you for many years to come.

Exercise 14:
Third Initiatory Working – The Sea

The third initiatory working of this text involves the casting out upon the waters. The time spent dwelling in the coracle is the third and final darkness, preceding the third and final rebirth. While a basket upon the ocean can seem quite artificial in comparison to the womb of the goddess Cerridwen herself, in many ways it's much more primal. While Cerridwen, being a goddess beyond flesh and blood, beyond the terrestrial manifestations, indicates a gestation in the spirit world, the world of the gods themselves is somewhat outside of the reach of space and time. Being flung upon the waters links the third rebirth to the first terrestrial mother, the great ocean, from which all life began. It harkens back to evolution, the tides of time far beyond a human stretch. This is where Taliesin rejoins his memory to the memory of the Earth, to all living and now dead creatures, from history and beyond, to gain a longer arc of time and perspective, leading him all the way back to his origin among the stars, as he'll later claim. This ritual evokes the rebirthing powers of the primal sea and the ladies of the sea.

The aim for this ritual is dream-like and nonlinear. You should take your time with it. While there is intention, there is no goal. For this ritual, you will need:

Ambient Dream-Inducing Music (no hard beats or voices. An ocean sound generator is acceptable or "ocean drum" if someone is playing for you. You'll also need a device or instrument to play the music)
Dark Cloth or Cloak (big enough to cover your body)
Single candle

Ideally if you could do this rite safely near the ocean, listening to the tides, so much the better, but I understand that is not feasible, or safe, for everyone. So your better option is the music.

You can start by setting up your altar if you so desire, but out of all the exercises, the altar is needed least in this one, since you are "going away" from your home base and into the world. If you are lighting candles, light only one, for it will ultimately be the light you first see when you are "drawn" from the bag. Before you get too far, you can prepare yourself further by doing **Exercise 3: Three Cauldron Activation** or even repeating **Exercise 13**.

Prior to beginning, you might want to learn and practice what is known in yogic traditions as the ujjayi breath. The ujjayi breathing is known as "ocean breath," and while its translation is usually associated with victory, yogis also believe this is the way we first breathe when we are born into the world, before our attention is grabbed by outside stimulation. I'm not sure how scientific that is, but the imagery of the newborn, as well as the ocean sound, plays into our rebirth ritual. The practice helps build upon power through retaining prana, expressed as body heat, but it also relaxes, regulates blood pressure, and oxygenates the blood. It can be done continuously during yoga sessions. It helps the practitioner be present, aware, and grounded, yet energized and meditative. As we prepare for entering into the world, it's an excellent breath to practice in this rite.

The breath itself is a powerful, diaphragmatic breath in and out through the nose, where you first fill the lower belly, then chest, and lastly the upper chest, or clavicular area, and then exhale in reverse, from the top of the lungs, then chest, then lower abdomen.

The trick to creating the ocean breath, rather than just a simple three-part lung breath, is to move the glottis as air moves in and out of the respiratory system. With a narrowed throat passage, the air creates a rushing sound reminiscent of the ocean. The breath is slow and even, with equal inhale and exhale, and practiced with simple control. When done correctly, there should be no tension or stress to the practitioner. It can be easier to "hear" breath through the mouth. Once you have the hang of it, try it through the nose. You might find you still leave the mouth open as you breathe through the nose.

When ready to begin, gather all your material, start your music, and create a sacred space. Again, you can adapt your own traditions or follow the method detailed here as before.

Using your wand, stirring stick, or hand, cast a ring of light starting in the north and moving clockwise around your working space.

Say:
By the Sacred Cauldron that dwells within the heart of Annwn, I cast this cauldron circle.
I call upon the Waves of Creation to flow from within me, about me, and all around me.
I call upon the powers of the cauldron to guard me from all harm. So mote it be.

Holding your arms outstretched, evoke the powers of the two and the three. Say:

By the vaulted arch of the cosmos,
I call upon the Lord of Death and Darkness to my left
And the Lord of Light and Life to my right.
May you ever hold the cauldron's brew.
Hail and welcome.

By the fires warming the cauldron below,
I call upon the Three Ladies, the Three Who Are Nine Who Are Three Again
Maiden, Mother, Crone
Stars, Earth, Underworld
Future, Present, Past

May you ever initiate change.
Hail and welcome.

For the quarter calls, rather than calling upon the animal powers of the last empowerment, we shall do something different, in alignment with the rebirth and origin of Taliesin. We shall call upon the Earth, Moon, Sun, and Stars.

Start by facing east, and evoke the spirit of the east.

To the east, I call upon the spirit of the Moon, pulling the tides of the Great Ocean.
Please bring your blessings to this circle, and teach me the ways of tide and time.
Hail and welcome.

Face south, and evoke the spirit of the south.

To the south, I call upon the spirit of the Sun, shining blessings upon the One Land.
Please bring your blessings to this circle, and teach me the ways of light and life.
Hail and welcome.

Face west and evoke the spirit of the west.

To the west, I call upon the spirit of the Stars, keeper of the Hidden Mysteries.
Please bring your magick to this circle, and teach me the ways of cosmos and creation.
Hail and welcome.

Face north and evoke the spirit of the north.

To the north, I call upon the spirit of the Earth, source of all that lives
Please bring your magick to this circle, and teach me the ways of love and law.
Hail and welcome.

Stand in the center and evoke the spirit of the center.

To the center, I call upon the spirit of the Ocean Mother, Mother of Time and of Space.
Let me be reborn by your waters.
Let me dream beyond the Sun and Moon.
Let me dwell among the Stars.
Please grant me a vision of my True Purpose here upon the Earth.
So mote it be.

Gather yourself under the blanket covering and enter the third darkness. Start your ujjayi breath. Float upon the sounds of the music, of the ocean. You have been cast into the sea in your coracle. You have been cast into water. You have been cast into darkness. You have been cast into a sea of stars. Flow with the cosmic flow and dream.

Enter the dream of the sea, where all life evolved. Enter the primordial dream of all life, from the first cells, the First Mothers, all the way to our current state of evolution, with flora, fauna, and fungus. All the realms of life that have evolved and passed and all the new ones developing in the future. See the patterns of evolution as if in fast forward, watching the evolution of life that has led us here.

Enter the dream of the stars, where our true consciousness descended from and will return to again. Enter the cosmic flow beyond your work upon the Earth, in patterns of evolution that have nothing to do with the Earth, being so far removed. See the patterns of the cosmos that led to its formation, from the start of creation to the igniting of stars, to the spinning of planets. See your place among this cosmic dance.

These two, the sea and stars, give you perspective on life of the below and life of the above.

A circle of stars reminds you of the pearl-rimmed cauldron of the nine maidens. From the nine maidens, you might be guided to seek your inspiration. Hold your intention for your vision of true purpose. Breathe like the ocean. Gaze into the darkness, and let the images of your guidance take form in the ring of pearly stars. You might even get a new name in this vision, to embody your purpose and inspiration of awen.

When you feel the vision is over, your body will get heavier. Cease the ujjayi breath. Prepare to return out of the "sack" and receive light on your radiant brow. As you take the covering off and begin to sit up, ask yourself, "Who or what is taking me out?" What is the first thing you think of or the last thing you "see" in inner vision before you open your eyes? Gaze at the single candle. Feel its light reach your upper cauldron and fill it with light, meeting the light already dwelling within you. If you have decided upon a spiritual name, or received one in the ocean dream vision, speak your name out loud now. If you have not, simply speak the name you use out loud now. Anchor yourself, and your new awareness in this name. With it spoken, you are reborn. Rest. Reflect.

We release the cauldron starting in the center.

I thank the Lord of Death and Darkness.
I thank the Lord of Life and Light.

I thank the Three Ladies of Black, Red, and White.
Hail and farewell.

To the center, I thank and release the spirit of Mother Ocean
Mother of Time
Mother of Space
Thank you for all your blessings.
Hail and farewell.

Face north and release the spirit of the north.

To the north, I thank and release the spirit of the Earth, mother of love and law.
Thank you for all your blessings.
Hail and farewell.

Face west and release the spirit of the west.

To the west, I thank and release the spirit of the Stars, teacher of the cosmos and creation.
Thank you for all your blessings.
Hail and farewell.

Face south and release the spirit of the south.

To the south, I thank and release the spirit of the Sun, father of the light and life.
Thank you for all your blessings.
Hail and farewell.

Face east and release the spirit of the east.

To the east, I thank and release the spirit of the Moon, lady of the tides and time.
Thank you for all your blessings.
Hail and farewell.

Facing your starting direction, and moving in the opposite rotation of how you created your sacred space, hold out your wand, stirring rod, or hand, and while infinitely expanding the circle, say:

By the Sacred Cauldron that dwells within the Heart of Annwn, I release this circle.
May all things return to their place and time.

Yet may the changes in this cauldron reverberate throughout the cosmos.
So mote be it.

Extinguish the candle and incense as needed. Ground and balance yourself as needed. Stop any music. Record your experiences in your journal and reflect upon them. Does the vision make sense? Do you have a next step for your divine purpose? Are you feeling the flow of awen within and around you, guiding you?

With the third birth, the last darkness of initiation, one can potentially wake to the continuous thread of consciousness that is the illuminated body of initiates. From this perspective, all initiates are like cells within the body of another, greater being. We have always known this to be true, but this is a conscious realization of it. Different facets of this one being are called different things. We might look at such terms as Christ consciousness, Krishna consciousness, or Buddha consciousness, each named after a different mainstream manifestation of a religion popularized in modern metaphysics, and see that by reaching a similar level of initiation and consciousness, one becomes united with such religious figures as Christ, Krishna, or Buddha. One realizes their own nature is already so, but drops away all that prevents that attainment. These are simply different cultural terms for an illuminated adept or enlightened master.

Less popular but no less applicable is the idea of a Hermes consciousness, a Merlin consciousness (as I was taught in the Western Mystery traditions) or even a Taliesin consciousness. Hermes, Merlin, and Taliesin seem to be figures – perhaps energetically one and the same and perhaps not – who transcend time periods, single cultures, and sole manifestations like other historic figures. They are shapeshifters and magicians. According to alchemical tradition, Hermes took many forms to bring civilization to the world, including:

Thoth/Tehuti – The Egyptian god of knowledge and culture

Seth – The second son of Adam in Judaism. Said to be the author of the Emerald Tablet

Moses – Also known as Thutmoses III and prophet of the Jewish tradition. The second smashed tablet brought down with the Ten Commandments was said to be a new copy of the Emerald Tablet.

Athothis – A deified being of Sumeria dating near 3400 BC

Hiram Ibif – From the Freemasonry tradition, dating near 2670 BC

Imhotep – Deified Egyptian scribe god dating near 2650 BC

Zoroaster – Founder of Zoroastrianism near 650 BC

Enoch – Jewish figure in both Biblical and apocryphal texts. Associated with the archangel Metatron and cosmological journeys through the heavens.

Idris – Islamic prophet equated with Enoch. Also the same name as a Welsh giant and astronomer.

Hermes – Messenger god of the Greeks

Mercury – Messenger god of the Romans

Hermes Trismegistus – Syncretic form of Hermes and Thoth. Often considered an incarnation of both gods come to teach humanity about alchemy and magick.

Buddha – Mahanirvana Tantra states Hermes and Buddha are the same being, come to teach humanity.

Much in the same way that the poetry of Taliesin is attributed to one consciousness, but very obviously written by many hands, *The Corpus Hermeticum* is attributed to Hermes but written physically by many scholars, Taliesin himself tells us of his many incarnations. He speaks this in the Court of King Maelgwn. The king asks him what he is and where he comes from, and he answers:

Primary chief bard am I to Elphin,
And my original country is the region of the summer stars;
Idno and Heinin called me Merddin,
At length every king will call me Taliesin.

I was with my Lord in the highest sphere,
On the fall of Lucifer into the depth of hell
I have borne a banner before Alexander;
I know the names of the stars from north to south;

I have been on the galaxy at the throne of the Distributor;
I was in Canaan when Absalom was slain;
I conveyed the Divine Spirit to the level of the vale of Hebron;
I was in the court of Don before the birth of Gwdion.
I was instructor to Eli and Enoc;
I have been winged by the genius of the splendid crosier;
I have been loquacious prior to being gifted with speech;
I was at the place of the crucifixion of the merciful Son of God;
I have been three periods in the prison of Arianrod;
I have been the chief director of the work of the tower of Nimrod;
I am a wonder whose origin is not known.

I have been in Asia with Noah in the ark,
I have seen the destruction of Sodom and Gomorra;
I have been in India when Roma was built,
I am now come here to the remnant of Troia.

I have been with my Lord in the manger of the ass:
I strengthened Moses through the water of Jordan;
I have been in the firmament with Mary Magdalene;
I have obtained the muse from the cauldron of Caridwen;
I have been bard of the harp to Lleon of Lochlin.
I have been on the White Hill, in the court of Cynvelyn,
For a day and a year in stocks and fetters,
I have suffered hunger for the Son of the Virgin,
I have been fostered in the land of the Deity,
I have been teacher to all intelligences,
I am able to instruct the whole universe.
I shall be until the day of doom on the face of the earth;
And it is not known whether my body is flesh or fish.

Then I was for nine months
In the womb of the hag Caridwen;
I was originally little Gwion,
And at length I am Taliesin.
   — from "Taliesin" in *The Mabinogion*

The poem identifies him with Merddin, or Merlin. The Christian era tale aligns Taliesin's mythology with the Christian creator and the folk myth of Lucifer's fall, as well as the Biblical lore of Absalom, Nimrod, Noah, Moses, the cities of Sodom and

Gomorrah, and the New Testament figures of Jesus and Mary Magdalene. Pagan lore includes the mythology of Wales with Don, Gwydion, and Arianrhod, as well as Alexander the Great, India, Rome, and Troy. It shows a figure that could not have experienced these things in one lifetime.

Is he one figure remembering many past lives? Is it one order of magicians, with a guiding purpose and current of the group consciousness? How could that order be terrestrially organized? Most likely, it is not. Is it an inner plane order manifesting through individuals across time? If so, the name Taliesin is simply one perspective on it. There is a thread of consciousness, of bards and magicians, that manifests in many places and many times in a non-linear way.

In the Irish traditions, one word that possibly describes a non-linear form of reincarnation is tuirgen. As defined in *Cormac's Glossary*, tuirgen is "a successive birth that passes from every nature into another... flowing through all time from beginning to end." Essentially everything is constantly becoming everything else, with no particular hierarchy or humanly understood order.

While everything is becoming everything else, that sliver of consciousness that identifies as the magician, the alchemist, the poet, bard, Druid, or Witch, is called in the modern Witchcraft traditions the One Sorcerer, or One Witch. It is the one consciousness with many expressions. It is the spirit of Witchcraft itself. We are all expressions in a particular zone of space and time, but there is an underlying oneness of our purpose and work, even if we don't subscribe to the theory. Is this One Sorcerer Hermes? Is it Merlin? Is it Taliesin? Maybe. Perhaps those are three names we can call it, but it's more than any of those specific descriptions. Or perhaps they are three subsets of something greater.

To truly embody the living awen, start framing your perspective in the larger arc of time. What is your soul here to do in this lifetime, and what is the long-term plan of your soul's work? What is the work of this timeless tradition to which we all belong? Identify with the Taliesin that was in Sodom and Gomorrah, Troy, India, at the Tower of Nimrod, in the ark of Noah, at the fall of Lucifer, and on the throne of the Distributor. Then you will understand the true nature of the One Sorcerer.

The Magicians of Poetry and Song

Once there is initiation into the poetic mysteries, the power of word, story, song, music, and prophecy is at the tip of the tongue of the new bardic initiate. Today we tend to think of magick in terms of potions and candles, but the power of the word is first and foremost, and we find practitioners of it all across our mythic traditions. It is not limited to devotees of Cerridwen, or even the Celts exclusively. It's part of our global esoteric traditions, and an understanding of one part can help you understand the patterns of the whole.

In the Mediterranean, most prominent is Orpheus, the world teacher of the Age of Taurus. Orpheus is credited as the founder of the Orphic Mysteries, mysteries anchored in poetry, sound, song, dance, story, and music. Occult tradition tells us he was the world teacher of the great celestial month of Taurus during the most ancient Greek period, the time of the Minoan civilization and the building of great monuments. It was the time when the bull was worshipped and sacrificed. He played the lyre, a type of Greek harp, and legend says he could charm all living creatures as well as the very stones of the Earth themselves with his music. The Greeks revered him as the greatest of musicians. His role as world teacher is not unlike Jesus of Nazareth as the world teacher of the Age of Pisces. Taliesin's final rebirth on May Eve, when the Sun is in the sign of Taurus, points a finger to the type of mysteries embodied by Taliesin's tale and helps align him with the Taurean world teacher. Orpheus and Taliesin have some common points, even more so if you align Taliesin with Merlin.

In his tale, Orpheus lost his wife Eurydice to a premature death and seeks her out in the underworld, charming Lord Hades and Queen Persephone and bargaining with them to release her. They agree...on one condition. Eurydice is to follow him back as his shadow, and he must not look back at her until he's returned to the light of the land of the living. At the last moment, fear and doubt overtake him, and he looks back, condemning her to the underworld. Not looking back is a theme of many religious and magickal cults. He wandered the land in his depression and was torn apart, or initiated, by the wild followers of Dionysus, and some believe Orpheus to be an incarnation of Dionysus. Others viewed him as a son of Apollo, a god of prophecy and healing as well as the light of the Sun. The maenads cast Orpheus' severed head into a river, where it eventually floated upon the shores of the Isle of Lesbos and inhabitants built a shrine for him. The muses took his lyre to the heavens to create the constellation of Lyra.

Orpheus is part of a long tradition of sacred severed heads that continue to reveal information, including figures such as Bran, Mimir, and John the Baptist. The link between music, poetry, and prophecy aligns quite well with the teachings from the Taliesin tradition. One of the most famous quotes attributed to the Orphic Mysteries – found in a gold funerary talisman, an Orphic Tablet – also relates well to the Taliesin lore: the "region of the summer stars." While not directly attributed to Orpheus, it this phrase speaks to the mystery of Orpheus and the realm of the dead:

Thou shalt find to the left of the House of Hades a spring,
And by the side thereof standing a white cypress.
To this spring approach not near.
But thou shalt find another, from the Lake of Memory
Cold water flowing forth, and there are guardians before it..
Say, "I am a child of Earth and starry heaven;
But my race is of Heaven (alone). This ye know yourselves.
But I am parched with thirst and I perish. Give me quickly
The cold water flowing forth from the Lake of Memory."
And of themselves they will give thee to drink of the holy spring.
And there after among the other heroes thou shalt have lordship.
— From the Funerary Gold Plates from Petelia, South Italy, 4th-3rd century B.C.

While less mythic than Orpheus, Pythagoras, a pre-Socratic philosopher, is also shrouded in mystery. We know he certainly was a historic figure, and most of us are familiar with his contributions to mathematics, including the Pythagorean Theorem much dreaded by high school math students, but most are less familiar with his contributions to religion, natural philosophy, and esoteric music. He is one of the first philosophers on record to relate mathematics and music in terms of proportions and geometry. He saw music as mathematics in "time." Pythagoras was also a proponent of the Music of the Spheres theory, that the planets are in a divine ratio to each other and produce a harmonious music sound heard by adepts and subtly influencing us. He would prescribe music as medicine, both metaphysically to align the soul, purify the mind, and clear the emotions, but also to heal physically and maintain health. His healing intention was to bring about harmony between soul and body using music, performing "soul adjustments" to bring one back in alignment with the cosmos, a term he coined for both creation and the underlying harmony of creation.

Pythagoras is well known for his Seventy-One Golden Verses, a series of oft-quoted guidelines attributed to him. They are popular in many esoteric and occult circles, particularly those influenced by Neoplatonist schools of thought:

1. First worship the Immortal Gods, as they are established and ordained by the Law.

2. Reverence the Oath, and next the Heroes, full of goodness and light.

3. Honor likewise the Terrestrial Daemons by rendering them the worship lawfully due to them.

4. Honor likewise your parents, and those most nearly related to you.

5. Of all the rest of mankind, make him your friend who distinguishes himself by his virtue.

6. Always give ear to his mild exhortations, and take example from his virtuous and useful actions.

7. Avoid as much as possible hating your friend for a slight fault.

8. Power is a near neighbor to necessity.

9. Know that all these things are just as what I have told you; and accustom yourself to overcome and vanquish these passions:--

10. First gluttony, sloth, sensuality, and anger.

11. Do nothing evil, neither in the presence of others, nor privately;

12. But above all things respect yourself.

13. In the next place, observe justice in your actions and in your words.

14. And do not accustom yourself to behave yourself in anything without rule, and without reason.

15. But always make this reflection, that it is ordained by destiny that all men shall die.

16. And that the goods of fortune are uncertain; and that just as they may be acquired, they may likewise be lost.

17. Concerning all the calamities that men suffer by divine fortune,

18. Support your lot with patience, it is what it may be, and never complain at it.

19. But endeavor what you can to remedy it.

20. And consider that fate does not send the greatest portion of these misfortunes to good men.

21. There are many sorts of reasonings among men, good and bad;

22. Do not admire them too easily, nor reject them.

23. But if falsehoods are advanced, hear them with mildness, and arm yourself with patience.

24. Observe well, on every occasion, what I am going to tell you:

25. Do not let any man either by his words, or by his deeds, ever seduce you.

26. Nor lure you to say or to do what is not profitable for yourself.

27. Consult and deliberate before you act, that you may not commit foolish actions.

28. For it is the part of a miserable man to speak and to act without reflection.

29. But do the thing which will not afflict you afterwards, nor oblige you to repentance.

30. Never do anything which you do not understand.

31. But learn all you ought to know, and by that means you will lead a very pleasant life.

32. In no way neglect the health of your body;

33. But give it drink and meat in due measure, and also the exercise of which it needs.

34. Now by measure I mean what will not discomfort you.

35. Accustom yourself to a way of living that is neat and decent without luxury.

36. Avoid all things that will occasion envy.

37. And do not be prodigal out of season, like someone who does not know what is decent and honorable.

38. Neither be covetous nor stingy; a due measure is excellent in these things.

39. Only do the things that cannot hurt you, and deliberate before you do them.

40. Never allow sleep to close your eyelids, after you went to bed,

41. Until you have examined all your actions of the day by your reason.

42. In what have I done wrong? What have I done? What have I omitted that I ought to have done?

43. If in this examination you find that you have done wrong, reprove yourself severely for it;

44. And if you have done any good, rejoice.

45. Practice thoroughly all these things; meditate on them well; you ought to love them

with all your heart.

46. It is those that will put you in the way of divine virtue.

47. I swear it by he who has transmitted into our souls the Sacred Quaternion, the source of nature, whose cause is eternal.

48. But never begin to set your hand to any work, until you have first prayed the gods to accomplish what you are going to begin.

49. When you have made this habit familiar to you,

50. You will know the constitution of the Immortal Gods and of men.

51. Even how far the different beings extend, and what contains and binds them together.

52. You shall likewise know that according to Law, the nature of this universe is in all things alike,

53. So that you shall not hope what you ought not to hope; and nothing in this world shall be hidden from you.

54. You will likewise know, that men draw upon themselves their own misfortunes voluntarily, and of their own free choice.

55. Unhappy they are! They neither see nor understand that their good is near them.

56. Few know how to deliver themselves out of their misfortunes.

57. Such is the fate that blinds humankind, and takes away his senses.

58. Like huge cylinders they roll back and forth, and always oppressed with innumerable ills.

59. For fatal strife, natural, pursues them everywhere, tossing them up and down; nor do they perceive it.

60. Instead of provoking and stirring it up, they ought to avoid it by yielding.

61. Oh! Jupiter, our Father! If you would deliver men from all the evils that oppress them,

62. Show them of what daemon they make use.

63. But take courage; the race of humans is divine.

64. Sacred nature reveals to them the most hidden mysteries.

65. If she impart to you her secrets, you will easily perform all the things which I have ordained thee.

66. And by the healing of your soul, you wilt deliver it from all evils, from all afflictions.

67. But you should abstain from the meats, which we have forbidden in the purifications and in the deliverance of the soul;

68. Make a just distinction of them, and examine all things well.

69. Leave yourself always to be guided and directed by the understanding that comes from above, and that ought to hold the reins.

70. And when, after having deprived yourself of your mortal body, you arrived at the most pure Aethyr,

71. You shall be a God, immortal, incorruptible, and Death shall have no more dominion over you.

— from *The Golden Verses of Pythagoras and Other Pythagorean Fragments* (Firth)

In Homer's *The Odyssey* there is the character of Demodocus, a poet visiting the court of King Alcinous on the island of Scheria. Some might describe Demodocus as the healer of Odysseus, through the preparation of three songs. Odysseus has ended up in the court of Alcinous after spending seven years in captivity on an island, leaving on a raft and almost being drowned by Poseidon until he can swim to shore with some help from the sea nymph Ino. To say he is exhausted and traumatized at this point in his adventure would be an understatement.

The first is a song about Odysseus and his disagreement with Achilles at Troy. Odysseus bursts into tears, for that event brought him great pain. Blind Demodocus and the rest of the court are unaware of the identity of Odysseus, but King Alcinous notices his tears and directs the feast outdoors to competitive events. The games are followed by another song from Demodocus, now singing about the affair of the gods Ares and Aphrodite behind the back of Hephaestus. Odysseus asks Demodocus to sing a third and final song, offering a large piece of his own portion of port from the dinner feast to Demodocus. The poet sings a story about the Trojan Horse and the sacking of the city of Troy. Again Odysseus bursts into tears. King Alcinous notices him once again and confronts him, asking who he really is. Odysseus then tells his tale of his return to Troy, including his trials with the Cyclops, the sorceress Circe, his travels to the land of the dead, his encounter with the sirens, and his battles with Poseidon. It is the songs of Demodocus that lead to his catharsis, this reliving and acceptance of his past trauma and mistakes, and then the continuation of the story. The music triggers a healing capacity within the hero. In *The Shamanic Odyssey: Homer, Tolkien, and the Visionary Experience* by Robert Tindall with Susana Bustos Ph.D., the authors argue it is also the acceptance of his own rejected feminine nature and his own unconscious, as embodied by the mysteries of the sea and his feminine adversaries.

In Celtic myth, the Irish god Lugh visits Tara, the home of the gods, at the Court of King Nuada of the Silver Hand. There, demonstrating his many skills and his value to the Tuatha De Danann, the Children of the Goddess Danu, he begins to play a harp after winning a stone-tossing contest against the god Ogma. He first puts the gods to sleep peacefully with his playing. As they awaken, he plays a slow, mournful song that makes them cry in sorrow. The music turns, growing faster with cheer, until both the song and their cheers grow louder, and the hall is filled with laughter. He then stirs them towards battle against their current oppressors, the Fomorians. Along with his skill as a warrior, a historian, a chess player, a smith, a craftsman, and a sorcerer, he is also a magical musician in the tradition of Orpheus and Taliesin.

In a similar vein to our Welsh Taliesin is the Irish bardic figure Amergin. Amergin is of the race of Milesians, what are considered ethnically the modern Irish, and cosmically, the human race, as opposed to the Tuatha De Danann, the gods of the race of Lugh. The three goddess queens of Ireland give them permission to settle, insisting the Milesians must name the island after the queens: Ériu, Banba, and Fódla. While we might see them as three individual beings of the Tuatha, in many ways they are literally the spirit of the land of Ireland. But despite this, the Tuatha put up an initial resistance. Eventually, rather than fight the Milesians to the death, the Tuatha relinquished control after the death of their three kings by the Milesians and chose to dwell beneath the land. During the fight, Amergin evokes the spirit of the land of Ireland, in a poetic invocation known as "The Song of Amergin." Its shapeshifting imagery is very reminiscent of the Taliesin style of poetry, showing it as a common factor in Celtic lore. There are many translations of "The Song of Amergin," but this is the one I first learned and have used in ritual:

The Song of Amergin

I am the wind that blows across the sea;
I am a wave of the deep;
I am the roar of the ocean;
I am the stag of seven battles;
I am a hawk on the cliff;
I am a ray of sunlight;
I am the greenest of plants;
I am the wild boar;
I am a salmon in the river;
I am a lake on the plain;
I am the word of knowledge;
I am the point of a spear;
I am the lure beyond the ends of the earth;
I can shift my shape like a god.

Caedmon, a Christian bard, is one of the first Anglo-Saxon poets on record. While in Ireland, he would vanish whenever a song started or a harp would play in the local pub, for he could not sing and join with everyone. While escaping one such episode, he went to tend animals in a stable and fell asleep. There, in a dream, a man ordered him to sing of the first creation, and he did so. Later, in telling this dream to another, he was brought before the Abbess and asked to sing, and he did so! Though not trained in music or art, he received divine initiation into the magick of the bards and the healing power of song. He used his voice to connect people to divinity.

Story, poetry, and song help us connect to divinity by helping us answer the great questions of life: Who are we? Where are we? Why are we here? Where did we come from? And where are we going? When we have a connection to our past and hope for our future, we are able to be more fully in the present and in the presence of our divinity.

The Great Song

All of these practitioners demonstrate the underlying power of the song and of the word. Many creation stories start with "the Word" or Logos. Early Greek philosophers simply used the term to mean discourse or argument (which then meant a reasoned or well-ordered point of debate) until the Stoic philosophers equated it with an animating force of the universe. Later Christian philosophers adopted it, and Jesus Christ was seen as the incarnation of the Logos, the Word of God that creates the universe with the words "Let there be light" in the Book of Genesis.

Today, global occultists would see a similar function in the Hindu teaching on Om or Aum, the divine sound that creates, sustains, and dissolves the universe on all levels. Om speaks to the more primal sound of creation, and returns us to the idea of the universe created by song, by dance, by story. Pythagoras thought of it as the Music of the Spheres, but we know it goes beyond the planets to the stars, and to the very empyrean beyond.

I use the term Oran Mor, a Celtic term said to mean Great Song, meaning that all life is participating in the Great Song of creation. The Oran Mor is the world song, the universal song. We each have our part to play, our note to sing. When using song in ritual, we are not simply retelling our history or relating a story that has already happened. The singing of the song is a ritual to be in the present moment of creation, really stepping outside of space and outside of time into a sacred space beyond both. Ritual song is to recreate and re-experience the mythic conditions of time and space, eternity and infinity. By participating in the song, you recreate the cosmos. You sing the world anew, fully present through song.

As we all have a part to play in the beautiful cosmic symphony, awakening to our own bard nature, to our own magician's word, is essential to our full participation. The gods have their role, but so do the animals, the plants, and minerals of the very Earth. Humans, as part of the animal realm, also have our own role. The alchemy we experience is an alchemy of song, of harmony and proportion, literally and metaphorically.

In Irish myth, the good god known as the Dagda had a harp named Uaithne. Uaithne, also called Daur da Bláo, was made from the finest of oak and played "Four Angled Music." It would play the Music of Mirth, bringing joy; the Music of Grief, making all weep; the Music of Sleep; making all slumber; and the Music of the Seasons, which would order the seasons and turn the Wheel of the Year. Only with the proper playing of the harp would summer follow spring, and spring follow winter, winter follow fall, and fall follow summer.

One could argue that keeping the old ways, venerating the old gods, and celebrating the seasons of the Earth and Sun and Moon help keep the seasons in their proper order, and honoring the planets and stars in their alignments maintains the harmony of the spheres. That is at the heart of many Pagan and Witchcraft traditions. We are a cult of the Moon, Sun, and stars. Like many tribal people celebrating the equinoxes, solstices, and other holy days, we do so to "keep up the day" for all.

There is said to be a language and song of the animals. In the ancient ages before us, our ancestors could speak to the animals, before we forgot they were our family too.

Many generalized Native American tales (now told for popular culture) speak of times when the animals spoke to humanity, implying a return to nature can return this connection and communication again. Often specific tribes will have a cultural hero or ally in the form of an animal, giving particular aid to the people. Among the Algonquian people of the American Northeast, it is the woodchuck. The Navajo have coyote. The Ojibwe legends have talking birds. White Buffalo Calf Woman of the Lakota is a buffalo who transforms herself into a human woman to talk to the people, for they have lost their ability to speak to the animals.

In shamanic traditions, all medicine animals are said to have their own song or dance, and when performed correctly by a healer or the one seeking healing, health and balance are restored. This is not so far off from Pythagoras' soul prescriptions with musical modes and rhythms.

In the ancient Norse legends of the hero Sigurd, the hero kills the dragon Fafnir and bathes in his blood to gain invulnerability and drinks the blood to learn the language of birds and beasts.

The language of birds in particular has been associated with magicians and philosophers across the world as a perfect language, before humanity learned to speak so many confusing tongues. It is considered to be a pure tongue, perhaps the language of angels and of humanity before we fell out of nature and forgot the song.

In alchemy, the language of the birds is also known as the Green Language, also connecting it to the plant world of the alchemist. The magician king Solomon, the adept Apollonius of Tyana, as well as Democritus, Anaximander, Tiresias, Melampus, and Aesopus were said to be speakers of this language. In medieval France, the language of birds is linked with the Troubadours, who in turn have associations with the Celtic bardic tradition and the teachings of the Holy Grail and Arthurian mythos.

Up to the modern era, cunning men, Witches, magicians, and mystics are said to share a special relationship with the animals. Alex Sanders, co-founder of the Alexandrian tradition of Wicca, was said to be able to charm the birds right out from the trees. Today many magickal practitioners feel a kinship with a special animal familiar, a type of animal, or even all animals, and use their psychic abilities to transmit and receive communications with them.

In the world of the plants, those who work deeply with plant spirit medicine know that all plants vibrate, hum, and sing. As their flowers bloom, the song becomes more present and intricate. Ritualists working with plant medicine will sing with or sing to the plants to unlock their own healing powers on a soul level.

In the Amazonian and Peruvian healing traditions, indigenous healers would receive a healing song from the plant spirits themselves, known as an icaro or ikaro in

Quechua. The icaro is the ultimate expression of the shamanic power and the relationship between plant and healer. They can be given in dreams, visions, or rituals, evoking a supernatural presence of the divine, influencing all present with the spirit of the particular plant associated with that icaro.

The Huichol of the Sierra Madre Occidental range in Mexico, a people who have shared much of their lore and mysticism with Westerners, use song in a similar way during peyote ceremonies, and their ritual use of song is not unlike the tale of the Irish god Lugh in the court of Nuada. As documented in *The Shamanic Odyssey,* the Huichol start in "mode of the orphan," with the intention of creating sorrow, sleep, and forgetfulness. The second mode is known as the "mode of the flowers" to bring joy, expansion of consciousness, and a sense of timelessness. Together, they produce a healing catharsis.

In a similar vein to the rebirth and renaming of the boy Gwion Bach to Taliesin, the Algonquins make a potion called wysoccan from the plant datura, a well-known Witch's herb used in young male initiation ceremonies. The wysoccan is given repeatedly to the boys over twenty days during the ceremony. The effect of the herbal potion was to "un-live" their childhood and relieve them of their memories of the past and be reborn anew as men in the tribe.

Returning to plant consciousness restores us to the first garden, the primordial consciousness of humanity before agriculture. Our most common myth is the Garden of Eden, but there have been many paradise lands from which humanity has been expelled or forgotten. It is the dream culture of the ancients that offered a state of perfect, profound peace. With initiation into the plant world, you can hear their song better and find harmony with it as you add your own notes to the world song.

Lastly, we have the mineral world in the great song. The minerals are probably the purest of our notes, the clearest of our vibrations, anchoring the lower tones of the song of the Earth. Though many consider them un-living, remember that they too were moved by Orpheus' music, right along with the animals. The mythic Lia Fail, of Ireland, is the stone of sovereignty, said to cry out when the rightful king of the land would stand upon it.

Science has recognized literal singing stones, as in volcanic basalt rock that has a higher interior iron content. The inner rock is under tension, creating a sound when struck, much like a bell or hammer. Most famous are the singing stones of Brittany. Yet there are many singing stones of different composition, said to sing or ring out under certain circumstances and times of year. Standing stones are arranged to reverberate whatever music or song is played in their presence. Many believe that is one of the many purposes of Stonehenge, to serve as an amplifier.

Various traditions of Native American lore tell us that stones are the record keepers and storytellers. In one beloved tale from the Seneca nation, an orphaned boy hunting birds for himself and his new foster mother is out in the forest without much hunting success. He sits upon a large stone to eat his lunch, and a voice from nowhere asks, "Shall I tell you stories?" He is frightened because no one is there, but soon realizes it is the stone speaking to him.

The boy asks the stone, "What does this mean, to tell stories?" The stone answers: "It is to tell of things that happened a long time ago." The boy agrees and listens all day, returning with only a few birds. The stone makes him promise not to tell anyone. His foster mother sends another boy out to look for him, who also agrees to listen to the stone's stories. They return with a few birds and no answers for the foster mother. The foster mother then sends two hunters after the boys on the next day. The two hunters and the two boys all listen together until the stone tells them to bring the whole village the next day to listen. They do. The stone tells them all beautiful stories of the past, of creation, stories involving people living in the sky and animals speaking to each other and to humans. The stone made the people promise to retell these stories to their descendants for all times to come, improving the life and happiness of the people with stories. Then the stone was done telling its stories and fell silent.

By looking at the various musicians of the Oran Mor – at least on Earth and as far as we can "hear" in the music of the spheres – we can see how the work of Cerridwen's initiation prepares you to work more deeply on these levels. We have the animal totems of the chase. We explore the green world in the hut and potion. We rebuild ourselves from the minerals, as embodied by the cell salts, which resonate with the seasons and the zodiacal heavens, in the womb. We flow with the sound, the song of the seas, and return to the world to do our part, and sing our note, within the great song

Musical Correspondences

While a historic and philosophical understanding of the role of music, story, and song is quite important, it certainly doesn't replace practical instructions and occult techniques. Contemplate the following associations in language and music when creating your own bardic magick. The knowledge can seep into you intuitively, expressing itself in unconscious and unusual ways, or the correspondences can be used to consciously construct language, poetry, and music that directly evokes certain powers and feelings. Ultimately either path – unconscious and intuitive or conscious and directed – must be touched by divinity. One cannot speak or sing with an empty heart and empty head. One must be illuminated from within, filled with the fire in the head, for the true magick to work. Our goal is that inspiration, that illumination of awen. Magickal tools, including these correspondences, are simply a means to an end.

Sacred Vowels

In modern English, there are five vowels recognized – A, E, I, O, U – with a sixth – Y – sometimes operating as a vowel. Early in my magickal training, I was introduced to a five-vowel/ five-element correspondence system for evoking magickal energies:

Earth	A as in "day"
Air	E as in "we"
Water	O as in "no"
Fire	I as in "eye"
Spirit	U as in "you"

Chart 14: Five Elemental Vowels

While this system served me well – and still does – it speaks to the elemental world of the microcosm and ignores the rich tradition of vowel sounds associated with the planetary sphere, or the macrocosm. We refer to the seven-vowel system as the Greek vowels, though there is evidence of their use (or the use of something similar) in many magickal systems, and occult tradition tells us the Greeks obtained it from the Egyptians, like so many mysteries. We find notations of sacred sounds, particularly the seven vowels in the Mithraic Mysteries and the Greek Magical Papyri as part of the barbarous names of power.

We associate the letters with the seven wandering planets of ancient astrology as mentioned through the writings of Aristotle and Hippocrates, and we see their use as a way to work with the mythos of the Music of the Spheres, but in truth, we don't know which sound corresponds with each letter. The ancient writers didn't leave us a correspondence chart or explicit directions.

Two systems are most often followed, one proposed by esoteric scholar Manly P. Hall, in his book *The Secret Teachings of All Ages*. He proposes starting with Alpha as the Moon, the sphere nearest to Earth, and ascending in the Chaldean order of the planets that is also encoded in the Qabalistic Tree of Life. While attributed to Hall, Abbé Jean Jacques Barthélemy proposed it first in 1787, while the Secret Teachings was published in 1928. This appears to be the dominant system for most modern occultists using the vowels.

Greek	Letter	Sound	Manly P. Hall	H.C. Agrippa
Alpha	A	A as in "father"	Moon	Saturn
Epsilon	E	Eh as in "bed"	Mercury	Jupiter
Eta	H	AY as in "day"	Venus	Mars
Iota	I	EE as in "tree"	Sun	Sun
Omicron	O	OH as in "old"	Mars	Venus
Upsilon	Y	UE as in "glue"	Jupiter	Mercury
Omega	W	AW as in "law"	Saturn	Moon

Chart 15: Seven Sacred Vowels in Alphabetical Order

Famous German occultist Henry Cornelius Agrippa, who preserved so much esoteric lore today in his *Three Books of Occult Philosophy*, proposed a different system, attributing Saturn with Alpha and then moving down the Chaldean order, as influenced by his work with the Hebrew alphabet. Notice how in both, the Sun has the same association, Iota.

Esoteric scholar Joscelyn Godwin suggested in his exploration of the vowels in *The Mystery of the Seven Vowels* that rather than following an alphabetical order, the tonal or harmonic order is the key to understanding their associations. This yields two more options, depending on the Moon or Saturn starting order, and again, yields the same sound for the Sun, but in this case, alpha, the first. Perhaps for solar-oriented cults as found in Egypt and the mysteries of Mithras, assigning the Sun as the first alphabetical letter has some significance.

Greek	Letter	Sound	Moon Order	Saturn Order
Iota	I	EE as in "tree"	Moon	Saturn
Eta	H	AY as in "day"	Mercury	Jupiter
Epsiolon	E	Eh as in "bed"	Venus	Mars
Alpha	A	A as in "father"	Sun	Sun
Omicron	O	OH as in "old"	Mars	Venus
Omega	W	AW as in "law"	Jupiter	Mercury
Upsilon	Y	UE as in "glue"	Saturn	Moon

Chart 16: Seven Sacred Vowels in Tonal Order

Along with the vowels, occult tradition has assigned consonant sounds to the elements. These correspondences can be found in *The Goodly Spellbook: Olde Spells for Modern Problems* by Lady Passion and *Diuvei.

Element	Consonant Sounds
Earth	g, gh, k, kh
Water	z, zh, s, sh
Air	d, dh, t, th
Fire	b, v, p, f

Chart 17: Consonant Sounds

One could continue the study by looking deeper into the magickal associations of the Hebrew and Greek Letters, the various Germanic Rune systems, and the Celtic Ogham alphabet.

Druidic teacher and author Kristoffer Hughes of the Anglesey Druid Order suggests the hidden secret of the symbol of awen is in the three rays and four "spaces" within and around the three rays, creating the seven sacred vowels. In the Welsh language, the seven sacred vowels, as detailed in Hughes' book *From the Cauldron Born*, are:

Vowel	Short	Long
A	Mat	Farmer
E	Let	Bear
I	Pit	Meet
O	Lot	Lore
U	Ill	Limb
W	Look	Fool
Y	Up	Under

Chart 18: Welsh Vowels

The three rays of awen are embodied by the vowels O-I-W, with the spaces in-between and around for A, E, U and Y. Awen contains all seven sacred letters and their associations, not unlike the Egyptian and Greek mysteries of other occult systems.

Scales

Scales refer to the organization of pitch, rather than vowel sound of a note. The familiar seven-note major scale is demonstrated to many people not trained in music through the popular song "Doe-Re-Mi" or "Doe a Deer" from the movie *The Sound of Music*, but this is not the only form of scale available to musicians or occultists.

For an elemental association with the scales, we have what are known as pentatonic, or five-note, scales. Most people in the Western world are conditioned to think of a heptatonic, or seven-note scale, as the traditional scale, but five-note scales are common in world folk music, blues, country music, and traditional Chinese music. Even if you have little conscious knowledge of five-note scales, you'll find there is a familiar quality to pentatonic scales, as you have probably been listening to them for all your life.

Each of the five elements – with their corresponding vowel in the elemental system above – is taught as having a corresponding note in the musical scale relative to the starting note, known as the tonic. The starting note is marked as "Do" and followed up the scale with "Re", "Mi", "So", and "La," skipping "Fa" and "Ti" with the octave of Do in the traditional familiar seven-note major scale. Do, Re, Mi, So, and La are the primary notes of the pentatonic scale. In a C scale, they would be the notes C, D, E, G and A respectively.

Element	Pentatonic Note within a scale	Notes
Earth	Do	C, D, E, G, A
Water	Re	D, E, F#, A, B
Air	Mi	E, F#, G#, B, C#
Fire	So	G, A, B, D, E
Spirit	La	A, B, C#, D#, F

Chart 19: Elements with Pentatonic Notes

Each of the elements is also associated with a different type of pentatonic scale. Each type of pentatonic scale has its own qualities, and in this system, are said to align with the energy quality of the element. The name of the Pentatonic Scale is given here, along with the "white" notes on a piano that would correspond with it, for those seeking to experiment with the sound without having to learn the sharp (#) and flat (b) notation systems in music.

Element	Pentatonic Scale Name	Notes	With Octave
Earth	Major Pentatonic	C, D, E, G, A	C
Water	Blues, Major	G, A, C, D, E	G
Air	Egyptian, Suspended	D, E, G, A, C	D
Fire	Minor Pentatonic	A, C, D, E, G	A
Spirit	Blues, Minor	E, G, A, C, D	E

Chart 20: Elements with Pentatonic Scales

Drawing once again from the ancient Greeks for musical inspiration, we look to the Greek modes of music. The modes are seven-note melodic scales, each evoking different quality and mood. They have become a staple of Western music, and two have been dominant forms of musical expression, in the form of the Ionian mode, now often called the natural major scale, and the aeolian mode, or natural minor scale.

There is great confusion around the modes and metaphysics namely because the modern modes and names are not the ones used in the ancient world, and the same names were adopted, adapted, and changed in the rise of Gregorian chant music of Europe. Occultists of the medieval world were drawing upon references from both the ancient Greeks and their own time period, but what we are using today, inspired and drawing from the past, is different, and without a level of detailed study to the evolution of music beyond the scope of this book, it would be difficult to parse out the various historic stages and associations. For our purposes we will be looking at some of the systems I've been taught, found, and experimented with in modern magick.

Since there are seven primary modes recognized, it is natural for occultists to associate them with the seven planets. Much like the vowels, there are different schools of thought on the appropriate correspondences. I know of two different systems of correspondences with the planets.

The modes are traditionally ordered in this way, so examining the correspondences, we can find some patterns. If playing the modes on the white keys of the piano, one simply starts at C to find the first mode, Ionian. Then to find the second mode of Dorian, play the white keys starting with D. The pattern works for all seven modes, as it relates the tonic, or starting note of the mode, to its place in the major scale. The interval pattern gives the same information, using T for the whole tone, one step up from the previous note, or "s" for semi-tone, or half-step up from the previous note.

Then when we look at the patterns of planets, we can see in System 2 we have the Chaldean order rising, as found in the Tree of Life, starting with Venus. In System 3, we have the order of the planetary days of the week. In System 1, there is no traditional pattern of astrology that I can recognize.

Due to the evolution of Gregorian chant and the division of modes beyond an octave, various modes have been extended from the traditional seven most musicians learn to include things like Hyperdorian, Hypolydian, and Hypophrygian. They also include an eighth called Hypomixolydian. Most occult correspondence traditions in the medieval era, including those of Agrippa, focus on the Gregorian chant modes of the time, while most Pagans today rather focus on the Greek. Interestingly enough, the work of Agrippa in *Three Books of Occult Philosophy* associates nine muses with the Gregorian modes of the time, as well as a verse to remember them. The traditional qualities are combinations of qualities from the musical theorists and composers Guido of Arezzo (995–1050), Adam of Fulda (1445–1505), and Juan de Espinosa Medrano (1632–1688).

Mode	System 1	System 2	System 3	Scale
Ionian	Sun	Venus	Sun	Standard Major
Dorian	Saturn	Sun	Moon	Minor with a Raised 7th
Phrygian	Venus	Mars	Mars	Minor with a lowered 2nd
Lydian	Mars	Jupiter	Mercury	Major with a raised 4th
Myxolydian	Jupiter	Saturn	Jupiter	Major with a lowered 7th
Aeolian	Moon	Moon	Venus	Natural Minor
Lorican	Mercury	Mercury	Saturn	Neither Major nor Minor

Mode	Notes	Interval Pattern	Qualities
Ionian	C D E F G A B	T-T-s-T-T-T-s	Clarity, Brightness, Happiness, Health, Friendship, Good Will
Dorian	D E F G A B C	T-s-T-T-T-s-T	Serious, Discipline, Tame Passions, Folkloric, Timelessness
Phrygian	E F G A B C D	s-T-T-T-s-T-T	Mystical, Passion, Jealousy, Can Incite Anger
Lydian	F G A B C D E	T-T-T-s-T-T-s	Happy, Energy, Bright Fiery, Will, Intention
Myxolydian	G A B C D E F	T-T-s-T-T-s-T	Angelic, Pleasure, Sadness, Ecstasy, Success
Aeolian	A B C D E F G	T-s-T-T-s-T-T	Sadness, Darkness, Calming, Soothing, Cooling, Feminine
Lorican	B C D E F G A	s-T-T-s-T-T-T	Tricksters, Invisibility, Dissonance, Spirit Summoning, Witchcraft

Chart 21: Modes and Magickal Correspondences

Mode	Planet	Muse	Note	Traditional Quality
Silence	Earth	Thalia	—	—
Hypodorian	Moon	Clio	E	Sad, Tearful
Hypophrygian	Mercury	Calliope	F	Tender, Tempting
Hypolydian	Venus	Terpsichore	G	Pious
Dorian	Sun	Melpomene	A	Serious, Happy
Phrygian	Mars	Erato	B	Vehement, Angry
Lydian	Jupiter	Euterpe	C	Happy
Mixolydian	Saturn	Polyhymnia	D	Angelical, Youthful
Hypomixolydian	Fixed Stars	Urania	—	Perfect, Very Happy, Knowledgeable

Chart 22: Modes and the Muses

"Silent Thalia we to th' Earth compare,
For She by music never doth ensnare;
After the Hypodorian Clio sings,
Persephone likewise doth strike the bass strings;
Calliope also doth chord second touch,
Using the Phrygian; Mercury as much:
Terpsichore strikes the third, and that rare,
The Lydian music makes so Venus fair.
Melpomene, and Titan do with a grace
The Dorian music use in the fourth place.
The fifth ascribed is to Mars the God
Of war, and Erato after the rare mode
Of th' Phrygians, Euterpe doth also love
The Lydian, and sixth string; and so doth Jove.
Saturn the seventh doth use with Polymny,
And causeth the Mixed Lydian melody.
Urania also doth the eighth create,
And music Hypo-Lydian elevate."

— from *Three Books of Occult Philosophy* by Henry Cornelius Agrippa

I'd suggest looking to these qualities, and even more importantly, playing them and seeing what qualities spring to your own magickal mind, choosing the system or creating the associations that work best for you.

If you want to relate the modes to the muses, take the muse-planet association on **Chart 22** and apply it to the mode-planet association that works best for you. Explore your awen, your magickal inspiration, using these tools of scale to help you and keep track of what results you have with specific systems for future use.

Magick of Meters

If tone is music in the range of vertical space, going up or down in pitch, meter is music in the range of time, moving horizontally through the seconds, minutes, and hours. Rhythm is the pattern of sound in metered time, determining how long or short a sound, or note, is played, while the tempo is the speed at which it is played. The rhythm combined with the pitch creates the melody, and the speed it is played can influence the mood and quality it evokes.

In Western music, we notate meter in ratios, while music is divided into measures (also known as bars). The fraction tells us how many beats are in a measure and what note value is given a beat within the measure. For example, a 3/4 time signature tells us there are three beats (top number 3) per measure, and a quarter note (bottom number 4 as 4 indicates a division of four, or quarters) gets a beat. 3/4 time is that of a traditional waltz. Most popular rock music is in 4/4 time signature, and different styles of music can place different emphasis on different beats. In 4/4 rock music, the emphasis is in the second and fourth beats, with the second beat stronger, while in classical 4/4 music, the emphasis is on the first beat, then the third beat.

Occult tradition associates a few common time signatures with the elements, as they evoke the "feel" of the elements to some practitioners. They can be helpful when both composing music and chants, as well as when creating drumbeats for shamanic journeys, basing the pattern of the beats on one of these time signatures.

Signature	Elemental	Qualities and Uses
4/4	Earth	Grounded, solid, general trance purposes
3/4	Air	Stimulating mind, memories, expression
6/8	Water	Emotional healing, flow, feeling
9/8	Fire	Energy, inspiration, creativity, power

Chart 23: Magickal Meters

Instruments

Lastly we have elemental associations with certain instrumentation. Many are simply common sense. Percussion and low notes have a natural dense, earth association. Woodwind instruments have air qualities. Use this list if you are seeking to really flow with musical and magickal composition.

Element	Instrumental Correspondences
Earth	Drums and percussion of all kinds, low-toned instruments such as the bass
Water	Strings (violin, cello, viola), harp
Air	Woodwinds, high-pitched instruments
Fire	Brass, electric guitar
Spirit	Keyboard instruments, harp, bells

Chart 24: Magickal Instrumentation

EXERCISE 15:
The Story of Your Life

You are the author of your own experience. You are the chronicler of your own tale. We often get immersed in our own story, and when done so consciously, we are master magicians writing our own biography and prophesying that which we wish to happen. Soon we enter the true flow of living awen and manifest through the tongue that cannot lie. When we are unconscious, we repeat unhealthy stories, creating patterns that disempower us. The narrative is seemingly out of our own hands, yet we are the one perpetuating it. The retelling of our own story of life can help us detach from it and stop identifying with it so strongly, as the Taliesin myth teaching us our origin is far beyond this life. Use your story as a tool, as an aid. What would your story sound like from someone else's point of view? That is another truth, but neither it nor your own version are the absolute truth.

Take some time first to observe and second to contemplate friends and family. Remember and listen to their story. Listen when they speak their story, even in day to day conversation when they don't realize it. How do they characterize themselves? Hero? Victim? Rarely a villain, though they can be the villain in someone else's story. Are they in an epic adventure, looking at all obstacles as grand tasks to be completed with honor and courage, or solved with wisdom and curiosity? Are they a repeating weekly sitcom, with no major change or evolution, but repetition of small crises? Are they in a tragedy, or in a romance with their sadness? Think of all the genres, too many to name here, and examine the themes. Their lives don't have to be restricted to one theme, and in certain phases of life, the story can change.

Now more importantly, and more challengingly, observe your own life. What is the story you are telling yourself? What is the theme? How do you frame your character? What roles do other people fill in your story? Does this story support your vision, your work in the world? Is your story filled with living awen? For most of us, the answer is no. But now you have perspective to change that story. How would you like to change it? Changing it doesn't change the events of your life. You are not rewriting reality, but you are reframing your experiences to a narrative that supports the living flow of awen.

For my own story, in my younger days growing up as a closeted gay man, raised Catholic and being told the story that I was wrong or sinful, on some level I decided to accept that story as true. I first was depressed about it. Then I tried to embrace it. But it went against my very nature. I tried to be mean. I tried to revel in not caring, and the typical teenage rebellions that lead into college followed. Many did lead me to wonderful things, forcing me to break out of expectations by abandoning the expected career trajectory of math and science for music. I tried to play the self-destructive, moody artist, unconsciously creating dramatic situations to fuel my music and art.

My first burst of awen, of awareness, came in my Witchcraft training, and the revelation that the philosophy of interconnection and interdependence on every level was not just a philosophy, a nice idea. Our thoughts, emotions, words, and actions reverberate as a song on the web of life, influencing ourselves and all others as we are in turn influenced by all. We have to maintain an inner strength and discipline to continue the good and helpful influence and not be pushed off our center by outer and often-hidden inner forces. I began to learn about the gods and myths and occult stories, and I started to see myself in those mythic terms instead of as a struggling and suffering artist. Suddenly, I could do anything, and had to choose wisely. My story changed, and for the better. My music career became part of the new story, the darkness before the light. Every part of my experience served my new story, but reframing it gave it different meaning for who I was and who I chose to be.

So what is your story? Do you wish to change it? Make a prophecy of your life and create it with the tongue that cannot lie. For this exercise, write a short work in the vein of a simple biographical sketch. It can be a story, a poem, or a song. For some, it might be more of a physical work of art like a painting or sculpture, or even a movement-based work, like a dance. Express your story. If contemplating music, you can work with the magickal correspondences of music above, or simply create, and then later look at the notes, sounds, and instruments you chose, to see some of the inherent magick in your intuitive choices. Make it the story you wish to live. Start with the flow of awen into your three cauldrons and create who you are meant to be.

Part Three: Mysteries of the Cauldron

Chapter Seven: The Adventures of the Child of Light

By the debt of the poison
A truthful man in a cage
Caught by a wicked king, all in a rage
Calls to a strange child sucking his thumb
Hapless bards gathered and all are struck dumb
Singing my songs and the truth is made
Fortunes raced, and dug, and all debts repaid
Journey now with the company of the head
When only seven returned from the quest
Through seven revolving gates of dread.

Most magickal practitioners tend to focus only on the initiation of Taliesin and forget he went on to do many things, and has a great body of lore associated with him beyond the first tale of Cerridwen. If we equate him as Merlin, or as a Merlin, or a member of an Order of Merlins, then he has even more tales recorded in myth, legend, folklore, and popular culture. Does he manifest in other Celtic heroes with magickal childhoods, like Lleu, Pryderi, and Mabon? Do we see him beyond the shores of the British Isles, as he himself has told us he has spanned, and look to the myths of Orpheus, Dionysus, Apollo, and Hermes? After our own initiatory adventures, do we see him in ourselves?

The point of being reborn as a child of light, of finding inspiration, is to then go do something with it. The great mystery of initiation is to actually begin, where so many today feel that initiation is the end, the reward at the end of a period of training and the validation from others. The graduating initiate is asked to go out into the world, and put this new magick to use. The initiate will be challenged in similar ways to the initiatory challenges, and must understand the secret key that the initiation never ends. The cycle continues, and our rites and rituals were to prepare us to live consciously through the initiations of life. The true difficulty is where one begins after this rebirth. We have answered the sacred questions: Who am I? What am I? Where am I? Now we must ask another: What do I now do?

Elphin ap Gwyddno Garanhir

Taliesin has a special relationship with Elphin, son of Gwyddno. But why? The waters of the sea, carrying Taliesin in the third darkness, bring him to Elphin. Water – the sea, the cosmic ocean, the abyss or the void – all are manifestations of the divine creatrix, another manifestation of the Goddess. They embody the will of fate in this moment, the guiding intelligence of the Goddess initiator in a more subtle form, on a global or cosmic scale. Where does the sea bring him for his final rebirth? To Elphin, son of Gwyddno Garanhir.

Taliesin, still as Gwion Bach, unintentionally wrongs Elphin's father, killing his horses by poisoning the stream with the remains of the cauldron brew that ended up in the waters. From that day forth, the stream was renamed "Poison of the Horses of Gwyddno" because the devastation was so great, and the source unknown to Gwyddno and the local populace.

While I've heard some versions of the tales blaming Elphin for the horses' death, having him take the horses to the stream, that is not in all versions of the tale. But it does emphasize that Elphin was considered almost supernaturally unlucky and worried his father greatly. Gwyddno had only one son, and Elphin is described as "hapless" and "needy." His father believed he was born in an "evil hour." His story is that nothing goes right for him.

As a lord of his own castle, Gwyddno Garanhir had a weir on the strand between Dyvi and Aberystwyth. Traditionally the value of one hundred "pounds" was drawn from the weir – most obviously fish, and quite possibly salmon – on May Eve. Gwyddno's wise advisors told him to send Elphin for the May Eve drawing to reverse his luck and give him his start in the world.

Initially, there were no fish in the weir. One of the weir-ward aides believed Elphin destroyed the virtue of the weir, yielding only a leather skin, having no idea the treasure of the child of Taliesin resided inside. The first act of poetry from the reborn Taliesin is to recite a consolation to Elphin, to urge him to cease his sadness, remind him he has notable qualities, and to promise to protect him and turn his fortunes around by being of "more service to thee than three hundred salmon":

Fair Elphin, cease to lament!
Let no one be dissatisfied with his own,
To despair will bring no advantage.
No man sees what supports him;
The prayer of Cynllo will not be in vain;
God will not violate his promise.
Never in Gwyddno's weir
Was there such good luck as this night.
Fair Elphin, dry thy cheeks!
Being too sad will not avail.
Although thou thinkest thou hast no gain,
Too much grief will bring thee no good;
Nor doubt the miracles of the Almighty:
Although I am but little, I am highly gifted.
From seas, and from mountains,
And from the depths of rivers,
God brings wealth to the fortunate man.
Elphin of lively qualities,
Thy resolution is unmanly;
Thou must not be over sorrowful:
Better to trust in God than to forbode ill.
Weak and small as I am,
On the foaming beach of the ocean,
In the day of trouble I shall be
Of more service to thee than three hundred salmon.

Elphin of notable qualities,
Be not displeased at thy misfortune;
Although reclined thus weak in my bag,
There lies a virtue in my tongue.
While I continue thy protector
Thou hast not much to fear;
Remembering the names of the Trinity,
None shall be able to harm thee.
— from "Taliesin" in *The Mabinogion*

Why does he offer his service to Elphin? From the perspective of the initiate, there are many reasons. Rebirth does not wipe the slate clean as many believe. Most people upon rebirth lose their memory of their previous life, but not Taliesin. Not only does he remember Gwion Bach and the "court of Caridwen" where he has "done penance" but his memory becomes cosmic. One could say as an initiate, he remembers everything there is to remember about the nature of the soul and the history of the world. So from this view of events, he must also know of the death of the horses of Gwyddno.

The horse is a sign of British sovereignty, and in the Celtic traditions, a totem of many different goddesses embodying sovereignty. We have the goddesses Epona, Rhiannon, and Macha all relating to the horse, the land and kingship by right of the goddess queen. Seasonal plays in England and Wales have the horse-skull hobby horse procession, with the May Day "Obby Hoss" and the spectral Mari Lwyd poetry challenge in the Yuletide season in Wales.

The death of a lord's horses is a form of sacrifice and indicates something in relationship with the sovereign and the land. To sacrifice doesn't simply mean to kill, but to make sacred. Yet the horses were not killed by intention and reverence. They were killed through unintended consequence. Did the deaths of the horses serve a higher purpose in this greater initiation? Possibly. We will soon learn all was not right with the king of this land. King Maelgwn, brother to Gwyddno and uncle to Elphin, later became a focus for young Taliesin.

Taliesin was responsible for the death of the horses even though it was not his intention. Even though his life was reborn from that of Gwion Bach, he knows as a mystic that initiation leads to opportunities to redress past wrongs in new ways, to rebalance and redeem, to be free once the balance is restored. The "karma" so to speak is balanced, and the initiate can move more into the consciousness of "what must be done," known today as the right action, or dharma, or the True Will of the modern magician.

And lastly, even if Taliesin reborn is not responsible to Elphin or Gwyddno in any way, the initiate knows you work with whoever and whatever shows up. To be in this cosmic consciousness means a certain level of metaphoric – and in the case of the sea, literal – "going with the flow" and examination of what life brings to you. A good friend of mine, Christopher Giroux, often reminds initiates and ministers in the community, "It might not be your fault, but it is your responsibility," referring to the wisdom of Granny Weatherwax, a character from the *Discworld* novels of Sir Terry Pratchett. While you might not have intentionally caused something, or you might be one link in a larger chain where the cause did not originate with you, if you have the awareness that you can heal, resolve, or restore a situation, then it becomes your responsibility to do so.

Taliesin is raised by Elphin, and his wife and Elphin's fortune and riches continued to grow, either by the very presence of the child or more likely through listening to his counsel. In Taliesin's thirteenth year, Elphin and Gwyddno are invited to Christmastide in the court of their relative, King Maelgwn.

There in the court, the praises of King Maelgwn are sung by all, declaring him the greatest king of the world, and his wife the queen having the most virtue and his bards being the most skillful. When it comes Elphin's turn, he does not diminish the king, but boasts of his own virtuous wife and his own bard – Taliesin. For this trespass, Maelgwn imprisons Elphin in the tower and sends his own son Rhun to "enquire" about the virtues of Elphin's wife, seeking her ruin.

Taliesin warns his "mistress" or adopted mother about Elphin's imprisonment and Rhun's approach, and urges her to disguise a serving girl as herself. She does, dressing her up and placing her rings upon the poor girl. It appears that Rhun "disgraced" the serving girl, thinking her the lady of the castle, seemingly drugging her drink and cutting off her finger bearing the signet of Elphin, to return to Maelgwn.

Maelgwn brings Elphin down from the tower to show him the finger and ring and "prove" his wife's virtue is false. Elphin examines the finger and declares that it was not his wife for three reasons – due to the size of the finger, the state of the nail, and the roughness from kneading dough. For these reasons he declares it is not his wife's finger. Maelgwn sends up to the tower again, declaring he will remain unless he can prove his second boast about his bard. Taliesin tells Elphin's wife that he will free her husband, his master. When she asks how, Taliesin speaks this poem:

A journey will I perform,
And to the gate I will come;
The hall I will enter,
And my song I will sing;

*My speech I will pronounce
To silence royal bards,
In presence of their chief,
I will greet to deride,
Upon them I will break
And Elphin I will free.
Should contention arise,
In presence of the prince,
With summons to the bards,
For the sweet flowing song,
And wizards' posing lore
And wisdom of Druids,
In the court of the sons of the distributor
Some are who did appear
Intent on wily schemes,
By craft and tricking means,
In pangs of affliction
To wrong the innocent,
Let the fools be silent,
As erst in Badon's fight,
With Arthur of liberal ones
The head, with long red blades;
Through feats of testy men,
And a chief with his foes.
Woe be to them, the fools,
When revenge comes on them.
I Taliesin, chief of bards,
With a sapient Druid's words,
Will set kind Elphin free
From haughty tyrant's bonds.
To their fell and chilling cry,
By the act of a surprising steed,
From the far distant North,
There soon shall be an end.
Let neither grace nor health
Be to Maelgwn Gwynedd,
For this force and this wrong;
And be extremes of ills
And an avenged end
To Rhun and all his race:*

Short be his course of life,
Be all his lands laid waste;
And long exile be assigned
To Maelgwn Gwynedd!
   — from "Taliesin" in *The Mabinogion*

Taliesin makes his way to the castle and finds himself in a place in a quiet corner, casting a spell upon the bards with only his finger, lips, and two "words": "Blerwm, blerwm." No one really notices the strange child. When it comes time for the bards to sing the praises of the king, they are struck dumb, only saying, "Blerwm, blerwm" when attempting to speak. The chief bard, Heinin Vardd, is able to speak only after being struck on the head with a broom, and he then blames the child in the corner, who is brought to the king and revealed as Taliesin.

Taliesin goes on, unmatched by any of the king's bards, to chastise them and prophesy their destruction. He prophesies about a creature from before the flood. Soon Taliesin summons a storm that blows open the doors of the castle. Fearing the castle will fall upon them, the king quickly frees Elphin and brings him before Taliesin, and with a magickal verse, Taliesin unfastens the silver chains binding Elphin.

I adore the Supreme, Lord of all animation,
Him that supports the heavens, Ruler of every extreme,
Him that made the water good for all,
Him who has bestowed each gift, and blesses it;
May abundance of mead be given Maelgwn of Anglesey, who supplies us,
From his foaming mead horns, with the choicest pure liquor.
Since bees collect, and do not enjoy,
We have sparkling distilled mead, which is universally praised.
The multitude of creatures which the earth nourishes
God made for man, with a view to enrich him;
Some are violent, some are mute, he enjoys them,
Some are wild, some are tame; the Lord makes them;
Part of their produce becomes clothing;
For food and beverage till doom will they continue.
I entreat the Supreme, Sovereign of the region of peace,
To liberate Elphin from banishment,
The man who gave me wine, and ale, and mead,
With large princely steeds, of beautiful appearance;
May he yet give me; and at the end,
May God of his good will grant me, in honour,

A succession of numberless ages, in the retreat of tranquillity.
Elphin, knight of mead, late be thy dissolution!
— from "Taliesin" in *The Mabinogion*

In this verse, he looks to the supreme god as a giver of gifts – mead, food, beverage, and clothing – and then compares Elphin, as the one who gave Taliesin wine, ale, and mead, to the supreme, entreating the supreme to liberate Elphin.

His song ends with several parts known in the tales as "The Excellence of the Bards," "The Reproof of the Bards," and "The Spite of the Bards." He then shows Elphin's wife – with all her fingers – to the court, declaring her virtue.

Taliesin goes on to urge Elphin to bet the king that Elphin has a horse that is better and can beat the king's best horse in a race. And Elphin does. They set a time, place, and course. The race is held at a place known as Morva Rhiannedd. The king brings twenty-four horses, and Elphin just one with a rider. Taliesin gives the rider twenty-four twigs of burnt holly to place in his belt. He instructs the rider to overcome each of the horses and strike the horse with one twig, which will cause it to fall. Once he has overcome all twenty-four of the king's horses, his own horse will stumble, and his hat should be thrown where the horse stumbles. The rider overcomes all of the king's horses, doing as instructed with the holly twigs, and finally throwing his cap where his own horse stumbles, winning the race.

Taliesin then take Elphin to the cap upon the ground and bids men to dig in that spot. Soon they find a large cauldron, and within the buried cauldron is gold. Taliesin declares it is thanks to Elphin for pulling him out of the weir thirteen years ago and raising him as his own. A pool of water is formed in the hole dug to retrieve the cauldron, and this pool is now called Pwllbair.

Strangely, after all of this, the king, assumed to be King Maelgwn, calls for Taliesin and asks him about the creation of man. Taliesin answers with a poem: "One of the Four Pillars of Song." He goes on to prophesize to the king of things that should be in the world. And there ends this version of the Tale of Taliesin.

It should seem strange to later serve the king who appeared to be his enemy. Why would Taliesin do that? One could say on a terrestrial level, he had no choice. The king is still the king, despite freeing his prisoner and losing a race. Yet this all proved that the king had no power over Taliesin, and in truth, Taliesin had power over the king. But it wasn't personal power. Taliesin didn't install Elphin, or his father Gwyddno, as king, even though they were both of royal blood. While he graciously "repaid" Elphin, it wasn't personal.

Throughout his poetry there is an identification that goes beyond the personal. The supreme god, identified as "'renovator," "Supreme, Lord of all animation," "Ruler of every extreme," and "Supreme, Sovereign of the region of peace" is referenced, and despite much of the Christian overlay of form and terminology, speaks of something sublime and mystical. Taliesin speaks of the whole world, the stars and heavens, and identifies himself not with one kingdom, but as "Chief of the bards of the west." When all is done and his debts are repaid, he works with who is before him – in this case, Maelgwn – to advise, inform, and answer his questions. This starts a long line of his work for the sovereigns of the land. While the role of the true bards of his caliber is to speak necessary truth to power, like the fool and the child, his role is to also serve the sovereign as an embodiment of the sovereignty of the land.

When one looks at his act of magick to repay Elphin, one may ask if it too, like the death of the first horses, serves a higher purpose in furthering the rebalance and restoration of the land. It's unclear if the burnt holly twigs simply gave the horses a "blow" so he could overcome them to win the race, and they were not truly harmed. Or in a version the horses could not "pass" the holly twig that was cast down upon the ground, creating a form of magickal barrier, allowing Elphin's slower, weaker horse to win. The rider was specifically instructed to strike them "over the crupper, and then let that twig fall." The crupper is part of the tack gear to prevent the saddle from riding up upon the horse. Perhaps the magick simply unfastened the saddle and left the horse riderless, though it doesn't specify. Many take the image of the burnt twig to have somewhat sinister connotations, and believe the "blow" implies the horse was harmed or killed. Holly is associated with power and the withering wintertide, with red berries and sharp leaves. Today's magicians associate it as a tree of Mars, and in healing, a remedy that induces and heals anger.

In any case, horses alive or horses dead, there is again a mystery of the horse as Goddess, as the land, and as Sovereignty by whose grace the king rules. We might hope and believe that something then shifted in King Maelgwn. Humbled, he could possibly rule more justly and seek better counsel than those who would lavish praise with no critique. In the repayment of Elphin, we can see the possible restoration of sovereignty to the land, all unfolding in what appears to be unrelated – or at the very least unintended – consequences. Through this work, Taliesin is serving a higher purpose in the renewal and restoration of the kingdom and land, practice on a small scale for the greater tasks to come.

Before we look beyond to these greater tasks, we should examine the poems in this tale. When seeking direct knowledge, receiving answers that seem personal, but which are truly beyond the personal sphere, indicates you have learned many skills.

Through the three darkness trainings are three areas in which to seek answers:

First Darkness	Repetitive Actions	Inhibitory Trance Stirring, Swaying Mantra, Mudra Chanting "ah-ou-en" Ogham Hand Positions Herbal Sacraments Lower Cauldron Energy Work
Second Darkness	Shamanic Journey	Exhibitory Trance Drumming, Ecstatic Body Posture Offerings, Minerals & Homeopathics Shape-shifting Awakening the Heart Middle Cauldron Energy Work
Third Darkness	Dream Visions	Inhibitory/Exhibitory Dreaming, Sound, Music Storytelling, Inner Listening Aligning with the Flow of Awen Upper Cauldron Energy Work

Chart 25: Magickal Techniques of the Three Darknesses

These techniques can be used separately or in various combinations as you see fit.

The Excellence of the Bards

What was the first man
Made by the God of heaven;
What the fairest flattering speech
That was prepared by Ieuav;
What meat, what drink,
What roof his shelter;
What the first impression
Of his primary thinking;
What became his clothing;
Who carried on a disguise,
Owing to the wilds of the country,
In the beginning?
Wherefore should a stone be hard;

Why should a thorn be sharp-pointed?
Who is hard like a flint;
Who is salt like brine;
Who sweet like honey;
Who rides on the gale;
Why ridged should be the nose;
Why should a wheel be round;
Why should the tongue be gifted with speech
Rather than another member?
If thy bards, Heinin, be competent,
Let them reply to me, Taliesin.
 — from "Taliesin" in *The Mabinogion*

"The Excellence of the Bards" is a poetic challenge to Heinin and the bards of Maelgwn's court to answer these "big" questions to prove their excellence as bards. He asks them about the first man made by God in the beginning, asking things that would not be answered in their Biblical creation myths. He goes on to ask the reasons for the nature of things, such as the hardness of stone and the sharpness of thorns. While these are the questions no one but the bard, the magician, or the mystic would seek an answer to, the seeking and finding beyond the personal consciousness is the realm of true excellence.

Exercise 16:
Seeking Your Excellence

Take out your journal and write down five questions that have no obvious answer. These questions should be in the same poetic vein as those above, like the nature of "Why is water wet?" or "Who is like clouds?" Notice none of the questions are looking for a scientific "how" to explain the mechanics of the world, but instead each ponders the poetic "why" it should exist in that form, the implication being why should it exist at all given all the possibilities of the universe.

Once you have questions established, seek the poetic answer to these questions through any of the techniques from the three darknesses. You can seek the answers to all five questions at once or in five separate sessions, one for each of your questions, varying the techniques to find what is most effective for you.

Creatively express your answers through poetry, song, story, art, craft, or dance. You can ask a trusted mentor to give five questions instead of creating them yourself.

The Reproof of the Bards

If thou art a bard completely imbued
With genius not to be controlled,
Be thou not untractable
Within the court of thy king;
Until thy rigmarole shall be known,
Be thou silent, Heinin,
As to the name of thy verse,
And the name of thy vaunting;
And as to the name of thy grandsire
Prior to his being baptized.
And the name of the sphere,
And the name of the element,
And the name of thy language,
And the name of thy region.
Avaunt, ye bards above,
Avaunt, ye bards below!
My beloved is below,
In the fetter of Arianrod
It is certain you know not
How to understand the song I utter,
Nor clearly how to discriminate
Between the truth and what is false;
Puny bards, crows of the district,
Why do you not take to flight?
A bard that will not silence me,
Silence may he not obtain,
Till he goes to be covered
Under gravel and pebbles;
Such as shall listen to me,
May God listen to him.
  — from "Taliesin" in *The Mabinogion*

"The Reproof of Bards" is a chastisement of the bards of the court. Young Taliesin goes on to describe a bard as imbued with genius and not to be controlled, and then essentially says they are not bards due to their behavior and lack of understanding. They cannot tell what is true and what is false, so they cannot silence Taliesin.

A difficult part of our spiritual path is to offer impersonal rebuke when another is not living up to the role of their office or their claimed duties. The classic role of the bard or wizardly advisor is to tell the king when a mistake is being made, to speak truth to power, or in the case of Taliesin here, to call out injustice and demand justice. Later this role falls to the jester of the court, who can speak freely without fear of recrimination, or the prerogative of the child or the fool to tell the emperor he has no clothes.

First and foremost, we must address our own wrongs and failures and continue to do so through an active practice of introspection. Then we must apply our vision to the world, to speak when words need to be spoken and to take action when action needs to be taken.

It's important to understand that this is not rooted in the personal. Any anger over injustice is a righteous anger on behalf of the all, not the one. It's not about addressing personal slights and insults. While it is important to do that too, for your own personal healing and balance, the reproof of a bard is from the perspective of the greater good, without attachment or reward.

Exercise 17:
Speaking Reproof

Examining your life and what is before you – the state of your community, country, and world – are there any issues that need voice? Certainly there are. What are inspired beyond the personal day-to-day, requiring a greater voice of a bard?

Even if the issue is unclear, use any combination of techniques from the three darknesses to seek an expression to that voice, just as you did for **Seeking Your Excellence** in **Exercise 16**. When you have found an expression of your voice for this issue or situation, express yourself. Share it through words, song, or other artistic or political medium. Don't be attached to an outcome, but do as you feel guided in the flow of awen. The very act of putting it out there for others is an act of magick that can bring change, even if the change is not clear to you. One pebble can inspire the landslide of change in a situation, having others respond to your work.

The Spite of the Bards

Minstrels persevere in their false custom,
Immoral ditties are their delight;
Vain and tasteless praise they recite;
Falsehood at all times do they utter;
The innocent persons they ridicule;
Married women they destroy,

Innocent virgins of Mary they corrupt;
As they pass their lives away in vanity,
Poor innocent persons they ridicule;
At night they get drunk, they sleep the day;
In idleness without work they feed themselves;
The Church they hate, and the tavern they frequent;
With thieves and perjured fellows they associate;
At courts they inquire after feasts;
Every senseless word they bring forward;
Every deadly sin they praise;
Every vile course of life they lead;
Through every village, town, and country they stroll;
Concerning the gripe of death they think not;
Neither lodging nor charity do they give;
Indulging in victuals to excess.
Psalms or prayers they do not use,
Tithes or offerings to God they do not pay,
On holidays or Sundays they do not worship;
Vigils or festivals they do not heed.
The birds do fly, the fish do swim,
The bees collect honey, worms do crawl,
Every thing travails to obtain its food,
Except minstrels and lazy useless thieves.
I deride neither song nor minstrelsy,
For they are given by God to lighten thought;
But him who abuses them,
For blaspheming Jesus and his service.
— from "Taliesin" in *The Mabinogion*

While quite immersed in Christian symbolism and culture, the sentiment expressed in "The Spite of the Bards" is beyond reproof to outright condemnation of those who embody falsehood, vanity, laziness, greed, and immorality, causing harm to the innocent. In short, it is spite for the corrupt.

Humans tend to either believe they are entirely beyond reproach and blameless with undeserved self-esteem or have a poor enough self-image to be extremely hard on themselves and all actions. The truth is somewhere between, and it can take the process of rebirth, of initiation, to see the truth.

Rather than starting by looking to vent your spite upon others who might deserve a strong rebuke, it can be best to start at home with yourself. This entire part of the tale of Taliesin is about taking responsibility for past actions, even if harm inflicted on others, or harm inflicted on oneself, was not the intention. So let's look to take self-responsibility.

Exercise 18:
Resolving Spite

While it's easy, or at least easier, to seek our own excellence and reprove others, it can be quite a bit harder to look at times when we have been false, vain, lazy, greedy, and immoral, even if that was not our goal. It is hard to look at when we cause harm, even when not intended.

Journal on past harms you have caused others, looking for three specific points to focus upon:

- The first, a time when you have harmed another, intentionally or otherwise.
- For the second, a time when you have harmed yourself.
- And the third, a time when your actions have harmed a group or community.

Can you reflect upon each one and see the reality of the situation, rather than an emotionally charged memory? Entering into the awen, to the consciousness that comes from the cauldron that animates a Taliesin, one can see from above, not impersonally, but transpersonally, in the context of your entire life.

Again, using the techniques of the three darknesses, seek out healing and resolution for the three experiences. The answer might be found in metaphysical technique or in outer work. Your guidance from the cauldron might tell you to seek out those you have wronged and apologize, and you should only do that if such an apology won't cause more harm and distress to the recipient. The inspiration of the cauldron consciousness might tell you to perform a specific ritual, make an offering, receive a type of healing, or otherwise move the energy. While the vision itself might resolve what is held, the most profound usually have some real world action you will be responsible to do. Cerridwen, Taliesin, and the spirits cannot do it all for you, with no effort on your part.

One of the Four Pillars of Song

The Almighty made,
Down the Hebron vale,
With his plastic hands,
   Adam's fair form:

And five hundred years,
Void of any help,
There he remained and lay
   Without a soul.

He again did form,
In calm paradise,
From a left-side rib,
   Bliss-throbbing Eve.

Seven hours they were
The orchard keeping,
Till Satan brought strife,
   With wiles from hell.

Thence were they driven,
Cold and shivering,
To gain their living,
   Into this world.

To bring forth with pain
Their sons and daughters,
To have possession
   Of Asia's land.

Twice five, ten and eight,
She was self-bearing,
The mixed burden
   Of man-woman.

And once, not hidden,
She brought forth Abel,
And Cain the forlorn,
   The homicide.

*To him and his mate
Was given a spade,
To break up the soil,
   Thus to get bread.*

*The wheat pure and white,
Summer tilth to sow,
Every man to feed,
   Till great yule feast.*

*An angelic hand
From the high Father,
Brought seed for growing
   That Eve might sow;*

*But she then did hide
Of the gift a tenth,
And all did not sow
   Of what was dug.*

*Black rye then was found,
And not pure wheat grain,
To show the mischief
   Thus of thieving.*

*For this thievish act,
It is requisite,
That all men should pay
   Tithe unto God.*

*Of the ruddy wine,
Planted on sunny days,
And on new-moon nights;
   And the white wine.*

*The wheat rich in grain
And red flowing wine
Christ's pure body make,
   Son of Alpha.*

The wafer is flesh,
The wine is spilt blood,
The Trinity's words
  Sanctify them.

The concealed books
From Emmanuel's hand
Were brought by Raphael
  As Adam's gift,

When in his old age,
To his chin immersed
In Jordan's water,
  Keeping a fast,

Moses did obtain
In Jordan's water,
The aid of the three
  Most special rods.

Solomon did obtain
In Babel's tower,
All the sciences
  In Asia land.

So did I obtain,
In my bardic books,
All the sciences
  Of Europe and Africa.

Their course, their bearing,
Their permitted way,
And their fate I know,
  Unto the end.

Oh! what misery,
Through extreme of woe,
Prophecy will show
  On Troia's race!

A coiling serpent
Proud and merciless,
On her golden wings,
  From Germany.

She will overrun
England and Scotland,
From Lychlyn sea-shore
  To the Severn.

Then will the Brython
Be as prisoners,
By strangers swayed,
  From Saxony.

Their Lord they will praise,
Their speech they will keep,
Their land they will lose,
  Except wild Walia.

Till some change shall come,
After long penance,
When equally rife
  The two crimes come.

Britons then shall have
Their land and their crown,
And the stranger swarm
  Shall disappear.

All the angel's words,
As to peace and war,
Will be fulfilled
  To Britain's race.

— from "Taliesin" in *The Mabinogion*

The poem entitled "One of the Four Pillars of Song" is Taliesin's answer to the King about the creation of man. It is one of those big mystery questions, even beyond the questions in seeking excellence. The big questions are not just personal, stemming from a place of self, or idle curiosity on how the world works. The big questions are collective: Who are we? Why are we here? Where did we come from? What are we doing? Why? What's next? It is the purpose of the bard to seek and reveal an answer to the question, knowing every answer is just a single perspective, and that there are as many answers as there are bards and magicians. And there is a bard or magician in each and every one of us. But when one connects to the flow of awen, to the cosmic consciousness of the cauldron that is at the beginning and at the end of all things, there is an underlying unity and wisdom to the answers of a true bard in the flow. The difference is in the poetic expression.

Exercise 19:
Seeking A Pillar

This task is incredibly simple and incredibly complex all at the same time. Ask yourself a big question that needs answering. Using any of the techniques learned thus far, seek your answer to this question. Encode the answer upon your creative expression, your own work of art. Share it as you see fit, but don't think your answer will be everyone's answer to the big question. Hopefully your answer will help inspire their own.

The Company of Bran

Where does Taliesin go after his coming of age with Elphin? Based on his poetry, one could answer "anywhere he wants!" I would also say "any when he wants" as well, as I don't think we can follow the adventures of the mythic poet in any chronological order. There might be mortal men named Taliesin in history we can track down, but the spirit of Taliesin is not bound by time and space, and in many ways, the Goddess of the Cauldron is asking you to unbind yourself from your linear notion of self and the world.

If you attempt to follow Taliesin linearly, you will find the fallacies in such a path and open yourself to the paradox of the mysteries, that contradictory things can be simultaneously true on a higher plane of consciousness. But the frustration and madness in the attempt can help fuel our quest, so let us try to look at Taliesin linearly.

The Hanes Taliesin as translated by Lady Guest has a lot of Christian elements to his dialogue. Much of his poetry references Old and New Testament events and images. Despite the wondrous magick of potions and shapeshifting harkening back to a potentially pre-Christian Pagan time in Wales, the "birth" of Taliesin appears to be firmly in the Christian era if we are to date it historically. We know it generally corresponds with the fragments found in *The Book of Taliesin*, and that all of these manuscripts were historically written in the Christian era, so their scribes could have adapted and added to older folk tales. And they most likely did over a long period of time, both through the oral tradition and what was written. Yet, they did see the spirit of Taliesin firmly planted in this Christian era.

In one simple line, Taliesin is included in the story known as the Second Branch of *The Mabinogi*:

"Branwen the Daughter of Llyr." In a very complex story with both mythic and possible historic connotations, Taliesin is named as one of the seven escaping survivors from the great battle in this tale. Notable companions in his escape are Pryderi and Manawyddan, each with their own mythic tales:

"In consequence of that the men of the Island of the Mighty obtained such success as they had; but they were not victorious, for only seven men of them all escaped, and Bendigeid Bran himself was wounded in the foot with a poisoned dart. Now the seven men that escaped were Pryderi, Manawyddan, Gluneu Eil Taran, Taliesin, Ynawc, Grudyen the son of Muryel, and Heilyn the son of Gwynn Hen."

— "Branwen the Daughter of Llyr" from *The Mabinogion*

Is this the same Taliesin? We have no reason to think otherwise. It doesn't appear that Taliesin is a common name like John or Mike today, but a name of particular distinction. Yet does this Taliesin predate the one found in the birth story we have been carefully exploring? Since the stories are not given in a clear chronology, beyond the ordering of the four Branches of *The Mabinogion* in sequence where Taliesin is not a primary character of the four branches, it's unclear.

The translation is missing the obvious Christian references found in Taliesin's story, indicating an older version, if not an older tale itself. While framing itself as history, the central focus of the tale is of course around Branwen, but also Bran's magick cauldron. Another major clue is found in the stature of the characters, particularly Bran.

While it is never stated explicitly that he is a giant, Bran is described as a giant. How? When he crosses the waters between Wales and Ireland to rescue Branwen and punish King Matholwch, he does so by carrying the provisions on his back and wading across the waters with his ships, for no ship can contain him. Matholwch's men think they have spotted a floating forest with trees and a mountain on the sea when there was not one before, but Lady Branwen informs them that what they are seeing is the ships of her kingdom and her giant brother. The ridge they see with two lakes to either side is his nose and two eyes.

Giants appear throughout these tales, indicating some elder power, a titanic force predating humanity, involving what occultists would call the gods before the gods. Remember the story around the cauldron of Bran, the cauldron named Pair Dadeni. In the teachings here, I have associated it with the element of water and rebirth, for it is a cauldron of resurrection. Bran tells Matholwch he obtained the cauldron from two giants named Llassar Llaesgyvnewid and Kymideu Kymeinvoll. They came to Wales from Ireland. Is Kymideu Cerridwen? Or some form of the Goddess of the Cauldron? Is Llassar Tegid Voel? In the tale of Taliesin and Cerridwen, while Tegid is named a giant, Cerridwen is not explicitly called a giant, but she can probably change her size and shape in human form as much as she could as an animal. She is also never called a goddess, yet today we see her as such. Likewise, in the tale of Branwen and Bran, Bran is considered a giant, but Branwen is not depicted as so, but they are both siblings from the same father, another primal god, Llyr, who is the sea itself. Giants among human-sized beings depicts a transition from the elder times to the more modern times, a time when the gods and humanity walked together upon the Earth, and all things were possible.

While the tale is named for Branwen – and she is key to the story – in many ways this branch is just as much, if not more, about the mystery of Bran. Who is Bran? What is going on? And how does Taliesin fit into this?

While we think of Wales and England as separate parts of the greater United Kingdom, it's important when looking at this time period, even in its mythology, to think of Bran the Blessed, the King of Wales, as the sovereign of the entire landmass. There were no English as we know them today. The Welsh are the native Celtic people of lower Britain, with the Scottish to the north. Historically, the area was filled with related but diverse Celtic tribes and people. Mythically, this speaks of a time when they were one, when later stories, such as the tales of King Arthur, speak more to their fragmentation in our historic understanding.

Bran is the giant king, the sovereign of the land. Branwen, though his sister, is the embodiment of the goddess of the land, the bestower of sovereignty. To make an alliance with Ireland, she is betrothed to Matholwch. She freely goes, in contrast to the frequent kidnappings of Queen Guinevere by other kings, human or faery, seeking rulership.

Remember the root of the problem actually came from Branwen and Bran's cousin Efnysien, who insulted Matholwch and led to the grudge and mistreatment of Branwen. Branwen sent for her brother, and he came to her rescue with "sevenscore and four countries" with him. And in the final battle, it was Efnysien who destroyed the cauldron from within, killing himself in the process by bursting his heart. The living were not meant to go into the Cauldron of Regeneration. They had to enter the gates of death first.

At the end of the war with the destruction of the cauldron, Bran is struck in the foot with a poison dart, reminiscent of the stories of Chiron, an immortal who would not die but who would possibly remain in pain due to poison or who could not travel due to the foot injury. Bran strangely requests, while still alive, that the seven survivors, including Taliesin, cut off his head. It will remain "pleasant" and uncorrupted while they travel, acting as good company for the men. They are instructed to bring it to the White Mount in London, where the Tower of London is today, and bury it facing east towards Europe. It will act as a talisman of protection and guardianship for Britain. He goes to tell them they will travel quite a long time, finding a hall where they will be distracted by a wondrous feast, sealed away from the world by the song from the Birds of Rhiannon. Once the doors to this realm are opened – including a door to Aber Henvelen leading towards Cornwall – they will have to continue their journey to London.

Branwen was initially the eighth survivor but did not last long on the trip. When returning to Wales, the Island of the Mighty, she dies of a broken heart and is buried upon the banks of the Alaw in Anglesey in north Wales. The seven continue their journey. Her power is returned to Wales.

As the seven journey with the head, they encounter many other people upon the road, asking them about the news of the land. A new king named Caswallawn, Son of Beli, has risen up by overthrowing Caradawc, son of Bran, who was left in charge of the seven princes when Bran left for Ireland. Using the magick of the Veil of Illusion, Caswallawn killed the seven, and Caradawc could only see the sword slaying them but not Caswallawn as the perpetrator. Caradawc died from a broken heart as well.

In Harlech, the seven and the head stop to eat, drink, and rest. They are joined by the Birds of Rhiannon, seemingly both present and far away across the sea simultaneously. Their pleasant song entrances the men for seven years. They find a hall overlooking the ocean and continue their feast there. Two doors of the hall are open, but the third, looking towards Cornwall, is closed. Manawyddan recognizes it as the door they must not open.

Their days and nights are filled with regaling and feasting, filled with joy and having no understanding of the passing of time. Bran is with them as a head, just as he would have been full-bodied. They are not stricken with grief or pain. They all remain another fourscore (four times twenty, or eighty) years. This time is known as the "Entertaining of the Noble Head" in contrast to the time before as the "Entertaining of Branwen and Matholwch." The seven are known as the Assembly of the Wondrous Head or the Company of the Wondrous Head.

Heilyn is the one to open the third door to see if it were true, what was said about it. And he opens the door and it looks to Cornwall and Aber Henvelen, and he learns the prophecy is true. The spell is broken, and their joy is broken. The misery, loss, and suffering are returned to them. The weight of grief from the loss of their lord Bran, and of his sister Branwen, is upon them. They cannot return to feasting, drinking, and mirth, so they journey onward. They complete their quest, burying the head of Bran, and as long as the head is buried and concealed, no true invasion ever comes from the east. In Ireland, five pregnant women survive and give birth to five sons, leading to the five divisions of Ireland we know today.

What are the teachings hidden in the second branch? On one level, it is the continued tale of sovereignty told by the Celtic people, involving the mysteries of the land, the goddess, and the people. The blow struck by Matholwch to Branwen is described in the triads as the "third unhappy blow" to this island and bringing great grief.

The cauldron mystery brings life from death, the rebirth of the flesh in the story of the soldiers, but pointing to the rebirth of consciousness for the initiate. Yet the cauldron of rebirth was not available to Bran. With its destruction and the death of the elder blessed titian Bran, a new age dawns. Bran as king is compared to the later Arthur, where one is truly divine and the other is very human. Each are the stewards of their own age, and it is Arthur who is blamed for letting invaders into Britain by digging up the head of Bran in a fit of ego, not wanting to share credit or responsibility for protecting the country with a dead god-king. From there the invasions from the east increase if the myths are to be believed, leading to the Romans and the Saxons. We will look further into the resurrection myth in Chapter Nine, comparing Bran's cauldron with the depictions of the Gundestrup Cauldron and the Arthurian connection to the grail in Chapter Eight.

Remaining then, is a profound mystery in the Assembly of the Wondrous Head. Here we have the motif of a severed head, predicting what will happen on the journey, and how it should be used talismanically. There is resonance with other severed head myths, including those previously mentioned of Orpheus and John the Baptist.

The concept of the severed head plays into cultic practices. The Celts were considered famous for head hunting. Severed heads on the battlefields in Ireland were known as Macha's acorns, for an aspect of the triple Morrighan, goddess of war and queen of sovereignty. Illuminated Druids and bards would have "Fire in the Head " to indicate a magickal state of inspiration. We can find head "ball" games among the ancient Mayan. The ancient site of Göbekli Tepe shows headless carvings and evidence of a "skull cult," and we even have the Catholic skull relics of Saint Catherine of Siena and St. Oliver Plunkett. There is something magickally illuminating about the imagery of skulls and heads, with their obvious connection to knowledge, wisdom, and the inspiration of awen.

In British seasonal lore and village dances and plays, we have images of the sword dance and beheading games. Men would dance with swords around the neck of a poor "old king" forming a "knot" in the shape of the pentagram or hexagram. Do they speak of older myths, to the roots of the Christmas "game" of the Green Knight, found in the myth of Sir Gawain and the Green Knight? Once Gawain lops off the Green Knight's head, the Knight simply picks up his own head and continues speaking and moving about until he restores it, showing a level of mastery beyond normal life. A similar Irish tale of beheading is found in the Feast of Bricriu, with a giant and the hero Cú Chulainn.

In the Norse sagas, we have the tale of Mimir. It is unclear if he is one of the gods or possibly a giant, but he is beheaded during the Aesir-Vanir War, the battle between the "sky" gods of Asgard and the "Earth" gods of Vanaheim. His head is magickally preserved by Odin, the leader of the Aesir, with herbs and incantations, and placed into a well that feeds the World Tree. The Well of Mimir is sometimes equated with the Well of Fate, and other times considered separate, depending on the interpretation. Odin goes to the head often for wisdom and advice.

Bran, Mimir, the Green Knight, Orpheus, and John all have in common the aspect of continued voice, and either continued magickal power or newfound magickal power. We don't know how wise Mimir was to begin with, but after going in the well, he seems to know quite a bit. Orpheus and John were both prophets, but appear to be elevated even further after their death and beheading. The Green Knight gets his body back with no real consequence, and in many ways, he becomes the true initiator of Sir Gawain into the mysteries. Bran began as an elder god, a king, and possible magician, but afterwards has aspects of the seer and prophet in his powers, until finally focusing upon the act of being a guardian for the nation.

With the assembly, the seven and the head seemingly step outside of time, into what might be considered a "summerland" paradise of eternal feasting, drinking, play, and mirth. All sorrows are forgotten, at least for a time. The Birds of Rhiannon, with their paradox of being both near and far at the same time, play a key role in this magick, as does as the boundary of a sealed door. Rhiannon is another goddess of sovereignty in *The Mabinogion*, with her own trials and not a cauldron, but an enchanted bottomless bag.

While a character in the assembly, Taliesin doesn't seem to do much specifically. Is he the bard, entertaining the feast? He is not the leader of the group. He is not the one to break the spell and open the door. Yet he is present in the time beyond time and space beyond space of the eternal now. There is a mystery in being able to enter the eternal moment. One both simultaneously steps into the flow and steps out of it, like the paradox of being both near and far. There is an ageless immortality and joy that comes from being in the moment, when all your needs are met, yet experiencing at the same time a separation from the rest of humanity, without focus on the past or goals of the future.

The implication of "entertaining the noble head" is that the seven are working to support the head of Bran, though magickally, one might think it's the other way around. Who knows what the head of Bran the Blessed was sharing with them? Perhaps they were showing their skills, knowledge, and stories, a form of release. Perhaps he was filling them with something new and different to continue their journey. When the door was opened, his magick didn't diminish the grief, but they still had the strength to carry on, and after such a long time suspended between worlds, like the realm of faery, they could be fortified and rejuvenated.

When we step outside of time, in the space of our ritual circles, or in deep meditation, many believe we are spared the ravishment of that time while in sacred space, and we thereby extend our lives and are rejuvenated. You'll find in the practice of magick, that many practitioners stay quite young for a long time, spending so much of their life between the worlds and beyond time. They perceive time not in a linear stream, but in the true cycles of mythic time and are constantly renewed.

Exercise 20:
Seeking the Wondrous Head

Where is Bran's head now? Good question. Some would say that it is long gone, decayed once dug up from the hill of the Tower of London. Others might believe that since it existed beyond time and space, part of it will always exist beyond time and space, and like Taliesin, we can join the Assembly to partake in the mystery of the head and the Birds of Rhiannon. Taliesin did nothing specific, for we, each in our turn, are

Taliesin on this journey. We each step into the assembly and take our own role, experience our own wisdom, along with the other six compatriots. Together we find the eternal oracular head that still awaits us in the assembly hall of the Castle of Carousel.

You will need:

Cauldron
Small High-Pitched Bell(s)
White Candle and Candleholder
Skull or Head Effigy
Myrrh incense

    Place an altar before the consecrated cauldron, and place the white candle to rise up out of it. If possible, place a skull or head effigy before the cauldron, "looking" at you. Today, small-to-large carved crystal skulls are quite popular. A doll's head, a broken statue head, or anything else that embodies the severing of the head from the body can be the focus if it is evocative to you. You could even use the sugar skulls used in ancestral folk traditions in central America. The Birds of Rhiannon are compared to the chiming of small bells heard by spiritualists, when entering into a deep trance state to commune with the dead. One of my earliest teachers used small high-pitched bells to help induce a meditative state. Upon a length of braided cord she had nine small brass bells of various sizes, and she would shake the gathered cord to let the bells ring. I use something similar in my rituals today. And lastly, once you are ready and have lit the candle, burn myrrh incense. Myrrh is a resin used in embalming and preserving the flesh, and while not traditionally Celtic, is evocative of the deep levels of the otherworld. If incense is not an option, you can anoint the candle with myrrh oil.

    When ready to begin, light the white candle, then touch the effigy of the head and say:

I seek to experience the Assembly of the Wondrous Head.
I seek to be one of the seven.
I seek the mystery of the oracle, of the talking dead.
I seek the Wonder of Bran of the Cauldron
The Wonder of Mimir of the Well
The Wonder of the Green Knight of the Chapel
The Wonder of Orpheus of the Isle
The Wonder of John of the Waters
Oracles and prophets, tell me what I need to hear.
Speak so I may listen to your wisdom.
Awen.

Ring the bells gently. Gaze into the "eyes" of your head effigy. When you feel the connection, close your eyes. Gently run energy from the depths of the Earth into your lower cauldron, middle cauldron, and upper cauldron, and then drawn down the heavens to your upper cauldron, middle, and lower, and into the Earth. Feel the flow like the flow of the rivers and seas associated with many of the oracles.

Some will keep the bells gently ringing as they visualize, while others will put the bells in their lap. Either way, envision a great tree before you, with a trunk larger than you have ever seen. It stands in this time of twilight, and you are unsure if it is dawn or sunset, but everything is illuminated in a soft, warm light. In the roots of the tree is an ancient wooden double door. The roots are almost growing over it, but you know it can open. You hear the otherworldly birds in the branches of the tree, singing like soft bells. Knock on the doors. Slowly the doors swing open towards you, revealing a dark passageway.

You follow the passageway deeper into the tree, into the Earth itself. The walls of the corridor are made from the moist Earth. They seem to pulse as if alive all around you. Small torches illuminate your way, and you wonder who lit them. How did they know you would be coming?

At the end of the tunnel is another set of double doors. You hear something, like a gathering, behind the doors, but the sound is muffled and faint. Again you knock, and they open, revealing a marvelous feasting hall. There in the center table is a large head, severed upon a plate. The eyes are open, and it is singing. Surrounding the head are all manner of foods, drinks, and treats. Despite being startled by the head being so alive, you see some of your favorite things upon the table, again, as if the event was planned to include you. There are six others gathered in this place. Many of them are cloaked, so you can't see them very well. They are dancing and playing. They won't stay still.

This realm is a paradise realm, a place of enjoyment. While our ancestors saw the Summerlands as endless feasting, drinking, and merriment, your idea of paradise might be something different. As you look around the room, you can see other aspects of paradise that speak to your heart and mind. What would be paradise for you? If it truly would be, you will see it there somewhere in the room, or in one of the many chambers leading off from this central banquet hall.

As you move into the party and mingle, trying to figure out exactly what to do in this bizarre scene, you realize that these six people are all people you know, or at least wear the faces of people you know. Each of the six is someone who was very important upon your life path, who is very important, or who will be, and those who will be important might be the only ones there unknown to you. This realm is beyond the bounds of space, time, and linear thought.

Explore and enjoy these chambers. Partake in your fill of paradise. Here all your worries are left behind. Here is nothing but bliss and play. Enjoy yourself fully. You might find yourself talking to the other six guests. Even though they wear familiar faces, they might not be the people you know in your day-to-day life, for here they are also beyond all their own worries.

After a time, the rooms grow noisier. The people become more boisterous. Soon, the severed head starts singing, and sings a note that cuts through the din. Everyone stops what they are doing and faces the wondrous head of the oracle.

At first it sounds like the head is speaking gibberish, but soon you hear words for you and only you in the verse. The head speaks the words you do not want to hear, but you need to hear. The head speaks of what must be done, in your own life, and for the betterment of your people, and the evolution of the world. The head speaks of the mystic will and prophecy. What is your role? Listen.

When the head is done speaking, everyone is silent. You each turn and see a closed door. You each move toward that closed door, and when you open it, the spell of paradise is broken. You affirm you will remember all the head has said to you and make your way through the door, back through the spiraling tunnels of the tree. You return through the double door in the roots and close the door behind you. Soon, it is as if the doors were never there to begin with. Only the roots remain. The tree fades from your mind, and as you gently open your eyes, you gaze at the burning candle in the cauldron, and the head before you.

Thank the spirit of the wondrous head and ground yourself. Snuff the candle out or let it burn to its completion. Then, like the head of Bran, take the head effigy and face it in the direction of your challenges. You do not necessarily have to bury it, and you can use it again to commune with the oracular head. But ideally it should face where you might feel a challenge is being directed. For myself, I have the crystal skull face the window of my office/altar room. It helps ward the space from undue influences.

With the opening of the door, you return to your own world of worries and concerns. But while reflecting upon any worries and concerns, think about the advice of the head. Record it. How may the wisdom help you better take action amid your concerns? How do your actions not only serve you, but your greater community and the world?

King Arthur

One of the earliest references to King Arthur's quest for the Holy Grail is found in "The Spoils of Annwn." Attributed to Taliesin, it implies his journey with Arthur to Annwn to seek its treasures, most specifically a cauldron. Again, only seven return from this "splendid labor" just as only seven returned with Bran's head. It seems as if you go anywhere with Taliesin, make sure you are one of the seven.

There are strange and splendid parallels between the tales of Arthur and Bran. In the tale of "Culhwch and Olwen," another collected by Lady Guest in her version of *The Mabinogion*, Arthur gathers a retinue of men to sail to Ireland for the cauldron of the Irish man Diwrnach. Again, we have a source of the magick cauldron in Ireland. The sea is often a vehicle not just for terrestrial travel, but otherworldly travel. In referencing this land as Ireland, is there some folk memory of seeking the otherworld island across the sea? In the tale accompanying Arthur is "Taliesin the chief of the bards" just as he is the narrator in the "Spoils." The text of "Culhwch and Olwen" also has a number of remarkable adventures within it; most popular among Witches and Wiccans today is the release of Mabon from his prison. It's a tale often recited and ritualized at the Autumn Equinox in the modern Wheel of the Year.

Is the journey for the cauldron in "Culhwch and Olwen" the same tale as the one recounted in "The Spoils of Annwn"? We will probably never know for sure, but they seem to be drawing on similar mythic ideas.

This cauldron in the "Spoils" poem is described not as one specifically of regeneration like Bran, but possibly one of earthly abundance, like the Dagda's. Unlike the Dagda's, there is a clear sense of creating food, but also refusing to boil the food of a coward. Despite having a culinary use, this unusual cauldron is lined with pearls. There is a "first word" from the cauldron, indicating aspects of inspiration, like Cerridwen's. And most importantly, it is warmed by the breath of the "nine maidens" found in Annwn. We have related them to the nine maidens of Avalon and the classical muses. It ultimately becomes one of the Thirteen Treasures of Britain guarded by Merlin. Whatever else the cauldron can do, we do not know.

Annwn is mentioned as the Celtic otherworld or underworld, ruled by its head, meaning "chief," not "severed head," though I find our use of the word "head" interesting in light of our stories with Bran. The chief of Annwn in various myths has been Arawn, the enemy of Hafgan; Pwyll, Prince of Dyfed and friend of Arawn; and Gwyn ap Nudd, Light, Son of Darkness, and faery king.

In the journey, a series of caers – often thought of as mounds, forts, or castles – are described, like gates descending deeper into the underworld. Though discovering their translations and use has been difficult, especially in determining which are considered separate caers and which are different names and descriptions of the same one, occult tradition provides possible translations and correspondences with a system of seven, relating them to the planets, chakras, and stages of alchemical initiation. Occultists like myself look at this as a possible map, a Celtic version of the descent into the underworld through seven gates. Like the Sumerian goddess Inanna descending to the underworld, we must pass the challenges of each gate.

Taliesin is along for the ride if Arthur is the primary hero here. In such tales, it can be helpful to take on the role of the primary character and see the other figures in the myth as the allies to your quest. We would believe, based upon his tale with Elphin, that Taliesin acts as guide and advisor to the hero, in this case Arthur, paralleling our concept of Merlin's role in the Arthurian myth, though Taliesin, unlike Merlin, seems to go on the adventures with Arthur.

Like Taliesin – going through successive stages to reach initiatory rebirth, facing darkness not once, but three times – Arthur must go through seven stages in this map. Again we have the familiar patterns of seven. We first learned them as the alchemical stages, forming a ladder to heaven or a staircase stepping down into the underworld. They follow the seven holy metals, the seven wandering stars (planets), the days of the week, and the chakras. We can now look to the seven caers as an addition to this map.

It is important to note this is a correspondence and comparison done by occultists looking into the Celtic Mysteries. Today we can piece together the stories and poetry, and we have no real proven knowledge of what the scribes and the earlier authors themselves intended to encode, if anything, in these stories. But we use them as tools for our own attainment to unlock new levels of awareness, even if that was not their original intention when created.

In the poem, the caers appear to go backwards from the top, much like the descent to the underworld the goddess Inanna takes. It parallels the body, starting with the crown and descending down into the underworld of the body, the base of the spine, and the robe of flesh itself. **Chart 26** shows the process in terms of alchemical process, rising up, while the poem below marks the unwinding return to the beginning, to the cauldron in the center of all of creation at the heart of the underworld.

While not considered the most up-to-date of translations, the 1868 version of *The Four Ancient Books of Wales*, as translated by W. F. Skene, are in the public domain and suit our purposes. The "Spoils" poetry comes from *The Book of Taliesin XXX* within *The Four Ancient Books*. Variations of the caer names are found in other places, and attempts have been made to collate various translations, including Skene's. I personally use the list of caers and possible translated meanings passed on to me by a mentor and used in my own community's initiation rites, as detailed in my previous book, *The Living*

Temple of Witchcraft, Volume I. Where they differ from the Skene names, I will notate in the text.

Calcination	Burning	Saturn	Caer Ochren	Castle of Dread	Lead	Castle of the Shelving Tide
Dissolution	Dissolving	Jupiter	Caer Fandy-Manddwy	Castle on High	Tin	Sea Castle
Separation	Dividing	Mars	Caer Goludd	Castle of Gloom	Iron	Castle of Death Castle of Trials
Conjunction	Uniting	Venus	Caer Rigor	Royal Castle	Copper	Castle of Royal Horn
Fermentation	Decay	Mercury	Caer Fredwyd	Castle of the Perfected Ones	Quicksilver	Castle of Carousal
Distillation	Refinement	Moon	Caer Pedryfan	Revolving Castle	Silver	Four-Cornered and Revolving Sky Castle
Coagulation	Unification	Sun	Caer Sidi	Castle of the Sidhe	Gold	Castle of the Zodiacal Wheel

Chart 26: Castles of Annwn

Caer Sidi

I WILL praise the sovereign, supreme king of the land,
Who hath extended his dominion over the shore of the world.
Complete was the prison of Gweir in Caer Sidi,
Through the spite of Pwyll and Pryderi.

No one before him went into it.
The heavy blue chain held the faithful youth,
And before the spoils of Annwvn woefully he sings,
And till doom shall continue a bard of prayer.
Thrice enough to fill Prydwen, we went into it;
Except seven, none returned from Caer Sidi.
— from *The Book of Taliessin XXX*

This verse references Pywll, Lord of Dyfed and later Head of Annwn, and his son, Pryderi, whose mother is Rhiannon. Their tale is in the First Branch of *The Mabinogi*: "Pywll Prince of Dyfed." Upon Pywll's death, Pryderi assumed the lands and forms his own kingdom. Pryderi then accompanies Bran to rescue Branwen in the Second Branch of *The Mabinogi*. Along with Taliesin and Manawyddan, Pryderi is one of the seven to survive and journey with the severed head of Bran as one of the Assembly.

The imprisonment of Gweir could be a central focus of the poem, that the impetus to journey was not just the spoils, or cauldron, but to rescue Gweir. While there are a variety of Gweirs associated with King Arthur's family, in this case Gweir could possibly be a reference to Gwydion, nephew to King Math and brother to Arianrhod. Gwydion is a magician who plays a key role in the Fourth Branch of *The Mabinogi*. Being held by a heavy blue chain is an image reminiscent of Elphin being held by a silver chain in the tower dungeon of Maelgwyn, though it can also be a reference not to silver, but to water, creating a prison not unlike that of Mabon. In fact, in the whole of *The Mabinogi*, various youthful characters in their imprisonment or exile are equated with Mabon, including Pryderi and Gwydion's nephew Lleu.

In Gwydion's tale, as a youth, he starts a war between the kingdom of his uncle Math and the Kingdom of Pryderi by stealing Pryderi's pigs. After three bloody battles where Pryderi loses, he agrees to settle the war by single combat with Gwydion, who ends up slaying Pryderi. So through the "spite" of the spirits of Pryderi and his father Pwyll, Gwydion is the first to enter the prison of Caer Sidi.

Prydwen, also Pridwen in several translations, is King Arthur's ship in both "The Spoils of Annwn" and "Culhwch and Olwen," and later the name used for his shield in Arthurian lore. In many ways, Prydwen is not an inanimate object, but a magical being in itself, and an ally to Arthur and his men. It is quite similar in nature to the ship of King Solomon which shows up in later grail myths of Sir Galahad in the Vulgate Cycle of the grail myths, where three spindles of wood were fashioned from a tree descended from the Biblical Tree from the Garden of Eden and used in the ship along with the sword of King David. Evidently, the party that went into Annwn could fill Prydwen, but only seven came out, implying a large ship sized to carry a large party.

Caer Sidi is considered the castle of both the stars and the faery folk. Despite meaning the Irish word Sidhe, occultists associate Sidi with both the Sidhe and stars. The Welsh term for faeries would correctly be Tylwyth Teg. Associating faeries and stars might sound strange to us today, but a great mystery is associated with the faeries and the starry beings, for esoteric folklore tells us the stars are within the Earth. The faery light, or Earth light, radiating out from the heart of the underworld is what sustains nature as much as the Sun in the sky. The faery beings weave the astral tides that are the vitality of nature and fate. Often deities of the Annwn are seen as stellar deities. Arianrhod's castle is seen both within the Earth and as the Moon or stars themselves. Caer Widon, the Castle of Gwydion, is considered to be the Milky Way.

The circle of north stars – including the mythologies of Ursa Minor and Polaris, Draco and Thuban, Lyre and Vega, Cygnus and Denab, and Cepheus and Al Deramin – all play a role in esoteric Arthurian and faery lore as the pole star of the Earth changes over time. If the axis of the Earth is seen as the great World Tree, often from the Northern Hemisphere, the open southern sky is "up" and the North Star is at the roots. The northern stars and the northern winds rise from the underworld of Annwn.

Caer Sidi is both the first and the last of the castles. If truly first in sequence, why would the prisoner be found in the first gate, singing before the treasures, instead of the last gate? On an epic adventure, it's like finding the horde of gold and the imprisoned princess in the courtyard, with no dragon or monster to be found. It's another understanding that from poetic sequences what is up is down and what is down is up in the initiation of the mysteries.

Caer Pedryfan and Caer Fredwyd

Am I not a candidate for fame, if a song is heard?
In Caer Pedryvan, four its revolutions;
In the first word from the cauldron when spoken,
From the breath of nine maidens it was gently warmed.
Is it not the cauldron of the chief of Annwvn? What is its intention?
A ridge about its edge and pearls.
It will not boil the food of a coward, that has not been sworn,
A sword bright gleaming to him was raised,
And in the hand of Lleminawg it was left.
And before the door of the gate of Uffern [hell] the lamp was burning.
And when we went with Arthur; a splendid labour,
Except seven, none returned from Caer Vedwyd.
    — from *The Book of Taliessin XXX*

The second stanza contains two castles, the first is Caer Pedryfan (also spelled Caer Pedryvan) and Caer Fredwyd (also spelled Caer Vedwyd). Are they the same? Some say yes. It is interesting to note that in our alchemical associations, one is silver and the other is quicksilver, very similar in color, yet entirely different.

It is in Pedryfan where the cauldron is described as being warmed by the nine maidens' breath, lined with pearls. Here it is described as refusing to boil food for a coward. It represents a test of virtue. Like an alchemist wanting to prove attainment to himself, if not others, he must turn lead into gold. To prove valor, the noble warrior must often prove his worth – to himself and to others – through such a magick cauldron. Celtic lore is filled with similar motifs. This cauldron revolves four times, and one can imagine some sort of challenge or trap to get into it, just at the right moment, linking a feat of courage and cleverness.

Lleminawg appears to a warrior in Arthur's company responsible for claiming the cauldron, whose name is strikingly similar to the character Llenlleawg in "Culhwch and Olwen." Strangely, a lamp is left burning, perhaps to guide the way of the warriors at the gate of Uffern, who as a figure, can be equated with Arawn, the King of Annwn, or as some would translate, Hell or the underworld.

Caer Fredwyd/Vedwyd is sometimes described as the Castle of Carousal or the Castle of the Perfected Ones. Is this the caer that describes the realm where the Birds of Rhiannon sing and the Assembly of the Wondrous Head gathers? If so, it might make sense that a cauldron that boils food as a reward – or better yet, provides food and drink (like the Dagda's) and is attended by nine beautiful maidens – would be found here. The Bran tale, however, has no second cauldron with the assembly, just a feasting hall with three doors. Is approaching from "below" the paradise a move to distract the heroes from actually finding a cauldron? It's hard to tell from the fragments we have left. I can only say my mentors and initiators divided Fredwyd/Vedwyd from Pedryfan/Pedryvan as two distinct levels, so I continue to honor those experiences and teachings by doing the same, though other options are available to you, as we'll see below.

Caer Rigor

Am I not a candidate for fame with the listened song
In Caer Pedryvan, in the isle of the strong door?
The twilight and pitchy darkness were mixed together.
Bright wine their liquor before their retinue.
Thrice enough to fill Prydwen we went on the sea,
Except seven, none returned from Caer Rigor.
   — from *The Book of Taliessin XXX*

In this stanza, we start with Caer Pedryfan/Pedryvan, giving some to think that Caer Fredwyd/Vedwyd is just another name synonymous with Pedryfan. Very little is said here, though Taliesin is again asking about being a candidate for fame. If taken to the fourth caer, synonymous with the heart, the lines of mixing "twilight" and "pitchy darkness" align with the operation of conjunction, though not conjunction of opposites, which would be light and darkness, but a twilight and darkness instead, so a minor unification that is signified by the fourth step. Is the twilight caused by the lamp at the gate? What does that lamp signify in our spiritual journey?

Wine is referenced and would make a connection to one title for the caer as the Castle of the Royal Horn, if we think of it as drinking horn for wine or mead, rather than trumpeting horn. Is this a sacramental drink or initiatory rite? Is this a sacred substance to bring one deeper? Is this a healing herbal liquor to unite the two sides of self? We do not know, but our modern traditions, ritual sacraments harkening back to the northern traditions of the blot and sumbel, link us with our ancestors, gods, and community. In Wicca, the Great Rite is the union of paradoxes, most explicit in the female and male symbols of the spear and cauldron, the blade and the chalice. Perhaps in this caer, we must seek connection between the darkness and light.

Caer Goludd

I shall not deserve much from the ruler of literature,
Beyond Caer Wydyr they saw not the prowess of Arthur.
Three score Canhwr stood on the wall,
Difficult was a conversation with its sentinel.
Thrice enough to fill Prydwen there went with Arthur,
Except seven, none returned from Caer Golud.
   — from *The Book of Taliessin XXX*

In this fourth stanza, we have both Caer Wydyr and Caer Goludd (also spelled Golud). Caer Wydyr is usually seen as the Castle of Glass or the Invisible Fort. It could possibly be a description of all seven castles, which are really only seven layers or gates to one mystery. All are in the spirit world, so all are invisible, like glass. The Isle of Avalon, now equated with Glastonbury, was also considered to be glass, just as one manifestation of the tower of Merlin was, glass or air, invisible to the naked eye. One could envision seven invisible rings or squares rotating, and one having to find the entrance to each as the task of trials.

A canhwr is a group of a hundred warriors, and three score (three times twenty or sixty) canhwr would presumably be six thousand warriors. Yet only seven men returned. Evidently the "difficult conversation" with the sentinel was more than an exchange of words. Charles Squire, who collates several versions of the tale in his 1905 book, *The Mythology of the British Islands*, interprets the sentinels in the revolving glass castle as ghostly or spectral. At this point, it seems to be the greatest challenge the heroes have faced upon the quest. Goludd can be translated as the Castle of Riches, though esoteric lore gives it the titles of Castle of Gloom, Castle of Trials, and Castle of Death. I aligned these titles – and considering their varied meanings, fittingly so – with the Solar Plexus. In alchemy, the third stage is assigned to Mars, associated with iron and the process of cutting and dividing. Here the seven are divided from the company of their many men, who might otherwise protect them. In other lore, the solar plexus is associated with the Sun, and material riches associated with terrestrial power and wealth.

Caer Fandy-Manddwy

I shall not deserve much from those with long shields.
They know not what day, who the causer,
What hour in the serene day Cwy was born.
Who caused that he should not go to the dales of Devwy.
They know not the brindled ox, thick his head-band.
Seven score knobs in his collar.
And when we went with Arthur of anxious memory,
Except seven, none returned from Caer Vandwy.
    — from *The Book of Taliessin XXX*

Caer Fandy-Manddwy, also Caer Vandwy in the text, is perplexing. To my knowledge, there is no clear myth left of Cwy. Evidently, he had a good birth and should not travel to Devwy, though we don't know why. There is an assumption from the poet that the listener would most likely be familiar with the tale, so there is no need for explanation. We also have the description of an ox with seven knobs on his collar and an anxious Arthur leading the way. Seven is a number that shows up quite often in mystical lore.

Another translation of "The Reproof of the Bards" in Taliesin's story with Elphin, translates the line "And the name of thy region" as "And the name of the head-band," leading Robert Graves in *The White Goddess* to speculate that the head-band that Heinin does not possess is the head-band of the "brindled ox" in this work. What bardic mystery surrounds the head-band is unclear to us today. By looking at both versions, is it bounding some religion associated with the head?

In our esoteric lore, this caer is described as a sea castle, or a castle high upon a cliff over the sea. The alchemical operation is dissolution, or drowning in the sea of emotion and spirit to release all that will join with the fluid power and allow all that will not be penetrated to sink to the bottom.

Caer Ochren

I shall not deserve much from those of loose bias,
They know not what day the chief was caused.
What hour in the serene day the owner was born.
What animal they keep, silver its head.
When we went with Arthur of anxious contention,
Except seven, none returned from Caer Ochren.
   — from *The Book of Taliessin XXX*

Continuing the trend, Taliesin as narrator in continuation of "not deserv[ing] much" from those who do not know "what day the chief was caused./ What hour in the serene day the owner was born." Perhaps this is another reference to Cwy's birth. Perhaps we cannot easily unlock the gifts of Taliesin as we don't know when Cwy was born either. Whoever he was, this chief sounds important. Arthur has shifted from anxious memory to anxious contention, and a mystery animal with a silver head is kept in Caer Ochren. Graves contends that it is the White Roebuck of the mysteries, the otherworldly Roebuck in the Thicket and emissary of the White Goddess of inspiration and mystery.

Caer Ochren relates to the previous water imagery, as the Castle of the Shelving Tide, but it is also titled as the Castle of Dread, being the first and the last of our gates, relating to the heavy guard of Saturn. It is also simply the Castle of the Otherworld:

Monks congregate like dogs in a kennel,
From contact with their superiors they acquire knowledge,
Is one the course of the wind, is one the water of the sea?
Is one the spark of the fire, of unrestrainable tumult?
Monks congregate like wolves,
From contact with their superiors they acquire knowledge.
They know not when the deep night and dawn divide.
Nor what is the course of the wind, or who agitates it,
In what place it dies away, on what land it roars.
The grave of the saint is vanishing from the altar-tomb.
I will pray to the Lord, the great supreme,
That I be not wretched. Christ be my portion.
   — from *The Book of Taliessin XXX*

The last stanza finalizes the adventure of the spoils in a strange and unconnected way. Here we have the most Christian references to monks compared to both dogs and wolves, acquiring their knowledge from superiors, as references to the Lord and Christ. The word "dog" implies an animal domesticated in the kennel, whereas "wolf" implies a wildness. Woven into this is the imagery of the elements and the natural world, of wind and water and fire, the night and dawn, the grave and the altar tomb. The motif of caer, of the boat, of Arthur and the seven seems abandoned, with no description of what happened to the cauldron, the prisoner, or their return. So again, it makes one question if this is the end of the quest or the beginning, seeking the knowledge of monks and blessings of the "Lord" and "Christ."

When we reverse it, we see a pattern that might make a bit more sense to the magical initiate. The company is guided across the sea or river through the magickal vessel of Prydwen. They arrive on the isle that is the gateway of Annwn. A lamp is left lit at the gate, to provide light to guide them back.

Caer Ochren	Silver-Headed Animal
Caer Fandy-Manddwy/Vandwy	Bridled Ox with Head-Band and Silver-Knobbed Collar
Caer Goludd	Difficult Conversation with Sentinel (Battle)
(Caer Wydyr)	Glass Castle
Caer Rigor	Mixing of Twilight and Darkness – Sacramental Drink
Caer Fredwyd/Vedwyd	Distraction by Paradise
Caer Pedryfan/Pedryvan	Find the Cauldron of Annwn
Caer Sidi	Rescue the Youth Gweir

Chart 27: Pattern of the Caers

In the first realm, the guide is the silver-headed animal. Silver or white animals in Welsh lore are often indicative of faery animals, allies from the otherworld, to distinguish them from traditional animals by their coloring. White deer and hounds are common heralds of the otherworld. This possible roebuck heralds the way into the otherworld, through Caer Ochren. We are also reminded of the serene day when a chief is born.

The second realm has another animal, this one a bridled ox, collared rather than the potentially wild faery animal of silver. Does the mystery of the ox provide them transport or access? Bulls, ox, cows, and even the extinct aurochs play strong mythic roles in European myth, and the ox and cows in particular in Celtic lore. Again we have a reminder of birth, a person now named Cwy. Do these caer have something to do with birth? Despite being reminded of a serene day, our hero Arthur is anxious.

The third caer, Goludd, is described as a difficult conversation with a sentinel, but this most likely appears to be a battle or challenge of some sort, and it appears despite possibly six thousand men going in, only seven survive to pass onward. While many might seek the mysteries, only a small number really get through the first gate. The first three caer, if aligned with the first three chakras, represent the lower cauldron of the belly. This is the cauldron upright in all people who are alive. Yet overcoming your own conflicted nature and moving onto the middle cauldron of the heart is something few truly do. In some understanding of energy anatomy, there is a "lock" or knot that has to be unlocked and passed, to reach the heart. Is this what Caer Wydyr, the Glass Castle is?

Onto the fourth realm of the royal horn, we have the mixing of twilight and darkness and the drinking of wine. I would believe this is the vestige of some sort of ritual sacrament required to go forward. It joins the nature of the caers before with the ones that will follow.

Next a paradise realm of Carousal, both a respite and a distraction from the quest, not unlike the realm the Assembly of the Wondrous Head found themselves in at the end of the Second Branch. The lamp is mentioned here, so perhaps it was left to light the way here, rather than at the start of the adventure.

We seemingly succeed in the next gate, finding the cauldron, and assuming it is still warm, the nine maidens, though little is mentioned of any encounter with them. Perhaps it is as it should be – that such things are a mystery.

If one stops there, then the company will not reach the castle of stars and rescue the youth Gweir. While the cauldron is quite a find, it is implied he is hidden in a chamber where more treasures are found, that he is, in fact, a bardic treasure, for he and his song are also hidden within the chamber, despite or perhaps because of, Pryderi and Pwyll's spite towards him if he is indeed Gwydion.

Only seven leave, but do they return back the way they came, or is the only way out to go through?

Exercise 21:
The Seven Caers of Annwn

This journey is a bit longer or more detailed than some of our others. It will help prepare you for the work of the Holy Grail in the next chapter. To enter the seven gates is to be changed, so be prepared that you wish to transform yourself and find the "youth" within the gates before you embark upon it.

7 Candles
9 Cups
9 Stones or Crystals
Cauldron
Pearls

On the altar before you, place your consecrated cauldron for this work. If possible, place a pearl necklace of any quality around the edge of the cauldron, or around the base of it. If only a few pearls are available, you can arrange them in a pleasing manner around the base of the cauldron. Around the cauldron place nine small glasses filled with pure water. Into the glasses drop ritually cleansed and blessed stones. They can be simple beach stones or rocks from your yard or polished crystals, whatever you feel suits the purpose to embody the nine maidens, the union of water and earth. Before the cauldron ringed by nine glasses, place seven candles of any color. Some prefer the rainbow, but they can be all white, or a mix of any colors in an arrangement that is pleasing to you. When ready to begin, light the candles, speaking one line about the caers with each candle lit.

I seek safe passage and safe return through the first gate,
Caer Orchen, Castle of Dread.
I seek safe passage and safe return through the second gate,
Caer Vandwy, Castle of the Sea.
I seek safe passage and safe return through the third gate,
Caer Goludd, Castle of Trials.
I seek safe passage and safe return through the fourth gate,
Caer Rigor, Castle of the Royal Horn.
I seek safe passage and safe return through the fifth gate,
Caer Vedwyd, Castle of Carousel.
I seek safe passage and safe return through the sixth gate,
Caer Pedryvan, Castle of Revolving Sky.

I seek safe passage and safe return through the seventh gate,
Caer Sidi, Castle of the Stars.
I call upon the Nine Maidens of the Cauldron.
I seek your blessing. I seek your wisdom. I seek your healing.
I shall prove I am not a coward.
I shall use what I gain for the betterment of the world.
Blessed be.

Close your eyes. Enter your magickal state of awareness using whatever techniques are most suitable for you. In your inner world, sense a vast body of water before you, as if you are on the shores of a great river, lake, or sea. The water is lapping at your feet as you feel the mist upon your skin. Out of the mist rises a great ship, a living ship that is your guide and ally. You board the living ship, and might feel the shades and shadows of other adventures joining you, as we know "thrice enough" to fill the ship, started the journey to Annwn, and only seven returned.

You journey for a time through the mist of the waters. The ship moves as if it is being magnetically pulled towards a distant shore. You might hear the murmuring of your shipmates, but it is as if they are ghosts, phantoms. You and the ship are the only things truly real to you.

The ship makes it to the shores of a mystical island, with a large earthen mound acting as its castle keep in the center of it. You disembark from the ship onto the shore, and find the path.

Before you is a mound of green earth, like a faery mound. Shining out of the mound's round entrance is a dark red light, a fire burning slow and strong. Near the entrance is a silver white stag, who looks at you and looks into you. The stag is challenging you to come, to enter the fire of the Castle of Dread. The mound opens and the stag leaps in. You are challenged to follow. You feel anxious with the challenge. Why did you embark on this quest in the first place?

You enter the first caer, and feel yourself surrounded by an orange-red ember-like glow. Everything is red hot. Everything is burning, including you. Everything that does not serve your work, that limits you, is burning away. Let it. Offer up all that does not serve to the fire. In the light of the fire you see a bright whiteness, and it is the stag. Taking the form of a horned god of white light, he challenges you. Are you ready to prove your bravery? Will you complete this quest?

If you pass the challenges, a new path is shown, leading out of the furnace of the first castle and towards a cool darkness. The path in the darkness will lead to the second mound, the second caer.

∙ ∙ ∙

There you hear the roar of the ocean, but know you are no longer near any water. The smell of sea spray is in the air. A soft dull orange light flows from the mound that is before you, like a softer lantern. You enter the mound, and realize your feet are wet. You are standing in a pool of water. You walk further into the mound, the water grows deeper, rising from your feet to your knees. Further still the water is up to your waist. This is the water of dissolution, drowning your emotions to dissolve the hardest of hearts. The water releases long-held emotions, long-held armor, so you can flow free. As you wade through the water, you come to a chamber where a bull or cow being wearing a collar of seven knobs awaits you. The cattle guardian challenges you to dive deep into your deepest feelings, your joys and your sorrows. Will you? The cattle guardian confronts you with memories that you might not want to remember. Are you willing to face them? As you do, the water rises, yet know you will not drown if you embrace your emotions. The water will sustain you as easily as air.

If you pass the challenges, a new path is shown. As you follow it, the water starts to recede. The path leads out of the second mound, and you know you are on your way to the third gate.

∙ ∙ ∙

You come upon no earthen or sea mound, but a castle made of iron and stone, solid and unyielding. From beyond its walls is a yellow-gold light shining. There at the entrance is a sentinel, a warrior guardian. The guardian stands with a blade. The first two figures, the stag and the cattle, were simply teachers. This one is truly a barrier. This one will offer you a trial, a challenge, and divide you from your unhealthy past. The sentinel may manifest his challenge in words or actions, poetry or martial combat. You can feel as if you are physically cut, bleeding away something that does not serve. As you do, you'll find that many of the threads and cords holding you back are also being cut, separated from you. The sentinel is a filter, and if it can purify, you will be given safe passage.

If you pass the sentinel's challenge, you are given entrance through the gate and enter the castle. You feel yourself walking through a glowing yellow-gold light, like walking into sunshine though there is no visible Sun. As you breathe, you breathe in the golden light, and are empowered and revitalized. All your previous wounds are not only healed, but you feel better than ever. The path through the castle leads to an exit, and a new path, heading towards the fourth gate.

∙ ∙ ∙

In the distance you see the mysterious fourth castle. Steeped in eerie green twilight, it is both enticing and frightening. Some truly otherworldly creature must dwell there. To your surprise, the entrance is unguarded. None bar your way. You enter the mound fort, and there is a central chamber with an altar upon it. As soon as you enter, the entrance leading you to the chamber closes and disappears. There is no other exit. As you look around, you see the altar has two bottles, each with a strange liquid, and a drinking horn. One liquid is bright, while the other is dark. Intuitively you know your challenge is to mix the right proportions of the two liquids into the horn. You take the challenge.

Once done, nothing happens. You realize you must also drink the liquid, embody the balance. You do, and you feel a strange sensation come over you. You feel yourself enter a new level of balance and harmony. A new doorway opens for you, and you follow the path out of the fourth caer and make your way through Annwn to the fifth castle keep.

• • •

You see a mound made from the roots of the trees, as if a larger tree had been on top and was cut off in the distant past. There is a double door, and you hear all sorts of noises coming from behind it. A blue light flecked with silver emanates from the roots. You realize this realm is familiar to you. It feels similar to the feast accompanying the wondrous head. You enter the realm through the gate, and realize that while there is a feast, there is no wondrous head this time. But the party is large. All manner of spectacle is going on. It is the most enticing party you have ever seen. Food is everywhere. Drink flows. Entertainment beckons. It is a strange mix of your wildest dreams, and it is easy to jump right into it.

Yet you realize this is a distraction. This is an immortal image of all the things that are temporary in life, that fall away. Pleasurable yes, for a time, but not something to make your only pursuit. They are the thoughts, feelings, and actions that we can get caught into repetitive cycles. They are not only the pleasures, for as you really look around at the party, you see the pains, the worries, the fears, and all we do to distract ourselves rather than face them. But they will decay.

With that in mind, you resolve yourself to find the exit. As you do, more characters seek to distract you, to bring you back to the party. Find the door. Leave the party behind. Make your way onto the sixth gate.

• • •

In the distance again is a perfectly shaped round mound, illuminated from within with a silver light. Around the mound are four pillars or towers or stakes, all illuminated from within, creating a strange mix of the circle and the square. If you look at it too long, too hard, the pillars and the mound appear to be revolving, turning, twisting. Are they on the ground? Are they in the sky? Both. Neither.

As you approach, you realize there is a small moat or flowing stream you must jump to make your way to the gate, and as you do, it can feel like the four rotating pillars are moving in a way to block you. You have to time your jump just right to cross their barrier and the stream.

If you successfully make it across, you enter a round chamber. There is the cauldron that cooks the true food of the feast. There is the cauldron that makes the universal medicine. There is the pearl-rimmed cauldron reflecting all of space and time in the silvery white spheres.

In the shadows are the nine maidens, who keep the cauldron warm by their breath. If you have made it this far, they will now work their magick upon you, to refine your essence, to strengthen your resolve, and empower your three cauldrons to act as one once again. They bless you with the gifts of awen once again. You are not to take the cauldron. You were never meant to take the cauldron. You are meant to visit with the cauldron and remember.

When done, they open a gate to lead you to the seventh and final chamber. From the darkness of their chamber comes a cavern of crystalline light, dazzling like the stars. There in the chamber is the Child of Light. Commune with the Child of Light. Become one with the Child of Light. This child is the true treasure of the deep.

The child will lead you out of the otherworldly realm, either back the way you came, as all is transformed, or on a new route that will lead back to the ship that brought you here. Keep the child in your heart, but like the cauldron, the child must also always remain in potential, in the heart of the deep.

You board your ship and sail back through the misty waters to where you began. Disembark when you arrive back where you began. Thank the ship as your ally and guide. Let the ship and waters fade from your mind's eye, and return yourself from a meditative state. Ground yourself. Journal upon what you have experienced.

Continuing in the line of Arthurian mythos, Taliesin has a friendship with Merlin. Appearing in the *Vita Merlini,* or *Life of Merlin* as a companion to this historic Merlin of the author Geoffrey of Monmouth, Taliesin speaks with Merlin at length for they have much in common. Merlin sends his sister Ganieda to ask Taliesin to come visit with him. Taliesin was evidently studying philosophy with Gildas the Wise. When he arrives, they speak of cosmology, and the virtues of rivers and kings and violent battles. By the end of *Vita Merlini,* under the leadership of Merlin, Ganieda, a man named

Maeldin, and Taliesin decide to retire in the woods away from cities and traffic within his glass hall of prophecy. Merlin, Ganieda, and one would imagine Taliesin all take turns making prophecies. The *Vita Merlini* ends with a prophecy from Ganieda and Merlin acknowledging that she now takes the mantle of prophecy for spirit has curbed his tongue.

The Prison of Arianrhod

Arianrhod is the great mystery in the work of Taliesin. As Cerridwen is the initiator of Gwion Bach – and often seems to be his nemesis but ultimately shapes him to be the magickal bard he is meant to be – we see a similar story between Arianrhod and her "son" Lleu. In the tale, she appears to be the villain, as her brother Gwydion plays the role of patron to Lleu, yet in the end, her three curses are like three stages of initiation for a warrior: Naming, Weapons, and a Bride. The betrayal of his bride leads to his "death" and rebirth through his eagle form, considered a very solar – or at the very least, light – manifestation of the divine. Is the battle between Lleu and Blodeuwedd's lover Gronw Pebr simply an agricultural tale of gods of light and darkness, summer and winter, or is there something else going on here? Lleu is also associated with the wren, and we have the Yuletide traditions of the wren as king of the birds being hunted and killed today on what is known as St. Stephen's Day, December 26, though modern celebrations use a fake wren on top of a pole as part of a seasonal mummers' parade. Lleu originally kills a wren to gain his name, but during the attack by Gronw Pebr, he shifts into the eagle and returns as the eagle, signifying a transformation through the cycle of the year. Some say Cerridwen makes a guest appearance near the end of the tale as the white sow at the roots of the tree eating his rotting, fallen eagle flesh. Many a myth of the World Tree has a great bird in the branches and a chthonic creature in the roots.

In "The Chair of Cerridwen," Cerridwen speaks of her admiration of Gwydion as the "most skillful" and she also speaks of Arianrhod in a perplexing passage of what might be both praise and blame:

Arianrhod, of laudable aspect, dawn of serenity
The greatest disgrace evidently on the side of the Brython,
Hastily sends about his court the stream of a rainbow,
A stream that scares away violence from the earth.
    — from *The Book of Taliesin XVI*

In the court of King Maelgwn, Taliesin says, "I was in the court of Don before the birth of Gwdion" and then later "I have been three periods in the prison of Arianrhod."

Don is the greater mother goddess, and her court or house refers to the family of land gods, though many of her children, such as Arianrhod and Gwydion, have stellar associations. Don is also associated with Beli, and the House of Beli relates to the sky gods. This also contrasts to the House or Court of Llyr, referring to the family of sea gods which includes Bran, Branwen, and Manawyddan. So Taliesin was in the court of Don before Gwydion was born. Since Gwydion appears to be in the first generation of children to Don and possibly Beli, this must be quite a long time, demonstrating that he may have had a role as bard in this ancient time to the court of gods embodying the land. While both Math and his nephew Gwydion have magician roles they play in the family, did Taliesin also have a role guiding the family of Don?

Taliesin was in the prison of Arianrhod not once, not twice, but three times? What is the prison of Arianrhod? Caer Arianrhod is the Fortress or Castle of Arianrhod, and while some think of it as the Moon, it is most likely the Corona Borealis, the Crown of the North. So despite having an Earth association with the House of Don, possibly due to Beli, Arianrhod has a stellar association, like her brother Gwydion. So one would imagine the prison of Arianrhod is in the Caer of Arianrhod, which is in the heavens. Why was Taliesin there? What did he do?

In "The Chair of Taliesin," the first thing he says is "I AM the agitator." Has he agitated or insulted Arianrhod? In the tale of Lleu and Gwydion, she seems quick to anger and displease, but so does Cerridwen in Taliesin's own tale. His role in so many stories seems to be to speak truth to power, but does this include a divine figure such as Arianrhod? Well, Gwydion appears to do the same.

The image of the chair comes up frequently in the bardic mysteries of Taliesin and speaks to a mystery and contest that still continues to this day. It refers metaphorically to the winner of the poetry contests, but harkens back to when the bard would have a chair next to the king. Many skilled poets would vie for the chair of the chief bard. We see that in the battles of words and magick between Taliesin and the Chief Bard Heinin in the court of Maelgwyn. The metaphor also extends to the idea of the seat of inspiration, a particular perspective where the flow of awen is strong.

In "Song Before the Sons of Llyr," Taliesin asks:

Shall not my chair be defended from the cauldron of Cerridwen?
May my tongue be free in the sanctuary of the praise of Gogyrwen.
The praise of Gogyrwen is an oblation, which has satisfied
Them, with milk, and dew, and acorns.
Let us consider deeply before is heard confession,
That death is assuredly coming nearer and nearer.
— from The Book of Taliesin XVI

Cerridwen appears both a judge and a contender of sorts – for it is her chair, cauldron, and laws – but she is recognized as skillful in the court of Don. In "The Chair of Cerridwen," she states:

When are judged the chairs,
Excelling them (will be) mine
My chair, my cauldron and my laws,
And my parading eloquence, meet for the chair.
I am called skillful in the court of Don.
   — from The Book of Taliesin XVI

Taliesin speaks of his chair in Caer Sidi in "Song Before the Sons of Llyr":

In the festivals of the Distributor, who bestowed gifts upon me.
The chief astrologers received wonderful gifts.
Complete is my chair in Caer Siddi,
No one will be afflicted with disease or old age that may be in it.
Manawyddan and Pryderi know it.
Three utterances, around the fire, will he sing before it,
And around its borders are the streams of the ocean.
And the fruitful fountain is above it,
The liquor is sweeter than white wine.
And when I shall have worshipped you, Most High, before the sod,
May I be found in the covenant with You.
   — from The Book of Taliesin XVI

With Taliesin's chair being complete, one has to wonder about all these different castles. Is Caer Sidi, castle of the stars in the end, or beginning, of the Spoils of Annwn the same as Caer Arianrhod, the Crown of the North, where Arianrhod must keep her prison? Are ultimately all these caers, at least the ones concerned with chairs and cauldrons, the same magickal place?

While we can consider the prison to be among the stars, is not Taliesin's home among the summer stars? While the realm of Arianrhod is most likely to the north, would not some of those stars be more prominent in the summer months? Would it be other stars associated with the warming of the year in other cultures, such as the Pleiades or Sirius? We don't know directly. If so, being anchored in the north – with the small circle of stars rotating around the north polar star – would be quite restrictive for one used to the journey of the wide arc of the ecliptic of the summer stars, forming a type of prison. But from the north – from the top of the pole or the bottom of the tree, depending on your perspective – you can see everything more clearly in a way that is obscured if you are passing with the tides of the seasons.

Is the prison of Arianrhod also the chair in Caer Sidi? The throne is a prison, and the prison is a throne. Three times is the classic number of initiation cycles. The three darknesses of Gwion, the three prohibitions of Lleu, and today, the three degrees of Wicca. We even see it in trade guilds – apprentice, journeyman, and master.

In folklore, there has been a link between Arianrhod and the Greek Ariadne, the keeper of the thread that leads Theseus from the maze of the minotaur. Robert Graves' work elevated her to a major goddess, though in Geoffrey of Monmouth's *Prophecies of Merlin,* we find the pair of gods, Janus and Ariadne, in a section sometimes known as the Apocalypse of Merlin. Occultists such as R.J. Stewart indicate her nature as a weaver goddess, relating her by function to Arete and Ananke, and through the *Prophecies of Merlin,* make the connection from Ariadne to Arianrhod. All weavers have a spinning wheel also associated with fate and fortune, and Arianrhod is also associated with the roundness of the Earth and Moon and the spinning of stars.

In modern traditional Witch lore, the Goddess of Fate resides in the spiraling castle or rose castle. Governed by the four kings of winds and the elements, here one had access to all realms of wisdom while awaiting rebirth, but first one had to cross the river to gain entry and walk the maze. The image of the spiraling castle comes from Robert Graves' work and is incorporated into the Witchcraft traditions of Robert Cochrane, with obvious roots to "The Spoils of Annwn."

In this vision, we seek our own time in the chair, and in the prison of Arianrhod, to see all things as they truly are, to find our inspiration. This journey is one of perspective. As so much of the work of Cerridwen was in the primordial – the dark hut, the belly and the sea – Arianrhod takes us upward to the stars for the bigger picture.

Exercise 22:
The Castle of Arianrhod

For this work we shall actually be seeking the prison of Arianrhod, to sit in her chair at the center of all things. You will need:

Cauldron
Water
Tall White Candle
Pen, Markers, or Paint
Journal

Place your consecrated cauldron before you. Fill the cauldron halfway with water and place a white candle so it is rising up out of the water in the cauldron. You can also use any incense that would have a lunar or stellar quality if you wish, such as a blend of mugwort, orris root, white cedar, cypress, white rose, lotus, vervain, star anise, poppy, camphor, storax, sandarac, and chickweed (starwort). Prepare yourself and your tools, and recite the incantation when you begin:

By the blessings of the Great Distributor
May my gifts be enough to endure my journey
As I seek the castle beyond all castles, the caer beyond all caers
I seek the revolving castle in the stars
I seek the revolving castle that is also in the heart of the Abred.
I seek Caer Sidi and the chair in the prison of Arianrhod
I seek to be the child beyond the cauldron that all heroes seek to rescue.
I seek to rescue myself at the center of all things.
Awen.

Close your eyes. Flow with the energy of the three cauldrons, first drawing energy up from the belly, heart, and head, and then down from the heavens into the head, heart, and belly, and down into the Earth. Softly recite the mantra of "awen" to enter deeper into a trance. Remember the three darknesses of Cerridwen. Now we seek the darkness of the night sky and the castle of stars.

Envision the great World Tree before you. The largest tree you have ever seen. It is the great tree where Lleu as an eagle retreated into its branches, eventually to be coaxed out by Gwydion. It is the tree that is fed by the well where Mimir's head is kept. To the right of it in the distance is the lake, and the island, where all of this began. To the left is the sea where you floated in darkness. Between them is a winding river. Above are the north stars. Gaze up at the north stars.

As you do, like the winding river, you feel a spiraling starlight descend slowly around the three. Like a river of stars, like a swirling spiral staircase of stars, a connection around the three and upward to the highest heavens. And you know you must travel the spiral upwards.

The spiral feels different for everyone. Some might feel as if they are swimming in a night sea of stars, swimming in the darkness. Others are walking a starlit path, a spiraling bent line of twilight faery light. Others are walking upon a staircase made of glass and light. Find your path, and ascend.

As you turn upward and around, gaze at the tree in the center of the spiral. It is the

Tree of Life, with a multitude of creatures living in it, strange fruit and nuts growing upon it. The leaves might change as you ascend, showing that it is all trees, and really not one tree.

As you ascend, you might find that you are passing familiar realms of the planets themselves, moving beyond the Moon, Sun, and wandering stars of the planets. Each might look like a bright jewel in the sky giving off a strange light.

Soon you pass higher than the tree and are surrounded in stars. The way becomes like a river or pathway of stars, and you enter the realm beyond the planets and into the firmament of fixed stars. They are all rotating against the Sun-wise direction of the north, all around the North Star as the celestial nail, the celestial mill, grinding the starry grain of the universe to make all of creation.

There in this realm you become a star walker, and search for Caer Sidi, Caer Arianrhod.

You will find a castle that is like glass, a castle that is made from clear light. You will find the castle that is revolving. You will find it is unlike anything you thought it would be.

You will need to cross a river of stars to enter the threshold. Cross the river as the gate opens for you. Enter the castle of stars.

Seek the center of the turning castle. There you will find the Prison of Arianrhod. You feel as if a thread of light is guiding you through the castle keep, like a thread guiding you through the labyrinth maze of light and dark. The prison of Arianrhod is the throne room of Arianrhod. She stands behind the throne in light and shadow, and upon the throne, you see yourself. Why are you there? How did you already get there?

You are there, awaiting yourself. You knew you would come to rescue yourself.

Approach Arianrhod, and approach your star self in the chair of the bard.

Speak with the goddess.

Speak with yourself.

Listen to what they have to say.

You will be guided to enter yourself, to take a seat upon the throne. Do so. Merge with your seated self, and suddenly your view of the universe changes entirely.

You can see through the glass castle, across the stars. You can see across space. You can see across time. You can see everything. And interconnecting everything is a web of starlight. You sit in the center of this massive web, this tapestry of light, and stretching all around you, in every direction, across all of space, across all of time, you see the interconnections.

What do you wish to know about? Simply thinking about something, asking yourself a question, casts your mind out across the cosmos. Ask and perceive. The information will not be linear, visual, or easy to understand. Often it will be complex and poetic and paradoxical. Allow and experience. Don't analyze or judge right now.

If you are feeling overwhelmed, remember all that has led you here. Remember the three darknesses. Remember the oracle head. Remember the seven caers. Call out to Arianrhod to help you, and she will place her hands upon your head or shoulders and guide your perception.

Take this time to explore. When you are done, you see a shadow approaching, walking towards you from the direction you came. As you look closely, focusing on who is approaching you, you see it is you, just as you would expect. You have come to rescue yourself. You hear yourself speak to you and the goddess, and you answer, now acting from this side of the conversation. As soon as your new self sits down into the chair, you are free. You follow the path back out, again following an invisible thread. As you go, thank Arianrhod for this time in her "prison."

You leave through the gate you came in and cross the river again. Behind you is the revolving castle. You follow the stellar path back out to the spiral. Everything is the same, yet completely different.

Follow the spiral back down the tree. Take notice of everything, particularly "new" things you didn't notice before.

Return to where you began. Thank the Tree and let it fade from your inner perception. Return your awareness to the world and come back to the world of flesh and blood, breath and bone.

Before doing anything else, take this time to make something creative, based upon your experience. Write verse or poetry. Draw. Paint. Do something to etch your experience into art.

When done, or when you have at least the framework of a new piece of art, fully ground yourself and journal in a more linear fashion about your experience.

• • •

Like Taliesin, I recommend repeating this ritual three different times, but you don't have to do it three times in a row. Return to it when intuition calls you to repeat it, as each time will offer a new perspective.

This last chapter on Taliesin proper is to illustrate that the final initiation, coming out of the bag with Elphin, is not the end of the story. One only graduates to go on to do great things in the world. If you seek the flow of awen, you will be expected to use it, and your journey may take you far and wide, across space and time.

Chapter Eight: The Hallow of the West

By the three unholy blows
Where the land turns to waste
Through questing for the grail hidden in a holy place
Kept by the Wounded King of Kings
And the Nine Ladies of the Springs
A lance, cup, cauldron, plate, and stone
The lock and the key to bring us home
Bright drink, dark drink, red drink we deserve
Through the trials and tasks we must ask
Whom do I serve?

The Holy Grail is such a beautiful and difficult mythos for the modern Witch and Pagan. The tale is so beautiful as it has no single form, but many manifestations and heroes. The literature of the grail is a living tradition, with both esotericists and fiction makers of novels, movies, and television shows adding to the body of work. It represents a beautiful place in our collective psyche where the relationship between Paganism and Christianity can be healed and renewed in sisterhood and brotherhood, between mystics from both traditions. Yet the difficulty is found in all the same reasons. There is no set mythos and formula, creating a lot of confusion as names, titles, and roles change in the stories. It stands between a Pagan and Christian worldview, making approaches to it from either perspective difficult when confronted with theologies and images outside of your acceptance and interest. This paradox of strength and weakness is honestly where the myth draws its power, always renewing itself.

In the systems already outlined, we have placed the healing function of the grail with the element of air, to be perceived as a pattern of health. While we can align it with underworld cauldrons, there is something particularly celestial about the Arthurian manifestation of the grail mythos. While its origins might be found with Cerridwen's greal, when presented to Arthur, it is aligned with the heavenly Christian father and his only son. While it is hidden upon the Earth, its origin – at least the part relating to Arthur's power in this mythos – is from on high.

Our common myths say it is the cup of the Last Supper, used by Jesus in the first Christian Eucharist ceremony. The transubstantiation of wine to blood was aligned with literal blood, when considered to be the cup that caught his blood from the crucifixion, or replaced with one of two cruets, one for his blood and one for his tears. This lends to the legends of Joseph of Arimathea establishing Christianity in Glastonbury, England, a place like the grail itself, where Paganism and Christianity intersect for redemption and renewal.

The most basic understanding of the grail myth in Arthurian lore is that it is the object of a knightly quest. In a common tale, the Round Table is created with one empty chair. The empty chair is kept empty until the knight who would find the Holy Grail appears and joins Arthur's company. The empty chair is later called the Siege Perilous. In different versions of the tale, either Lancelot or Percival or Galahad unknowingly sit in the chair, initiating the quest. In story and art, the grail is depicted in a vision that appears floating above the Round Table, ornately decorated with fine metals and gems, veiled and held aloft by two angels. The vision indicates that it is time to quest. For some, the initiation point is that there is peace in the land, with nothing left for the knights to do other than undertake some dangerous mystical quest. Later, the concept of the grail as the cure for the Wasteland of the kingdom evolved.

Everything else has become a permutation on this theme, popularized in the lore, literature, and media. Our esoteric understanding is an amalgam of many themes – direct quotes and images from the oldest lore mixed with direct alchemical insights from practitioners, received or channeled lore and popular culture. The lines of magickal training that trace their origin back to the schools of author and teacher Dion Fortune – considered by many to be the High Priestess or "shakti" heralding our new aeon – have inner teachings about the Arthurian myths. Dion stood at a crossroads, both historically and magickally. A devout Christian who sought out ancient magick and goddess mysteries, she found her way through not by denying any aspect, but by harmonizing her Christianity, Qabalistic magick, and her draw to the land of Britain that she loved and its nature mysteries through the material found in King Arthur's stories. The image of Morgan Le Fey played a strong role in her writing and magick, as seen in her fiction *The Sea Priestess* and *Moon Magic*. This "three fold way" as she called it was the foundation of her work in *The Magical Battle of Britain*, using meditation and magick to prevent Hitler's invasion of the United Kingdom during World War II.

Received teachings and past-life memories of those mythic times from her and members of her order continue to influence us today. For an understanding of the philosophical and direct practice of her Arthurian teachings, as they progressed through her schools, we have *The Arthurian Formula* by Dion Fortune, Margaret Lumley Brown, and Gareth Knight and *The Secret Tradition in Arthurian Legend* by Gareth Knight. The material continues to be developed through the work of author Wendy Berg, notably through *Red Tree, White Tree* and *Gwenevere and the Round Table*.

Just as it can unite or divide the Pagans and the Christians in mystical lore, the grail forms a bridge of restoration between Heaven and Earth, or for the occultist looking to sidestep the idea of above equals good and beneath equals bad, the macrocosm and the microcosm. Through the alignment of these two manifested patterns, we can reach beyond, to the unmanifest mystery, the ineffable.

In much of our Hermetic and Gnostic philosophy and theology, there is the idea that the perfect heavenly pattern has been broken or distorted upon Earth. Was it a cosmic accident? A rebellious action? A shattering of a vessel? An enticement or a trap? A human error? A great evil? The characteristic of that answer shapes the religion or tradition, creating a place of tension between the earlier Pagan models that see the world as natural and perfect and the greater force today of distortion through humanity's action. We don't see anything as being fundamentally wrong, but we do think humanity has forgotten how to see that things are right and therefore take action from this fundamentally imbalanced perspective. We are only outside of heaven because we cannot see the heaven all around us.

Yet if it were that easy and clear, wouldn't more people be living from that perfected perspective, leading the way for the rest of us? Since there aren't, Pagans believe the collective culture has placed a spell upon the world mind, particularly rooted in the magick of The Book, and all the prophetic traditions of the People of the Book that have spread across the world.

It is in the dynamic tension between the views of the world being damaged and the world being naturally whole that we find a solution to reconcile both. In the grail mythos, the Wasteland is the ultimate manifestation of the distortion of the world. Things go from natural, with its own struggles, to withering. The land is responding to the people. And what is the cause from the people? The answer lies in what the mythos calls the Dolorous Blows. There are three recorded Dolorous Blows, and they all involve women. But unlike the dominant understanding of the Christian mythos, the blame is not laid at the feet of women, but upon humanity's treatment of the divine feminine. You can see the themes of this lore in the Celtic myths of sovereignty, particularly in the tale of Branwen's mistreatment from the Irish King Matholwch, who gives her "the third unhappy blow" echoing the three Dolorous Blows in Arthurian lore.

The Three Dolorous Blows

The first of the Dolorous Blows involves the office of the sacred king. In fact all three deal with the role of the sovereign, but this is the only injury to the divine masculine. The king is harmed on the hunt, said to be gored by a wild boar. In other versions, he is injured by the spear from an enemy warrior, and as we'll soon see, the spear is one of the manifestations of the grail, one of the four hallows. While most myths will politely tell you his "thigh" was injured and he is now lame and can't walk (which could be also true), the real symbolism is that his genitals were gorged and he is no longer able to function sexually.

Our understanding of the Fisher King originates with the work of Chrétien de Troyes' tale of Perceval in *The Story of the Grail*, and then *Parzival* by Wolfram von Eschenbach. The origin of the king is often cited as the Pope, critiquing religious authority, or as an allegory for Jesus himself. The Pope leads the Church but cannot procreate. Esoterically, we look to the tale of Branwen to see her brother Bran as the prototype fisher king with a cauldron or grail. In Robert de Boron's *Joseph d'Arimathie*, the king is named Bron, not a far cry from Bran.

In Celtic traditions, the king must be physically perfect. We see that in the Irish tales of King Nuada, who loses a hand and goes to great lengths to have it replaced first with a silver one and then abdicates his throne until he can obtain a new flesh and blood, fully healed hand. Now take the damage of hand and apply that same standard of perfection to the phallus, a symbol of divine masculinity, even when obscured by Christian sensibility in the telling of the tale. I would say the only thing worse would be to cut off his head, but we can see how oracles can continue to perform as a severed head, while kings needing to produce an heir cannot.

The balance of the land is maintained through the relationship between the king and the queen, as embodiments of the people and the land. If there is no possibility of fertility between them, then there is no fertility of the land. But where does this danger come from? Cosmic evil? Or simply an accident of man and nature that happens, just as accidents can happen to us? It's the nature of the world itself that things change and there is danger. In *Parzival* there is a more religious theme. The "king" is wounded specifically for taking a wife and queen, as this grail keeper, as all grail keepers in the tale, are expected to be "chaste." If so, perhaps the evil comes from institutional or religious authority, justified by a story.

This damage of the sacred union causes the land to wither into the Wasteland, and the king to become the Fisher King of a lonely kingdom. Since he can no longer hunt, he fishes to fulfill his duty to the people of the castle.

The Fisher King strangely becomes one of the kings, if not the singular king, of the Grail Castle, and one can see the act of fishing as meditative, introspective, and reflective, as he fishes on a lake of still water. He is plumbing the depths of his psyche, the psyche of the kingdom, and reaching into the underworld. The fishing also has an allegory to the Christian mythology of Jesus Christ, as the world teacher of the Age of Pisces, being a "fisher of men." He feels trapped, because under normal circumstances, if he had a son, the son would then go on to become king, but this king is injured before he has an heir, so he becomes old before his natural time. The castle, called Corbenic, appears to move from place to place, spectrally, as if it is no longer anchored to the physical world, but to the ever-shifting currents of the inner planes.

We see this motif in the myths of the sacrificed god over the course of the year. In each story, the older god is replaced with a younger, more virile version of himself, or a young king trades off with an old king, as seen in the motif of the Oak and Holly Kings found in the agricultural plays of Britain and popularized in modern Wicca and Witchcraft. The sexual element is found in the myths of castration, often by a boar, as in the tale of the god Attis. In some version, he self-castrates to atone for cheating upon the goddess Cybele (giving reason as to why her own priests were eunuchs) and is then killed by a boar. Otherwise he is simply an agricultural and vegetative god killed by the boar embodying the winter tide. Likewise, the mortal lover of goddesses, Adonis, had his life cut short by a wild boar. Most famously, though not involving a wild boar, is the loss of Osiris' phallus when he is dismembered by his brother Set. For his resurrection, his sister-wife Isis has to fashion one from gold for his real phallus was devoured by a fish in the Nile River.

Celtic fishing stories also involve the Salmon of Wisdom, the salmon who eats the hazel nuts of wisdom and who plays a key role in the tale of Fionn mac Cumhaill, or Finn MacCool. Fionn's tale is a cognate in many ways to Taliesin. Both accidentally burn their thumb, suck it, and gain the wisdom and magick meant for another. Interestingly enough, it is a fish that takes Osiris' phallus in his own resurrection tale. Does the fish, as embodied in the teachings of the true Christ, play a role in the redemption? As the Holy Grail in these tales originates with Christ, we can't help but think so esoterically. Yet much of the actions of even the most noble knights don't seem very Christian from a New Testament perspective.

Despite being the king of one kingdom, the effects of this withering of the Fisher King reach all the way to the court of King Arthur, even though the Grail King is not Arthur himself. It shows how the power of sovereignty in a society is overlapping. The disruption of one kingdom leads to the disruption of all, a good point to remember when looking at the global stage. War in one nation will destroy the peace of all nations.

His healing, like ours, cannot occur on its own. Losing his virility, the Fisher King loses his agency to be an active psychic force and must be receptive, waiting for an outside agent to approach him. In this, he learns one of the great mysteries. On the outer planes, the male is active, and the female is receptive. On the inner planes, the male is receptive, and the female is active. He transforms his role from the seeker, the male, to the guardian, the keeper. The outside agent, the worthy knight, must play the active role, asking the right question. Simply by being asked this question, the Fisher King will be healed and the land restored.

The second of the Dolorous Blows comes from King Amangon and his men. The tale of Amangon is found in the French poem known as *The Elucidation,* giving us an introduction to another form of the nine sisters. Returning from a quest, they come upon a beautiful glade with nine maidens who are keepers of a sacred well and its restoring waters. They hold magickal gold goblets and offer hospitality of food and drink to weary travelers. Were these human priestesses of the well? Were they faery women? The tale, written in the Christian era, is unclear. Filled with violence and lust, Amangon and his men take more than they are offered, raping the nine women and stealing the gold cups. This transgression against the guardians of the well, in itself a form of the Holy Grail in the land, results in the well drying up and drought setting in across the land, creating the Wasteland. The Wasteland endures so long that the descendants of the maidens and their rapists become seven guardians of that place, encountering would-be grail knights on their journey. These seven along with the nine maidens must be healed as part of the curse of the Wasteland.

The third and last of the possible Dolorous Blows is more familiar to most modern fans of the Arthurian romances. It is the betrayal of the king. Sadly, as the most well-known, it also has the closest approximation of the Biblical fall from Eden in its theme. The wounding of the union of the king and queen comes through the betrayal by the most celebrated champion and knight, Lancelot. Emissary of the Lady of the Lake, of Avalon, in the court of King Arthur in Camelot, he has an affair with Queen Gwenivere, betraying his best friend Arthur. In the telling of the tale, many place the blame with Gwenivere, painting her as an Eve to Arthur's innocent Adam, yet modern renditions of the tale spread the blame to all three. Arthur is painted as too ambitious, too involved in the outer world of politics and power and not the inner reality his duty afforded him as priest-king for his people, embodying and mediating the divine solar forces to the priestess-queen, embodiment of the land.

In every version, there is a wounding of the sacred relationship between the king and queen – the divine masculine and feminine. Without the proper flow of energy, as shown more violently in the blow to the Fisher King, the land will fail and wither. The act is compounded by the possible divine "crime" of incest with his sister, in the conception and birth of Modred, who will go on to mortally wound his father/uncle Arthur and bring the downfall of Camelot while the best knights are off seeking the grail.

So which of these stories, if any, is true? What is the real reason? Just like life, there is not one reason. All of these reasons are true. Men are wounded, though the wound is necessary and divine and can lead to a greater wholeness. Women are wounded and have had violence brought upon them by men, as reflected in the greater patriarchal society's unthinking violence against the Earth and indigenous people, the children of the Earth closest to her. And from these wounds, men and women have betrayed one another. As we injure each other, we injure ourselves. To harm one is to harm all, including self. We have to recognize we are all wounded by these actions, these choices regardless of gender. We all have aspects of all genders within us while also being beyond all gender from a magickal perspective. Those who are non-binary have a special perspective in these mysteries, but are still participating in the wounding of the world and the process of healing the wound. There is no divine reason for this wounding, but when we let it fester, the unhealed becomes toxic, poisoning us all. All are necessary to come together to heal and renew. Failure to not take your part only leads to more destruction. The people and the land, the world, must find their new harmony together.

From the perspective of the occultist, the magician, the Witch, and the mystic, the three blows reveal something very important. They show us that when you look deeply at the world around you, you see we are still living in the Wasteland. This is the exile from Eden. This is the fall of Atlantis. This is the wandering in the desert. Our theology, politics, and technology – in short our entire society – emphasizes the separation. We know what has been done. The same story has been told and retold, creating the same actions. We must now heal this story, and tell a new one. When each takes responsibility, the poison can stop, and the healing begins.

Exercise 23:
Reflect upon the Dolorous Blows

When you review the Dolorous Blows, some powerful themes that can be applied to our own lives and path arise. I advise journaling on these themes and distilling the journaling down to bullet-point lists. This reflection will help you in later workings for this chapter.

The first blow is the wounding of the Fisher King. This reflection involves when we have been injured, be it by others or through bad luck or circumstance. What are your "injuries" and illnesses seemingly inflicted upon you by forces outside of your control? This list should include all the things you would categorize as "not your fault."

The second blow is the rape of the well maidens. In this reflection, review when you have done harm to another. Was it knowing and willful, or an unexpected consequence? Do you regret it, or would you do it again? Would more awareness and thought have prevented it? What were the consequences of your actions, even if you did not intend them? Is there a way to make reparations?

The last blow is the betrayal of the king and queen. For this reflection, we look at toxic situations we have knowingly participated in with others. We are not the sole victim. We are not the sole perpetrator, but our actions contributed to harm against self and harm against others. These are the "injuries," often of emotions, that we had a hand in creating, even if that was not our original intention. Lies told with "good" reason, hiding situations for our ease or benefit, betrayals because we were betrayed, and retributive behavior against those who wronged us are all a part of this third blow.

Restoration of Heaven

These blows disrupt the potential for the heavenly order to be established – or some would say re-established – upon Earth. In many ways, Camelot was the prototype. Camelot was the trial of the sacred city in the west after the fall of Atlantis. In the East, there are models of Shamballa, and some would say beneath the world is the perfect kingdom of Agartha, but in overt Western culture, Camelot was the experiment. In many ways, otherworldly Avalon was the ideal.

Sacred cities are described in terms of a balanced mandala, with symbols describing the elements and divine powers. The grail's permutations, its Five Miraculous Changes, give it the opportunity to fill any of these roles in the establishment of a new order. These forms – and the myths and symbols attached to them – grant five sacred purposes, not unlike those outlined at the start of this text in the many element-based manifestations of the cauldron. The keepers of these forms – the king, queen, knight, ladies, magicians, and priestesses – create archetypal patterns and a dynamic flow of energy between them in the mandala.

Each of the Five Miraculous Changes shows us something in need of healing, hence the need for the grail to take that form. With the spear, it is the woundings around sex and sexual violence, the root of the patriarchal wound. For the cup, our lack of true medicine to restore health and nourishment. The cauldron restores us from our disconnection with our own divine inspiration. The severed head is our fear of individual and collective death, while the stone is the regeneration of all nature through the secret science: the hope that we can repair what has been done to our world.

The cosmology of the heavenly template is also the cosmology of the soul. Through the quest, a new pattern must be established within, consciously with "all our parts" so that we can treat others from this place of wholeness and build something together. The soul is described as a kingdom, a sacred landscape interfacing with the landscape of a greater world. The court cards of the tarot, esoteric Qabalah, alchemy, and Jungian psychology all give us variations to characterize our consciousness and soul. In our age, the images can be chauvinistic and patriarchal, but it doesn't help us to write a new version without understanding intimately the old models. Many who do cease to see them in terms of outer role models understand the deep soul nature being expressed, how it is the expression of our time and the time before us, without judgment.

The King is on a level of awareness and divine consciousness, but not perfected. The Queen is intuitive and often has hidden powers to be drawn up or out into consciousness. When united together as the divine androgyne, they form what we might think of as the higher self or true self. The princess, the daughter, the spark of soul in the material world is lost to those in the castle. She is really an embodiment of the grail, or at least a keeper of the grail's power and mystery. While some hate the idea of a lost princess, she is really the key to everyone's perfection. The knight or prince is sent on a quest into the world as the conscious, but not necessarily fully aware, self. The round table – and the kingdom itself – gathers all our other parts, and the magician and priestess are advisors on both our sides, offering clues, directions, and gifts.

At heart, this grail provides the potential of the blueprint, the divine matrix, and can forge the link between the greater reality above, in precise and divine working order, to create harmony in the below, our world. By establishing that harmony, a chance is created to go beyond and within, to that which cannot be named. Camelot is the half-way point, where the struggle is clear, but the ideal is also established and striven for despite human mistakes.

Five Miraculous Changes

Magickal lore shows us that the grail can manifest in many different ways, and not all of them are the familiar cup many seek. The grail seems to take on the form of what is considered to be the sacred "hallows." They are the tools from primarily Celtic myth, though having some correspondence with other mystery traditions such as Mithraism that today's magicians and Witches see as embodiments of the four elemental "weapons." These are the same basic tools found in the modern tarot deck.

Traditionally the four hallows are a little less familiar and are associated with names and figures in Irish myth. There are often discrepancies between the sword and the spear and all their associations, stemming from different teachings about fire and air and their directions and tools.

Weapon	Owner	Description	Element	City	Wizard
Sword	Of Nuada	Dividing Sword	Air	Finias	Uiscias
Spear	Of Lugh	Lightning Spear	Fire	Gorias	Esras
Stone	Of Fal	Stone of Death	Earth	Falias	Morfessa
Cauldron	Of Dagda	Hollow	Water	Murias	Semias

Chart 28: Hallows the Tuatha de Danann

Even here, some of the elemental associations are interesting. While the Cauldron of the Dagda is assigned to water in Western esotericism, being the closest to the cup, its function is much more earthy, though we associate the zodiac sign of watery Cancer with the principle of nourishment.

In modern lore, the tools have become:

Tarot Suit	Tool	Element	Key Words
Swords	Blade	Air	Truth, Communication, Mind
Staffs	Wand	Fire	Will, Destiny, Victory, Passion
Coins	Penatcle	Earth	Sovereignty, Resources, Home, Money
Cups	Chalice	Water	Compassion, Emotion, Relationship, Family

Chart 29: Elements and the Hallows

When we look at the grail in what is known as the various "grail processions" filled with rich and confusing symbolism, the revealed grail is often not just a cup. The main things the grail can be include a chalice, a bleeding spear, a plate (often with a severed head upon it), a cauldron, or a stone that is usually described as a meteorite or emerald.

Each of these five shapes, as we have explored, contains a mystery, a different way to approach the grail. Each one has a sacred purpose, not unlike the five sacred purposes we initially put to the elements in the various cauldrons from myth. When comparing the cauldrons to the Five Miraculous Changes, you'll see a transformation amid the elements that can help you understand the interweaving of the elements in the mysteries. If we see the original grail as celestial and airy, linked deeply to speaking, to asking the all-important grail question, then we can see these elemental manifestations as subsets of the greater restoration of the heavenly idea. In some magickal lore, we describe these elements as being "of" the larger element, in this case, air.

Our original purposes of the cauldrons – abundance, rebirth, inspiration, healing, and transformation – are still our sacred purposes, but through the one thing, the grail, that can manifest in these five ways, the symbolism will be different. Each of the strange manifestations of the grail has a purpose and brings us closer to the realization of its mystery.

Chalice

Historic Form: Cup of the Christ from the Last Supper
Element: Water of Air
Sacred Purpose: Healing
Key Words: Forgiveness of Past Wrongs, Restoring the Divine Feminine

The first manifestation is the simple cup, the chalice. In Christian mythos it is recreated as the chalice of Holy Mass, to recall the sacrament of the Last Supper. Jesus shared this cup of his sacramental "blood" just before he knew he would be betrayed. It manifests as the Cup of Healing and Forgiveness, and it is this same shape the grail takes when appearing to the Christian Knights of the Round Table.

Spear

Historic Form: Bleeding Lance weeps for the Fisher King
Element: Fire of Air
Sacred Purpose: Rebirth
Key Words: Heals the Wounded King, Restores Relationship with the Land, Virility

The spear mysteriously shows up in the grail processions as either magickally weeping tears or bleeding of its own accord. It is obviously a manifestation of the phallus of the Fisher King, the wounding and grief of the divine masculine as embodied by the king, and now the grail. While not the most disturbing of the manifestations of the grail, it is still considered disturbing to some. The acceptance of what is followed by the asking of the grail question restores the vitality of the king. He is freed, and can be "replaced" by a new king and keeper, renewing the land itself. In the Christian mythos, the lance is the Spear of Destiny, or Spear of Longinus, the non-Biblical name of the Roman soldier who pierced Christ's side during the crucifixion. Folklore says it survived and that it allows the wielder to control destiny and be undefeated. Occult conspiracy theories claim that Hitler sought the spear in his conquest of the world.

Plate

Historic Form: Dish with the Severed Head of the Prophet
Element: Air of Air
Sacred Purpose: Inspiration
Key Words: Initiation, Speaks Prophecy from Outside of Life and Time

The plate or dish sometimes manifests alone, embodying the mystery of emptiness.

When appearing with a severed and perhaps bloody head, a new mystery is presented, but one we are already familiar with through the teachings of Bran and the comparisons with Orpheus. In these Christian tales, it is usually the head of John the Baptist, and we can make occult connections to mystical teachings of the Knights Templar, where John's severed head, speaking oracles and prophecy in a holy tongue, plays a strong role. The plate speaks what was, is, and will be – from the perspective beyond life and outside of time.

Cauldron

Historic Form: Cauldron of Annwn
Element: Earth of Air
Sacred Purpose: Abundance
Key Words: Cooks Food of a Noble Warrior, Cures Famine

From a grail mythos, the cauldron most often associated with the grail is the Cauldron of Annwn, the one Arthur sought through the various caers of the otherworld. It is the cauldron of food and abundance, as well as inspiration warmed by the breath of nine maidens. In many ways, when considering the word "spoils" as named in the title of the poem "The Spoils of Annwn," one might think he unfairly claimed the cauldron, stealing it and bringing it to the human world, and did not have permission to do so. Perhaps that is why only seven returned.

Stone

Historic Form: Emerald Fallen from Lucifer's Crown
Element: Spirit of Air
Sacred Purpose: Transformation
Key Words: Co-Creation, Restoration, Enlightenment

One of the most mysterious manifestations – and perhaps the most disturbing for those following traditional Christian theology – is that the grail is really an emerald that fell from heaven. This emerald was "carved" into the Holy Grail, and possibly is of the same substance as the Emerald Tablet of Hermes. From an alchemical perspective, it is the "one thing" that all things are made of. When crafting the Philosopher's Stone, we seek to make our own. One myth says the emerald was brought to Earth during the War of Heaven by the neutral angels, taking neither side in the battle. They called it the Ordo Lapsit Exillis, another name we use for the Philosopher's Stone. Another myth tells us that during the War in Heaven with the righteous angels fighting the rebellious, the leader of the rebels – the beautiful Lucifer, bearer of light – was knocked about and an emerald from his crown loosened and fell off, entering the Earth, becoming the grail – the key to restoring harmony within all spheres. Gnostic faery traditions echoing back to Scottish lore say that Lucifer is the emerald and his fall ignited conscious creation. Theosophists have a similar theology with a figure known as Sanat Kumara, hailing from Venus, whose descent initiates earthly life as the role of the Planetary Logos is assumed. Those looking for it physically claim the green silica tektite known as moldavite, formed from an ancient meteorite strike, as the Luciferian emerald.

When trying to sort out the strange and mysterious manifestations of the grail, it can be helpful to look to other grail explorers. An expert in the psychic search for the grail, author Andrew Collins is recorded by Avalonian scholar Paul Weston in his book *Avalonian Aeon* on seeking the true nature of the grail:

The grail is but a superficial image created in a modern age. The true Grail is a multi-dimensional crystalline complex that forms the blueprint to cosmic order and form, from the center of the universe, the moment of the big bang. It includes all life in this universe, its influence setting the standards of life for a cycle of time. It is the co-ordination of the cosmic pulse of life and exists on many levels, the heartbeat of the world, it's a cosmic computer, controller of the destinies of Time.

Notice that in all five miraculous changes, the grail does not become the sword. While Excalibur can be considered a "hallow" in the magickal sense, and an otherworldly gift from the Lady of the Lake, it appears that the questing knights already have their blades with them. The grail manifests as the other hallows they are less likely to have already.

With all this in mind, in the end it doesn't matter how the grail manifests. We study the past to try to better prepare, but it will appear as it will appear, and we must be prepared to receive the experience that we need, that is being offered to us by the cosmos.

The Elements and the Miraculous Changes

Obviously, when you look at these magickal tools, it's easy to see that any manifestation of the miraculous change and almost any mythic cauldron can embody any and all of the elements and powers. Upon deeper meditation and reflection, I questioned the discrepancy between the elemental associations I had for the primal cauldron of myth and the elemental associations for the five miraculous changes. The five changes of the grail came out of one manifestation of the mythic cauldron, our holy grail, but still, it appeared there was some pattern here to explore. Though meditation and vision work, my own understanding unfolded.

A magickal teaching separates three elements from the four, usually dividing earth or fire from the matrix. In the magickal teachings, as diverse as the Greek teachings on the triple power of Hecate to the houses of the Welsh gods outlined in *The Mabinogi*, we have a tripartite division of the world as Land, Sea, and Sky. Likewise, we see the same in the teachings of traditional Witch Robert Cochrane, in his mythos of the Clan of Tubal Cain. In it, three queens represent the elements of earth, water, and air, for fire is reserved for the blacksmith god.

Yet in the practices of ceremonial magick, the twenty-two sacred letters all have associations with sets of twelve for the zodiac, seven for the ancient planets, and three, known as mother letters. The mother letters are ascribed the elements of fire, air, and water, with manifestation, earth, doubled with the latter and assigned to Saturn. Earth is said to rise from the waters in this creation myth. Along with the elements and astrology, the letters have been corresponded with the trumps of the major arcana of the tarot, and the modern "outer" planets.

Letter	*Aleph*	*Mem*	*Shin*
Meaning	Ox	Water	Tooth
Value	1	40	300
Sound	A	M	S/Sh
Element	Air	Water	Fire
Alchemy	Mercury	Salt	Sulfur
Power	Equalizing	Silent	Sound
Planet	Uranus	Neptune	Pluto
Tarot Card	0. The Fool	XII. The Hanged Man	XX. Judgment

Chart 30: Mother Letters

The three mother letters through the tarot also speak of the grail quest. Grail knights such as Perceval start out as the divine fool, not really a knight at all. They wander the world, the Wasteland, not often knowing the consequences of their actions. Yet they have such divine potential at the start of the quest to truly fulfill it. That is also most of us. We start innocent and foolish. The Fisher King is the hanged man. He is stuck between life and death. He is stuck between the world and the waters he fishes. He is immobile, yet can see the situation and the problem at hand so clearly. He just doesn't yet have the power to do anything about it, until the grail knight visits him. Lastly is the procession of the grail, where the knight with the king encounters the aim of the quest and must ask a fateful question. Does he succeed in the quest, or fail? Will he bring about the end of the world as we know it and a renewal of a heavenly work, or leave the world as he found it?

The three mother letters also speak to the threefold sacrifice and initiation formula that is found in many traditions. Those in the Arthurian mythos would see it most closely in the older tales of Merlin. The initiate would be drowned, stabbed, and hung – relating to water, fire, and air. We find similar ritual death in the bog bodies, such as the famous Lindow Man. The retrieved and preserved corpse reveals stabbing, strangling, and being thrown into a body of water. The sacrificial death can also be found in the crucifixion. Christ was hung on the cross – which is both being raised in the air and mythically connected to the Hanged Man card – and stabbed in the side with the spear. Unlike Merlin, he is not drowned, for his initiation of water happened earlier, with John the Baptist.

My own inner explanations between the elements of the mythic cauldrons and the miraculous changes of the grail yielded a special transformative relationship between the elements of air, water, and fire. If you assign the whole Holy Grail mythos to the element of air and the principle of healing in the greater macrocosm of the mythic cauldrons, and then look at their subdivision as described above, you'll see the relationship between air, water, and fire.

Rebirth in the grail mythos comes from the regeneration of the king, of the phallus, as found in the spear. Rebirth in the macrocosm of the cauldron mysteries is found in the Cauldron of Bran, and the bodily regeneration of the soldiers of Bran and his enemies.

Healing in the grail mythos comes from drinking from the chalice, the holy cup. Healing in the macrocosm of the cauldron mysteries comes from asking the sacred question of the grail bearers and offering to serve.

Inspiration in the grail mythos comes from the words of the severed head, the prophecy of one who is found beyond life and time. Inspiration in the macrocosm of the cauldron mysteries comes from the cauldron of awen, the first cauldron of Cerridwen, and taking those three divine drops.

Grail Element	Miraculous Change	Principle of the Grail	Mythic Principle
Fire of Air	The Spear of the Grail	Rebirth in Healing	Rebirth Was Water
Water of Air	The Cup of the Grail	Healing in Healing	Healing Was Air
Air of Air	The Severed Head of the Grail	Inspiration in Healing	Inspiration Was Fire
Earth of Air	The Cauldron of the Grail	Abundance in Healing	Abundance Was Earth
Spirit of Air	The Stone of the Grail	Transformation in Healing	Transformation Was Spirit

Chart 31: Grail Elements

Abundance in the grail mythos comes from the cauldron of Annwn, boiling the food of one who is deserving and remaining cold for those who are cowards. Abundance in the macrocosm of the cauldron mysteries is the Cauldron of the Dagda, the never-ending Undry.

Transformation in the grail mythos is less clear. I would assign the stone, the Ordo Lapsit Exillis, as the restorative and regenerative force bringing heaven to Earth and Earth to heaven. It is the spark of light within matter seeking to redeem the world. Through the touch of the Philosopher's Stone, the lead is turned to bright gold and beyond. Transformation in the macrocosm of the cauldron mysteries is the alchemical crucible, our attempt to make the heavenly stone from our own world, and our own selves. It is our attempt to release and redeem, to create heaven on Earth. The stone is the bridge between the macrocosm and our microcosms. It is the divine matrix, and as Andrew Collins says, the "multi-dimensional crystalline complex that forms the blueprint to cosmic order and form, from the center of the universe."

Now other occultists might make the association of the stone to earth and the cauldron of Annwn to spirit, and that could be equally correct. One of the reasons I find for the separation of both the elements of earth and spirit is their unique nature. The element of spirit is within Earth, and Earth itself contains all elements. That is the reason the pentacle, the five-pointed star, is both a symbol of the common concerns of the material world and also the supreme symbol of the mysteries. The pentacle shows us the secret star that is within the stone, the star that is within all of us, the Venus star bearing the light of the heavens and the true form of healing. All we must do is ask, "How do I serve?"

The Three Sacred Drinks

When one looks at the sacred purposes of the grail, in the restoration of sovereignty, some basic themes come up. One must have their basic needs met, like food and shelter, and this comes through the purpose of abundance. It is the foundation for all other aspects, the bottom rung on a hierarchy of needs as described by the modern psychologist Abraham Maslow in 1943, though drawn from the teachings of the Blackfoot Nation. While a modern term, the principle is ancient. Once needs are met, true healing can be possible. One can feel safe enough to admit wrongdoing to others, to themselves, and their world. With safety they can ask for forgiveness and take restorative actions to address the situation to the best of their ability. With safety, we can address those who have harmed us, and when not possible, address the situation ourselves and how it affects us. Through healing there is the first rebirth of the self, and we may undergo many more rebirths, finding a regeneration and renewal in our relationship with ourselves, others, and the world by letting go of the past hurts and forgiving ourselves when we have hurt others. From this new perspective, we can seek inspiration and go with the flow of life, seeing things and taking action from a broader and more inclusive place. Lastly, we can transform ourselves, embodying the grail, becoming a catalyst for change. We can truly be of service to a higher good, offering aid to other people, the land, the ancestors, and the spirits.

Interestingly enough, the quest itself can be enough to undermine safety and shake us from our complacency to change. The first goal of the wilderness is to break our patterns of safety and truly look for authentic and essential security. It comes from a place where the seeker has already established security and then must break the pattern to really change. If all else fails, the knight could go back to the security of the court, and most of the failed grail knights do.

So with our concerns of safety, healing, and service, grail mythology presents us with three types of drinks, in an almost alchemical pattern.

Bright Drink – The bright, white, or clear drink speaks to our sense of nutrition, need, and safety. It nourishes and restores. In ritual, milk or water can be used for the bright drink.

Dark Drink – The dark drink is the drink of healing. It can bring on forgetfulness to let go of the past or simply to face our shadow, our own darkness, and consume it rather than run and reject it. Dark drinks can be a dark beer or ale, or a dark juice, such as pomegranate. If there is a dark drink you do not like the taste of, that makes the best of the dark drinks.

Red Drink – The red drink is the wine of the lord and indicates the sovereign of the area. It is the drink of stewardship, and calls upon us to act, to share in hospitality with others. The lord or lady of the keep must safeguard and develop the land not just for self, but for all of the community. Wine or red grape juice is appropriate for this drink.

For ritual work, I suggest adding the cell salts of different zodiac signs to the three drinks to imbibe them with a deeper healing intention, for the ritual working of the question.

Exercise 24:
Preparation of the Drinks

Before attempting the next ritual vision, obtain three liquids to be used for the bright drink, dark drink, and red drink. Just before performing the ritual, place into each a small amount of the cell salts listed.

Mythic Drink	Ritual Drink	Zodiac	Cell Salts	Bach Flower Remedy
Bright Drink	Water or Milk	Cancer Taurus Aquarius Sagittarius	Calcium Fluoride Sodium Sulfate Sodium Chloride Silica	Clematis Gentian Water Violet Agrimony
Dark Drink	Beer, Ale, or Juice	Virgo Scorpio Aries Gemini	Potassium Sulfate Calcium Sulfate Potassium Phosphate Potassium Chloride	Chicory Impatiens Cerato
Red Drink	Wine or Juice	Leo Capricorn Libra Pisces	Magnesium Phosphate Calcium Phosphate Sodium Phosphate Iron Phosphate	Vervain Mimulus Scleranthus Rock Rose

Chart 32: Three Drinks

If you would rather add another safe and subtle zodiac correspondence instead, such as a flower essence or gem elixir, please do so. I would also highly recommend the "twelve healers" of Dr. Edward Bach's original Flower Remedy healing system. Each is associated with a zodiac sign and its related issues, which I have listed here (**Chart 32: Three Drinks**) as an option for you. While the plants may not align with the traditional herbal astrological and planetary correspondences, Dr. Bach created a system that speaks deeply to the mental and emotional patterns in the twelve signs.

For the bright drink, Cancer is the sign of the nourishing mother. Taurus values pleasure and the home. Aquarius is the sign of friendship and social groups, while Sagittarius is the enjoyment of exploration and freedom, as the mentoring of a wise teacher.

For the dark drink, Virgo is the sign of the healer, helping us discern what to keep and what to release. Scorpio aids in the delving deep into our psyche and past. Aries requires us to take action and face our fears, while Gemini helps us look into how our minds might be tricking us.

Lastly for the red drink of leadership, Leo is the sign of the Sun King and sovereign, followed closely with Capricorn as the sign of responsible leadership. Libra seeks balance and justice, while Pisces is the spiritual leader, serving the divine principle of heaven.

These drinks will be used for the Grail Quest and the Consuming of the Emerald of the Grail Ritual that follows. They are particularly important to prepare for the grail ritual, to be ritually consuming all twelve energies in combination with the five sacred gifts.

The Quest of the Grail

Now that we have an understanding of the five, or more, potential manifestations of the grail in these stories, and how they can be related to the other cauldrons of myth, we must understand the Grail Quest. The tales hinge on the idea that the grail is someplace else, and one must go on a far and dangerous journey for the hope to encounter it. While the specific sequence and encounters are different in each version of the tale, essentially the knight must leave the familiar and go into a strange landscape filled with monsters and magickal knights. To those with a magickal eye, the journey away from the castle and court is a journey into the otherworld, a psychic landscape as much as a terrestrial world. While not explicitly stating it, their thresholds and borders are the same as the caers found in "The Spoils of Annwn," though the knights go questing alone, not with a company. In these tales, Arthur remains behind, and the knight is his agent.

Through the quest, the knight must both learn new information and pass tests to show what has been learned. This is quite like an initiatory journey through the underworld. As in the traditions of the Egyptians, Greeks, and later Christian Gnostics, which required certain code words, symbols, and signs to pass through the gates, this step is indicative of specific forms of knowledge and magick. Ideally, the word or symbol has no power on its own, but is empowered by the inherent characteristics of the initiate the symbol embodies and focuses. If you haven't done the spiritual work, having the codes without deep understanding will not help you. Later traditions most likely focused on the outer form, the talisman and correct words and sounds.

While today quasi-masonic initiation rites using Arthur as a foundation have similar passwords and handshakes, the Arthurian Romance seems to have no set of instructions. Each knight on the quest must wander until they stumble through it, or are guided by God to a wise character willing to help them.

Through the quest, the knight must ultimately grow as a spiritual being, embody the codes of chivalry (that time and place's understanding of reverence for the feminine), and demonstrate virtue.

The knight is challenged to combat and overcome fear, but also to make moral decisions, framed in the backdrop of medieval Christianity.

Through analysis of many versions, and looking to the rites and rituals based upon the story, there are five major points of the quest, with many variations.

Quest	Element	New Quality	Challenge
Wilderness	Earth	Security	Strips Us of Abundance
Questing Beast	Water	Compassion	Challenges Us to Be a Healer
Crossing the Bridge	Air	Authenticity	Confronts Us to Be in Spirit
Facing the Guardians	Fire	Virtue	Tests Our Reborn Self
Grail Procession	Spirit	Service	Requires Us to Transform

Chart 33: Points of the Grail Quest

Each of these stages has its own peril. And each of these steps has a key to move through it. As an occultist, it is natural to look at anything divided into five and assign elements to it. We could also further subdivide the quest in seven or nine. All of these stages are a simplification when looking at many variations of the mythic tale. There is a chapel in the wilderness that provides respite or teaching to the knight. There is usually more than one guardian and the tests are many, including the guardian as a king with his wife providing additional tests of virtue. There can be encounters at the lake with the Fisher King before realizing he is the keeper of the grail. And lastly the Grail Castle can contain two kings, a wounded younger king as the Fisher and an older, hidden king as the true keeper of the grail, surviving only on what the grail will provide for him. But for our fivefold exploration of the grail here in this chapter, we will simplify with five major stages.

The Wilderness of the Wasteland

Once the boundary of Camelot's territory is crossed, one enters into a wilderness of the Wasteland. While we might expect a Wasteland to be desert-like, and in some cases that imagery is used, often there is a wildness to a thick wood. This forest is unwelcoming. Food is hard to find. Poisons and thorny hedges block the way. Dangerous animals are hidden and hunting. The wilderness brings up all the knight's thoughts – and our thoughts as well – of "the other." This land is not centered on humanity. Humanity's civilization is the outsider here. To survive, there is a level of having to get back to "nature" but nature as it is said to be "red in tooth and claw" to quote Alfred Lord Tennyson. We have to leave the relative safety of civilization and its confinement. The wild can break the patterns of routine and obligation, the distractions of daily life and stress, to make us truly alone with our own self. Why do so many mystics go into nature alone to discover their purpose and power? Merlin runs wild in the woods and returns a prophet. Jesus wanders the desert for forty days and returns the Messiah. Wilderness brings out the primal, forcing us to shed many of the unnatural artifices we carry, the untrue thoughts and feelings, images, and projections. We must get lost in ourselves to be found. We get lost in our thoughts, feelings, and ideas, and to find our way through the overwhelming and disorienting, we have to find our own personal "true north" and sift through our experience to "tell the forest from the trees." The reality of our world becomes apparent when we have nothing but ourselves.

The obvious element to the wild woods is earth. This earth teaches us to find security in ourselves, as it strips us of communal security and sense of abundance. Food and shelter are not just around the corner. Can you trust yourself? Can you trust in nature? Can you return to the security the deer and the rabbit have, in the wild, not worry day to day in the way that humans worry? With that bottom foundation of Maslow's pyramid taken from us, we become destabilized for a time. It is in those periods of destabilization that the greatest changes, with new foundations, can be made.

Taming the Questing Beast

The knight will encounter some sort of monster that must be overcome. In the lore, this can take the form of the bizarre questing beast. It appears as a kind of khymera, a strange mix of many animals. In some tales, the hunt for the questing beast, not the grail, is the focus. It was originally described with the form of a large snake for a head and neck, the body of a leopard, the hindquarters of a lion, and the cloven hooves of a stag, making a monstrous sound of thirty hunting hounds within its belly barking. Though some scholars think it's a mangled description of the giraffe, the mythic origin of the beast is linked with a devilish birth from violence or incest. It appears to Arthur when he conceives Mordred with his sister. The questing beast represents all that is wrong in the realm of Camelot, and by extension, our world.

For modern knights on the quest, the beast is the embodiment of fear, chaos, and all that has gone wrong between us and nature. Our shame and guilt around our violent ways as well as our inner conflict around sexuality and sexual abuse are tied to the beast. The beast becomes a repository for a collective shadow, things we do not seek to bring to consciousness, but instead repress and cast out. And in that repression, these feelings haunt us as the beast, providing something external to blame and hunt.

The key to the beast in the quest is to not slay it. Slaying it will only create another. The beast must be tamed, truly embraced and shown compassion. This transforms the beast, and it is revealed for what it is, another creature, often pregnant, also struggling in the world. The element of the beast is water, as it embodies primal emotions and shadow feelings. It strikes terror in our heart. While the grail quest is about our own healing, right up front, we are confronted with the challenge to be healer first, rather than destroyer. We must offer the beast a sip from our own healing cup. We must show compassion for the suffering, rather than label it "other" and monster. If we do not, then we deserve it when others label us monsters and seek to destroy us. Here at this stage. the knight must realize that this adventure is different. It's not about who can kill the most foes and be the most skillful warrior. The grail knight must be strong and brave, but demonstrate these virtues in unusual ways. How different would our mythologies be if the knight spoke to the monster or dragon first, rather than jump into the battle immediately?

While the motivation must be altruistic, one might find the transformed beast willing to help the knight on the next stage of the quest.

Crossing the Sword Bridge of the Abyss

Past the beast and further into the otherworldly wilderness, the knight will spy the castle that becomes the focus of the quest. Yet the castle is not easy to approach. It is across a chasm, representing the vast and seemingly uncrossable distance between the human consciousness of the knight and what lies beyond in the castle of the grail. Magickal systems of attainment are full of images of veils, locks, barriers, and abysses to be crossed by the initiate.

In Arthurian lore, the key to crossing is in the form of either a secret passageway, tunnel, or bridge, each with their own challenge and dangers. One of the most evocative images is that of the "sword bridge," a giant sword or series of swords connecting both sides of the chasm. If it were a single normal sword, the knight could simply jump because the gap would be narrow to be bridged by a normal sword. The polished and sharp edge is up, requiring the knight to walk on the edge to cross. The implication is obvious: the knight will both have trouble balancing on such a fine edge and risks falling, but even if successful, can cut himself beyond immediate repair, potentially crippling him for life. The other side will also have exotic animal guardians, such as lions, signaling this is a realm of a king. When presented this option, there is also a tunnel that goes under the raging river in the chasm, surrounding the castle. To reach it, the knight would have to climb down the side of the cliff, so most choose the way of the sword.

Our elemental association for the sword – and this bridge hanging over the abyss – is air. Air is our communication with ourselves and others. It is the ideas we carry, also about ourselves and others. Air embodies truth, and how we express our truthful, authentic self. The wilderness should have already worked well in separating us from many of the ideas that may lead to a false sense of security. In our elemental manifestations of the grail, air is of inspiration, the truth spoken by the severed head. Fall the wrong way with the sword bridge, and the grail knight might also become a severed head. The key teaching of the bridge is to shed all ideas and identities of self that are not the truth, and to be clearly in the moment, the state of consciousness we have when we are "in spirit" or inspired, in the eternal now.

To ritually do this, the knight takes off his armor, shedding the defensive barrier that would be far too heavy to balance on such a perilous crossing. Initiates of the mysteries are asked to disrobe, to come nude, or as Wiccans say, skyclad, showing the literal and metaphysical shedding of outer identity, comfort, and protection. One is quite vulnerable when naked. At the same time, we all carry metaphoric armor to protect us emotionally and mentally. The sword bridge requires us to drop it all, to be in the moment, one with spirit, and trust in ourselves and the process. It only allows what is the essential self, the true self, to cross.

Guardians of the Gate

Either before attaining the Grail Castle through a confrontation in another setting (at another castle or keep) or at the various gates within the Grail Castle itself, the questing knight is challenged in some way. The challenge might be a seemingly more obvious challenge, and the challenger can be a returning character from an earlier portion of the story. The concept of "colored" knights as challengers and guardians is popular, including Green, Red, Black and Blue Knights, crossing streams with other Arthurian romances. The guardian will test the worthiness of the questing knight. The challenge can be in words and poetry, though asking what the questing knight has done to be worthy. Sometimes the challenging knight is unknowingly a friend, in the guise of another lord or king offering hospitality. In such situations, it is the wife of the king, the queen of the castle, who tempts and seduces the questing knight. Virtue is challenged, and the knight is asked pointblank a question about it, and must answer truthfully, despite wanting to protect the reputation of the queen. Truth must win out.

The elemental association with the guardian confrontation is fire. In our miraculous charge of the grail, fire is the element of the lance, the weeping spear, and speaks to the castration of the king, so it is only fitting that challenges of either "manhood" or sexuality are put before the questing knight. The spear's power is to renew and regenerate the king, to give him rebirth. In many ways, the "new" questing knight, from crossing the bridge, is challenged to put his truth into action. Virtue is not simply believing in something, but putting your worthiness in action as demonstrated by your behaviors. Speaking of virtue does nothing. Virtue is in the doing, or not doing, when tempted to move against your truth. Wands and fire are all about the actions we take to define who we are.

The Grail Procession within the Chapel of the Castle

The grail procession is one of the strangest and most mysterious points of the Fisher King mythos. To any ritualist, it points to the possibility of an actual ritual procession as part of some secret mystery tradition. The specific symbols vary, but it is a procession of spectral quality. In some tales, the procession is first seen wandering the wilds of the Wasteland in the beginning of the quest, like ghosts or faeries, singing an unearthly music, some form of Christian hymn. First illustrated in the story of Perceval, our hero is having dinner with the Fisher King. In each course of the meal, he sees youths carrying various items such as the lance oozing blood down to the hands of the squire who holds it; two gold candelabras of ten candles, each held by two young handsome men; and finally the grail cup itself by a young maiden. The grail of pure gold is set with every precious stone imaginable, finer than any seen before. Light shines from the grail that is so bright, it is described as the Sun, and the candle flames are like the stars, blocked out by the brightness of the Sun. The grail maiden is followed by another young woman carrying a beautiful silver platter. Perceval fails to ask any question about what he sees, fearing to be rude. He was taught this by the man who knighted him, but is later chastised by a "loathsome" or ugly woman, possibly under a curse, for failing to ask, "Whom does the grail serve?" Specifically the question refers to whom the procession was taking the grail, presumably to serve their meal, but it carries the larger implication of service and the grail.

So the original procession consists of a young male squire, two handsome boys, and two maidens, five in all. The first item is a symbol reflecting wounding, with its blood. Occultists see the Tree of Life and the Tree of Knowledge in the two candelabras, then ten candles for the ten realms of the Tree of Life, and then ten candles for their reverse, what is known as the Tree of Knowledge or Tree of Death. It is the tree of the broken universe below ours. Their light is united by the healing light of the grail, illuminated with jewels and gold. And these blessings are to be received in the world upon the plate. Occult lore tells us that the inhabitants of the Grail Castle are manifestations of all those seeking to be healed, not just the Fisher King. They are the nine Maidens of the Wells, and their seven offspring, the ladies and lords of the world who suffer until the grail restores the world. The castle holds their lost spirits and soul fragments.

The key to the grail procession is to ask the question, but it is not simply the process of asking. Perceval is being asked to change, to transform once again. He was taught not to ask questions by his first teacher, the one who knighted him, initiating him into the world of the knight. He is now challenged to become something else, and has to let go of old ways that no longer serve. That is the essence of becoming something new – the willingness to let go of what was once a guiding light and find a new authority in self, rather than rule or regulation. Through that willingness, we are able to be of greater service, as we will do what is correct and necessary in the moment, following our own inner guidance, rather than an outer authority figure. By being willing to transform and ask the question, the king would be healed.

So upon the quest's end, what does the knight have to do to take full advantage of any form of the grail? Fulfill the task embodied by the air element we assigned to this manifestation of the primal cauldron at the start of this book – ask the sacred question, "For whom does the grail serve?" Each of the five miraculous changes and five points of the quest are the support structure to that central mystery.

Really, all we have to do is ask any question that allows us to participate in the process of restoration. In the descent of Inanna, initiates are told the failure of Inanna when facing her dark sister of the underworld was in not asking, "Sister what ails thee, and how can I be of service?" Simply asking "What is going on?" and "How can I help?" implying service for the greater good, not ego satisfaction, is the key. When we can find that detachment from our own sense of need, we can faithfully serve, and in serving others, we also serve ourselves. Asking is holy. Asking is how we mindfully and purposefully, with full consent, participate.

EXERCISE 25:
The Grail Quest

Follow the path of the Grail Knight and enter the quest. This is a long vision working, and can be divided into several sessions where breaks are indicated. It can be helpful to divide it, reflecting upon your experience before going further to make sure you are ready for any changes it may trigger.

Ritual Items:

10 Candles: White, Gray, Black, Blue, Red, Yellow, Green, Orange, Purple, and Brown
Wand for the Lance
Chalice for the Cup
Stone (preferably green)
Plate
Cauldron
Bowl of the Bright Drink
Bowl of the Dark Drink
Bowl of the Red Drink
Incense, Charcoal, and Incense Burner
Water in Bowl
Salt in Bowl

Grail Quest Incense

3 Parts Frankincense
2 Parts Myrrh
1 Part Storax
1 Part Benzoin
½ Part Cedar
½ Part Cinnamon

Figure 24: Altar of the Grail

On an altar, prepare the grail hallows and candles. Have bowls prepared with the three individual drinks – bright, dark, and red. Face north and place the consecrated cauldron in the north, the wand in the east, the plate in the south, and the cup in the west. Place the stone in the center, and around it, the three bowls of the drinks. Place the bowl of water in the southwest and the bowl of salt in the northwest. Place the incense burner in the southeast and the incense bottle or bowl in the northeast. The candles can be arranged in any way you wish. Though a single candelabra of ten tapers is ideal, it is not necessary.

To start, add a pinch of salt to the water and dip your fingers in it. Those of a Christian persuasion might make the sign of the cross, while Qabalists may perform the Qabalistic Cross and Pagans the "goblin cross" of touching your brow, left breast, right shoulder, left shoulder, right breast, and back to the brow, forming a pentagram.

To create simple sacred space, light the incense charcoal and sprinkle the incense upon it. Take the incense from the center to the north and back to the center. Then move to the east and back to the center. Then to the south and back to the center. Finally move to the west and to the center. Hold the incense above you to the heavens and then back down near the floor before returning it to the center of the altar.

Light your ten candles in the following order – brown, purple, orange, green, yellow, red, blue, black, gray, and lastly white. This is the color order of climbing the Tree of Life, of approaching the godhead.

Using the skills you have learned, enter a meditative and visionary state to commune with the spirit world. Your intention is to walk the path of the grail knight and to see the Castle of Corbenic where the Fisher King keeps the grail.

Part One: Facing the Wild

Before you is the greenery of the forest trees. Part the trees with a rustling of leaves and step into the forest. You find yourself on a forest path. As you look around, it is a wild, sinister landscape that looms all around you. The forest is as much hedge as it is trees, with thick thorns and brambles making passage difficult. You find a sword in your hand, and you use it to cut your way through the overgrowth. This is not the fun adventure you had hoped and dreamed about. You feel frustrated, wandering, mindlessly slashing at things but getting nowhere. The rough spots of the trail alternate with desolate areas, where the land appears to have been poisoned. There is no life, no sound, just an eerie stillness. You can't help but wonder and think that you might have made a big mistake by taking this quest. You have left the safe world behind. You have left your home. You have left your bed. You have left all security behind.

In your wandering, you hear something faint in the distance, like the haunting melody of pipes, or a high-pitched choir. As you gaze through the branches, you see an eerie, otherworldly procession of what could be specters or faeries, solemnly walking as they sing a chillingly familiar tune. You can't understand the words. You move towards them.

The more you try to reach them, it is as if the branches of the forest itself are trying to block you. By the time you think you have caught up to them, they disappear. Yet the path is open once again, as if the procession has cut a well-worn path for you. The forest no longer fights you, and your way is now clear. Follow the path they have set. You now have more confidence that the path will lead to the Grail Castle.

While the path is easier, it is still strange and frightening. Amid the brush, you hear a disturbing noise of an animal, or a group of animals, yipping and barking. You look to your left and see a stream. By the stream is a strange, awful beast unlike anything you have ever gazed upon before.

There you see what you know is the Questing Beast. It is serpentine and feline all at the same time, larger than the largest horse, with the back claws of a lion, the spots of a leopard, and the long head of a snake. The front hooves strike the ground. From its belly, not its mouth, you hear the cries of a pack of animals seeking to burst forth from its body. The unearthly creature is unnerving, and you know by seeing it that you are no longer in the realm of humanity.

The very sight of it releases a primal fear within you. The hackles on your skin rise as you know it is dangerous. Just looking at it brings up every awful thing you've ever done, ever thought about. It is a beast embodying shame, violence, fear, and chaos. You are ill and overwhelmed by this nightmare, yet you know you must face it.

Go down to the river. Face it. Look truly and deeply at it. Welcome it. Tame it.

As you do, you realize it is not violent, but in pain. To tame it you must befriend it and help it. You must forgive yourself and forgive others. As you do, the beast changes in your eyes. You see the amalgam of different animals makes it look silly, something to frighten a child, not an adult.

Each moment you spend with it, it becomes smaller and more docile, more friendly. It soon sheds the form of beast and becomes a quite small fox, pregnant with a large litter. Can you offer the fox compassion? Commune with the spirit of this creature. It might shift its shape again to another animal, perhaps one you have already encountered in your cauldron journeys. Thank the fox.

When you feel you have transformed your situation with the Questing Beast, return to rest and reflect. Journal on whatever the beast brought up from your past, and how you feel about it now.

Part Two: Passing the Tests

Repeat the preliminary rituals with water, incense, and candlelight. Fix your mind upon the transformed beast once again. Return to where you left it and gaze upon the befriended animal. How does the animal look now?

If you have successfully transformed the beast, it will guide you, despite any of its own difficulties, along the path. In the distance, you see the path leading upward to a cliff, and across the cliff the silhouette of the great castle. You realize that is most likely the realm you seek, and you wonder how you will ever get there.

Step by step you make it up to the cliff, to the edge of the chasm. There the former questing beast turned fox leaves you. You look beyond and see what was once a magnificent castle, now somewhat dilapidated. You look down and see the roaring blue-black waters at the bottom of a very steep chasm. As you look deeply into the dark water, you wonder if it is water at all. The white rapids now appear like clusters of stars against the darkness. You realize this chasm is really the abyss, and those who fall in could be lost forever in a broken universe.

You see further down that the chasm is bridged by a very large sword, like the sword of a giant, longer than two lances held from end to end. The sword's edge is held up, with the hilt of the sword closest to you, and the point thrust into a tree on the other side. Also on the other side are two lions looking quite ferocious. One lets out a roar. You recognize the sword bridge from the stories and know you have to walk the blade's edge with a sense of uncanny balance, which could potentially maim your feet, or if you tried to crawl, knees and hands. What will you do?

Looking below again, you see the hint of a tunnel, a bridge beneath that crosses the abyss through the water, creating a water-bridge. To get there, you would have to climb down the cliff side and risk falling into the abyss anyway. Two choices are before you, the sword or the water. As a knight on a quest, you know you are called to the way of the sword.

To successfully cross the sword bridge, you must divest yourself of all armor, both metallic and spiritual. To be light enough to avoid being cut by the blade, you must shed your unnecessary traits and energies, including all pretense, masks, bravado, or disguises. You must be your truthful, honest, and authentic self. Strip away your armor and clothes, and as you do, release the subtle armor you carry with you. Become your essential self. Let go of your attachment to labels, good and bad, applied to yourself. Let go of your titles. Let go of your preferences. Let go of your stories, accomplishments, and even beliefs. You might even feel your flesh is falling from your skeleton, revealing pure spirit.

Unencumbered, cross the edge of the sword. Don't look down. Just focus on looking across. The lions hold your gaze, but soften in their stance. As you make your way to the other side, you begin to take form again, but a new purer form. The lions barely notice you now, but as you become more "solid" and "you" again, you feel lighter and truer to the essential self. You've shed a lot that no longer serves your highest purpose.

As you follow the path to approach the castle entrance, you realize the castle is somewhat circular, and might even seem like it's spinning. There are three main concentric rings surrounding a tower in the center.

Come to the first gate and knock on the door, a red door, announcing yourself and your quest. The gate opens and reveals a fearsome Red Knight holding a bloody spear.

The Red Knight asks you what you have done to deserve entry to the castle. What have you done that is brave, of service, that constitutes selfless good deeds? Can you answer?

Depending on your answer, the Red Knight will let you pass or challenge you in combat. If the Red Knight deems you worthy, you are allowed to pass into the first courtyard, the first realm. In this realm, the people all seem like ghosts, ephemeral and unreal. They barely notice you at all. They seem to be unhappy, stuck in routines. Observe them. You might see figures that are familiar to you and your life.

Make your way through the maze of the first ring, and you will find a door in the inner wall, a black door. Knock on the door, announcing yourself and your quest. The gate opens to reveal the Black Knight, larger than the red, carrying a long sword with a blade seemingly made from obsidian.

The Black Knight asks you what you have done that makes you unworthy to enter the castle, and you must be truthful. What is the worst thing you have done in your life? Can you name it? Can you take responsibility for it? If not, he will start naming the wrongs you have done to others, as if he can read your deepest memories.

If the Black Knight believes you are truthful and made amends in life, he will let you pass. If not, you will be challenged by his sword. If after this challenge, you are allowed to pass, you enter the second courtyard, the second realm. This is darker than the first. The inhabitants are more enfleshed, solid and real. They notice you. They are in tatters and in rags. They look ill and injured. As they look at you, you look at them, and you soon realize they are people whom you have harmed, directly or indirectly, in your life. They are seeking an apology. They are seeking a blessing. You must navigate your way through the crowds with love, blessing, and asking for forgiveness to make your way to the third gate.

The final gate of this inner wall is bright green. When you humbly knock on the door and announce yourself, the Green Knight opens it. This is the first guardian that seems glad to see you. While he has a green axe, it is not drawn but hangs on his back. Leaves and vines seem to be growing out from under his green armor. His skin is green. His eyes are green.

The Green Knight is the guardian of what is good, and asks you about the good you have received from others, the help you have been given. He asks you to name five things you are truly thankful to have received. Can you answer him?

If he is satisfied with your answer, the Green Knight allows you to pass through the third gate and move towards the tower that is the Castle of the Grail. The door that opens to the Grail Castle is crystalline, prismatically reflecting all colors. Look deeply at it.

Take this time to pause and return, remembering the door. Take a break because passing the bridge and the three guardians is a tremendous effort. Reflect upon what you shed, and the questions the three knights challenged you with. Even when you pass, they can leave you unsettled. Take the time to rest and integrate the changes you have made before seeking the crystal door again. When you are ready, return to part three.

Part Three: Encountering the Grail

Repeat the preliminary rituals with water, incense, and candlelight. Fix your mind upon where you left and bring your memory upon the crystal door to the Grail Castle. As you do, you see the door open, and entering from the left side of the tower is that strange and familiar procession of spectral figures, looking a little bit less spectral, yet still otherworldly. A parade of enchanted men and women carrying strange objects begins to enter the tower.

The procession is led by a young man and a young woman, each holding a candelabra of ten taper candles. Twenty flames enter the darkness behind the door. These two are followed by five more figures, each holding something close to their heart. They sing a haunting tune of the glory and power, of everlasting joy and to the destroyer of death. It echoes through the tower, and you realize the tower is a spiral staircase as the voices ascend. You decide to follow the procession through the crystal door and upward.

At first you assumed they were singing a Christian hymn, but now you are not so sure. The words appear to be praising the Goddess and her Child of Light. Their light leads the way upward, until they gather in an upper chamber. You enter the chamber illuminated with the twenty flames of the candles. Many figures are simply dark silhouettes. The five processional figures step through the two candle bearers, one by one, to present something to the group.

The first figure presents the lance. The lance is dripping. What is dripping from it? Perhaps it is water, tears, or even blood. The liquid flows to the hand of the bearer, and drips to the ground. Amid the shadows, you see a king enthroned upon a grand chair in the center, and you know this is the Fisher King. His wound is still bleeding, and the blood pools upon the floor. Beside him is a queen, gently weeping. Her tears fall to the floor, and soon the blood and the tears mix before them. The Fisher King asks us to all think about the wounds we have that will not heal. What is your wound? The bearer announces this is the hallow as it restores sovereignty through sexual sacrifice. With that, the bearer steps back into the darkness.

The second figure presents the cauldron. The cauldron is brewing a rich stew, and the aroma fills the chamber, making you feel both hungry and satisfied by what's in it all at the same time. For a moment, you see the Red Knight gathered with the figures amid the shadows. You remember the trial of the Red Knight. The bearer announces this is the hallow as it restores the abundance to the land by the courage of a hero. With that, the bearer steps back into the darkness.

The third figure steps into the light and presents the plate with a large covering upon it. The covering is lifted to reveal the severed head. The head of the ancients opens its eyes and looks around. It speaks, yet appears to say something or sing something different to everyone in the room. Amid those gathered, you notice the Black Knight, and he looks upon his obsidian sword and back to the head. You reflect upon the trial of the Black Knight, and the sword bridge. The bearer announces this is the hallow as it restores wisdom and inspiration to the world by giving up everything. With that, the bearer steps back into the shadows.

A fourth figure moves forward to the center and presents a stone. The stone appears dark at first, but when held up in the presence of all the candles, the light reveals it is a beautiful green stone. The dazzling emerald light reaches out to the hearts of everyone present, revealing an emerald in their own hearts. You see the Green Knight among those gathered in the shadows. The bearer announces this is the hallow as it restores heaven upon Earth through the light of transmutation. The bearer steps back into the darkness, but the stone continues to glow softly.

The fifth and final figure steps into the center, surrounded by the candlelight. She reveals from her heart the Holy Cup, the Sacred Chalice of the Holy Grail of Immortality. The light coming from the cup eclipses the light of the candles. The room is filled with light and all darkness is dispelled. You see them all – the two candle bearers, the five hallow bearers, three knights, the Fisher King and his queen and their court of ladies and lords. And behind the Fisher King, you see the elder king, the Grail King, smiling. The woman announces this is the hallow as it restores true healing by asking the only question that matters. Through the question, all that was unforgiven is now forgiven. Will you ask the questions?

> Why does the Lance bleed?
> When does the Cauldron boil?
> How does the Head speak?
> Where did the Stone Fall?
> Whom Does the Grail Serve?
> What do these wonders mean?
> And how may I be of aid?
>
> Listen to the answer deep within you.

If you do, the five bearers will come together, and the five hallows are clearly one, yet five. The five bearers bring their sacraments to all those attending, including you. A cup is brought to your lips. Gaze down. Is the drink bright, dark, or red? Drink.

Drink from the Grail and heal your own wounds.
Drink from the Grail and heal the wounds of your people.
Drink from the Grail and heal the wounds of the planet, the Wasteland.
Restore Camelot and Enchant the World!

The bearers come together again and become one, as the five hallows come together and become one. You see the knights are transformed into a Sun King, a Horned God, and a Green Man. Among them you see the nine ladies, those who are the nine sisters and muses. You see their seven sons. They are healed and whole. The Fisher King and his queen are no longer bleeding and weeping. The bearer of the grail offers the dazzling grail to the King behind the King, the true Grail King.

The chamber fills with light, and the Grail King ascends another set of stairs to the highest chamber of the tower, followed by the Fisher King and Queen, leaving you amid the twenty candle flames. One by one, the members of the court pinch out or blow out a flame, until there is only one left. The nine maidens each snuff a flame. The seven sons each snuff a flame. The three god-knights snuff a flame. And you are now asked to snuff the last flame. In the darkness, you feel yourself return magickally back to the realm of flesh and blood, breath and bone.

You are before your altar, with the ten candles and the three bowls. What color was your drink in vision? Pour that color drink into your chalice. Remind yourself of the questions again.

Why does the Lance bleed?
When does the Cauldron boil?
How does the Head speak?
Where did the Stone Fall?
Whom Does the Grail Serve?
What do these wonders mean?
And how may I be of aid?

Drink. Drink three times of your drink, and remember why you drink three times.

Drink from the Grail and heal your own wounds.

Drink from the Grail and heal the wounds of your people.
Drink from the Grail and heal the wounds of the planet, the Wasteland.
Restore Camelot and Enchant the World!

Take time to reflect and meditate. When done, snuff out the ten candles still burning in the order of white, gray, black, blue, red, yellow, green, orange, purple and brown. Offering the remaining two bowls of drink to the land as a further blessing.

Becoming the Grail

The Holy Grail can be approached from two perspectives, creating a third. All three are necessary in the creation of greater divine harmony. The first is the most obvious, and what most of the tales are about: the seekers of the grail. This includes the knights, emissaries of their kings to the world beyond the court. These are the people who have heard the call and are on the quest. Some might not be doing it consciously, but they're on the path nonetheless.

The second are the keepers of the grail. These are the guardians. Most Witches, magicians, and mystics already see themselves in this role. They don't identify with the knight. They want to be the lady of the lake or the wizard. But to be a keeper of the grail, you must first find it. Too few of us are born with a knowledge that the Wasteland is not reality. Perhaps more and more each generation, but for most of us, we need to go on the quest for healing ourselves before we can be a keeper of the grail. You see the idea that the grail knight goes on to replace the Fisher King as guardian of the grail. In some tales, there is a second, hidden king with the Fisher King. Called the Grail King, he is hidden away with the grail deep in the castle, presiding over the procession of the grail. In such tales, the healed Fisher King goes on to become the elder Grail King, and the questing knight, the seeker, becomes the finder, and takes a role in the lineage of Grail Kings, suffering and awaiting the next knight to find him. Strangely, we learn that despite the teaching contrary to it, personally finding the Holy Grail doesn't restore all the world. It just restores your portion of it. Everyone must find the grail to restore the entire world.

Becoming a keeper, a guardian, allows you to continue to participate, to serve rather than seek, and help the next generation. That is why many mystery traditions and magickal groups make it a requirement that you must teach or serve in some way, to usher in the next generation instead of just taking and not giving back. To do so would cause the mystery traditions to collapse. Magick without service invites corruption.

Along with the grail-keeping knights and kings, we have those in the procession, often believed to be another manifestation of the nine ladies and the attending faeries and humans who dwell in Avalon, the land of enchantment beyond. The theme of magickal places – be they Corbenic or Avalon, unmoored from physical reality – shows the grail is not in a place, but is a state of being, a state of consciousness. To be a guardian of the grail is to attain that state of consciousness. By doing so, you find yourself "showing up" where you are needed, and our very presence becomes a trigger for the potential healing.

In the attainment of the question and the transition to guardian, there occurs a balance of polarity, a reconciliation of opposites. One might see it in terms of polarity. The mystery is feminine, the seeker is masculine, at least from the outer worlds, and entering into mystery to be healed resolves the paradox, and one can embody both as needed. In the quest, we say the hunter becomes the hunted. You become that which you seek. As often quoted in the famous "The Charge of the Goddess":

And you who seek to know Me,
know that your seeking and yearning will avail you not,
unless you know the Mystery:
for if that which you seek,
you find not within yourself,
you will never find it without.
For behold, I have been with you from the beginning,
and I am that which is attained at the end of desire.

Through finding, you are transformed. Some fear that it means they are supposed to have all the answers or be one-hundred-percent balanced and healthy all the time, a living master or avatar of divinity. Finding and being a guardian and gateway for others in the mysteries simply means you are entering into adulthood. You will still have questions and problems. You will still be a seeker of knowledge and experience. But the thirst, the drive, the necessity will be transformed. Rather than wandering through a wasteland with no source of water, by finding it, you will have dug your own well. Your journey will continue to build up, engineer, decorate, and share from your well, and having a stable water source, you'll be able to visit other people's wells, but you won't have the desperation of being lost in a wasteland, always seeking.

With this, you realize the true embodiment, the final miraculous change of the grail, is to become the grail, to embody it yourself. You no longer have to seek it or guard it. You no longer have to keep it. You become the grail upon Earth. You embody the divine pattern in the greater below, as all the grails are reflected across time and space in the greater above. Through this becoming, you have greater access to embody the mystery beyond that which can be described. You overflow with blessings.

Some would consider becoming the grail as a mystery of blood lines. It is the oft-discussed mystery today, popularized by spy novels and movies, of the sang real, or "royal blood," that is found in the san greal, or "Holy Grail." Many have used this to seek a terrestrial messiah hidden in the bloodlines of queens and kings in Europe. The popular notion is that the grail is not a cup, plate, or bowl at all, but the womb. In the cosmic sense, all wombs are the grail, but to those seeking the mysteries amid conspiracy theories, the grail is the womb of Mary Magdalene, secret disciple of Jesus of Nazareth. After his crucifixion, she took his child to Europe, possibly France, beginning some of the Christian teachings the later Catholic Church would find heretical. Her descendants were said to be mingled with European royalty. While it's an interesting mythology, I don't think it helps you find the grail within, only without, in the form of a potential terrestrial leader as a second messiah. Others use the idea of the literal royal blood to create teachings of superiority for a particular ethnicity or culture, as the teaching becomes a veil for white supremacist groups. And those even further on the fringes focus on the possibility of extraterrestrial DNA as the key to the holy blood of the grail.

Much like those waiting for the second coming – be it of Christ, or in this mythos, the return of Arthur – the key to understanding the expression of that myth in the dawning Age of Aquarius is realizing that fulfillment is not in any one person or group, but in the fulfillment of all. One person bearing the sword of truth or finding the holy cup will not cure the Wasteland. All must seek and find it, and become it.

Exercise 26:
Consuming the Emerald of the Grail Ritual

This is a ritual to make the necessary alignments to become one with the inner grail. It should only be done after all the previous exercises of this book, but particularly those of this chapter, and you have had time to rest and reflect upon your work.
Altar and Tools:

Red or Orange Candle for the Belly Cauldron
Green or Blue Candle for the Heart Cauldron
Yellow Candle for the Head Cauldron
White Candle for Unity
Matches

Cauldron in the Center
(Green) Stone in the North
Cup in the West
Empty Plate in the South
Wand in the East
Small Cup or Bowl of the Bright Drink
Small Cup or Bowl of the Dark Drink
Small Cup or Bowl of the Red Drink

Figure 25: Consuming the Emerald of the Grail Altar Set Up

Begin by casting a ritual circle in any manner that is appropriate to you, looking back at our previous cauldron circles. I suggest holding aloft the wand or even your mixing spoon from our cauldron work – here acting at the "lance" or "spear" – and move counterclockwise around your space.

While most traditions only move clockwise, with the Sun in the northern hemisphere, we are moving not against the Sun for this rite, but with the stars, for when you stare at the north pole, the rotation of the heavens is counterclockwise.

Starting in the north, move counterclockwise around your ritual space with these words:

By the Spear, we create a boundary that none may sunder, protecting us from all harm.
By the Weeping Lance, we create a space where the perfect order can be made manifest.
By the Holy Rod, we create a circle of stars beyond the bounds of space and time.
I become Polaris, the Guiding Light, and all shall turn around me on this night.

Again call the quarters, starting in the north and going counterclockwise. Hold up each item from your altar, and when done, place it back down before moving onto the next.

To the north, I call upon the Element of Earth.
I call upon the Stone of the Heavens.
I call upon the Queen, Throne of the World who holds the King
Bringing Abundance to the Earth
and filling the cauldron with bounty.
Hail and Welcome.

To the west, I call upon the Element of Water.
I call upon the Cup of the Wells.
I call upon the Priestess, Mistress of the World beyond the Mist
Bringing Healing to the Earth
and filling the cauldron with nectar.
Hail and Welcome.

To the south, I call upon the Element of Air.
I call upon the Plate of the Severed Head.
I call upon the Prophet, Seer of the World who holds the Vision
Bringing Inspiration to the Earth
and filling the cauldron with truth.
Hail and Welcome.

To the east, I call upon the Element of Fire.
I call upon the Lance of the Lord.

I call upon the King, Lord of the World from the Deep Cave
Bringing Rebirth to the Earth
and filling the cauldron with light.
Hail and welcome.

I call to the center, to the Hidden God Beyond All.
Invisible in shape
Beyond all form
Your name is one and many and none.
Hail and welcome.

    Pour the Bright Drink into the Cup.

By She who rules the Tides of the World and creates Space
May we all find home.

    Pour the Dark Drink into the Cup.

By He who rules the Time of the World and shares Prophecy
May we all see clearly and be healed.

    Pour the Red Drink into the Cup.

By He who rules the Light of the World and bestows Divine Harmony
May we all become stewards.

    Place the Cup into the Cauldron in the Center of the Altar.

I bless this sacrament by the Cauldron of Annwn.
May it never go empty.

    Carefully lift the Cup and Cauldron up, and place the empty plate beneath it.

I bless this sacrament by the Empty Plate.
May it fill with wisdom.

    Touch the wand to the drink, drawing the wand out so that several drops will fall back into the chalice, like a weeping lance.

I bless this sacrament by the Holy Lance.
May you weep and bleed no more.

Place the stone into the Cup

By She who rules the Matter of the World and grants Sovereignty
I bless this sacrament by the Star and the Stone
May you become one with the True Grail.

Hold the Candle of the Belly to your belly without dripping or burning yourself.
Feel the light of your lower cauldron enter into the flame, your life.
Then bring that flame to the unlit candle of unity, and light it.
Say: *By Life*

Hold the Candle of the Heart to your heart without dripping or burning yourself.
Feel the light of your middle cauldron enter into the flame, your love.
Then bring that flame to the candle of unity, and add this flame to the first.
Say: *By Love*

Hold the Candle of the Head to your face without dripping or burning yourself.
Feel the light of your upper cauldron enter into the flame, your awen.
Then bring that flame to the candle of unity, and add this flame to what is already there.
Say: *By Awen*

Feel the three flames as one within the candle.
Lift up the cup and hold it over the flame of the unity candle.

In the name of the Nameless
In the shape of the Shapeless
In the form of the Formless
by the Hidden One Beyond All
May I be all things and may I be no thing.
May I be all that is necessary to embody the grail within the world
And recreate the Heavens upon earth.

Drink the sacrament without swallowing the stone in the cup. Pause. Reflect. Welcome the grail in all its forms. Become the grail in all its forms. Meditate or do anything else that you are called to do at this time. When you feel it is complete, release the circle.

To the north, I thank and release the Element of Earth.
I thank the Stone within
And I thank the Queen who holds the King.
Thank you for the blessing of abundance.
Hail and Farewell.

To the east, I thank and release the Element of Fire.
I thank the Lance within
And I thank the King who wakes from the Cave.
Thank you for this blessing of rebirth.
Hail and Farewell.

To the south, I thank and release the Element of Air.
I thank the Empty Plate within
And I thank the Prophet who holds the Vision.
Thank you for this blessing of inspiration.
Hail and Farewell

To the west, I thank and release the Element of Water.
I thank the Cup within
And I thank the Priestess from beyond the Mist.
Thank you for your blessing of healing.
Hail and Farewell.

Take the wand and move clockwise around the circle.

By the Spear, the Lance, the Holy Rod, we cast out this light to revivify the World.

Touch the ground to both anchor yourself and bless the world.

You might notice there is intentionally a lot of crossed symbolism in this ritual. The stone, which we have declared for spirit, is in the north where we would put the earth tool, rather than the center. It must "fall" and be brought to the center. The cup, which we have declared in the mythos, is brought from the west to the center, signifying the successful quest. The hero goes into the west to retrieve the grail, and has done so, bringing it back to "Camelot." The cauldron, which we have called the tool of abundance and the earth, is in the center of the altar, for it is the crossroads of the world where the people gather, our symbolic Camelot. In the earliest myth, during the hunt for the Cauldron of Annwn, Arthur and his six companions are successful and return with the cauldron. The material needs are generally provided for in the center of our mandala.

This simple ritual forms a pattern, the mandala we have talked about to restore the matrix of heaven upon the world. It requires that we each become a successful grail knight, that we each awaken the sleeping and healing Arthur and return to the world. Through the pattern, we bestow the five blessings upon ourselves and all the world. Through the pattern, we move from seeker to finder, from finder to keeper and guardian, and ultimately from custodian to the embodiment of all that we seek.

Through the consumption of the central symbol, we equate the grail with the ultimate and universal medicine of the alchemist, as well as uniting the concept of the blood and body of Christ with the emerald of Lucifer. In this sacrament, all polarities and paradoxes are resolved into the one thing and one mind from which we all take part.

Chapter Nine: The Cauldron of Resurrection

By the center to the edge
Three worlds shaped by unknown hands
The cauldron of rebirth came to us from far off lands
Lady of the Wheel, Lord of the Horns
Warriors in death become the horsemen reborn
Cattle of the center sacrificed by sword
Lions, wolves, and gryphon moving in accord
Judge and Hunter, Sea God of the west
Triple goddess of the deathly crows
Return me to the Isle of the Blessed.

We return from all of our mythic cauldrons and grails to end on one of the best real-world historic artifacts to be used in modern magick, the Gundestrup cauldron. Truly an artistic masterpiece, it has inspired many ideas in the Celtic occult revival. I was introduced to it through a detailed reproduction of the cauldron from a statuary company named Sacred Source that one of my first mentors had among her magickal items. Since then, not only have I obtained my own reproduction of it, but have been to many rituals where similar reproductions were used. There is something deeply evocative about the imagery contained within it. The original is now in the National Museum of Copenhagen, as it was found in a peat moss bog in Gundestrup, Denmark. While apparently crafted in Thrace around 100 B.C., the imagery is most likely Gaulish Celtic, and it is suggested that the thirteen panels depict a power foundational myth. For its functional use, it could have possibly been a "sacrificial" bowl to collect the blood of sacrificed bulls, as bull images are frequent in the art, or as a general offering bowl, for various foodstuffs offered to the gods. Some believe it was made for the entire purpose of being disassembled rather than remaining a fully functional cauldron, as a votive offering to the gods of the land and water.

Occultists believe that art, music, language, and story can be "contacted," meaning that there is an energetic link to a deeper intelligence related to its fashioning. The Gundestrup cauldron is certainly a contacted piece of art, and the imagery, when studied through ritual and inner vision, unlocks an amazing series of cauldron experiences for the magician. One must look through the thirteen panels and let the experience arise from each one.

From the study of both scholars and Celtic spiritual practitioners, a number of efforts have been made to pin down the identities of all the figures on the Cauldron, often claiming with authority exactly who the figure is or isn't. The truth is, we don't know. There was not a detailed commentary in the bog from its creators, owners, or users when it was found. We can make educated guesses, based on what we currently know of Celtic myth, realizing that much of the ancient Pagan Celtic past is really lost to us. We have divined inspired gnosis of who the figures are, but we should add that gnosis can only reveal who the figures are to the one having the gnosis. Your revealed knowledge is not my revealed knowledge. Beyond the more orthodox theories, more colorful suggestions have tried to tie it to the family of the Biblical Noah after the flood, or to the Egyptian gods, but most credit an Indo-European mythos for the basis.

One of the reasons I love it so much is that it is so mysterious. The gods are a mystery. Initiation is a mystery, and while we can understand the mechanics of how magick might work, the why of magick is still a beautiful mystery. Our magickal ancestors reach us from the ancient past, and reveal this mystery for us to resolve for ourselves, if we so choose. I love that there can be more than one "correct" interpretation, and by correct, I mean magickally effective. Whenever possible in my description, I describe the possibilities around each figure and panel as I have studied them, drawing from scholarly sources, fringe ideas, and personal gnosis. But in the end, this interpretation and understanding is my approach to the mystery here, shared with my own students and fellow practitioners. Use it as I do, or let it inspire your own understanding.

At its heart, in terms of our historic understanding of the magick contained within it, this cauldron seems to be closest to the Cauldron of Bran the Blessed, a cauldron linked to the mysteries of life, death, creation, and rebirth. One might think of it as embodying the primal cauldron in the heart of the otherworld, from which all things issue forth and to which all things return. With this perspective, the Gundestrup cauldron contains all possibilities in it, so therefore all possible interpretations can be correct for their practitioner.

Several key scholars have given their understanding and interpretation of the cauldron historically, archeologically, and mythically. Ole Klindt-Jensen was the first to argue for the Cernunnos interpretation of the horned figure, an idea that is disputed by G.S. Olmsted. Olmsted does the most with the mythology, arguing for a consistent story throughout the cauldron, and believes it to be a Gaulish prototype of the Táin Bó Cuailnge, the Ulster cycle of myths involving the hero Cú Chulainn. The horned figure is a form of Cú Chulainn. Henry Hubert, in *Rise of the Celts,* as well as P. Jacobsthal in his *Early Celtic Art* and Ellis Davidson with *The Lost Belief of Northern Europe* all contribute, among many others, to our mythic understanding of the various panels of the cauldron.

Some of the aspects scholars have to contend with in reviewing a "Celtic" artifact include the wide number of non-Celtic things associated with it, particularly in regard to the depicted clothing and creatures such as gryphons, lions, and winged horses. The images are so similar to Thracian metal work that most assume they are the creators of the actual cauldron, but for Celtic patrons, many stick to a Celtic-only origin theory. The ambiguity has only deepened the mystery for the occultist seeking to use these images for ritual purposes.

For me, the key to this work is entering into magickal vision with the images, and dealing with the animating forces behind their story. Each will act like a guiding spirit and present you with mysteries and trials to experience directly rather than simply read out. Having a good familiarity with the images and some possible interpretations can seed the mind to have the appropriate information to be able to interact with these living energies, providing the necessary common cultural vocabulary for some form of exchange.

You can apply classic pathworking visionary techniques to "enter" into each of the panels as a focus. You can also experiment with the ecstatic body posture technique as discussed in Chapter Five. Rather than using an inhibitory relaxation-focused meditative technique for a guided vision of the particular cauldron panel you've chosen, you can use a drumming or rattling music to induce trance and hold a posture that is depicted in the central character of the panel. The most famous is the "horned god" pose that is not quite cross-legged, with arms in a "V" holding a neck ring and a snake. To enter the consciousness of that picture, enter that pose and listen to the ecstatic rhythm. The body posture will unlock the mystery. You learned this posture in Chapter Five, along with the Aztec Corn Goddess shapeshifting posture. Now apply the same idea to the other panels. You will notice most of the deity figures have a central "giant" with a specific arm posture. Try sitting or standing while holding that arm posture and journeying with a repetitive drum or rattle sound to unlock that picture's magickal wisdom.

The meditations on each panel are rather short, giving guidance to find the "entrance" to an experience of wisdom embodied in it. At this stage, if you have been doing all the previous work of the cauldron, you should have developed a fair amount of skill navigating into and out of meditative work in the otherworlds and conducting ritual. The brief nature of the exercises gives you space to rediscover the mythic patterns and come to your own conclusions about their nature.

The Structure of the Cauldron

The cauldron itself was disassembled to be cast as an offering, and scientists have reassembled it. It has a rounded bottom with an interior design focused on a bull. Five interior plates describe fairly active scenes with humans and animals and what are assumed to be deities. A ring of seven plates forms the exterior of the cauldron, each one depicting a center figure, assumed to be a deity. Of the seven, three are female and four are male. The official names of the plates and their ordering comes from Klindt-Jensen, with the inner plates using capital letters (Plates A, B, C, D and E) and the outer plates lower case letters (Plates a, b, c, d, e, f, and g). These labels have been fairly consistent in their use by other scholars since their introduction and are the labels and order I will be using here. The titles accompanying the plates in the figures are mine, based upon meditative work, and are not part of the literature.

Cosmologists would wonder if the threefold division depicts a threefold division of the cosmos, a concept found in many cultures and most easily expressed in shamanic teachings, as many are based upon a central spire, an axis mundi of a tree or mountain, with a world above, a world below, and a world between. The world between, or the Middle World, is our world of space, time, and form. Below is a chthonic matrix from which reality springs filled with denser – but not necessarily evil – forces of regeneration, while above is a sky realm of perfect pattern and harmony.

Occultists of a Neoplatonic or Gnostic bend have the material world at the lowest point in the cosmology, depicted in the center of a circular mandala. Around it is the Psychic World, also known as the World Soul. The World Soul is the mediating force. Some think of it as the divine feminine, and it has been equated with goddesses such as Hecate or Demeter. We can think of it like the soul of Mother Nature, while the material world is the body of Mother Nature. The World Soul mediates the Nous, or Noetic World, which we might equate with the Divine Intellect, Divine Mind, or Cosmic Consciousness. Beyond the Divine Mind is the Absolute and Ineffable, also known as the One or the Good. In some cosmologies, each orbit of the planets, along with the fixed stars, represents various levels between the human world and the Ineffable.

Bridging between these models and also rooted in the image of the cauldron is a cosmology proposed by the controversial Welsh poet and nationalist Iolo Morganwg. Born Edward Williams, his legacy has informed a wide range of neo-Druidic, Neopagan, Wiccan, and Witchcraft beliefs. Being a great enthusiast of Welsh national identity and all things considered Celtic, his writings created a spiritual and philosophical vision, contributing to modern Welsh culture and national pride. He was self-taught in his academics and wrote on a wide range of topics, the most famous of his writings being published after his death as *The Barddas of Iolo Morganwg*. He attributed many of his own writings to other historical authors and sources and was accused of forgery after his death, though some during his lifetime suspected his sources. As a bard and man of vision, as well as a user of laudanum, he might have had difficulty differentiating between historic truth and poetic truth, putting forward his ideas as relics of antiquity because he felt being self-educated would not earn him the recognition an accredited writer and scholar would receive for original work. Whatever his motive, or lack thereof, his philosophy has made a lasting impression upon the bardic, Druidic, and occult worlds. His work has been developed through ritual, visionary meditation, and further philosophical comparisons in modern occultism, forging a legacy that often neglects to mention him by name. I've seen many a Witchcraft tradition pass off less familiar ideas as family tradition, and perhaps it is now, but we know the roots came from the Barddas as the vision of Iolo.

The cosmology of his Barddas is of concentric circles. The region of the inner ring represents Annwn, described in the multiple-ring cosmology as akin to the underworld. The realm of Annwn is where things begin, taking shape and form. At the center of the inner ring of Annwn is a cauldron. All is born from the cauldron. The middle of three rings is the realm known as Abred; it is the world we know, including material form, time, space, life, and death. Things taking form in Annwn can be born in the world of Abred, and with the known mythic journey, those of Abred can pass into Annwn and back again, such as the Welsh king Pwyll and Arthur and his band of seven men. Beyond the realm of Abred, further away from the cauldron, is the world of Gwynvyd. Gwynvyd is a realm of perfection and beauty. We could consider this the upper world or heavenly world. Those that are perfected must have journeyed from Abred, perfecting themselves and forging a home in Gwynvyd. Members dwelling in Gwynvyd are described as divinities or holy angels. Abred is a realm of necessity, or rather, the journey from Annwn to Abred and then onto Gwynvyd is necessity. Beyond the realm of Gwynvyd is Ceugant, the realm of eternity, or God alone, and only God can traverse it. Ceugant is equated with the Ineffable of the Neoplatonic scholars.

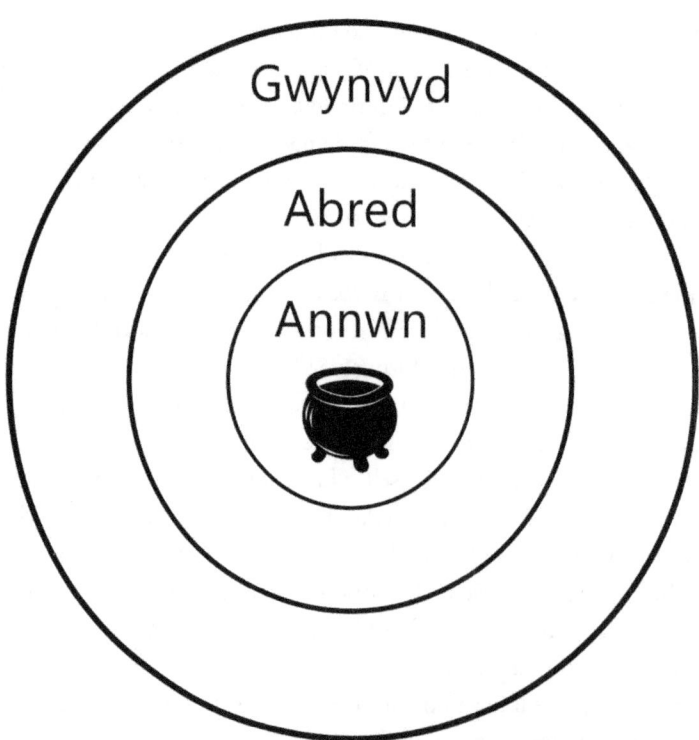

Figure 26: Three Realms in Concentric Rings

The cosmology particularly resonates with modern Witches, and it doesn't escape our notice that when we gather in a ritual circle, we recreate this model. Our magick circle is cast in three "rings." We often have a cauldron on the central altar where we perform ritual, burn incense, cast spells, or craft our potions. The gods of the Witches are usually of the underworld, and during ritual are called to the center. We stand in the world of flesh and blood (Abred) around the altar of the cauldron (Annwn). We feel the presence beyond our circle's edge of the Mighty Ones, the Mighty Dead of our tradition, those who have perfected themselves to reach Gwynvyd. We are like a cauldron within a cauldron within a cauldron, creating this cosmology of three realms.

Does the work of Iolo Morganwg accurately describe the Gundestrup Cauldron? The only true answer is that we don't know. If so, the bottom of the cauldron is Annwn, the inner ring of five plates would be Abred, and the outer ring of seven portrait plates would be Gwynvyd. That is feasible, though some favor the idea that the bottom center is the starry cosmos. The possible permutations are in the form of the sequence of Upper World, Middle World, and Lower World, in the form of the shamanic tree, or the neoplatonic scheme of material world (Middle World), World Soul (Lower World), and Nous (Upper World).

	Shamanic Models		Neoplatonic Models	
	1	2	1	2
Bull at Center	Lower World	Upper World	Middle World	Upper World
Five Interior Scenes	Middle World	Middle World	Lower World	Lower World
Seven Exterior Portraits	Upper World	Lower World	Upper World	Middle World

Chart 34: Three Worlds and the Cauldrons

The biggest question for me is if you emphasize the center of the cauldron as a point of creation and possibility (Lower World), a place of sublime stillness (Upper World), or a place of day-to-day experience (Middle World). All are valid choices, as we have no true and undeniable knowledge of the cauldron maker's philosophy, and in the end, if the symbols should aid us and our own world vision clashes with the creator, so be it. Use what works.

I tend to favor the first option out of all these possibilities, with the central animalistic figure being in the center of the cauldron, in the world of Annwn. The inner action scenes are the interactions between the people, gods and animals in Abred. The portraits on the outside are the perfected ones of Gwynvyd.

Yet there is also truth in the reverse, in the paradox, that the center of the cauldron is stillness, the perfect and holy amid the swirling of the world. We find stillness in the center. Yet does not the Cauldron of Annwn lead to another realm? Like the hypothesis of the black hole in one universe leading to a white hole in another. Each connects and contains its opposite.

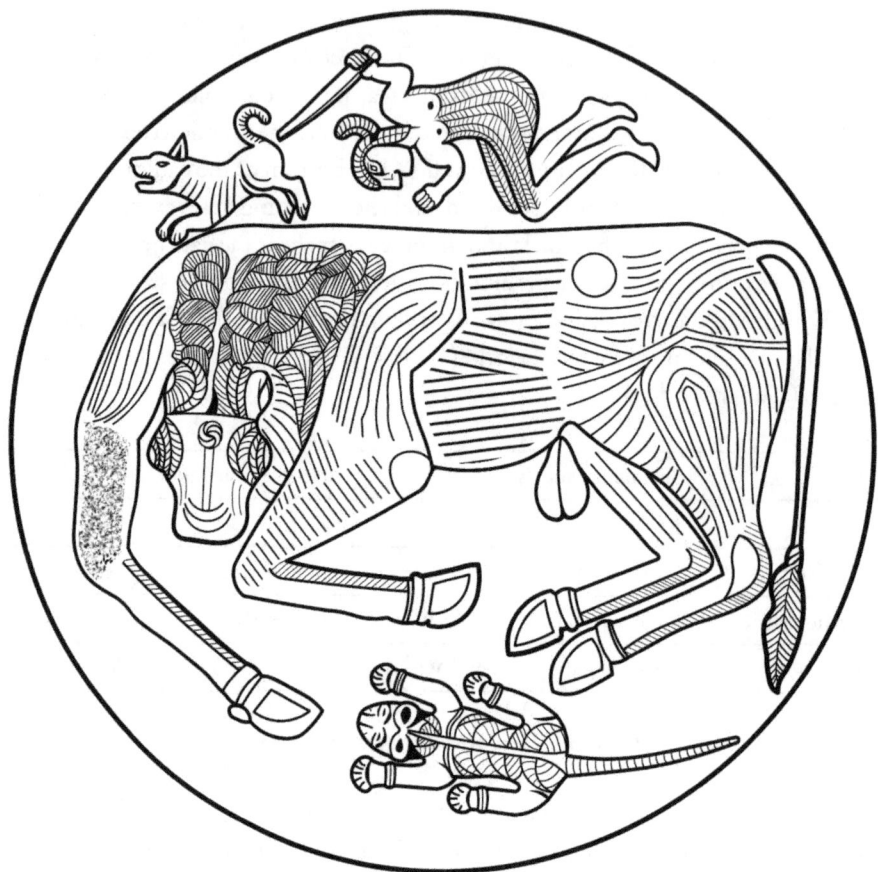

Figure 27: Bottom of the Cauldron

Bull at the Base Plate

At the center bottom of the cauldron, on the base of this incredible artifact, is a depiction of a bull in full detail. The bull appears to be laying on its side. There appears to be a place for his horns, which at one time stood out from the bull's head. Above the bull is a figure (whether it is a man or woman is unclear) with a sword or spear, chasing a dog. Beneath the bull is another dog, on all fours as viewed from above. The bull as well could be viewed as if we are looking at it from above, and in a sense we are, when we peer into the cauldron. Around the figures are ornamental patterns in a vegetative motif, with tendrils spiraling around the figures.

Trying to literally interpret the scene and its strange angels has given rise to a variety of scenarios. Is it a sacred hunt of the bull? The warrior with the dog is described as a hunter, seeking the bull. Perhaps the scene is a battle with the bull. Some see the bull as upright and about to charge. Others see the bull sinking and about to be sacrificed, with the figure "above" interpreted as "behind."

What myths can help us understand this base to the cauldron? Bulls and cows play a strong role in many world mythologies. Cows are revered as sacred in Hinduism, Jainism, and Buddhism, yet cattle are sacrifices in ancient Judaism and ancient Greek religion. Occultists view the age of cattle being prominent in religion and sacrifice as a part of the astrological Age of Taurus, ranging roughly from 4000 B.C. To 2000 B.C, depending on who you ask. In ancient Greece, we most likely have a bull cult in Crete, though our remaining images and myth comes to us through the tale of the Minotaur. While most think of him simply as a monster, some Witchcraft cult traditions in the modern age focus upon him as a manifestation of the god, under his name Asterion, or Starry One.

In traditional Zoroastrian religion, the Soul of the Earth is described as the Spirit of the Cow. In Egypt, Apis is the bull deity, often associated with Osiris, but it is the beloved cow-headed goddess Hathor, originally a consort to the Sun god Ra, who is associated with the Milky Way, love, and nurturance. Many believe the popular goddess Isis took on her role, and her horned crown or helmet emulates the horns of the cow. In many ways, Isis became the representative of the Magna Mater, or Great Mother, in the developing ancient world as her cult spread through the Roman Empire.

In the Lakota tradition, we have the divine prophet of White Buffalo Calf Woman. While not quite the cow or bull, as the buffalo is categorized as bison and not bovine, there is a sacred resonance of cattle with the buffalo. Legend says she brought seven sacred rites to the Lakota people, including the pipe ceremony, and today her legend is recognized not only among the Plains Indians and greater Native American community, but widely told in modern metaphysical and New Age traditions looking to find a closer relationship with the land of North America.

Though not Celtic, one Norse creation myth starts with a cosmic "cow" named Auðumbla, licking the ice giant Ymir, leading to the creation of beings and ultimately the nine worlds. Many find the sacrifice of Ymir's body to echo a common Indo-

European theme of the universe being created through the primal sacrifice of the first "man" – or in this case – giant.

In Celtic Gaul, the goddess Damona is associated with cattle, while in Ireland, we have the goddess Boann. Celtic literature is filled with cattle references, the most famous being the Táin Bó Cúailnge, popularly known as "The Cattle Raid of Cooley." The tale is the battle resulting from the theft of a very special bull by queen Medb and the opposition by Cú Chulainn. The scholar G.S. Olmsted perceived the entire Gundestrup Cauldron as a visual prototype to "The Cattle Raid of Cooley."

The ancient Irish reportedly had a ritual known as a tarbfheis, or tarb feis, meaning the "bull feast," as recorded in the tale of Serglige Con Culainn, or "The Sick Bed of CuCulainn." To find the new high king, a white bull is ritually sacrificed and a meal, a stew, is made of his flesh. A man chosen to be the seer, most likely a Druid or poet, would eat the flesh and drink the broth of the bull. Based on other similar tales and practices, we might assume the seer would be wrapped in the hide of the white bull and put down ceremonially to dream. Four Druids speak incantations over him, and with this magick, the dream will reveal the next king.

In another Irish tale, Togail Bruidne Da Derga, or "The Destruction of Da Derga's Hostel," the Druid's incantation is revealed to be one demanding truth, and if the dreamer lies about what he dreams, his death is the result. A similar technique is shown in yet another Irish tale, the "Life of St. Berach," where four Druids are placed upon the hides of sacrificed bulls, lying down upon rowan hurdles. They drink ale, call for the ancient gods, and will have divine inspiration. Returning to the Welsh, in "The Dream of Rhonabwy," a tale often collected in *The Mabinogi,* the main figure Rhonabwy sleeps upon a platform with a yellow ox hide, and in his dream, is taken to the court of King Arthur. Cattle and ox obviously have a connection to sleeping, dreaming, kingship, and prophecy.

Together these images and myths speak of the divinity of the bull, as both a starry beginning and relating to the heavens, as with Hathor and Asterion, but also as sacrifice and offering to the chthonic gods of dreams and darkness below. The Age of Taurus is said to be the time of the temple builders, including the pyramids and the famous palaces of Crete. The mysteries of the Age of Taurus were focused upon the ecstatic mystery cults of the goddess and prophets such as the Greek Orpheus. On a personal level, the spirit medicine of the bull is described as tenacity and the ability to stay the course. Cow spirit is about the nurturance and unconditional love of the divine mother. It is appropriate that where we begin and where we end with our cauldron work is with the bull.

You can do each vision sequentially, as you move from plate to plate, or you can choose to read them all entirely, analyzing the whole cauldron before attempting any of the vision workings. As the journeys are relatively short, allowing you the ability to interact with the figures and experience your own gnosis, you can even combine several of the journeys in sequence together.

Exercise 27:
The Divine Bull

Place your consecrated cauldron before you, or hold it in your hands in your lap. If possible, gaze into the center of the cauldron, and feel yourself gazing into the center of all cauldrons, everywhere, into the stillness of the center. Focus upon the darkness of the center of the cauldron. Breathe deep, close your eyes, and use your techniques to enter an altered state, either using inhibitory meditative techniques or exhibitory ecstatic techniques.

Enter the darkness of the cauldron. Sense the presence of the Divine Bull. Before you, you feel the power of the bull, horns slightly illuminated in the darkness. On either side of the bull is a dog, and next to the bull is a warrior with a spear, almost like a guard to the bull. The Bull Spirit feels like a god of creation in the center of the cauldron, and this is his court. Commune with the Bull God with respect and thanks. Learn any mysteries these spirits are willing to share.

They may ask for something in return, or some form of offering to be made to them. Negotiate your terms and only agree to actions and offerings that you can truly do. Affirm you will remember whatever is said, and when done, thank all the spirits. Return the way you came out of the cauldron. Ground yourself and record your journey.

Figure 28: Plate A Horned Animal Master

Horned Animal Master (Plate A)

The most famous of all the plates from the Gundestrup cauldron must be this first figure depicting a man with either stag horns or a headdress of stag horns, seven points on each side. He appears to be in a peaceful meditative pose conveying aspects of ritual, as he is wearing a torc, or Celtic neck ring. He is also holding one in his right hand and a ram-headed serpent in his left, with his arms bent at very precise angles. His right foot is tucked in at the groin and his left foot slightly extended. It's not unlike many yogic meditative poses. Comparisons of both pose and dress are made to show Eastern influences beyond traditional Western Celtic. Behind him is a faint leaf motif suggesting a forest, and around him are all manner of animals. With him is a small human figure, perhaps a boy, riding a fish or dolphin.

Many consider him the Gaulish Celtic god Cernunnos, or horned one, and he's been equated with various forms of the northern European horned gods of traditional Witchcraft. Qualities associated with him are wealth, success, fertility, and prosperity, yet there are no actual surviving myths of Cernunnos, just a partial inscription from the Gaulish time period in what is now France. Witches associate him as the god of the hunt, both being the hunter and the hunted, a guardian of nature and master of animals. Some see the horns as representative of the gateway, and he is the master of the gate between worlds. Sexual comparisons are made between him and the Greek Pan, another famous horned god, but there is nothing in this representation to suggest overt sexuality, such as a clearly depicted phallus.

At his right appears a stag bearing eight points on each antler, with a small bull strangely on top of the stag's back. Another bull is found to the figure's furthest upper left point. To his direct left is a hound. Above the hound is either a lion or possibly a boar, and that leaves a pair of creatures usually described as lions, having similar body shape and features to the upper lion/boar figure.

Along with Cernunnos, the figure has also been identified by the scholar G.S. Olmsted in The Gundestrup version of Táin Bó Cuailnge (Antiquity, Vol. 50) as Cú Chulainn in the Irish myth cycle. His archetype has more relation to Mercury than Cernunnos. Many Neopagans assume the child-like figure with the dolphin to be Dylan, son of Arianrhod and brother to Lleu. Soon after his birth, he escapes into the sea.

Could this panel be a depiction of shapeshifting? A union with the realm of animal consciousness? An initiation? The torc is a symbol of wisdom and power for warriors and Druids. The ram-headed serpent is the most unusual of the creatures, the most obviously otherworldly, and it appears to be whispering into his left ear.

EXERCISE 28:
The Master of Animals

Before doing this vision, look upon Plate A. Along with the reproduction here, search for this popular image in books and online. Really get the imagery into your memory. Focus not just upon the horned one, but upon all the animals and adornment. Then, when you firmly feel you know this image, begin.

Hold your cauldron in your lap. Breathe deep and gaze into the cauldron itself. Conjure the idea found in Plate A, the horned master of animals. Hold that idea to the center of the cauldron that is the center of all cauldrons. From this cauldron comes the magickal journey. Enter the darkness and close your eyes. Using the techniques you have learned, enter a trance state.

Find yourself moving through a forested land. The underbrush of leaves touches your face as you make your way through. Soon you find an opening. You come upon a grove. And in the twilight of the grove, you discover a strange gathering of animals – stags, bulls, lions, boars, and dogs, all together. There is a large, strange serpent there, with the horns of a ram. And amid them all is a horned man, a horned god. He is the master of animals.

The serpent moves towards him and makes its way to his left arm. In his right hand he holds a torc. Around his neck is also a torc. He motions silently for you to join him. Together, you sit upon the ground face to face, staring into each other's eyes, surrounded by these peaceful animals. Commune with the horned one. What mystery might he share with you?

You could get an intuition from the god about what to do and how to work more deeply with him, your animal allies, or animals in your life in general. He might also make suggestions on particular offerings and rituals to deepen this relationship. Listen and remember.

When done, thank him and all the animal spirits. Thank the spirit of the forest itself. Return the way you came to this scene, and rise up and out of the cauldron. Ground yourself and record your journey.

Figure 29: Plate B: Goddess of the Chariot

Goddess of the Chariot (Plate B)

In this second inner panel, the torso of a feminine figure is in the center, upon a stylized chariot. Each of the two wheels have six spokes each in a pattern that is similar to the popular Flower of Life sacred geometry. She is wearing a torc around her neck and gestures in some stylized manner. Around her are five animals. At the top of the panel appears two speckled animals with characteristics of both boars and elephants, including tusks. Their legs look too long for traditional boars, yet the appendage at their heads is not quite an elephant trunk, though it is generally accepted that it depicts elephants. Below them are two mythic creatures similar to gryphons. They are bird-headed with wings and horse-like bodies, yet claws instead of hooves. In the center beneath the chariot is a powerful-looking creature. Its head is a bit monstrous, with features that might suggest a feline or canine, while the legs look more bird-like.

Traditionally, this is assumed to be a lion or wolf. Combined, this goddess appears to have similarities to the Mesopotamian Inanna-Ishtar-Astarte complex of goddesses, being both a goddess of love and war, associated with the morning and evening star of Venus.

Ancient goddesses are often associated with animals, and in classical mythology rooted in Indo-European tradition, we find divine chariots pulled by terrestrial and mythic animals. Many gods were said to circle the heavens and maintain the orbit of the planets, seemingly moving around the Earth. The chariot is a "vehicle" for consciousness to travel and ascend to different realms. Selene and Helios pulled the Moon and Sun respectively from their chariots. Accounts differ, but in Ovid's account, Selene's chariot was pulled by bull or oxen. Hecate was said to have a chariot pulled by dragons. Astarte is known as the Mistress of the Chariot and Lady of Horses, as well as being associated with lions.

In the story of "The Cattle-Raid of Regamna" in *The Yellow Book of Lecan*, the Irish goddess known as the Morrighan, or the phantom queen, meets the hero Cú Chulainn while riding upon a chariot pulled by a "one footed" red horse. Their encounter does not go well, for he does not know who she truly is and treats her with disrespect. The Morrighan declares them to be enemies if he will not be with her, and prophecies ways to attack him until transforming into a crow, and Cú Chulainn realizes his mistake. If the Gundestrup Cauldron is a proto-depiction of the Táin Bó Cúailnge and this tale precedes it, perhaps the archetypal force in this panel is akin to the Morrighan. While modern Witches are partial to Morrighan, the figure could just as easily, and in the view of scholars, be Queen Medb, another primary figure in "The Cattle Raid of Cooley." While having different cultural associations than the goddesses related to the figure of Astarte, all of these female figures are queens with associations of love and war. Their key to the mysteries is in the sovereignty of the king through the right relationship with the goddess. The chariot is a vessel to transport one between the worlds and transport on the battlefield which is life.

The chariot image is also used in the work of Plato as a metaphor for our soul. In his work *Phaedrus*, Plato depicts a charioteer, acting as reason or logic, driving a chariot of two winged horses. One horse is good nature and noble, embodying the moral impulse and measured response, while the second causes trouble, embodying passions, appetite, and irrationality. The first horse is immortal, while the second horse is mortal. The charioteer has to get them to act together and move the soul towards enlightenment. This metaphor is to show us how difficult the journey can be, and why. The charioteer, our reason, has to decide what traits to encourage and what goals to seek. The white horse seeks to bring us up towards the heavens while the dark horse brings us towards the world. An unskilled charioteer will lose control and crash.

According to Plato, the souls follow the path of the gods towards enlightenment. It is a rare soul who achieves enlightenment and can rise above to see the world as the World of Forms, its true nature. This is the realm of Beauty, Justice, Truth, and Goodness. Some reach this perspective some of the time, and enter in and out of the World of Forms. Reaching it nourishes the horses and their wings. The gods have perfect immortal horses. The human's horse, lacking a special nourishment from attaining the World of Forms, will lose their wings. Some lose control of the second horse, described as a black horse in contrast to the white, and are pulled all the way back down to Earth. The descent down is representative of the rebirth process into a new life. Plato described nine kinds of incarnations one can take, based upon how much truth the soul has seen approaching the World of Forms.

1. Philosophers and Lovers of Beauty, Culture, and Love
2. Kings and Civic Leaders who abide the laws
3. Politicians, Estate Managers, and Businessmen
4. Bodily Health Experts (Doctors and Healers)
5. Prophets and Mystery Cult Members
6. Poets and Artists
7. Craftspeople and Farmers
8. Sophists and Demagogues
9. Tyrants

Those higher on the list, closer to the heavens, will find it easier to regrow the wings of their horses, due to the amount of truth they have seen in the World of Forms, helping to nourish the wings' growth. Those lower on the list will have a longer time regrowing the wings, and feel more trapped in the world. Today philosophers argue about his meaning on this teaching, as with many of his other teachings. Was this a literal transmigration of the soul, or a figurative teaching tool on the morals of society? Those of us today looking at this list probably think that leaders, politicians, and business managers should go lower on the list, and elevate artists, craftspeople, farmers, and mystery cult initiates.

Similar teachings of the chariot as an image for the soul's journey are found in the *Upanishads* of India. Rather than the chariot being the soul, in this teaching, the body is the chariot. The true self is the passenger of the chariot. The intellect, known as buddhi in these teachings, is the charioteer. The mind itself, separate from the intellect as the mind is a tool, is the reins to the horses. The metaphor is particularly found in the famous tale of *The Bhagavad Gita,* where the god Krisha acts as the charioteer and advisor to the main figure of the tale, Prince Arjuna. The battlefield is the battlefield of life, and Krishna and Arjuna discuss duty and what must be done. While the metaphor is a chariot and war, the deeper metaphysical idea is the concept of dharma, or right action. In Western magick we might call this true will, or the duty and purpose of your soul.

One can easily see the esoteric symbols and meaning of the Chariot card from the Major Arcana. In the lore of ceremonial magick, influencing our understanding of the tarot from a Qabalistic perspective, are the chariot teachings of Jewish esoteric lore. Called the Merkava, or Chariot, there is the concept of a chariot of angelic force used to ascend the gate of heaven and encounter "God." The chariot is aligned with the mysteries of angels and spinning wheels. Sometimes, it is described as a chariot of fire pulled by horses of fire, or a whirlwind of fire and light. The prophet Elijah used it to ascend into heaven.

Modern New Age traditions have fused it with other ideas, using Egyptian terms and creating the name Merkaba, referencing a geometric light body or light vehicle for our consciousness, based upon the image of the star tetrahedron. Interestingly enough, the underlying teachings of the Merkaba, through the popular New Age author Drunvalo Melchizedek, is based upon the geometry of the Flower of Life, the essence of the shape found in the chariot wheels of this panel of the Gundestrup Cauldron.

Figure 30: Flower of Life

Exercise 29:
Goddess of the Chariot

To start this journey, gaze deeply upon Plate B. Use the image above, but if you can find a good quality photo in a book or online, use that to really get the depth and detail of the image. Allow the symbols and figure to move deeply into your memory. Then, when you feel ready, begin this work.

Hold your cauldron in your lap and gaze deeply into the center. Breathe and relax yourself. Relax into your body. Relax into the cauldron itself. Enter the darkness and close your eyes. Using your meditative techniques, enter a trance state.

Find yourself gazing out upon a vast open green field, like the field where cattle would graze. Upon the horizon, you see movement. There, in the distance, you see her, a woman upon a chariot, being pulled by some creatures you can't quite make out.

Every moment, they draw closer to you. You feel anxious despite their distance, as if their power reaches far before their bodies ever do. What are the creatures pulling the chariot? How many are there? Do they seem fantastic, or are they animals that would normally pull a chariot? These figures are from the otherworld, so they can defy your expectations.

Do the animals move in harmony? Are they working together, or against each other? Does the goddess charioteer, this lady of animals, have control? With every moment, they draw closer.

Soon she is upon you. Encounter the Lady of the Chariot and her beasts. Is anyone else with her? Notice her torc. She may gesture to communicate with you. She could challenge you. Watch. Listen. Learn. Commune with this goddess. What does she teach you about herself, the beasts, the chariot? Perhaps she will teach you how to guide your own chariot through life as well.

Part of the communication could be information on how to work deeper with her, and how to make offerings and give thanks for this work, here and now. Use this information to build a relationship with the lady and her beasts. Affirm you will remember all, and when done, thank her and the beasts. She will turn and continue on her journey, either forward on a new mission, or back the way she came.

Bring your awareness back to the darkness itself. Feel the cauldron within your lap. Withdraw from the darkness of the cauldron you have consecrated. Rise up and out, affirming your connection back to your own body of flesh and blood, breath and bone. Ground yourself as needed and record the details of your journey.

Figure 31: Plate C The God of the Broken Wheel

The God of the Broken Wheel (Plate C)

The central figure of the third inner plate is a bearded god holding half of a wheel, akin to a chariot wheel. Most describe the half wheel as broken in half. There are eight clear spokes of the wheel on the remaining side, and he holds it in another posture that appears to be a ritual gesture. To his right is a smaller figure, believed to be the horned god of Plate A, as both have similar dress, and this figure is wearing a smaller horned cap, if not the full staghorn regalia. Beneath him is the horned serpent, also from Plate A. The two could be described as struggling for the wheel, resulting in it breaking. Around the figure are animals. They can be seen as either two rows of animals, the lower row moving towards the main figure's right side, with the upper row moving left, or a continuous circle of animals moving clockwise around the pair of animals. The lower row is the familiar griffin creatures, appearing in a triad, while the upper row has the lion or wolf-like creatures from previous plates. Decorating the background is the ivy plant motif.

What is possibly occurring in this panel? Who are the figures? Olmsted sees this as a confrontation between a young Cú Cuchulain and the bearded god-king Fergus, acting on behalf of Queen Medb. The horned serpent in this position could be the manifestation of the Morrighan in the form of an "eel" who has her ribs crushed under the foot of Cú Cuchulain in part of the traditional tale. Are the hounds helping Cú Cuchulain? Are the gryphons abandoning or defending Fergus? And what does the incomplete wheel mean? The panel is not clear to our modern minds. Others identify the bearded figure as Taranis, the Gaulish god of thunder and lightning, whose main symbol is the wheel and whose tree is the oak. He was equated with Jupiter by the Romans. Wheels are famous symbols of cycles – Sun wheels, Moon wheels, zodiac wheels, and the modern Neopagan Wheel of the Year. Philosophers describe the cosmos as wheels within wheels, interlocking rings, and our cauldron itself is a form of a wheel. Is the younger god in battle with the older bearded god, playing out some cycle of the year, like our popular idea of the Oak King and Holly King battling for the waxing and waning season? Is the battle a form of initiation? We would have to encounter the God of the Wheel to know for ourselves. And this figure will return in the outer Plate E again.

Exercise 30:
God of the Wheel

Gaze deeply upon Plate C, again looking at the reproduction here, and any available images and photos of the actual cauldron. Let your mind dwell on the scene of the animals surrounding the two figures who seem to be battling over a broken or incomplete wheel. When ready, start this journey.

Again hold your cauldron in your lap and gaze into the center. Breathe deeply to relax yourself. Use your techniques to enter a trance and close your eyes, entering the darkness of the cauldron.

Find yourself in a wooded realm again, navigating through the underbrush. Light trails through the openings in the canopy of trees. Soon you enter a place with a clearing, much like that of the horned god figure, but instead of a realm of peaceful animals, this has animals moving about, dancing or fighting. The feeling is generally of chaos and wildness. They are otherworldly creatures, not just animals you would encounter in a forest. There are winged gryphons and strange creatures that appear both canine and feline. And in the center are two godlike figures.

The first is larger, taller, stronger, and older. He is a bearded figure, holding a wheel of some sort. He is struggling with a smaller, younger, clean-shaven man. They are struggling over the wheel.

Make your way through the chaos of the animals if you can, or observe the whole scene from a distance. What are they doing? How are they acting? Do they speak to each other? What do they say?

Only the horned serpent notices you. Perhaps it will come speak to you. What does it say to you? Listen to the serpent's wisdom. Understand its teachings with the gods and the wheel. Affirm you will remember whatever is said. When done, thank the serpent, if not the animals and gods, and return back the way you came in, returning through the darkness of the cauldron and back to an awareness of your body. Ground yourself and record your journey.

Figure 32: Plate D The Sacrifice of the Bulls

The Sacrifice of the Bulls (Plate D)

In what might be the most straightforward depictions upon the cauldron, the fourth inner plate shows what everyone seems to agree is a bull sacrifice. Three nearly identical bulls face three nearly identical men; the central one has a jacket and the other two do not, but all three are bearing swords, seemingly to slay the bulls. The bulls do not seem to be attacking, but static and subdued. Beneath each bull is a dog-like creature. If one of the figures, most likely the central figure, is a Cú Chulainn prototype, and since he and the Irish wolf hound share a name, having the allies or totem of the dogs working with him, facing the same way, would make magickal sense. Above the bulls are three cat-like creatures, also facing the same direction as the men and dogs.

The key to this panel seems to be triplicity: three men with three bulls, three dogs and three cats arranged essentially in three levels of action. This echoes all that we've said about the triple nature of the cosmos and cauldron. This sacrifice is occurring in all three worlds at once, on all three levels of being at once. The bull in the center of the cauldron now exists in all three worlds. To sacrifice means to make sacred, to offer. To make offerings on all three worlds is to make an offering for the deep gods of the inner world; the realm of the land, community and nature; and the realm of the perfected ones.

A common concept ascribed to both Celtic and Germanic traditions is the triple death. Mythically it is compared to a threefold initiatory process, as found with gods and saints, though we find literal examples of it in what appear to be sacrificial bog bodies such as the Lindow Man. His throat was cut, he was strangled by a cord, and he was hit on the head, and of course for good measure thrown into a watery grave.

Odin is a god undergoing a triple-death initiation, being hung from a tree, stabbed in his side, and starved for nine days and nine nights until grasping the magick of the runes. Merlin in his wild man form, Myrddin Wyllt, foretells of a boy's death three different times, despite being presented with the boy in different disguises, an effort to "trick" the seer. He predicts the boy will fall from a rock, that he will hang, and he will drown. People think Myrddin is an obvious charlatan since he did not realize it was the same boy. This boy grows older, and as a man partaking in a hunt, he falls from a rock, is caught in a tree, and hangs down with his head in the water by the tree and drowns. Merlin later prophesies and experiences his own death by falling, stabbing, and drowning. A group of shepherds send him over a cliff. Falling upon a stake left below by fishermen, his head plunges beneath the water, and he drowns.

World	Lindow Man	Odin	Myrddin's Prophecy	Myrddin's Death
Upper World	Strangled	Hanged	Falling	Falling
Middle World	Throat Cut	Stabbed	Hanging	Stabbed
Lower Wolrd	Blugeoned	Starved	Drowning	Drowning

Chart 35: Triple Death

The three deaths can be representative of the three worlds, or as some speculate, sacrifices to three different deities.

EXERCISE 31:
The Triple Sacrifice

Work with Plate D as you would the other plates, closely examining the images on the diagram and any other images of it you can find. Let the images move deeper into your memory and consciousness.

Hold the cauldron before you and start by gazing into its dark center. Close your eyes and enter a trance state. See the triple bull sacrifice of the fourth interior plate of this fantastic cauldron.

Before you, feel the presence of three mighty creatures, the three bulls. As your sense of them becomes clearer, where are you? Outside? Perhaps a grove? Or are you in a beautiful temple? There are three large cat-like creatures and three dog-like creatures, as well as three men, preparing to sacrifice the bulls. Look to the shadows. Look to the spirits. Who has gathered with you?

Do the bulls have any connection to the first bull you have met? If so, how?

Witness the sacrifice, and try to witness it on all levels. It is occurring in three worlds at once. How are the worlds connected? Are there really three bulls, or just one? Perhaps the men, the dogs, or the cats will be able to communicate with you, or perhaps they will be silent, and just allow you to witness this rite.

When the work is complete, affirm that you will remember everything that has occurred and bring your awareness back as you entered, returning through the darkness of the cauldron. Return your awareness to the world around you and to your body. Ground and record the details of your journey and any insights you gained through experiencing the triple sacrifice.

Figure 33: Plate E Cauldron of Rebirth

Cauldron of Rebirth (Plate E)

The last of the inner plates depicts a scene hotly contested by scholars, but which makes clear sense to most initiates of the mysteries, depicting ideas we've studied already. Can the initiates be sure this was the intention of the artist? Of course not, but out of all the plates, this one puts into action the familiar magickal teachings. To the left of the plate stands a giant figure with either a ponytail or tasseled cap. The figure is considered a god, based upon the hair, but it could easily be a goddess, as the hair is reminiscent of a profile view of the figure in Plate B. The giant holds a vessel of some sort, usually considered a cauldron, and next to the giant is a canine figure leaping upward. At the bottom of the panel comes a row of six warriors with shields. Some are carrying a fallen tree along with their shields and spears. They are followed by a single figure without a shield, carrying a sword instead of a spear and wearing a more elaborate helmet. These seven are followed by three who are playing carnyxs, Celtic musical instruments consisting of a long thin tube adorned with a stylized boar's head. The giant is 'dipping" a figure into the vessel headfirst, and above the tree, heading away from the giant, are four decorated figures on horseback. Before them, as if leading the way, is the ram-headed serpent.

Each horseman figure has a special helmet. The first has a downward-turned crescent, the next small horns with knobs at the end similar to the younger figure in Plate C, the third a helmet with a boar on top of it (reminiscent of the sword bearer in the lower row), and the last with a bird upon it. A modern occultist – even recognizing the Celts did not have a four elemental system we are familiar with – might still be tempted to equate the four with the elements. The crescent would be water, horns would be earth, the boar would be fire, and the bird would be air.

To most of us, this panel easily depicts the cauldron of regeneration and rebirth. The bottom row embodies either prepared warrior initiates or fallen soldiers heading to the realm of the dead. The giant is a primordial deity, not unlike Bran, Dagda, or even Cerridwen. Those of a lower station, foot soldiers, get reborn through a turn in the cauldron and rise as horseman with the special designations of the crescent, horn, boar, or bird. Their totem guide, the otherworldly ram-headed serpent, leads them to return to the world. Perhaps the lower-level swordsman with the boar helmet and the musicians are already initiates, aiding the deity along with the totemic canine. This panel depicts the central teaching in the tale of Branwen. The Cauldron of Rebirth must remain in the hands of titans, for when it is given to human hands, just a king, it becomes a tool of war, resurrecting creatures, not initiates. The cauldron is not meant to be a weapon, but a vessel of regeneration.

If the cauldron is depicting one singular story and not many connected stories, is our hero from the previous panels the knob-horned warrior third in line to leave? As this is a cauldron moving in cycles, we then must ask, is Plate A really Plate A,? Or is this the fate of our hero after initiation, to become one with the forest and the animals?

Do the knobbed horns grow into true stag horns? Does the tale perhaps begin with the confrontation with the Goddess of the Chariot? Can one go for another round before entering the third zone of the outer cauldron ring? Is this the key experience, the gateway between the world of the inner panels and outer panels?

Exercise 32:
Cauldron Initiation

Study the details of Plate E along with any available images or reproductions. Really seek to understand the mysteries of those leading into and those leaving the giant figure and the cauldron vessel. Only then, with this image firmly planted in your consciousness, perform this working.

Gaze into your cauldron in your lap and breathe deep. Close your eyes and enter a magickal mindset. Feel yourself marching forward in the darkness. Step by step, you sense the presence of others around you, and as they become clearer, you realize you are marching in a line with fellow warriors. There is the mournful music of pipes playing behind you– are they accompanying you on your journey? Are you dead? Are you injured? It's unclear. Perhaps you were the bull sacrificed before this journey, and you now travel to the world of the cauldron. No matter what really happened, you are certain you can sense an immense presence before you, in the distance.

Soon the march brings you and your fellows to the grove of a great deity. The deity has the cauldron of rebirth, of regeneration. The deity is placing each person, one by one, into the cauldron to be reborn. You watch the next person enter the cauldron, and when taken out again, they are still and silent. They are reborn in a majestic new form, like the best version of themselves. The newly reborn quickly mount a beast of the other world and are decorated with arms that reflect their true inner nature and spiritual powers. One by one, you approach the deity. Soon it will be your turn.

The divine one gathers you up – and into the cauldron you go once more. Feel yourself swirling in the cauldron. You sense the branches, leaves, and flowers of an amazing tree. You see the presence of the ram-headed serpent swirling in the cauldron with you. It is as if it is a part of you, and it speaks to you in an almost silent whisper, of your impending rebirth.

You feel "cooked," and when you are done, the deity plunges their hands back into the liquid of the cauldron and pulls you forth. You are reborn, garbed in the armor and weapons that best embody your true nature. What do you look like? How do you feel?

You are placed upon an otherworldly mount. What does it look like? How does it work with you? Like a beast from the chariot, you have entered into a new level of power. What do you feel like right now? Thank the deity and take your leave, as others have done before you, for others will follow you into the cauldron, in this cycle of rebirth and return. You can feel as if the horned serpent is leading you back.

Follow the procession leading from the cauldron deity to the world. Wrap yourself back into the darkness and return back to the world. Return back to the presence of the world of flesh and blood, breath and bone. Return back to the world of your surroundings, but return with this sense of transformation from the cauldron. Ground and record what you remember, including any messages from the deity or your time in the cauldron.

The seven outer panels are portraits of various giant figures, most likely deities, with small figures surrounding them. For our purposes, we must ask ourselves, are these the giants of the underworld, the primal titanic forces, or do the giants represent the "perfected one" of the realm of Gwynvyd? Are they the forces mortals are subjected to in the middle world of space, time, and form? Or are they ever-present in all three, like the three sacrificed bulls, one for each world simultaneously, with our approach determining the mystical "place" or quality of our interaction with these figures?

You can perform the workings for these seven plates as seven distinct events or work with them in sequence within one larger meditation.

Figure 34: Plate a The Judge of Heroes

The Judge of Heroes (Plate a)

A bearded giant, differing from our last bearded god with the broken wheel, holds two smaller figures, each by an arm, while their free arm is holding or balancing an animal, usually believed to be a boar. His posture is similar to the god of the broken wheel, a posture that will become very familiar in this cauldron art. He wears either a coronet or crown-like headdress or has very stylized hair with a stylized beard. The smaller figure to the giant's right, our left, has a dog beneath his feet, while the opposite figure has a winged horse. As with the gryphons, it is strange to find Pegasus in a Celtic artifact from this time period.

Olmsted equates this figure with a Gaulish precursor to King Cú Rói, the magickal Irish king of Munster in the tale of Cú Chulainn. He often plays the role of a judge or arbiter in contests. In the previously discussed tale of Bricriu's Feast, his verdict for Cú Chulainn is contested, and he takes the role of the trickster in a form of the Beheading Game more clearly illustrated in the Green Knight tales. Cú Chulainn's rivals, Conall and Lóegaire, contested Cú Rói's judgment, so he appeared to them in a disguised form and offered to let them behead him, but only if they agreed to allow him to then behead them. He does the same to Cú Chulainn, and out of the three, only Cú Chulainn submits to the disguised Cú Rói's axe. Later in the tale, Cú Rói's and Cú Chulainn are set against each other, and ultimately Cú Chulainn kills Cú Rói. His son, Lugaid mac Con Rói, makes an agreement with Queen Medb and the children of others who were killed by Cú Chulainn, and ultimately kills Cú Chulainn.

If this is depicting a competition involving the boar, then the spiritual powers of the boar should be examined as a part of this plate. Boars have a strong role in Celtic cultures, so much so that the Celtic neck ring, or torc, often has ends shaped to be a boar. Boars have a powerful warrior spirit, a fierceness and danger, as seen in their tusks. In many forms of the Indo-European myths of the sacrificed god, the boar is the animal lord killing off the old king. Boars are clannish, living in large social groups with lots of social contact, another reason they are important to tribal and clannish people. While we tend to look at majestic creatures like the lion or dragon as the totem of kings, King Richard III of England took the boar as his coat of arms. The spirit of the boar asks us to face our opponents with courage and bravery. Boars also root around the underbrush, digging up roots and mushrooms. Being lower to the ground than some other regal animals, they can teach us to use the resources that are unnoticed by most and find the treasures right beneath our noses.

Exercise 33:
The Boar Judge

Look deeply upon the figures in Plate a before beginning the working of the Boar Judge. Get into a meditative position with your cauldron in your lap or hands. Gaze into the cauldron's interior darkness. Close your eyes and enter a trance state. Enter the otherworld.

Find yourself entering a wild wood – you are on the hunt for something. Or is something on the hunt for you? The boar! You remember it now. You are hunting the dangerous game of the boar, yet the boar can easily turn around and attack you. Other hunters are in the woods. Others are also being hunted. You know this is a ritual of sacred kingship, of the dangers of the wild woods and the role of the hunters to help their people and the people to support their warriors. You know the spirit of the boar, fierce and clannish. Do you catch the boar? Does the boar harm you? Keep hunting.

Soon you hear the shrill call of the hunting horn, and you know the contest is over. You follow the sound to a grove, and there is the bearded god king, inspecting all the warriors' prey. Watch and listen carefully. What does he say to you?

When this work is done, the warriors go their separate ways back to the civilized world of their villages. You know it is time for you to return to your own village, your own world, and enter back into the darkness of the cauldron. Return to your world and to your body. Ground yourself and record your experience and messages.

Figure 35: Plate b The Sea God

The Sea God (Plate b)

A large male figure, possibly bearded but without a mustache, holds in the familiar ritual pose two creatures described as sea horses or sea dragons. Beneath him are two reclining figures of small stature, connected by long, two-headed animals, with one head facing each.

Henry Hubert considers this central figure a sea god, such as Manawydan and Manannan, though with his titanic proportions, I would think it would be Llyr or Lir, as the primordial sea god wrestling with monsters, not the traveling sea god. Omlsted, keeping in the Irish Ulster cycle of mythology, considers this figure to be Froech, a character who fights a water dragon and is severely wounded by the monster and requires healing from the faery women or Sidhe. He later goes on to fight against Queen Medb. At the end of his tale, he is drowned in a river while fighting with Cú Chulainn.

The double-headed creature has been a greater source of speculation. Is it a monster attacking the two human figures? It could be a depiction of a "fire-dog" or metal frame that is set across an open hearth, usually ornamented with bulls' or rams' heads at each end. If that is the case, the men are not being attacked, but are reclining and most likely enjoying a feast. As the ocean is considered to be another realm, or an entrance to the ancestral otherworld where the newly dead are joined in feast with their ancestors, perhaps this ocean god is also the ferryman, as Manannan is, bringing heroes to the otherworld upon death. Ellis Davidson proposes this otherworldly interpretation of the panel.

Exercise 34:
The Sea God

Look deeply upon the figures in Plate b before beginning the working of the Sea God. Get into a meditative position with your cauldron in your lap or hands. Gaze into the cauldron's interior darkness. Close your eyes and enter a trance state. Enter the otherworld.

Hear the crashing of the waves and find yourself upon the seashore. You can smell the salt sea air and feel the cool mist. The water goes wild with waves, and you realize there are creatures in the sea – serpents, dragons, monsters – it is hard to tell. But the sea is a wave of chaos, and the waves come more violently upon the shore. It is a fearsome scene.

Soon, rising up from the waves, is the god of the sea. He battles these chaotic creatures, seeking to bring them to harmony. Observe the battle of the sea. Others may gather at the shore with you to watch the sea god. They might take time to speak with you as you all watch the momentous strength of the sea god, who, after some distress, manages to tame the beasts of the sea and restore the natural order to the world of waves.

When you feel your experience is complete, return to your world and to your body. Ground yourself and record your experience and messages.

Figure 36: Plate c The God of Three Figures

The God of Three Figures (Plate c)

Another classically bearded god, this time with a torc neck ring, has his arms outstretched. To his right is a figure described as a "boxer" due to his posture and hand positions. To his left is a leaper figure. Both are reminiscent in style and dress of the inner panel figures, and the leaper is almost the same figure as one on the inner base with the first bull. On his left shoulder is a smaller horse and rider moving away from him. Could these three be the three bull slayers of Plate D? We don't know. The central figure seems well disposed towards them, but are they attacking him? Again, we don't know. Is there a thread to show us the leaper from the base is the horned "hero" in the inner plates who has made his way here? There is very little scholarly supposition on the nature of this plate and its figures.

Exercise 35:
The Mystery of the Three

Look deeply upon the figures in Plate c before beginning the working of the Mystery of the Three. Get into a meditative position with your cauldron in your lap or hands. Gaze into the cauldron's interior darkness. Close your eyes and enter a trance state. Enter the otherworld.

Before you, surrounded by darkness and shadows, you sense four figures. Three are closer to your size and stature. One is larger. Do they seem familiar to you at all? The three human-like beings are gathered around a more titanic figure. What are they doing? Do they say anything? Do they notice you? Observe the Mystery of the Three, and see what wisdom can be gleaned here for you.

When you feel your experience is complete, return to your world and to your body. Ground yourself and record your experience and messages.

Figure 37: Plate d The Stag Hunter God

The Stag Hunter God (Plate d)

Here we have another large portrait of a god in the similar raised-hand position, but this time, no other human figures are around. His beard and hair are ornate, and his mood can be described as satisfied by the depiction of the eyes and mouth. The god holds two stags by their hind quarters. The plate is decorated with ivy and an angular zig-zag pattern at the top.

While it might be tempting to see this as a manifestation of a stag god, the god himself is not stag-like, and if he were supporting the stags, they would probably be upright around him. They are clearly caught, and possibly dead. Deer and stag hunts and otherworldly deer are common themes in Celtic myth, so it is hard to relate him to any single figure or deity. In the work of Olmsted, he is identified as the Gaulish equivalent of King Segamain, an Irish High King whose mother was said to be the goddess Flidias, of the Tuatha de Danann. She is a goddess associated with fertility and cattle who later became associated with the deer in an attempt to equate her with deer maidens, leading her to be portrayed in a manner similar to the Greek Artemis. Traditionalists would see this as a mistake and would restore her cattle-only associations. In the legend of Segamain – due to his mother's magick during his reign – the wild doe gave milk to his people just as the domesticated cows would.

The magickal teaching around the stag relates to the teaching of the hunter and the hunted, and the duality of being that which you seek. Horned gods are often paradoxically described as hunter gods, though if they embody the stag, they are what is being hunted by humans. In poetic Witchcraft lore, this is referred to as the Roebuck in the Thicket, the elusive white stag embodying the poetic mysteries of the goddess. The hunt for the roebuck is the hunt for the truth in the mysteries. The term was popularized first by Robert Graves and then later Robert Cochrane in the form of Modern Traditional Witchcraft.

Exercise 36:
The Stag Hunter

Look deeply upon the figures in Plate d before beginning the working of the Stag Hunter. Get into a meditative position with your cauldron in your lap or hands. Gaze into the cauldron's interior darkness. Close your eyes and enter a trance state. Enter the otherworld.

You enter an otherworldly wild wood. You are again hunting, this time on the trail of the roebuck, the stag of the forest and thicket. Rather than participating in a contest against others, there by your side is the god who is the Stag Hunter. He is your ally and companion on this hunt. Work with the hunter god to see the stag. Follow his directions, his lead. Let him help you understand the nature of the stag's power, and why we seek it.

Do you find the stag? Do you succeed in your hunt? The hunter does! Speak with him about the nature of the hunter and the hunted, and how in the duality of the two, there is simply the hunt itself.

When you feel your experience is complete, return to your world and to your body. Ground yourself and record your experience and messages.

Figure 38: Plate e Divine Trinity

Divine Trinity (Plate e)

A central goddess with her hair in two pigtails is ritually gesturing towards her chest rather than outwardly like most of the male figures of the cauldron. On either side are two male figures, but they are depicted larger than the more human-sized heroic figures of the other plates, indicating they too are gods. To her left is a cleanshaven face wearing a torc, and to her right is a bearded figure. Both have their arms raised, fingers curled towards the palms and thumbs gesturing away from the hands toward where their ears should be. Around them again is the leaf design.

Is the central goddess figure on this plate the same as in Plate B? Her gestures and hair are similar. Is the god to her right the same as the god of the broken wheel in Plate C? Olmsted identifies the female figure as Medb and the man to her right as Fergus, as in the other plates. Olmsted concludes the remaining figure is her husband Ail and that this plate depicts the insatiable nature of Queen Medb in regard to sex.

From a mystical point of view, it's hard for a Witch to not see the mystery of the great central Goddess with the dual god, one of youth, clean-shaven, and one of elderhood, bearded. She is the eternal Earth and cosmos, and they are waxing and waning of the seasons and tides of nature. Each battles the other to be the consort of the great goddess, ruling for half of the year. While today Witches celebrate this shift at the solstices, or even possibly the equinoxes, the Celts most likely divided seasons at the times we call Beltane and Samhain, with the new year starting with the waning season heralded by Samhain, just as their days start with sunset.

Exercise 37:
Triple Divinity

Look deeply upon the figures in Plate e before beginning the working of the Triple Divinity. Get into a meditative position with your cauldron in your lap or hands. Gaze into the cauldron's interior darkness. Close your eyes and enter a trance state. Enter the otherworld.

Through the otherworldly mist, you sense the three divinities. Before you is a central goddess, and to either side, a young god and an older god. Do they acknowledge your presence? Will they communicate with you? If not, simply observe them. What are they doing or saying to each other? The three will either let you have a glimpse of their mystery, or they will obscure themselves from you. At times they will be welcoming and allow you to enter their dialogue. Learn as much as you can from this observation or interaction.

When you feel your experience is complete, return to your world and to your body. Ground yourself and record your experience and messages.

Figure 39: Plate f Triple Goddess

Triple Goddess (Plate f)

This plate focuses on a central goddess, again with two pigtails. One arm, her right, is raised to lift up a small bird, while her left arm is across her chest. The small bird is similar to the bird helmet of the resurrected horsemen of Plate e. She wears a torc or other collar necklace. She is "attended" by two smaller female figures. To her right is a seated woman, with a lion-like creature running upward above her head. To her left is a woman attending to her hair. A third figure, possibly male, is fallen by her chest. While we might be tempted to think she is cradling the third figure, it appears outside, not inside of her left arm. Next to this figure is an upside-down dog, also possibly fallen away. At the top of the plate are two larger birds, described as eagles or ravens.

Due to their similarities, this could be the same goddess. We can assume Medb, though the upper birds give us the possibility of the Morrighan if they are ravens or crows. We have three feminine figures on this plate, indicating for the first time a potential triad of feminine power that is common in the depiction of the Morrighan and other Celtic goddesses, though the imagery does not suggest their equality. One is central while two appear to be supportive. Could the fallen figure be the hero and his hound totem, the fallen Cú Chulainn? Despite being killed by the hand of others, many would blame the Morrighan for the death of Cú Chulainn. She prophesied his end and placed upon him a geas, a sacred prohibition, to never eat the meat of a hound for it was his namesake. He also had a geas to never refuse the hospitality of strangers. With these two geas in place, she fatefully arranged a stranger to offer him dog meat, which meant that in either case he would break a geas and open himself to mortal danger. Is the small bird, the soul bird, a depiction of the higher self, set free to travel and enter the otherworld upon death? Many advocates of the triple soul model of consciousness – myself included – believe the higher soul can take the form of a bird. Was the bird on the helmet on the resurrection panel an expression of the higher self, unified with the warrior after initiatory rebirth?

Exercise 38:
Triple Goddess

Look deeply upon the figures in Plate f before beginning the working of the Triple Goddess. Get into a meditative position with your cauldron in your lap or hands. Gaze into the cauldron's interior darkness. Close your eyes and enter a trance state. Enter the otherworld.

Follow a long corridor, a long hallway, that leads to the throne room of the bird goddess. There, a central goddess is attended by two other female spirits. They could possibly be children attending her, little girls braiding her hair. Around them are birds such as crows or perhaps eagles. What kind of birds do you see?

At her feet is the body of a fallen warrior and a wolf dog. Who are they? Have you seen them before? Commune with the great lady of the bird before you. Ask her about her mysteries and her role.

When you feel your experience is complete, return to the way you came and come back to your body. Ground yourself and record your experience and messages.

Figure 40: Plate g Goddess of Rebirth

Goddess of Rebirth (Plate g)

The final outer plate depicts another female figure, possibly the same female divinity of all the previous plates, with her arms crossed upon her chest. She again wears a torc and has two pigtails on either side of her head. There are two figures to either side of her. To her right is a man struggling with a lion, or he could be embracing a large feline or canine animal. To her left is the leaping figure, returning from our cauldron base and Plate c. They again are surrounded by a background of the ivy leaf pattern.

From a magickal perspective, the goddess is holding the "death" position of ritual magicians and Wiccans, imitative of the Egyptian god Osiris and the many sarcophagi of that mystical land. If the figure on the right is struggling with a lion, it would easily recall one of the labors of Hercules, his battle with the Nemean lion. He eventually slays it and ends up with an impervious hide as magickal armor, though heroic battle with lions can pre-date the tales of Hercules. When I look at this plate, I see the same man in two different moments. There is a unification with the totemic animal self, an embrace. Unified and perfected, there is a leap back, to return to the center of the cauldron and begin the journey again with the first primal bull figure. The hero figure is like an avatar, reborn to teach the people about these mysteries by embodying them again and again.

Exercise 39:
Goddess of Death

Look deeply upon the figures in Plate g before beginning the working of the Death Goddess. Get into a meditative position with your cauldron in your lap or hands. Gaze into the cauldron's interior darkness. Close your eyes and enter a trance state. Enter the otherworld.

Journey through the darkness and mist to the realm of the Goddess of Death. There she greets you not with many beasts, as she has done before, but with one, your own beast. What do you see? Strangely, the beast attacks you, and you have to resolve this conflict, outwardly and inwardly. Can you make peace with the beast?

If you do, she opens the veil between and teaches you the way to "leap" between the worlds. Will you learn this from her?

When you feel your experience is complete, return to your world and to your body. Ground yourself and record your experience and messages.

When looking at these plates and seeking them in vision, we can see many patterns for us to work in ritual and meditation in communion with the primal powers. While there might be more male figures than female, if the cauldron is considered a whole magickal relic, the interaction with this goddess figure is an important point of the panels.

Through this artifact and the art from it – as well as all the stories we have reviewed in this book, from the Holy Grail back to the primal mother of the cauldron, Cerridwen – we can see the goddess and the cauldron and find the divine mystery for ourselves. Through this we embody the light and inspiration of the divine child. From darkness we bring the light and thereby transform ourselves, our people, and the world.

Appendix: Invocatory Poetry

As I worked through the themes of each chapter, art and poetry bubbled up in my consciousness. I used both the words and pictures as a means to unify my experience. May you use them in the same way, and may these words inspire your own words of poetic inspiration.

By fire, water, earth, and air
Seeking the depths of the mysteries
Going where few would dare
Lord of Darkness and Lord of Light
Ladies of Fate who shape cosmic night
Source of creation as the divine womb
and the destination of destruction as the divine tomb
Cauldron of Mystery, open the gate
So I may pass through you freely
And become a stirrer of fate.

By head, heart, and belly wise
Flowing with life, joy, and sorrow
To catch the emerald prize
Cauldron of Abundance and Cauldron of Rebirth
Prize of all prizes, both beyond all worth
Cauldron of Inspiration and Cauldron of the Grail
Bringer of awen and piercer of the veil
Cauldron of Transformation, the alchemist's holy stone
The secret of the royal road
that leads to our true home.

By the daughter of blessings
By the son of disgust
By the mother of wisdom whom none could trust

Father of Giants unseen and unheard
Blind man of the hut barely speaking a word
Boy thrown into darkness stirring without end
Divine nectar to mix and nectar to blend
Releasing three holy drops, enchanted and charmed
The secret brew of the lady
Used to heal and to harm

By the darkness of the hut
In the school of the cave
Where the cauldron boils hot by the work of the slave
Balms of the field, banes of the hedge
Diving deep these waters we dredge
Day after day and week after week
Searching for that which none may speak
Cracking the cauldron and poisoning the plot
Seeking the light of freedom beyond
By remembering all we've forgot.

By hare and salmon, bird and seed
By dog and otter, hawk and hen
To the threshing room floor and the bitter end
Chased on the Earth and chased in the deep
Running to avoid the eternal sleep
Chased in the air and chased on the floor
Womb, tomb, gate, door
Red mad mother seeking my guts
Tricking and turning and twisting
All to escape that dark hut.

By the flowing of the river
In the darkness of the bag
Taken to the shores far from the hag.
Rescued by a fool right upon the weir
Light from darkness dispelling all my fear
Hold me up as the radiant brow
and I fulfill an unspoken vow
To him I shall be loyal and true
Till my time unfolds once again
And I'll know exactly what to do.

By the debt of the poison
A truthful man in a cage
Caught by a wicked king, all in a rage
Calls to a strange child sucking his thumb
Hapless bards gathered and all are struck dumb
Singing my songs and the truth is made
Fortunes raced, and dug, and all debts repaid
Journey now with the company of the head
When only seven returned from the quest
Through seven revolving gates of dread.

By the three unholy blows
Where the land turns to waste
Through questing for the grail, hidden in a holy place
Kept by the Wounded King of Kings
And the Nine Ladies of the Springs
A lance, cup, cauldron, plate, and stone
The lock and the key to bring us home
Bright drink, dark drink, red drink we deserve
Through the trials and tasks we must ask
Whom do I serve?

By the center to the edge
Three worlds shaped by unknown hands
The cauldron of rebirth came to us from far off lands
Lady of the Wheel, Lord of the Horns
Warriors in death become the horsemen reborn
Cattle of the center sacrificed by sword
Lions, wolves, and gryphon moving in accord
Judge and Hunter, Sea God of the west
Triple goddess of the deathly crows
Return me to the Isle of the Blessed.

Bibliography

Agrippa, Henry Cornelius with James Freake and Donald Tyson. *Three Books of Occult Philosophy.* St. Paul, MN: Llewellyn Publications, original 1651, 1992.

Andrews, Ted. *Animal-Speak: The Spiritual & Magical Powers of Creatures Great & Small.* St. Paul, MN: Llewellyn Publications, 1993.

Andrews Ted. *Animal-Wise: The Spirit Language and Signs of Nature.* Jackson, TN: Dragonhawk Publishing, 1999.

Bartlett, Robert Allen. *Real Alchemy: A Primer of Practical Alchemy.* N.p.: QuinquanglePress, 2006.

Bartlett, Robert Allen. *The Way of the Crucible.* Lake Worth, FL: Ibis Press, 2009.

Bergquist, Anders & Timothy Taylor. "The Origin of the Gundestrup Cauldron." Antiquity, vol. 61, 1987, pp.10-24.

Bromwich, Rachel, ed. *Trioedd Ynys Prydein.* Rev. ed. Cardiff, Wales, UK: University of Wales Press, 1991.

Clifton, Chas S., ed. *Shamanism and Witchcraft.* St. Paul, MN: Llewellyn Publications, 1994.

Cowan, Eliot. *Plant Spirit Medicine.* Newberg, OR: Swan Raven, 1995.

Cowan, Tom. *Fire in the Head.* San Francisco, CA: Harper San Francisco, 1993.

Culpeper, Nicholas. *Culpeper's Complete Herbal: Over 400 Herbs and Their Uses.* London: Arcturus Publishing Limited, 2012.

Deerman, Dixie (Lady Passion), and Steven Rasmussen (*Diuvei). *The Goodly Spellbook: Olde Spells for Modern Problems.* New York: Sterling Publishing, 2004.

Firth, Florence M. *The Golden Verses of Pythagoras and Other Pythagorean Fragments.* Krotona, Hollywood, CA: Theosophical Publishing House, 1904.

Flemming, Kaul. "The Gundestrup Cauldron Reconsidered." Hoboken, NJ: Acta Archaeologica, vol. 66, 1995, pp. 1-38.

Fries, Jan. *Cauldron of the Gods: A Manual of Celtic Magick.* Oxford: Mandrake, 2003.

Godwin, Joscelyn. *The Mystery of the Seven Vowels.* Grand Rapids, MI: Phanes Press, 1991.

Graves, Robert. *White Goddess: A Historical Grammar of Poetic Myth.* New York: Farrar, Straus and Giroux, 1966.

Grimassi, Raven. *The Cauldron of Memory.* St. Paul, MN: Llewellyn Publications, 2009.

Hall, Manly P. *Secret Teachings of All Ages.* Mineola NY: Dover Publications, 1928, 2010.

Harner, Michael. *The Way of the Shaman.* Tenth anniversary edition. San Francisco: Harper & Row, 1990.

Harris, Mike. *Awen: The Quest of the Celtic Mysteries.* Oceanside, CA: Sun Chalice Books, 1999.

Hughes, Kristoffer. *From the Cauldron Born.* St. Paul, MN: Llewellyn Publications, 2013.

Knight, Gareth. *The Secret Tradition in Arthurian Legend.* York Beach, ME: Samuel Weiser, 1996.

Matthews, Caitlín. *Celtic Wisdom Sticks: An Ogham Oracle.* London: Connections Book Publishing Ltd., 2001.

Matthews, Caitlín. *Mabon and the Guardians of Celtic Britain.* Rochester, VT: Inner Traditions, 2002.

Matthews, Caitlín. *Singing the Soul Back Home: Shamanism in Daily Life.* Rockport, MA: Element, 1995.

Matthews, Caitlín, and John Matthews. *Encyclopedia of Celtic Wisdom.* Rockport, MA: Element, 1994.

Matthews, John. *The Celtic Shaman.* Rockport, MA: Element, 1992.

McColman, Carl. *Complete Idiot's Guide to Celtic Wisdom.* New York: Alpha, 2003.

McLean, Adam. *The Alchemical Mandala*. Grand Rapids, MI: Phanes Press, 2002.

Melchizedek, Drunvalo. *The Ancient Secret of the Flower of Life, Volume 1*. Sedona, AZ: Light Technologies Publications, 1998.

Melchizedek, Drunvalo. *The Ancient Secret of the Flower of Life, Volume 2*. Sedona, AZ: Light Technologies Publications, 2000.

Merry, Eleanor C. *The Flaming Door: The Mission of the Celtic Folk-Soul*. Edinburgh: Floris Books; 5th edition, 2008.

Miller, Jason. *Advanced Practical Planetary Magic*. Jason Miller, 2013.

Morganwg, Iolo. Ed. by J. Williams Ab Ithel. *The Barddas of Iolo Morganwg, Vol. I*., Abred.-Gwynvyd.-Awen., 1862. London: Forgotten Books, 2007.

Nash., D.W. Taliesin. *The Bards and Druids of Britain*. London: John Russell Smith, 1858.

Olmsted, G.S. The Gundestrup version of *Táin Bó Cuailnge* (Antiquity, Vol. 50), 1987.

Peacock, Thomas Love. "The Cauldron of Ceridwen." *The Poems of Thomas Love Peacock* edited by Brimley Johnson, London: George Routledge & Sons, 1907

Rennie, James. *Alphabet of Medical Botany, for the Use of Beginners*. Charleston, SC: Nabu Press, 2011.

Sanders, Alex. *The Alex Sanders Lectures*. New York: Magickal Childe, 1989.

Skene, William F. *The Four Ancient Books of Wales*. London: Forgotten Books, 2007.

Spence, Lewis. *Mysteries of Celtic Britain*. Malibu, CA: Siena Publishers Association, 1998.

Stewart, R. J. *The Miracle Tree: Demystifying the Qabalah*. Franklin Lakes, NJ: New Page Books, 2003.

Stewart, R. J. *The Mystic Life of Merlin*. London: Arkana, 1986

Stewart, R. J. *Prophetic Vision of Merlin: Prediction, Psychic Transformation and the Foundation of the Grail Legends in an Ancient Set of Visionary Verses*. London: Arkana, 1986.

Stewart, R. J. *Spiritual Dimension of Music: Altering Consciousness for Inner Development.* Rochester, VT: Destiny Books, 1987.

Tindall, Robert with Susana Bustos, Ph.d. *The Shamanic Odyssey: Homer, Tolkien, and the Visionary Experience.* Rochester VT: Park Street Press, 2012.

Wilson, Peter Lamborn. *Ploughing the Clouds: The Search for Irish Soma.* San Francisco: City Lights Publishers, 2001.

Yeats, William Butler. *The Wind Among the Reeds.* London: Elkin Matthews, 1899

Online Resources

Adderley, Mark. "'Pa Gur' and 'The Spoils of Annwn.'" Arthuriana: Arthur Complete. *http://faculty.smu.edu/arthuriana/teaching/lecture_welsh-lit_adderley.html.*

Ash, Sima. "An Overview on Homeopathic Cell Salts." *http://www.healing4soul.com/articles/homeopathy/44-an-overview-on-homeopathic-cell-salts.* 16 July 2014.

"The Battle of the Trees." *The Book of Taliesin VIII.* From *The Four Ancient Books of Wales, http://www.maryjones.us/ctexts/t08.html.* 16 July 2014.

Bonewits, Isaac. "21 Lessons of Hogwash: An Excerpt from *Bonewits's Essential Guide to Druidism*." *http://www.neopagan.net/21-Lessons.html.* 12 Dec. 2011

The Book of Taliesin (Peniarth MS 2). *http://www.maryjones.us/ctexts/llyfrtaliesin.html.* 10 Nov. 2011.

Branin, Mary. "The Celts & The Sea: History, Myth, and Cosmology." *Keltria: Journal of Druidism and Celtic Magick*, Issue 31, 1996. *http://www.keltria.org/journal/d-bran-c.htm.* 20 Nov. 2008.

Brodhead, Peter. "The 12 Tissue Salts or Cell Salt Remedies – Fundamental Homeopathic Remedies: A lecture presented by Peter Brodhead CN." 22 May 2001, *http://www.brighterdayfoods.com/PDFDocs/l/LR72WHCKJQ1V9LTGKT8CGWX7TM5B1NP5.PDF.* 16 July 2014.

Guest, Lady Charlotte (translator). *The Mabinogion.* 1877, Sacred Texts, *https://www.sacred-texts.com/neu/celt/mab/index.htm.* 6 Dec 2011.

Garrison, Omar. "Zodiac Sun Signs & Cell Salts" *https://pathwaytoascension.wordpress.com/category/zodiac-cell-salts/.* 23 May 2016.

"The Gundestrup Cauldron – Mythology and Cosmology: The Native Way of Understanding Cosmos." *http://www.native-science.net/gundestrup-cauldron.htm.*

"The Gundestrup Cauldron." *https://www.sacredsource.com/Gundestrup-Cauldron-12-1_2/productinfo/GCM/*

"The Gundestrup Kauldron." *http://www.unc.edu/celtic/catalogue/Gundestrup/kauldron.html*

Hutter, Shane. "The Pentagrammic Scale." *http://koseye.blogspot.com/2009/01/pentagramic-scale.html.* 30 Jan. 2009.

Leonardo. "Greek Vosels and the Chaldean Planets." 17 Dec. 2009, *http://voces-magicae.com/2009/12/17/greek-vowels-and-the-chaldean-planets.* 15 Jan. 2018.

Morgan, Iolo. The National Library of Wales. *http://www.iolomorganwg.wales.ac.uk:80/index.php.* 23 Jan. 2018

Millesima, Iulia. "The Dangerous Journey into the Gundestrup Cauldron." *https://www.labyrinthdesigners.org/alchemy-art/the-dangerous-journey-into-the-gundestrup-cauldron.* 7 Feb. 2018.

"Mode." Wikipedia: The Free Encyclopedia. Wikimedia Foundation, Inc, 22 July 2004, *https://en.wikipedia.org/wiki/Mode_(music).* 15 Jan. 2018.

"Nerium." Wikipedia: The Free Encyclopedia. Wikimedia Foundation, Inc, 22 July 2004, *http://en.wikipedia.org/wiki/Nerium.* 8 June 2014

"Objective Art: The Musical Modes (Octave Structures) of Ancient Greece." *http://objectiveart01.tripod.com/greek_modes.htm#.* 15 Jan. 2018

Pengwerin, Gareth. "A Taxonomy of the Major Keltic Deities and Their Interface with the Human Organism." *http://www.geocities.com/tyghet/taxonomy.htm.*

Reade, W. Winwood. "The Veil of Isis; or, Mysteries of the Druids." 1861, Sacred Texts, *https://sacred-texts.com/pag/motd/motd.htm*

Roth, Harold. *http://www.alchemy-works.com/primula_veris.html.* 13 May 2014.

Roth, Harold. *http://www.alchemy-works.com/oenothera_biennis.html.* 8 June 2014.

Serith, Ceisiwr. "Seeking the Wisdom of the Ancestors: A Form of Indo-European Divination." *http://ceisiwrserith.com/ritual/theory/divination.htm.* 2 June 2015.

"Sisymbrium officinale." Wikipedia: The Free Encyclopedia. Wikimedia Foundation, Inc, 22 July 2004, *http://en.wikipedia.org/wiki/Sisymbrium_officinale.* 8 June 2014.

Synodic Archives. Kazan University, 1909. No. 635:135, V.XXV., Case 337, page 257, Year 1752, Kazan, Russia *http://ifo.00.gs/Wonders_in_the_Sky.htm.*

"Trachelospermum jasminoides." Wikipedia: The Free Encyclopedia. Wikimedia Foundation, Inc, 22 July 2004, *http://en.wikipedia.org/wiki/Trachelospermum_jasminoides*. 8 June 2014.

"Wrightia antidysenterica." Wikipedia: The Free Encyclopedia. Wikimedia Foundation, Inc, 22 July 2004, *http://en.wikipedia.org/wiki/Wrightia_antidysenterica*. 8 June 2014.

About the Author

Christopher Penczak (Salem, NH) is an award-winning author, teacher, and healing practitioner. As an advocate for the timeless wisdom of the ages, he is rooted firmly in the traditions of modern Witchcraft, but draws from a wide range of spiritual traditions, including shamanism, alchemy, herbalism, Theosophy, and Hermetic Qabalah, to forge his own magickal traditions and create educational and community opportunities designed to encourage you to do the same. His many books include *Magick of Reiki, Spirit Allies, Ascension Magick,* and *The Mighty Dead.*

Along with his partners, Steve Kenson and Adam Sartwell, Christopher cofounded the worldwide Temple of Witchcraft tradition and religious nonprofit, drawn from the system found in his popular *Temple* series of books. Together, they support Witchcraft as a spiritual tradition and a means to transform the individual and the world. They also formed Copper Cauldron Publishing, a company dedicated to producing books, recordings, and tools for magickal inspiration and evolution.

Christopher maintains a teaching and healing practice in New England while working in the Temple community, but travels extensively, lecturing, offering rituals and intensives, and leading sacred site retreats across the world. For more information about his work and the Temple of Witchcraft community, please visit *christopherpenczak .com* and *templeofwitchcraft.org.*

www.ingramcontent.com/pod-product-compliance
Lightning Source LLC
Chambersburg PA
CBHW080724300426
44114CB00019B/2482